Circles of Meaning

The twenty-two relationships
of a spiritual life and culture – and
why they need protection.

A Study of the Sacred, Part Two

Circles of Meaning

The twenty-two relationships
of a spiritual life and culture – and
why they need protection.

A Study of the Sacred, Part Two

Brendan Myers

MOON
BOOKS

Winchester, UK
Washington, USA

First published by Moon Books, 2012
Moon Books is an imprint of John Hunt Publishing Ltd., Laurel House, Station Approach,
Alresford, Hants, SO24 9JH, UK
office1@o-books.net
www.o-books.com

For distributor details and how to order please visit the 'Ordering' section on our website.

Text copyright: Brendan Myers 2011

ISBN: 978 1 84694 745 2

A CIP catalogue record for this book is available from the British Library.

Design: Stuart Davies

Printed in the UK by CPI Antony Rowe
Printed in the USA by Offset Paperback Mfrs, Inc

We operate a distinctive and ethical publishing philosophy in all
areas of our business, from our global network of authors to
production and worldwide distribution.

CONTENTS

Overture

A Day in the Life

We awaken in the morning. We shower, eat the breakfast, kiss the wife, tussle the children's hair, and send them out the door to school. Then we start up the car, fight the traffic, grab the coffee from the drive-through, fight the traffic again, park the car, and rush past the homeless people, making sure never to make eye contact with anyone. We arrive at the workplace, and give eight hours or more of time to the very important task of moving things around from one place to another: raw materials, documents, computer files, machine parts, ad copy, finished product, and money. Why do we do this? Because other people are depending on us, so that they too can move things around from one place to another.

Everywhere you go, you see things in motion, and people and machines at work. Everywhere you see roads and rails carrying things-that-have-to-be-moved-around over every landscape, every ocean, and every skyline. Everywhere you see *busy*-ness, occupying nearly every square meter of livable land on Earth. Everything is in motion, and nothing is still. Why do we do this? Because someone is giving us money to continue doing it.

All the while, we tell ourselves little stories. We say anyone can become one of the country's lawmakers, or even its head of state. We say anyone can start a business, and that anyone who works hard enough can get very rich. And on the personal level we tell ourselves that we can think and believe and say whatever we want, marry anyone we want, play any kind of games, make any kind of art, work at any kind of job, seek any body of knowledge or education, join or quit any kind of association, subscribe to any religion, or even do none of these things. We can follow any way of life we choose. Why do we tell ourselves these stories? Because these are the stories of freedom, and we all want to be free.

At the end of the day, we go from the working-place to the shopping-place and spend that money. We buy food, clothing, maintenance for the house, fuel for the car, toys for the kids, and other toys for the adults. Everywhere you look, you see posters, billboards, signs, electronic displays, and labels, telling you how to spend your money. You find them on the walls of city buses, inside and out. You find them painted on the sides of buildings. You find them in your home, and printed on your clothing. You find them on your television and in your newspapers, magazines, and websites. You find them inside your mind. They tell you what you should look like, how you should act, what to say, how to live, what to do, and who you are. And most of us do follow along, most of the time. Why do we do this? Because we fear that if we do not do this, no one will love us, and we all want to be loved.

Then with plastic bags packed and plastic money spent, we take our plastic treasures home. We kiss the wife, eat the dinner, and send the kids off to play computer games in a sound-proofed basement. After that, we retire to a different room to watch the movie, drink the wine, kiss the wife again, and go to bed.

Why do we do this? So that tomorrow, we can do it again.

And why will we do this tomorrow? So that we can do it again the next day.

And when you go to bed in the evening, you try to rest and let it go, but the demands and consequences of the day vibrate in your head and trouble your sleep. You do your best to convince yourself that the noise is an acceptable price to pay for your prosperity, your freedom, and the love of others around you. Or you simply take a sleeping pill and chemically wash it away. Soon we will rise in the morning, and do it again. And why shall we do it again? So that we can do it all over again the next day.

And then, on the day after that, we can do it again.

And then, after *that* –

And *then* –

But really – why, why, please, *why* do we do this?

I suspect that most people really don't know anymore.

But we do know that *something is wrong*, even if we don't know exactly what. This sense of the wrongness of it all has perhaps been on people's minds since the very first cities, many thousands of years ago. How did we come to this? What is wrong here? Why do we stay stuck in it? What alternatives exist? How can we discover the solutions we need? Why do so very few of us live truly meaningful and worthwhile lives?

Friends, if you can spare a moment from this neurotic routine of ours, I'd like to share with you my own explanation.

The Labyrinth of Fear

Our world is utterly saturated with fear. We fear being attacked by religious extremists, both foreign and domestic. We fear the loss of political rights, a loss of privacy, or a loss of freedom. We fear being injured, robbed or attacked, being judged by others, or neglected, or left unloved. We fear succumbing to an exotic pandemic disease, or losing our homes to catastrophic storms induced by climate change and global warming. We fear the social breakdown that abortion, divorce, and same-sex marriage will supposedly cause. We fear foreign immigrants with their strange customs, coming to our neighborhoods to take our jobs, drain our welfare state, or commit crimes. We have existential fears such as the fear of death, fear of freedom itself, fear of the afterlife, fear of being 'unreal' (a surprisingly common one, although difficult to describe), and fear of loneliness and isolation. You might boast of having none of these fears. Yet there is a part of your mind which knows that certain boundaries must not be crossed. We see certain consequences befalling the unprepared, the disbeliever, the nonconformist, the Socratic gadfly. And so we supervise ourselves. We subscribe to moral and political values that separate us from each other, instead of unite us, such as competition, and individualism. We immerse ourselves in escapist mass entertainment, such as 'reality TV' programs. We support fanatical politicians and preachers. Our politicians, in turn, support dictators and tyrants in other countries, all in the name of 'security' and 'stability'. And we arm ourselves to the teeth, and pray to God to be saved. Thus even when we say we have no fear of these things, fear still governs our minds.

Let me draw attention to a special complication in the way fear affects our minds. I hope you will agree that what I'm about to describe is real, and that if it doesn't exactly cause all of our problems, it certainly participates in many of them, and worsens them. The problem I wish to describe is, in its essence, the same problem faced by the builder of a labyrinth who, on finishing his labyrinth, finds that he has sealed himself up inside it. Consider a few simple examples:

1. An interior decorator paints himself into a corner, and then can't move out of that corner without spoiling the paint job and getting his clothes dirty.
2. A carpenter builds a beautiful wooden fishing boat in his workshop, only to find that the finished work is too large to fit through the door.
3. A socialite wants to be well-liked by the people around him. Therefore every time he is invited to a party, he promises to attend. Sometimes he agrees to so many party invitations that he double-books himself. He becomes unable to fulfill many of his promises. He thus creates a reputation for himself as an unreliable busybody.

These introductory examples are perhaps rather silly. In the first example, the solution is quite obvious: the painter will have to just accept that he will get dirty as he crosses the floor. The carpenter in the second example will have to disassemble his boat

4

and reassemble it elsewhere, or else perhaps demolish one of the walls of his workshop. The painter and the carpenter can laugh about their mistakes later. And all three of them could have saved themselves their trouble with a little bit of forethought. But the socialite in the third example will have to sacrifice some of his pride. He may have to change his habits, and make realistic promises rather than numerous ones. And yet he may be unwilling to do so: if he's like most people, he thinks that admitting his mistakes must entail a loss of face.

In ethics, the notion of rational self-interests has a certain prestige. A right, for instance, is now normally defined as an interest of sufficient importance that the rights holder can place others under a duty to have that interest fulfilled. And in Utilitarianism, the notion of interests underlies one of the standard definitions of utility itself: the satisfaction of one's rational desires. We also find it in modern economics, which explains consumer behavior in terms of people's willingness to spend money in pursuit of their interests. As just about everyone now knows, the pursuit of rational self-interest can produce self-refuting strategies for success. People sometimes do what they think is in their best interest, but produce a bad situation for that person and perhaps also for others involved. The best known philosophical account of such situations is a logic puzzle called the Prisoner's Dilemma. This puzzle was first invented by American mathematicians working for the RAND corporation. But it was put into its best known form and given its name by Canadian born mathematician Albert Tucker. Here's one version of the dilemma.

Suppose you and an accomplice have committed a crime. The police have evidence sufficient only to give each of you a short jail sentence, and they want to get a confession fully implicating both of you. They separate you, and tell you that if your accomplice doesn't confess you'll get one year in jail if you confess, but two years if you don't confess. If your accomplice does confess, then you'll get three years if you confess, and four years if you don't confess. They also say that the same deal is being offered to your accomplice.[1]

Well, do you confess, or not? The dilemma presupposes that all prisoners are motivated by rational self-interest, and rational self-interest presumably includes getting the shortest jail time possible. To get the shortest sentence, one year, it's in your interest to confess. But your accomplice reasons the same way, so he confesses too, which sticks both of you in jail for three years. Suppose you stay silent instead. Then you have to decide whether you trust your accomplice to co-operate, which gives you both two years; a much better result than three. But if you co-operate by staying silent and the accomplice defects by confessing, you both get the maximum sentence, four years.

The prisoner's dilemma is a model of any situation in which two or more people or groups, who aren't communicating with each other very well, pursue what they think is in their self interest. But they instead produce a result that is actually contrary to their self-interest. It does not show that co-operation is always more successful than narrow selfishness, as it is often interpreted to mean. Rather, it shows that under some circumstances, when the structure of penalties and rewards is arranged in a certain way, co-operation is a better strategy for success than selfishness. The serious question here is not just a matter of whether self-interest is self-refuting. It is a question of how well real-world problems resemble the prisoner's dilemma. And this question can be answered easily: lots of real-world problems *do*, in fact, resemble the dilemma. Robert Axelrod, for instance, observed that the dilemma can explain the spontaneous cease-fires across the trench battlefields of the First World War. Soldiers had an interest in not being shot as they gathered their wounded, or as they celebrated Christmas dinner. So they refrained from shooting their enemies, and trusted that their enemies would reason the same way.[2]

Yet sometimes a real-world situation is much more than a matter of self-interested behavior producing bad results. It is also a case of the choices which someone makes, in pursuit of some interest, which produce bad consequences *and also trap him into affirming those bad consequences as if they were good*. Or, to explain another way: the bad consequences cannot be undone without repudiating some part of the pursuit of one's interests. And this may seem like a fairly straightforward thesis, nothing too original, but for two qualities which I shall shortly explain. Real-world examples of prisoner's dilemmas tend to have these two qualities, but the logic puzzle as normally expressed does not account for them very well. When those qualities are present, they render the prisoner's dilemma into something I'd like to call *the labyrinth of fear*.

In art, a labyrinth is a geometrically designed maze, with harmonious proportions. Unlike mazes, labyrinths usually have a single path leading from the beginning to the end. There are usually no branches, false paths, or dead ends. Also unlike mazes, the beginning is always at the edge and the end is always in the center. In that respect they are perhaps better compared to mandalas. The oldest labyrinths are prehistoric carvings on cave walls and various stone artifacts. One finds them in classical Greek and Roman times, for instance on Cretan coins. One also finds them in mediaeval religious art, for instance laid in the stonework floors of mediaeval cathedrals. As works of art, I am quite fond of them; I find them very beautiful. That very aesthetic quality is also one of the qualities of the labyrinth of fear. Like the labyrinths of art, the labyrinth of fear also has a direct path from the center to the outside. One can escape from it easily enough by following the thread back to the door. For unlike mazes, there are no dead ends and confusing branches to keep the prisoner trapped. Rather, he is held within the labyrinth by the hypnotic and mesmerizing design of the labyrinth itself. The prisoner is proud of his workmanship and entranced with the sight of something that is his own doing. At the same time he fears what might lie beyond its walls. Therefore he stays where he is: he remains unwilling to leave.

To show how this may work in matters more serious than floor painting and boat building, here are a few more examples.

4. A person enjoys eating pizza, hot dogs, hamburgers, sugary breakfast cereals, chips, pop, beer, hard liquor, and rich desserts. This food is cheap, readily available, and pleasurable to eat. But after ten years of eating nothing else, he finds himself morbidly obese, suffering from type-2 diabetes and various substance addictions. He may have difficulty washing himself, and may be in serious danger of an early death from liver and kidney failure or heart disease. Strangers in public places also taunt and jeer at him because of his weight.

5. A person wishes to be physically attractive. He therefore spends hours each morning and evening on maintaining his appearance. He submits to various surgical procedures such as Botox injections, liposuction, and facelifts. He replaces his entire wardrobe several times a year, at great expense. As a result, he may indeed be regarded as attractive by many of the people around him. However, he may also have gained a psychological obsession. He compulsively checks his appearance in every available reflective surface. Most if not all conversations with his friends concern recent fashion trends, and judgments of other people's looks. He may feel traumatized at the discovery of minor physical imperfections, such as moles, grey hairs, or age wrinkles. He may place himself on a starvation- diet to achieve thinness, and thereby threaten his physical health as well.

6. A person wishes to live 'the good life', with the fanciest cars, the most high-tech computers and electronics, the biggest house, the most fashionable accessories, the most exotic vacations. He makes impulse purchases of clothes, food, books, and novelties, and to justify these purchases he tells himself, "I've had a bad day today," or "I deserve it.". To pay for this lifestyle, he gathers together as many credit cards, bank loans, payday advances, and other sources of money that he can, and spends the money as fast as he can. A few years later he finds that his total debts outweigh his total assets, and his monthly minimum payments are greater than his actual monthly income. His creditors may take him to court to garnish his wages or take away his savings. His landlord may evict him for non-payment of rent, or his mortgage holder might repossess his house, in either case leaving him homeless.

Each of these examples may look like straightforward cases of someone intending benefit for himself but producing harm instead. But there is more than that going on. These people remain committed to their situations, even with consequences like these, because they perceive that their situation is a product of their choices. It is something that they have positively *willed*. They therefore usually reject all criticism or advice from others concerning how the situation is not in their best interest. You have all heard the argument: "It's my choice, and it's a free society, so I can do whatever I want." Indeed this reason for remaining within the labyrinth may create the illusion of freedom. The prisoners may even believe that their locked and stressed circumstance is a situation that they actually *want*. As the prison is made by the hands of the prisoners, so the prisoners think themselves still free.

Furthermore, the center of a labyrinth houses a monster. The word 'labyrinth' first appears in Greek mythology, and refers to a maze-like structure built by the architect Daedalus to imprison a minotaur. In the labyrinths of fear just described, the prisoners live in a social environment where various punishments are assigned for those who live different lifestyles. The junk food addict may find that junk food is cheaper and more readily available than fresh whole food. He may have eaten nothing but fast food and junk food his whole life, and so when offered a plate of fresh home-cooked traditional food, he might not touch it. (I've personally seen this happen.) So if he doesn't eat junk food, he might not eat at all. The fashion addict is surrounded at almost all times by images of beautiful people, for instance in fashion magazines, advertising, films, pop music, and television. He feels he will be judged by others in accord with how closely he resembles such people. The same mass media also encourages the debt-stricken person to seek out still further lines of credit to maintain his material standard of living. He may also have been duped by a sales pitch deliberately calculated to deceive him about hidden fees and other obligations. A former student of mine who once worked as an insurance salesman disclosed to me that his company's sales pitches are scripted very carefully, right down to certain specific words and phrases that the salesman must say. Some of those sales phrases require the salesman to lie to the customer, or to divert attention away from 'the fine print'. In financial matters, almost every social message we see today tells us to intensify one's lifestyle, rather than change it. Yet this message is contributing to a serious social credit crisis. A recent study found that household debt in Canada averages $100,879, and that the average household debt in Canada is 150% of the average household income.[3] The individual trapped in his labyrinth also knows that if he changes his ways, he will probably be socially punished. The junk food addict who suddenly switches to healthy food will be accused of having joined the tree-hugging hippies. Think of Homer Simpson telling his daughter Lisa, "You don't make friends with salad!" The fashion lover who decides to wear less makeup and more ordinary clothes, and who no longer obsesses about his waistline, will have 'let himself go'. The yuppie who stops keeping up with the Jones's will have 'dropped out'. In these ways the labyrinth is not simply a matter of one person failing to be responsible for his own life. It is also a comprehensive social environment which rewards the choices which create the labyrinth, and which punishes the choices which enable escape from it. That structure of reward and punishment creates fear. And that fear is the second quality which distinguishes the labyrinth of fear from an ordinary case of thwarted self-interest.

Probably the first description of this situation in philosophical literature is in Book 2 of Plato's *Republic*. There he described the "city with a fever", the "luxurious city" and "the city of pigs" (372d-374a). In this city, increasing demand for luxury goods leads to the depletion of local resources, which in turn leads to warfare with neighboring cities to replenish those resources. As Plato says,

> ... the land, I suppose, that used to be adequate to feed the population we had then, will cease to be adequate and become too small. Then we'll have to seize some of our neighbors' land if we're to have enough pasture and plough land. And won't our neighbors want to seize part of ours as well, if they too have surrendered themselves to the endless acquisition of money and have overstepped the limit of their necessities? (*Republic* 373d)

Presumably, none of the citizens of this city originally wanted war: they originally wanted comfort, wealth, and pleasure. But neither are they willing to reduce their material standard of living once they exceed the bounds set by the physical carrying capacity of their environment. That wealth and pleasure hypnotizes them into being unable to contemplate a change in their lifestyle. This impasse, according to Plato, inevitably produces war. It seems to me that it also traps the citizens of the luxurious city into actually wanting war, the very opposite of what they originally wanted.

A second example from philosophy appears in Thomas Hobbes' *Leviathan*. Hobbes had been translating the work of Thucydides who described the reasons behind the outbreak of the Peloponnesian War. Those reasons had to do with Athens' growing power and wealth and influence, and Sparta's fear of what Athens might do with that power. Hobbes was also a serious student of the civil war then breaking out in his own country. (*Leviathan* was published in the same year that the English Civil War ended: 1651.) In the first stage of Hobbes' analysis, people find that they are approximately equal to each other in terms of power. While one man might be stronger than another, he could be overcome by a weaker person "either by secret machination, or by confederacy with others, that are in the same danger with himself." (*Leviathan* 13.1) But even while people are equally powerful in that way, they might find themselves in a competition for scarce resources. This, in turn, produces never-ending warfare. In Hobbes' words:

And from this diffidence [distrustfulness] of one another, there is no way for any man to secure himself, so reasonable, as anticipation, that is, by force, or wiles, to master the persons of all men he can, so long, till he see no other power great enough to endanger him. (*Leviathan* 13.4)

The idea here is that any person or group involved in a competition with another similar person or group may find it in the interest of their security to launch a first strike. But they will also reason that the other person or group has the same interests, and thus the same reason for striking first. This ultimately produces, in Hobbes' words, "continual fear, and danger of violent death, and the life of man, solitary, poor, nasty, brutish, and short." (*Leviathan* 13.9)

A third philosophical account of the Labyrinth of Fear is in *Phenomenology of Spirit*, by G.W.F. Hegel, also published during a time of extraordinary political conflict. In this case the conflict was the Battle of Jena, in the year 1806, fought between the armies of Napoleon Bonaparte and Friedrich Wilhelm II. An anecdote about Hegel's life suggests that the final pages of this text were written while the battle was actually happening just outside his apartment window. One of the cornerstones of the text is a discussion which philosophers today call the Dialectic of the Master and the Slave. It occurs about a hundred pages into the text, following a discussion of Self-Consciousness, by which Hegel apparently means the awareness that an individual self may have of his or her own existence, and also the meaning and significance that may be assigned to that existence. That discussion concludes with the statement, emphasized with italics in the original text, that "self- consciousness achieves its satisfaction only in another self-consciousness." (Hegel, *P of S*, § 175) And a few paragraphs later he repeats: "Self-consciousness exists in and for itself when, and by the fact that, it exists for another; that is, it exists only in being acknowledged." (*Ibid*, § 178) In other words, a self is able to assign meaning and significance to its own existence only through an acknowledgement from another. We do not really assign that meaning to ourselves; rather: we look for others who will assign it to us. Or, what is perhaps more accurate, we look to others for confirmation of the value we assign to ourselves. I'll lay aside for now the argument by which he arrived at that conclusion; let it suffice for the moment to say that Hegel regarded it as something like a necessity in the evolution of the world-soul. Next, Hegel finds that when one independent self meets another, it "...must proceed to supersede the *other* independent being in order thereby to become certain of *itself* as the essential being." (*Ibid*,§ 180) The need to supersede the other arises because the self cannot easily nor automatically get from the other the acknowledgement it craves. And that, in turn, is the case because:

> … the other is equally independent and self-contained, and there is nothing in it of which it is not itself the origin. The first does not have the object before it merely as it exists primarily for desire, but as something that has an independent existence of its own, which, therefore, it cannot utilize for its own purposes, if that object does not of its own accord do what the first does to it. (*Ibid*, § 182)

So here we have two houses, both alike in dignity. Both are self-contained in their own existence (i.e. their own being-in-itself) but seeking an acknowledgement of the meaning and worth of that existence from one another. But neither can 'use' the other for that purpose, for neither of them are 'objects' passively available for that kind of use. You cannot use another person like a tool in your workshop or a piece of furniture in your house. And yet that is precisely what the Hegelian self-consciousness needs the other to be. This leads us to a kind of impasse: "Each is indeed certain of its own self, but not of the other, and therefore its own self-certainty still has no truth." (*Ibid*, § 186). And in that impasse, they enter into a life-and-death struggle to win from each other the acknowledgement of mastery that they seek.

> Insofar as it is the action of the *other* [that the self seeks], each seeks the death of the other… Thus the relation of the two self-conscious individuals is such that they prove themselves and each other through a life-and-death struggle. They must engage in this struggle, for they must raise their certainty of being *for themselves* to truth, both in the case of the other and in their own case… (*Ibid*, § 187)

But this struggle is self-refuting, because:

> This trial by death, however, does away with the truth which was supposed to issue from it, and so, too, with the certainty of self generally. For just as life is the natural setting of consciousness... so death is the natural negation of consciousness... which thus remains without the required significance of recognition. Death certainly shows that each staked his life and held it of no account, both in himself and in the other; but that is not for those who survived this struggle. (*Ibid*, § 188)

So, we end up with a situation like that of a plantation owner who, knowing that the slaves might not acknowledge his mastery freely, therefore demands that acknowledgement from them at gunpoint. But by doing so he takes away from them the very freedom without which they cannot give that acknowledgement. He might, instead, acknowledge the freedom and the self-sufficiency of the slaves, so that they in turn can acknowledge his own. But that would mean assigning to the slaves the very freedom and self-sufficiency that he wants for himself. Each party in the Hegelian dialectic ends up in exactly the same spot where each began, but with the additional element of fear. This fear, according to Hegel, awakens the mind of the person in the position of the slave, and assigns to the slave and not the master the exalted status of being-for-himself. (cf *Ibid*, §196) But this fear also holds both parties in a perpetual stalemate with each other.

Those three accounts, from Plato and Hobbes and Hegel, help illustrate the fear part of the labyrinth of fear. Another text of Hegel's gives us a curious parable which, to my mind, helps understand the hypnotic part of the labyrinth. It appears in his *Lectures on Aesthetics*, and runs as follows:

A boy throws stones into the river, and then stands admiring the circles that trace themselves on the water, as an effect in which he attains the sight of something that is his own doing. This need traverses the most manifold phenomena, up to the mode of self-production in the medium of external things as it is known to us in the work of art... The universal need for expression in art lies, therefore, in man's rational impulse to exalt the inner and outer world into a spiritual consciousness for himself, as an object in which he recognizes his own self.

(Hegel, *Introductory Lectures on Aesthetics*, § 49)

Hegel is speaking of art here, not human relations. But he is speaking of a similar phenomenological insight. Each person wishes to know that his or her existence is meaningful. One way to know that is to observe changes in the world which we have made; it is to do things (like make art) which have an effect on the world. As I see it, the labyrinth of fear combines these two things. We have on one side the impasse in the life of a person who, motivated by fear, pursues his safety in a self-defeating way. On the other side we have the hypnotic quality of the ripples in the water, which is the sight of the product of one's own labor. This is precisely what we see in City of Pigs, the Hobbesian Trap, and the Dialectic of the Master and Slave. Those situations, troublesome as they are, nonetheless serve as ripples in the water of the world which the stone-thrower can point to as evidence of the significance of his existence. Even as the impasse of such situations involve fear, they show us that we exist, and that our existence has some kind of meaning. Hence why, I think, those who build labyrinths of fear around themselves are often most unwilling to change their circumstances and set themselves free.

The Labyrinth of Fear is in some ways broadly similar to the other philosophical cases. The people of Plato's City of Pigs pursue wealth and luxury, but they get war. The people in a Hobbesian 'state of nature' pursue security and personal freedom, and they too get war: in fact a war of "every man against every man" in which "nothing can be unjust." (*Leviathan* 13.8 and 13.13) The Hegelian consciousness which seeks the "elevation of its existence to truth" instead produces a 'trial by death' with another being also seeking the same thing. Similarly, the prisoner's dilemma describes such a situation, but in more sober and mathematical terms. The prisoners want to be released, but so long as they pursue that interest in a narrowly selfish way, they get longer jail terms instead of shorter ones. Of these four accounts, only two of them explicitly mention fear. But it still seems to me that fear is the primary motivating force at work in all of them. It is arguable that self-interest is the primary force here. But in each of these cases, there is a stage in the game at which negative interests like fear-avoidance become greater than positive interests. To put it in terms of the aforementioned prisoner's dilemma, some prisoners might choose to always confess, knowing that the accomplice will probably confess too, and thus he consigns himself to jail for three years. But he does this because the fear of getting four years is stronger in him than the will to co-operate and possibly get only two years. A few more examples may serve to help understand this: and here's one from history.

7. In Iron Age Celtic, Anglo-Saxon, Scandinavian and Germanic society, a victim of certain kinds of crimes could recruit his family to inflict a similar crime upon the offender or his family. This was thought of at the time as fair and just, because it restored the relative position of the two parties. However, in this situation, the original victim would become a new offender, and the original offender would become a new victim. That new victim would therefore recruit his family to inflict a similar harm upon the original victim's family. The new offender and his family is thus victimized again, and seeks retri-

bution again. The result is an escalating spiral of violence. And if the original offence was murder, the situation becomes a spiral of retributive killing which can continue long after the initial incident is forgotten.

Historically, this situation was called 'the blood feud'. Sometimes the payment of a fine (in Irish, an 'eric'; in Anglo-Saxon, a 'wergild') could settle matters. But only one hold-out whose pride got the better of him could start the cycle anew. Fear is involved here: the fear of the power of the offender, the fear of the loss of face that might result from not punishing violence with more violence. A hypnotic effect is also obtained here too, as the vicious circle of the blood feud takes on a life of its own, giving people purpose, even if a murderous one. This example may seem very distant to us, and the ridiculousness of it all may seem plainly obvious. However, contemporary situations with almost exactly the same logic do exist. For example:

8. Someone feels aggrieved by something that another person said or did. He therefore gossips about that person and his actions, in order to convince others that the offender is a bad person. To maximize the effect of this gossip, he includes descriptions of unrelated incidents that occurred in the past, maybe years in the past, but which involve the same person. He may also mix half-truths, exaggerations, and lies into those stories. If others are sympathetic to the original offender, then the victim accuses them of 'bias', and demands that his side of the story be heard, in the interest of "fairness" and "hearing both sides". But he refuses to hear any view but his own, and may even take steps to prevent other views from being heard. He recruits others to gossip maliciously about that person. Sometimes he makes threats against that person, or describes how he might be "not respon-

sible for his actions" if he ever meets that person in a public place. He uses Internet social networks or cellphone text-messaging to harass and bully that person. He may also speak maliciously about that person's friends, family, and other associates. Meanwhile, the original offender, upon learning of the gossip which the victim is espousing, commences his own gossip campaign. He uses the same strategies to discredit the other person and to justify his actions.

The harm caused by malicious gossip is social and psychological, but it follows exactly the same logic as the Iron Age blood-feud. Instead of attacking someone's body with knives and swords, it attacks a person's reputation, social connections, and peace of mind, using malicious words and social manipulations. The attacks can cause sleeplessness, nightmares, headaches, uncontrollable shaking of limbs, unstoppable crying, and other symptoms resembling post-traumatic stress. It can worsen existing psychological problems such as anxiety disorders or clinical depression. It can render people unable to function in their jobs, or unable to parent their children. On some occasions, it has been known to drive people to suicide. But at the same time, the instigator of the malicious gossip often finds he cannot easily desist. The gossip campaign gives him purpose. If it is pointed out to him that his gossip is excessive and hurtful, he portrays the harms he causes that person as deserved and fair, because of the original harm caused to him. And if he's like most people, he won't want to admit that he is wrong, because that will entail losing face.

People can also trap themselves by doing things not only in response to what another person does, but also in competition against them, especially when scarce resources are involved. For instance:

9. A landscape experiences a drought, and so a thirsty man goes to a nearby water well to drink. He sees other thirsty people rushing to the well, and he knows that there is not enough water in the well for everyone. So he rushes to the well to be among the first to get water. He takes with him the largest bucket to get as much water for himself as he can before there is none left. But everyone else does the same, causing the well to run dry much sooner, and causing many other needy people to go without.

10. A ship has sunk at sea, and the survivors tread around in search of a handhold in the wreckage. One lifeboat remains. Each survivor knows that it will save his life, and also knows that there is not enough space on the lifeboat for everyone. But each swims toward it anyway, as fast as possible, and each pulls himself on board. Soon the lifeboat has too many people clambering to get on, and it flounders and sinks.

In those examples, the labyrinth of fear is created through the concerted action of a number of people. They trap themselves because of what they see others doing. A real-world parallel to these cases is the depletion of important and non-renewable energy resources such as petroleum. A report by the United States Army published in early 2010 said that "By 2012, surplus oil production capacity could entirely disappear, and as early as 2015, the shortfall in output could reach nearly 10 million barrels per day." In words that reminded me of Plato's parable of the city of pigs, the report also reminded the readers that "the Great Depression [of the 1930s] spawned a number of totalitarian regimes that sought economic prosperity for their nations by ruthless conquest."[4]

Another variation can be created not in the knowledge of what others are doing, but in the absence of that knowledge. We can trap ourselves with the fear of what another person *might* do. For instance:

11. A professional athlete, wishing to win more often and more gloriously, decides to inject himself with steroids. He also reasons that his competitors will likely have discovered the same drugs. To preserve his advantage he therefore takes more of them, and takes them more often. Perhaps he becomes more successful for a short while. But the end result is the destruction of his health, and the loss of prestige and credibility for his whole sport and virtually all athletes associated with it.

Like the prisoner's dilemma, the labyrinth of fear is a situation in which people pursue what they believe is in their interest, but produce a situation that no one wants. You may recognize the logic of Kant's Categorical Imperative here. Yet unless someone somewhere takes the initiative to step out of the prison, the poisoned situation will affect everyone. The athlete, for instance, knows that by doping he also puts his whole team at risk. In the summer of 2010, for instance, a football player at the University of Waterloo, in Ontario, Canada, tested positive for human growth hormone. The police arrested him for trafficking, and the university suspended the whole team for a season.[5] But we can see this version of the labyrinth operating on larger scales, with bigger stakes. Here are two more examples.

12. A businessman wishes to make money. He reasons that if he can sell his products for a lesser price than his competitors, people will choose his products instead of similar ones made by his competitors. Therefore he aims to reduce his production costs as much as possible. He also reasons that his competitors in the market will have the same wish as himself, and a similar plan for fulfilling that wish. He therefore locates his factory in a poor

country where industrial safety laws are very lax, and where he will not have to pay the workers more than a few pennies per unit. He authorizes the use of poor quality materials, or even toxic materials, when those materials are cheaper. The end result might be lower prices for consumers, and greater sales and profits for himself. But the result may also include poor quality goods, an exhausted and exploited workforce, and organized campaigns to boycott his products, or even his entire industry, in protest against moral and political injustices that he and his industry perpetuates.

Many investors and businesspeople believe that 'business is war'. It's a war against other entrepreneurs in the market: for one business to succeed, others must fail. It's also political. Warren Buffet, widely regarded as the world's most successful investor, told a CNN journalist: "It's class warfare, my class is winning, but they shouldn't be."[6] The practical results of this point of view, however, were seen in the sub-prime mortgage crisis of 2008, when the entire world's economy collapsed. I shall examine that case in closer detail later in this book. For the moment, let us turn to one more example of the labyrinth of fear, where those who cause others to be afraid end up trapped by their own fears:

13. A politician wishes to gain more power in his country. He reasons that if he is able to describe a great threat to the country, and depicts himself as the person best able to protect the country, then the people will vote for him. Yet he also knows that his political competitors also want power, and he reasons that they might hit upon the same strategy. He therefore tries to imagine the most frightening threat possible. He entertains the very worst and darkest of fears. He will name at least one national enemy: the 'red menace' of Soviet communism, or the 'merciless hordes' of

Islamic terrorists, the 'flood' of illegal immigrants. He will play up the danger of that enemy. The Soviets have sleeper cells in our communities, the foreigners are draining our welfare state, and the Muslims are building a nuclear bomb. These claims might not be true, but he can successfully gain and hold political power by convincing others to believe them. But he also ends up ruling over a population of fearful and paranoid people. He will have to maintain an extensive security surveillance network, and to ensure that network functions properly he may have to suspend some of his people's civil liberties. He may also find himself in a war with his enemy which, because the war justifies his rule, he cannot allow to end, and therefore will never win. But the war will certainly kill thousands or even millions of people, and destroy infrastructures and ecologies on a large scale. Finally, some of his people will eventually grow tired of living in fear. They will organize protests against him, and rally support for his political opponents.

Robert Grenier, retired former director of the CIA's counter-terrorism center, was told by a mentor of his to "always remember that fear drives the system." The fear he referred to is the fear of being blamed if something bad happens. As Grenier himself told a journalist:

In the world of national security, it means that if threats are not foreseen, if dots are not connected, if warnings are not issued and, God forbid, something bad happens, there will be hell to pay. And while the costs of a false warning will be negligible, a failure to warn could be catastrophic. Given this reality, it is no wonder that government bureaucracies behave as they do. I cannot recount the number of times when I have been forced to share information on a potential threat which I knew – knew as well as mortal man can know anything in this vale of tears – to be invalid."[7]

Yet the exercise of power via fear traps tightest not the person who is afraid, but the one who teaches the fear. Malidoma Somé, an Aboriginal Elder and writer from Burkina Faso, observed this effect on the people who were attempting to Westernize and Christianize his country.

When power comes out of its hiddenness, it shrinks the person who brought it into the open and turns that person into a servant. The only way that overt power can remain visible is by being fed, and he who knows how to make power visible ends up trapped into keeping that power visible... Whoever creates that kind of visible power must then stay in the service to that which he creates. To display power is to become servile to it in a way that is extremely disempowering. This is because the service is fuelled by the terror of losing the fantasy of having power.[8]

If I understand the elder correctly, I think he is saying that a person or group that exercises power over another, especially oppressive or coercive power, soon finds that he must *continue* to exercise power. The exercise of power mesmerizes him. At the same time he comes to fear the loss of power. (By the way, a similar observation was made by Chancellor Palpatine in the film *Star Wars III*.) That fear compels him (or them) to continue exerting power. Even if this exercise of power transforms the wielder into a tyrant, he simply cannot stop. His fear of losing power will compel him to continue behaving in a tyrannical way. You can see this happening on small scales, such as in arguments on Internet-based discussion forums, where belligerent speakers defend untenable positions in order to avoid losing influence or attention. You also find it on large scales, such as in the actions of a military force occupying a foreign country, which refuses to loosen their grip on things even as it becomes too costly to keep it. Think of former American president George W. Bush refusing to 'cut and run' from Iraq, even while it was becoming increasingly obvious that his army could not stop the insurgency.

When the labyrinth of fear emerges from choices made in response to or anticipation of other people's choices, as it did in the last several examples, then it also tends to be characterized by a deadlock of initiative. Everyone knows that something is wrong and everyone knows that something must be done. But *everyone is waiting for someone else to make the first move*. The hypnotic quality of the situation keeps everyone holding on, unwilling to let go. And since everyone is waiting for someone else to take the initiative, the result is that no one takes the initiative. Thus the athlete reasons that if he stops doping, he might lose the race. The promise of sporting victory hypnotizes him, and the fear of defeat drives him. The business investor reasons that if he stops using cheap labor and cheap materials, other businessmen will take over his share of the market, and he might be forced out of the market. The promise of wealth hypnotizes him, and the fear of poverty drives him. The politician reasons that if he downplays the fear, another politician will accuse him of "weakness", of not being a patriot, or even of being sympathetic to the enemy, and he might lose the election. If a terrorist attack actually did happen, he will be accused of complacence, and unreadiness. The promise of power hypnotizes him, and the fear of powerlessness drives him. And so each of them trap themselves, and remain trapped.

But *life does not have to be that way*. There is *nothing* natural, inevitable, or necessary about the labyrinth of fear. We *can* liberate ourselves. There *are* better ways to live. Someone has to take the initiative to love and trust her fellow living creature, and set us all free.

Who will it be? Who will it be?

The Circle of Meaning

I feel I need to apologize for beginning this thought-opera on such a dissonant chord. But I think it important to understand our problems clearly and properly. Such clarifications contribute to our wisdom, and also make our problems easier to solve.

Yet this book is not just about social and moral problems. It is about people and relationships. It is about what our lives might look like if we were not so profoundly governed by fear. As we have seen, fear tends to emerge from disordered and dysfunctional relationships. For one of the deepest and most debilitating fears we endure is the fear of *other people*. We fear what they might do or say, how they may act, whether they will judge you, harm you, steal from you, interfere with your life, perhaps kill you, or simply ignore you. The liberation from fear requires a better understanding of our relationships, and a rectifying and a healing of our relationships. In that sense, this book offers not one way, but twenty-two ways, to escape the labyrinth.

I also think that liberation from fear requires a sense of the sacred. For just as our fears emerge from our relationships, so does the sacred. Obviously the idea of the sacred is very complicated. But we may generalize very broadly and say that the sacred is something claimed to have a special place in our thoughts, feelings, and practices. This may be helpful: but describing that place can be very difficult to do. Often, therefore, people resort to the language of mystery. They say things like, "The sacred is an experience, and impossible to put into words." Or, "You have to make a leap of faith," or "Happy is he who has not seen and yet believes." But I've never been very satisfied with settlements like that. They seem to divert attention away from the question, instead of toward a solution. They cause the process of inquiry to *stop* just at the point where the process gets interesting.

When we think of the words 'the sacred', we do not normally think of relationships. We mostly think of 'things' We look to sacred places, like the mountain of Croagh Patrick, in Ireland;

26

sacred buildings, like Khajuraho Temple, in India; sacred music, such as Gregorio Allegri's *Miserere*, and sacred texts, like the Tao Te Ching. Sometimes we speak of sacred people, like priests, prophets, saints, shaman, seers. Or we might say someone is an elder, or that he is somehow 'very spiritual'. Sometimes we treat non-religious things in a sacred way, such as a national flag, or the trophy cup of a professional sports league. But as I hope this book will show, these things are sacred not simply because of what they are. They are sacred because of the relations between people which involve them. The sacred, I shall say, is *that which acts as your partner in the search for the highest and deepest things*: the real, the true, the good, and the beautiful. The name I'd like to give to the kind of relationship that gives us a chance to find such things is *a circle of meaning*.

Many spiritual and philosophical traditions already put human relationships, and the values needed to sustain them, at the center of attention. In a text called *The Doctrine of the Mean*, one of the most important texts of Confucianism, we find a discussion of "The Five Relations". Part of this discussion reads as follows:

> There are five universal ways [in human relations], and the way by which they are practiced is three. The five are those governing the relationship between ruler and minister, between father and son, between husband and wife, between elder and younger brothers, and those in the intercourse between friends. These five are universal paths in the world. Wisdom, humanity, and courage, these three are the universal virtues. The way by which they are practiced is one.[9]

The general idea is that all human relationships are variations or elaborations of this basic five. Thus in Confucian society, no one needs to think of anyone else as a stranger or an enemy. Everyone can find one of these five ways of relating to whoever they meet. It might be a familial relationship, as in the case of parents and children. It might be a relation of social function, of which the relation of 'ruler and minister' is the model. Modern examples might include the relation of landlord and tenant, or manager and employee. It might be a relationship of an older to a younger person, or of friends (or potential friends). This idea became immeasurably influential on Chinese society. The virtues of wisdom, humanity, and courage are noted here not because of their own merits, but because of the way they support the five relations.

In *The Book of Mencius*, another significant Confucian text, the values that maintain the five relations are specified more particularly for each, and with a final unifying addendum:

> ... between father and son, there should be affection; between ruler and minister, there should be righteousness; between husband and wife, there should be attention to their separate functions; between old and young, there should be a proper order; and between friends, there should be faithfulness. Emperor Yao said, "Encourage them, help them, aid them, so they discover for themselves [their moral nature], and in addition, stimulate them and confer kindness upon them.."[10]

The idea of sacred relationships also appears in the writings of other spiritual traditions. Jesus Christ taught his followers: "Where two or three are gathered together in my name, there am I in the midst of them." (Matthew 18:20) Similarly, attributing a moral as well as sacred dimension to our relations, he said: "Whatsoever you do to the least of my people, you do to me." (Matthew 25:40) Consider also this passage from a Hindu scripture called the *Taittiriya Upanishad*:

> One should not be negligent of duties to the gods and to the fathers.

Be one to whom a mother is as a god.
Be one to whom a father is as a god.
Be one to whom a teacher is as a god.
Be one to whom a guest is as a god.[11]

In Hinduism, all living things share in the presence of the Atman, the 'Self' that is the immanent and universal presence of God. Thus when you meet another person, you are also meeting the presence of God, dwelling in that person. Treating that person with the same respect that you would treat a god creates a circle of meaning between everyone involved.

Many spiritual people today believe that the most important knowledge in life comes from within oneself. "Follow your heart" is the mantra of our time. And some of the world's best known religious heroes achieved their spiritual victories by their own effort. Siddhartha Gautama achieved his Buddha-hood alone, beneath a tree, in a deep forest, far from others. Jesus defeated the devil in the desert, with help from no one else; he also took upon himself the despair of the world while alone in the garden of Gethsemane. The founder of Bahá'í, a mystic who took the name of Bahá'u'lláh, withdrew from his family and community to live as a hermit in the mountains of Kurdistan, in northern Iraq, for two years. I am well aware of the power and the peace that can be discovered in solitude. Yet one quickly finds that these great 'solitary' religious heroes did *not*, in fact, find their visions or win their victories entirely on their own. In every case, they had *teachers*. Even the Buddha, himself a champion of individualism, had several teachers, such as Alara Kalama, and Udaka Ramaputta. Jesus also had various teachers, although to find them, one must look to the apocryphal writings, as the official gospels omit large parts of his early life. For some religious visionaries, a supernatural being takes on the role of teacher, as in the case of the angel who dictated to the prophet Mohammed the text of the Koran. Others rejected what they learned, and developed their own system of thought and practice. But even so, their 'new' system developed as a reply to, an alternative to, or even in competition with whatever system they rejected. The Buddhist doctrine of *dukkha* (emptiness), for instance, is an inversion of the Vedic concept of *atman* (world-soul, higher self), which he learned from his Vedic Hindu teachers. Moreover, after their time as students, they gathered followers and disciples, became teachers, and shared their ideas in various ways. In every account of the life of a person who discovered or professed some important spiritual idea, the story always includes the human relationship between a teacher and a student.

Nor need we be limited to religious accounts. We've already seen a philosophical account in the first premise of Hegel's Dialectic: "self- consciousness achieves its satisfaction only in another self-consciousness." We find affirmations of the importance of human relations just about everywhere. In the warrior culture of Iron Age Europe, friendship ranks among the very highest of values. A strophe of the *Havamal*, for instance, affirms the value and importance of human companionship.

> Young and alone on a long road,
> Once I lost my way
> Rich I felt when I found another;
> Man rejoices in man.[12]

And here it is again, in the Islamic poetry of Omar Khayyám:

> Here with a loaf of bread beneath the bough,
> A flask of wine, a book of verse – and Thou
> Beside me singing in the wilderness –
> And Wilderness is Paradise enow.[13]

Finally, many miles and many years away in Ireland, The Poet wrote these wonderful lines about how friendship endures the transfigurations of time:

> ... think about old friends the most:
> Time's bitter flood will rise,
> Your beauty perish and be lost
> For all eyes but these eyes.

These simple lines, to my mind, express a primary proposition about human life: we find our greatest fulfillment in the company of other people.

We can also find support for this idea in the sciences. In 1992, the Italian neurologist Giuseppe di Pellegrino was examining the MRI scans of a monkey while it was eating some nuts. He found that that the exact same neurons in the monkey's brain became active when the monkey was not eating but was merely observing one of the researchers eating.[14] Other scientists, following up on this discovery, are finding that empathy, the ability to identify with the situation of another being, is part of the very neural structure of the brain. As noted by scientists Stephanie Preston and Frans de Waal, the evidence so far suggests that "perception and action share a common code of representation in the brain."[15] This is now referred to as the "perception-action hypothesis" of brain physiology.

> We hypothesize that empathic understanding comes when the subject's own representation of the emotion or situation is directly activated by perception of the object's. The representations activated in the subject in turn activate physiological and behavioral responses that are processed to the response phase unless inhibited. (Preston & de Waall, *Ibid*)

To put it in more ordinary terms: our brains are naturally structured for sociability and for empathy. We are 'hard wired' for relations with others. Thus, I think there is an important truth in the claim that human happiness dwells primarily in human company. There may be various pleasures and satisfactions that emerge from solitude and even from loneliness. Yet it is the touch, the gaze, the kind word, and the companionship of good people which produces the most valuable sense of fulfillment we can know.

A Study of the Sacred

Many writers who discuss social, moral, and spiritual problems, including the same ones I will be discussing in this book, use a theoretical or abstract approach. They proclaim certain values, analyze them in their unsullied theoretical purity, and then apply them to practical situations. Although we can learn much this way, I think this might be the wrong way to go about it. For our purpose is not just to analyze concepts and interpret events. Nor is it just to grasp the essence of things. It is also to reduce suffering and to edify human life. For a conversation about social and moral problems is not just about values. It is also about peace, war, adventure, death, tragedy, comedy, history, love, sex, growing up, growing old, happiness, suffering, thinking, working, dreaming, politics, imagination, mystery, psychology, music, art, poetry, health, time, reality, truth, magic, and life. There is simply no such thing as a moral or ethical value that dwells apart from somebody's way of being in the world. Therefore, instead of examining values and then applying them to our relations, I'd like to turn the thing around, examine our relations first, and then see what values emerge from them.

In the coming pages, I'll study twenty-two special relationships. Each of them is a way to escape the labyrinth of fear and create a circle of meaning. Some are distinctly personal, such as between couples, friends, and families. Some are more public, such as the relationship between a performer and the audience. Some are animist in nature: they concern relations with our environments. And some are existential, as they concern the larger immensities in which we live and die. The relations I've chosen to discuss here are obviously not the only possible ones which could fit this criteria. I'll have much to say about some, and only a little to say about others, but I don't wish to imply that some are more important than others. I present them not only for contemplative purposes. I also hope that readers of this book will *experiment* with them, in search of ways to make their sacredness more visible in their lives. Some chapters, therefore, include a few activities for you to try. I encourage you to treat your relationships as circles of meaning, and then see what happens, and talk about what you see. If we can craft our relationships like works of art, no less beautifully than the way we build temples and sing songs, then perhaps we can build worthwhile lives for ourselves and for each other, for the whole world, and for future generations.

Around three years ago, when I started conceiving the sacred as a mode of relationships, I suddenly found my research material all around me, everywhere I looked. I still did a lot of my research in libraries, like philosophers usually do, but I also found that I could treat almost anything as a philosophical text: recipe books, for instance, or magazines about wooden boat construction. Any text in which you can find a basic proposition, and an argument to support that proposition, is a philosophical text. Some such texts are better than others, of course, but that is not a denial of the basic point that philosophy happens everywhere. Moreover, since I was exploring the extent to which our spiritual ideas emerge from relationships, I also saw my friends and other people already around me as philosophical resources. I asked various people which of their relations were most important to them. I compared the lists until I settled upon the relations that seemed the most frequently mentioned. Then I sought out people I knew who were intensely involved in those relations. I spoke to chefs, gardeners, musicians, academics and scholars, policemen, vendors at my local farmer's market, school teachers, artists, hunters, medical doctors and nurses, First Nations Elders, a blacksmith, a luthier, a mechanical engineer, a timber-frame house builder, a dog trainer, and many other kinds of people besides. I spoke to them in their homes and workplaces, in public streets and in bars and restaurants, at festivals, at weddings and funerals, at concerts, and any place where I happened to meet them. I did some of this work while touring to promote one of my previous books, and so I was able to speak to people in six Canadian provinces and five European countries.

Sometimes I would examine a person in a Socratic way: asking questions designed to ascertain what someone actually believes, and also to ascertain whether there are any logical contradictions in what he believes. But most of the time, I found it better to resist the urge to play Socrates, and simply listen respectfully to what the person had to say, and then to thank them for teaching me. Socrates, although I do not doubt that he was a philosopher, often questioned people as if he assumed there was always a fault in other people's reasoning, and his job was to find it. For my own Socratic search, I thought it better to assume that people's beliefs are generally rational and sound, unless there were outstanding reasons to assume otherwise. To each person I spoke with I usually started with the same four questions. Why do you do what you do? What is the most significant relationship involved in doing what you do? What values, if any, are needed in order to be good at what you do? I also asked the person to tell me an interesting story about his or her work. Sometimes I also asked a few follow-up questions. But for the most part, these four questions were enough to draw out the most interesting philosophical material.

Although I gathered many curious anecdotes and proverbs this way, I wasn't just collecting random folklore. I was also pursuing a twofold thesis. In the first fold, I explore the idea that of all things in this world which we consider sacred, that is, of all the things which can act as your partner in the search for the highest and deepest things, *other people are most important*. The second fold of my thesis is more like a method. It seems to me that the best way to escape from the labyrinth of fear is to describe what human relationships can be like when not governed by fear.

I explore this twofold thesis in a rather anecdotal way. I offer stories, propositions, possibilities, and accounts of conversations with people, rather than systematic arguments and conclusions. I present each chapter almost as a stand-alone discussion: you could even read them out of order. I present some evidence which I think supports the twofold thesis, but I leave it to you to decide how strong that support really is. Nor does this book offer any definitive or final *solutions* to the problem posed in the discussion of the labyrinth of fear. I do, however, try to offer *ways to discover solutions*. My hope is that if we create better relations with each other, and learn better ways of communicating, then we might be able to avoid imprisoning ourselves in labyrinths of fear. And we may also accomplish the more life-affirming goals which the architects of the fear-labyrinths pursued in misguided ways. An eclectic account of things, like the one I am about to lay before you, might be the best way to explore these possibilities. One can see the shape and size of a cloud from a distance, but never measure it up close with a ruler. One can see the position of a shoreline from atop a cliff that overlooks the sea. But the precise edge of the sea itself, changing in each moment with rolling waves and moving tides, cannot be marked with a solid line. In a similar way, the general shapes of our relationships are easier to measure than their fine details. Thus an anecdotal approach might be curiously more appropriate than a purely analytic approach.

Yet I do introduce a few philosophical principles in this book. As you might expect, some of them are moral values, such as courage, honour, generosity, openness, trust, respect, and love.

35

But I also discovered that these moral values are islands that emerge from the deeper waters of metaphysics and epistemology. Here is a list of the most important ideas I discovered in those waters.

- Misercorpism (first introduced in chapter 1): a special variation of the labyrinth of fear.
- Perceptual Intelligence (ch. 2): a means of relating to one's environment, using the intelligence of the physical senses.
- The good and worthwhile life (ch. 4): the 'end' or the 'aim' of ethics, recalling Aristotle's concept of *eudaimonia*, which means 'happiness', 'flourishing', or 'blessedness'.
- Tradition; Blood and History (ch. 5): referring to how ideas and values are transmitted from one person or generation to the next.
- Ritual, custom, and drama (ch. 6): referring to the ways we put moral principles into action.
- Symbiotic Identity (ch. 7): a way of understanding how one's identity grows together with other people's identities.
- Dwelling (ch. 10): another way of understanding one's relationship to an environment.
- Excellence (ch. 11): the quality of things which makes them appear 'just right'.
- Alternatives to war (ch. 13): the search for ways of relating to each other which, by their nature, exclude violence and killing.
- Magic and Wonder (ch. 15): referring to the way we relate to that which is mysterious or hidden.
- Reason (ch. 17): a method of empowerment and enlightenment.
- The Immensity (various places), a word which indicates the presence of the highest and deepest things.

Some of these ideas may seem very complex, and at first glance their place in our relationships may not be obvious. But don't worry: they are only names for ideas, experiences, and realities that just about anyone can grasp. In the pages that follow, I hope to show how they help dispel fear, and how they both emerge from, and help create, the experience of the sacred in our lives.

I have called this kind of work 'a study of the sacred'. To some readers the word 'sacred' may suggest a kind of untouchability, as if sacred things must be approached like fragile archaeological relics. But I have in mind nothing of the sort. Many sacred places, for example, are used for more than just religious rituals. They are also used as music and theatre venues, courts of justice, sports fields, and sometimes as specialized markets. As an example of a multi-purpose sacred place, consider the Hill of Tara, in Ireland. The site is the original location of Ireland's ancient high kings, and also a burial ground for many of those kings, including Lóegaire, the last pagan king of Ireland. Tara is also the place where St. Patrick lit his Samhain fire to announce the arrival of Christianity. Today the hill is used for ceremonial purposes by Catholics and by modern Druids: two very different religious traditions. Tara is also a traditional site for political demonstrations. Before the Easter Rising in 1916, people held huge public rallies there to call for Ireland's independence from Britain. More recently, it has been used by environmental campaigners opposed to a nearby motorway development. It is also sometimes used as a sports field by local teenagers. In the same way, our relationships are often involved in many kinds of purposes, and sometimes conflicting purposes. They might be connected to our highest values and aspirations, or our most everyday and down-to-earth activities.

Moreover, although this is a study of the sacred, I know that religion can trap people in labyrinths of fear too. Religion can impose fear on non-practitioners with convert-or-starve 'charity' programs, or with outright warfare. It can impose fear on its own members, using witch-hunts and the threat of excommunication.

And a devout practitioner can impose fear on himself: he might fear being tortured in the afterlife as a punishment for his sins. He might live a rigorously puritanical life in order to quell that fear, even if the religion he professes doesn't require it. And like other labyrinths of fear, religion can hypnotize the prisoner into thinking himself still free. A sacred relationship might not be just a mode of association: it may also be a mode of conflict. A famous temple could be the site of a long tradition of violence, for instance when two or more groups argue over who has the right to enter, or what kind of ritual can be performed there. The Dome of the Rock, in Jerusalem, is an example of such a long contested place, and I'm sure the reader already understands why. Similarly, a sacred relationship between people may also include a tradition of conflict, alongside a tradition of co-operation. People might argue and fight over who can be involved, what aims or goals should be pursued, whether outside parties should have a stake in what happens, whether anyone should be in charge, or what the whole point of the relationship really is. The circle of meaning is just as subject to breakdown and failure as any other kind of relationship. Yet the language of the sacred may still be the best way to understand our problems, and heal our broken relations. When we treat the materials, the settings, the activities, and especially the people of our relationships as *sources of revelation* about the highest and deepest things in life, then we give to ourselves a real chance to escape the labyrinth and live genuinely worthwhile lives.

Acknowledgements and Dedication

As lengthy as this book is, still it began as something much larger. The original plan had 36 chapters, for instance. At one point the introduction grew so long by itself that I eventually decided to publish it separately (under the title Loneliness and Revelation). Nearly fifty people contributed to this work as interview informants, over three and a half years. I simply do not have the space to thank them all. I only regret that I did not use everyone's contribution equally. Space constrained me, as did time. I give special thanks to those who agreed to let me publish their words here: I do hope each of you feel that I have represented your thoughts fairly, and used them respectfully.

With pride, with love, with hesitation (because this book is so long!) and with respect, I dedicate this book to one individual, and one group of people. The individual is my good friend Juniper. Her kindness and support, and her love, especially when I was frustrated and grumpy about things, is appreciated more than I can express.

I also dedicate this book to the group of people who, although they don't know it, are more responsible for inspiring this work than anyone else, over the last half-dozen years or so. Every one of them are dedicated, industrious, honorable, and full of life – virtuous, in the original heroic sense of the word. They are the staff and volunteers of Kaleidoscope Gathering, and I feel humbled and proud to be included among them. I do hope that a few of the ideas in this volume contribute something to the community we are building together.

Brendan Myers
Ottawa, Ontario, Canada
April 2011

I

Body and Mind

When speaking of sacred relations with others, including the most intimate others, we might first speak of the relations within ourselves. (The fashionable wisdom of our time demands that all discussion of the sacred begin with the self.) The most obvious and visible of these are the relations of the body. In every experience of my life, whether in the interior realm of my heart and mind, or the external world that I perceive with the senses, I am also experiencing my body. I feel heat and coldness in contrast with the temperature of my own flesh. I feel texture in contrast with the friction of my own skin. I see light and color through the lenses of my eyes. I hear music through the instrument of my eardrum, as well as in the harmonic resonance of some of my bones. It is with the body that we move and speak and act. It is with the body that we see and touch other people and the world. It is with the body that we experience all our feelings and emotions. It is with the body, and mainly through the voice, the eye, the face, and the hand, that we reveal to other people the contents of our hearts and minds. It is with the body that I know myself to be an individual, different than others, possessing my own identity. For my body is particularly my own, unlike any other body. It has its own unique shape, appearance, and its own DNA code. And I have exclusive possession of it: only I inhabit my body, no one else, and I inhabit only this body, not any other. And finally, it is the body that is mortal and which some day comes to death.

Yet in looking at the relations of the body, problems quickly appear. For the body is the site of so many conflicts among differing religious and cultural traditions. Consider as an example the different ways that religious traditions treat hair. Some require practitioners to keep it cut short. Others want some or all of it covered by scarves and cloths. Some groups require their practitioners to shave it completely off. Other groups encourage their members to grow it long, and might recommend distinct ways of braiding it, such as dreadlocks. Some traditions require men to grow beards. Finally, in countries where a form of fundamentalism is part of the political climate, people can be ostracized, taunted in public, arrested by the authorities, or even physically assaulted by vigilantes, because of the way they show (or do not show) their hair.

Some of these issues might be treated as differences of culture about which it isn't necessary to get too excited. But superficial differences sometimes point to more serious theological commitments, which in turn become sources of conflict. I'm almost sorry to begin the body of this book on such an unpleasant note. But it seems important to me to get certain problematic assumptions out of the way. Just as one cannot plant a garden until first one has cleared the weeds, so one must first identify and discard faulty thinking in order to enjoy good thinking.

Made in the Image of God

Many religious and philosophical traditions treat the spirit and the body as two separate and distinct things. The spirit is a kind of 'ghost in the machine', immaterial and incorporeal; it belongs to a realm of pure thought and feeling. It also survives death, to reincarnate again on earth, or to move on to an otherworldly realm. This idea can inspire glorious works of art, and admirable acts of service and self-sacrifice. But it also entails a denial of the spiritual significance of the body. It appears most prominently in Christian Scripture, for instance Paul's letter to the Romans:

> My inner being delights in the law of God. But I see a
> different law at work in my body – a law that fights against

the law which my mind approves of. It makes me a prisoner to the law of sin which is at work in my body. What an unhappy man I am! Who will rescue me from this body that is taking me to death?

(Romans 7:22-24)

Christian physical disciplines are some of the most well-known results of this attitude. Flagellation, fasting, celibacy, corporeal punishment, and even requirements for colorless or constrictive clothing, are products of the idea that the body must be disciplined or punished for the sake of the mind and the soul.

Permit me to identify this idea with the name of *misercorpism*. Let this word designate any doctrine, practice, idea or teaching which disparages the body, or which privileges the mind or the spirit or the soul over the body, to whatever extent.

But the Abrahamic tradition also holds that a human being is made in the image of God (Genesis 1:26) and that the human body is the temple of God (1st Corinthians 6:19). This idea can sanctify a body, and make it holy. In the early Italian Renaissance, this idea seems to have been expressed in sculptures and paintings of nudes. Historian Kenneth Clark described a painting that the council of Florence commissioned Michelangelo to create. It depicted a group of Florentine soldiers taken by surprise while bathing (for which reason the council rejected it). But a preparatory sketch still exists, and Clark says that sketch "was the first authoritative statement that the human body – that body which, in Gothic times, had been the subject of shame and concealment... could be made the means of expressing noble sentiments, life-giving energy and God-like perfection".[16] Michelangelo's sculptures, such as his famous *David*, also suggest the idea that the body is the instrument for expressing spiritual forces. The contemporary Wiccan practice of worshipping 'skyclad' (that is, naked) is perhaps intended to convey a similar idea about the dignity and divinity of the human body.

Yet the principle of 'made in the image of God' exists in Christian thought in an unresolved tension with other, more disparaging ideas about the body. Consider the passage from Genesis that is often read out at funerals: "For thou art dust and unto dust thou shall return." (Genesis 3:19) When the prophet Abraham addressed himself to God, he also identified himself with dust and ashes (cf Genesis 18:27). Paul's aforementioned complaint about the different law at work in his body is only one example from the New Testament. There are others, such as Paul's claim that precisely because the body is the temple of God, it therefore does not belong to you. "Do you not know that your body is a temple of the Holy Spirit within you, which you have from God? You are not your own. You were bought with a price: therefore glorify God in your body, and your spirit, which are God's." (1st Corinthians 6:19-20). He similarly tells the people of Galatia that if they indulge in various bodily pleasures, such as eating, drinking, and sex, then they will be denied access to the Kingdom of Heaven (Galatians 5:19-21). To Paul, this principle generates a duty to control physical desires, and particularly to abstain from extramarital sex. Christianity seems to have inherited the Stoic idea that only the mind, not the body, is made in God's image. This idea can also be found in the work of Boethius, Cicero, and Marcus Aurelius, no less than in Early Fathers of the Church. Saint Augustine, for instance, claimed that resurrected saints have no need to eat! (cf *City of God*, Book 13, Ch 22, pp 18-19). Even Michelangelo's magnificent nude sculptures, glorifying the beauty of healthy and strong human beings, still privilege the mind and spirit over the body. An unfinished sculpture of his, called *The Prisoner* (even though there are no chains nor shackles), resembles a man struggling to free himself from the stone in which he is still half-encased. Clark says this work expresses "Michelangelo's deepest preoccupation: the struggle of the soul to free itself from matter."[17]

Christianity did not invent misercorpism. We find it in pre-

Christian Greek and Roman philosophy too. It appears in the works of Plato, who in *The Republic* argued that one must master the demands of the body to become a philosopher (cf 430d-432b). Here's a short text called "The Dream of Scipio", in which Scipio Africanus, a student of Cicero's, dreams of a conversation with his grandfather. At one point the grandfather says:

> Rest assured that it is only your body that is mortal; your true self is nothing of the kind. For the man you outwardly appear to be is not yourself at all. Your real self is not that corporeal, palpable shape, but the spirit inside.[18]

Disparagements of the flesh like this appear frequently enough in the religious literature of the East as well. The proposition that life is inherently miserable is the first of Buddhism's four Noble Truths. The *Samyutta nikaya*, an important Buddhist text, says: "The body, monks, is soulless. If the body, monks, were the soul, this body would not be subject to sickness... Thus perceiving, monks, the learned noble disciple feels loathing for the body..." Another Buddhist text makes a miraculous claim about the bodies of enlightened Buddhists which reads a lot like what Augustine said of the body of a resurrected saint: "Reverend Ánanda, the Tathágatas have the body of the Dharma – not a body that is sustained by material food. The Tathágatas have a transcendental body that has transcended all mundane qualities." (*Vimalakirti Sutra*, Ch 3) Passages like these suggest that Buddhism rules out in advance anything desirable, beautiful or good about corporeal embodiment. Certainly, it cannot reasonably be denied that much of the world *is* unhappy. Murder, disease, warfare, enmity, tribalism, grief, anger, and the like, do darken many people's lives. But misercorpism sees these unhappy conditions in a non-accidental association with embodiment. Whatever the Buddhist perceives, he finds it involved in various embodied attachments, and therefore *inherently* in a state of suffering. Nor is this program a merely incidental part of its general system: in fact this loathing for the body, prescribed by Buddhism, is part of its method for achieving enlightenment. As the aforementioned passage from the *Samyutta nikaya* continues: "feeling disgust [for the body] he becomes free from passion, through freedom from passion he is emancipated..."[19]

Nor is Buddhism the only Eastern source of misercorpism. The Yoga Sutra, an important text in Hinduism, asserts that the seeker should practice five observances, the first of which is cleanliness: "By cleanliness is meant disgust with one's body, and cessation of contact with others." (*Yoga Sutra*, 2.40) The Chandogya Upanishad, one of the holy books of Hinduism, says:

> O Maghavan, verily, this body is mortal. It has been appropriated by death. [But] it is the standing-ground of that deathless, bodiless Self. Verily, he who is incorporate has been appropriated by pleasure and pain. Verily, there is no freedom from pleasure and pain for one while he is incorporate. Verily, while one is bodiless, pleasure and pain do not touch him. (*Chandogya Upanishad* viii.xii.1)

It's clearly true that embodied life involves both pleasure and pain, and that it involves death. But from these propositions, *it simply does not follow that the body is therefore without value.* Let us assume that one who is 'bodiless' is freed from bodily pleasures and pains. Yet from this proposition it does not follow that the appropriate strategy for handling the problems of life is a retreat into some escapist fantasy concerning the immortal soul. There is no polite and diplomatic way to say it: these arguments are non sequiturs. But since they are supported by thousands of years of tradition and ritual and history, we no longer see them that way. As a final example of misercorpism from religion, consider this selection from the *Maitri Upanishad*:

... in this ill-smelling, unsubstantial body, which is a conglomerate of bone, skin, muscle, marrow, flesh, semen, blood, mucus, tears, rheum, feces, urine, wind, bile, and phlegm, what is the good of enjoyment of desires? In this body, which is afflicted with desire, anger, covetousness, delusion, fear, despondency, envy, separation from the desirable, union with the undesirable, hunger, thirst, senility, death, disease, sorrow, and the like, what is the good of enjoyment of desires?[20]

Certainly, it is undeniable that the body is subject to injury, disease, and death, and that these conditions can be obstacles to full human flourishing. If the body is a home of joy, as I have affirmed earlier, nevertheless it is a home that is fragile and vulnerable, subject to invasion. For this reason, many Eastern traditions claim that sustainable spiritual fulfillment cannot be found in bodily enjoyments like food, or sex, or even exercise. The purpose of such claims is to turn one's attention toward the soul, and to discourage people from getting 'stuck' in the thought that the body is the whole of their being. There may be some merit to this purpose. Yet I cannot help but find myself suspicious of any teaching, however old and venerable, which disparages the body so systematically.

Religious texts are not the only places where we find profoundly disordered attitudes toward the body. Consider smoking, binge drinking, drug abuse, sedentary lifestyles, bad eating habits, and bad hygiene. Those who work in high-pressure jobs, such as in sales or in corporate management, often deprive themselves of sufficient sleep, in order to be more productive and competitive. People also treat themselves poorly when they get sick: they simply drop a few pills and go back to work instead of taking a few days of rest. Some industries, such as the fashion and design industry, and the weight loss industry, veritably encourage disordered bodily relationships. They teach people to feel disgust with the natural shape and size of their own bodies, and they reward punitive diet regimes. Invasive forms of body modification, like cosmetic surgery, can be included here, when borne of a refusal to accept the beauty of a healthy body just as it is. The results of disordered bodily relationships are often serious physical diseases like as anorexia, bulimia, obesity, type-2 diabetes, alcohol-related liver disease, and lung cancer. I won't claim that these disordered bodily relationships have philo-sophical roots in religion, because I don't know that for sure. But some of them seem to be borne of a similar attitude, which views the body as a kind of adversary, or obstacle, which gets in the way of the higher and deeper things, be they material, or immaterial. The main difference between religious and non-religious misercorpism is the type of weapon. Instead of coarse-fiber shirts and flagellation whips, the weapons are crash diets, punitive exercise regimes, binge-and-purge eating cycles, invasive surgical procedures, and pharmaceutical interference in the body's chemistry.

Expressiveness and Asceticism

In both ways of thinking about the body described so far, both positively as an instrument and vehicle of life, and negatively as an earthy baggage, subject to disease and disability, what resolution is possible? In my view, a healthy and flourishing spiritual life must involve a categorical rejection of miser-corpism, in any of its forms. The good life must find a way to acknowledge the reality of the body's fragility and ailments without at the same time declaring it evil, or an obstacle to spiri-tuality. The good life must find a way to affirm the goodness of the body, and to involve care for the body in one's spiritual practices.

The way to find that relationship might be by using a propo-sition like this one. Whatever you love, you love it with of your body. For it is with the body that you move and act in the world. It is with the body that you speak, gaze, approach, and touch other people. The use of one's own body in all that you love appears not just on the obvious dimension of sexuality, but also through any other act of kindness bestowed upon others: smiles, winks, kind words, gifts of generosity. A similar proposition also applies to thoughts, feelings, and the interior life. For all one's internal thoughts and emotions correspond to biochemical events in the brain: an electric signal in the synapses, a release of neuro-transmitter chemicals, etc. Mystical or religious states of consciousness also have these biophysical correspondences. Researchers at the Massachusetts General Hospital found that people who regularly practice meditation have a larger cerebral cortex, particularly in the areas responsible for processing sensory information. They have also found which areas of the brain become active, and which neurotransmitters are involved, during meditative trance states. The relationship appears to go in both directions: meditation also helped slow the atrophy of certain parts of the brain, thus promoting longevity.[21] Someone might object by saying, "I am not a bodily being having a spiritual experience; I am a spiritual being having a bodily experience." But that proposition is precisely what we must *examine*, and so we cannot assume it as true from the beginning. I suspect it is a very subtle and hidden form of misercorpism.

For reasons like these, we should therefore care for the body for the sake of other things that we also care about. For many purposes this instrumental argument may well be sufficient. But I think it does not fully remove the shadow of misercorpism. Imagine a woodcarver who loves to create works of beauty from wood, but hates his chisels and hammers and knives. Or, imagine a weaver who loves making tapestries but hates her loom. Such a person effectively hates part of his or her own profession. The solution to such obviously absurd situations is to encourage that person to find other tools, or else find another line of work. But the person who resents or despises his or her own body does not have analogous options. He or she effectively hates part of what it is to be alive, human, and herself. Such is the nature of the wrongness of misercorpism: it is categorically incompatible with the affirmation of the goodness of one's own life. (Well, someone experiencing apotemnophilia[22] or gender-identity disorder[23] could pursue a surgical option. But I am concerned with misercorpism *tout court*, the resentment of the body as such, not the resentment of one of its isolated features.) The seeker who wants enlightenment for mind but not body, or for heart and soul but not eyes and ears, has effectively cut himself into pieces. His enlightenment, however profound on one plane, remains shadowed by that discord. Might there be a way of explaining the significance of the body without encountering this error? I shall now try to find one.

Let us assume as a first proposition the obvious truth that your life, whatever else it may be, is also the life of your body. Whatever way of being in the world you practice, and whatever personal identity you possess, it is a bodily way of being, it is a bodily identity. Obviously we use our bodies in practical ways: to lift things, to avoid hazards, to move, to help others, and so on. But we also move our bodies *expressively:* your way of using your body reveals something of who you are. Your standing posture and walking gait reveals something of your confidence, your excitedness, your purposefulness, your self-esteem, or the absence of these dispositions. Your presence also appears in the tilt of your head as you gaze at someone, the shape of your smile, the tones and rhythms of your speech, the way you touch someone else's body, especially the body of someone you love. These habits, these ways of in-*habit*-ing your body, configure your bodily way of being in the world. Your body's condition is only partly the responsibility of your genetics: your habits and your lifestyle choices also configure its condition. Thus we also see on the body the traces of how we habitually use it. You might have the athletic body of one who exercises regularly. You may have the yellow teeth and sagging skin of a chain smoker. You may also have the traces of certain events in your life: a scar from a childhood injury, or from a surgical procedure, for instance. These traces reveal one's personal history, another important feature of personal identity. Philosopher John Casey described how some of the ways we inhabit our bodies have ethical significance. Taking the virtue of courage as an example, he wrote:

> We can certainly understand courage as purely a disposition of soul, or a disposition to choose and pursue certain ends. Yet if we are interested in the *phenomenology* of courage we will be interested in the way in which a brave man characteristically 'inhabits' his body. One could say that his intentions toward the world – the way in which he confronts it as a brave man – inhabit his body... Although the metaphor is by no means perfect, it is better to say of physical courage that the brave man inhabits his body in a particular way.[24]

This phenomenology of the body enables us to think of at least some of our moral values as *bodily* values.

Taken together, the habits by which we use the body, and the changes that affect the body as a result, *reveal who you are*. Thus we have a reason to care for the body not for the sake of other things, but rather for its own sake. We should care for the body because caring for the body is the same as caring for the self, and the goodness of caring for the self is (or should be) self-evident.

A spiritual life must, as a first order of priority, involve caring for the body. But what practical form must that care assume? At the risk of sounding a little strange, may I say that the practical form of the bodily life-affirmation is *asceticism*. This word first appears in the English language in the seventeenth century, already associated with unpleasant things like fasting and physical punishment. But its origin is in the friendlier Greek words *askeitikos* and *askein*, which mean to exercise, and particularly to train yourself for athletic competition. *Askein* is still a discipline of the body but involves empowering and feeding the body, not punishing it. It is concerned with transforming, strengthening, and perfecting the body, to realize the body's full potential. Furthermore, the word *asceticism* is related to the name of *Asklepius*, the Greek god of healing. So the arts of medicine, nutrition, and hygiene are also forms of asceticism. To keep the body clean and to feed it properly, so to prevent disease, and to learn how to use and enhance the healing abilities of the body when it is injured, are also spiritual activities. Finally, although it is a bit distant, *askeitikos* is related to the Greek word *kosmos*, which means 'glittering'. This is the origin of the English word 'cosmos', meaning the stars above, and the word 'cosmetics'. Thus to practice asceticism is also to *decorate* the body, and make it shine like a star!

Many spiritual traditions have an asceticism of this positive kind among its customs. They develop the powers and abilities of the body to affirm the spirit and produce a greater awareness of the presence of the divine. Yoga is perhaps the most well-known of these practices. Its exercises are intended not to divide but to harmonize body and mind. The numerous forms of oriental martial arts like Kung Fu and Tai Kwan Do also aim for a similar benefit. We could add to the list the more gentle motions of Tai Chi, the whirling Sufi dances and turns, the 'grapevine' circle-dance of the ancient Greek dithyramb, the gymnastic sexual postures of Tantra, and so on. I have a friend who teaches Middle Eastern belly dancing. She told me that one of the reasons why she teaches it is because, "I also love the way women leave a belly dance class, mostly standing taller and a little bit more in love with their bellies. That's one of my favorite parts of teaching this dance!" (A. Shaherezade, 2009)

The point of such disciplines is to master the body, but not in the manner of curbing its desires, suppressing its needs, or interfering with its powers. It is, rather, to transform those desires and needs, and also to extend its powers, in order to transform the body into a spiritual body, that is, a body that expresses the spirit completely. When the body has been empowered, using it becomes pleasurable and enjoyable. Participating in the world with an empowered body promotes the consciousness that life is good. This is an asceticism which affirms our groundedness in the world. Although earlier I wrote that Eastern thought is often capable of severe misercorpism, the whole story is more complex than that. An branch of Hinduism called Tantrayana, for instance, has five sacraments, all of which are activities of bodily pleasure: *mada*, wine; *matsya*, fish; *mamsa*, red meat; *mudra*, herbs and grains (i.e. bread); and *maithuna*, sexual intercourse. There are favorable views of the body to be found in some Hindu scriptures as well. For instance, a passage from the Katha Upanishad says:

Know thou the self (*atman*) as riding in a chariot,
The body as the chariot.
Know thou the intellect (*buddhi*) as the chariot-driver,
And the mind as the reins.
The senses, they say, are the horses,
The objects of sense, what they range over.
The self combined with senses and the mind
Wise men call "The Enjoyer".[25]

The famous Analogy of the Chariot also appears in other Hindu sacred writings. It expresses the idea that the body is the home and the vehicle of the soul, and that it is perfectly acceptable to use the body as an instrument of pleasure.

In the Western tradition, there is a whole catalogue of virtues which are bodily in character. Grace and beauty, courage and strength, and even temperance (i.e. the virtue of a disciplined appetite) are some of them. This should come as no great surprise. For many of our most cherished religious principles and ideas are what they are precisely because of the shapes and the natural functions of our bodies! In his novel *Foucault's Pendulum*,

Italian philosopher Umberto Eco effectively deconstructed thousands of years of theological discourse by showing how that discourse presupposes a phenomenology of the body. Here is how one of his characters explains it:

> Archetypes don't exist; the body exists. The belly inside is beautiful, because the baby grows there, because your sweet cock, all bright and jolly, thrusts there, and good, tasty food descends there, and for this reason the cavern, the grotto, the tunnel are beautiful and important, and the labyrinth too, made in the image of our wonderful intestines. When somebody wants to invent something beautiful and important, it has to come from there, because you also came from there the day you were born, because fertility always comes from inside a cavity, where first something rots and then, lo and behold, there's a little man, a date, a baobab. And high is better than low, because if you have your head down, the blood goes to your brain, because feet stink and hair doesn't stink as much, because it's better to climb a tree and pick fruit than end up underground, food for worms, and because you rarely hurt yourself hitting something above – you really have to be in an attic – while you often hurt yourself falling. That's why up is angelic and down devilish.[26]

The idea that Eco wants us to understand is that we place the realm of purity and spirituality and goodness 'above' us, and the realm of evil, profanity, and death 'below' us, simply because of the way we live in our bodies. A healthy and strong human body walks erect and upright, with its head at the top. We also find the flying birds, the air we breathe, and the lights of sun and moon and stars, above us: these are phenomena which symbolically correspond to freedom and the spirit in numerous cultures. A body that is asleep, injured, diseased, or dead, is a body lying prone, horizontal, parallel with the surface of the earth. Thus 'below' has its malevolent associations. At the same time wisdom and secret mysteries come from 'below', from the belly where food is transformed into nutrition, and from the womb where egg and sperm meet to create new life. The sacredness of the 'below' also appears in the rigs and furrows of the field where the seeds of our crops are germinated, the wells from which drinking water is drawn, and the mines and quarries where we find gold and diamonds and precious minerals.

Men's Bodies, Women's Bodies

So far I have been writing as if all human bodies are homogeneous. But this is obviously not true: human bodies come in many shapes and sizes. We are tall, short, slim, round, muscular, spindly, dexterous, clumsy, tough, or fragile. We come in two sexes, male and female. Around one out of every thousand of us are both male and female at the same time. And some people deliberately transition from one gender to another through surgery and hormone therapy. We also come in at least four basic races: Caucasian, Aboriginal, Asian, and African, and each of these categories include thousands of distinct ethnicities. And then each individual body has its own distinctness. Faces, fingerprints, iris patterns, scars from childhood injuries, tattoos and piercings, and so on, are all unique to the body which has them. Even genetically identical twins have subtle differences: for instance, one tends to be a few millimeters taller than the other. It follows that one's bodily being-in-the-world is never an abstraction. A human body is always a *particular* body: it is my body, or yours, or his or hers. Therefore one's bodily being-in-the-world is also highly particular.

Women have a few distinct bodily experiences which men never have: ovulation, menstruation, childbirth, lactation, and menopause. The first book to study the psychology of menstruation was *The Wise Wound* by Penelope Shuttle and Peter Redgrove (first published 1978, revised 1986). They found, for instance, that some women are able to predict the onset of their ovulation and menstruation hours or even days in advance, and that women who could predict their cycles experienced them differently. (I am informed by several of the women in my life that the ability to predict ovulation and menstruation can actually be *taught*.) Furthermore the experience can have profound spiritual significance. As Shuttle and Redgrove state in their introduction, the book itself came about when the two of them studied Shuttle's dreams over a five-month period and noted certain patterns and changes that corresponded to her menstrual and ovarian cycles. Redgrove is a Jungian psychologist, so his analysis was guided by the Jungian idea that dreams are the body's primary way of communicating its condition to the mind. With that guiding hypothesis, he and Shuttle found that during certain days of the menstrual cycle a woman might dream of meeting a strange or supernatural person, who comes to help or to heal. This person is often male, not female, representing what Jungians call the *animus*; they also found that this dream-being may not be entirely human.

Although this may seem strange to some (perhaps especially to male readers of this book), Shuttle and Redgrove compared the menstrual dreams of various people to the experiences of shamanism and witchcraft. For one of the only universal observations about shamanism in every culture where it is practiced is that the shaman endures some kind of physical trauma in his or her youth. He or she has a severe physical injury, a debilitating disease, or the like, some months or years before training as a shaman. The spirit-helper comes to his or her dreams during the healing process. This phenomenon is very well documented for male shaman, but what is less well documented is that women may also become 'shaman' in a similar way. If the accident of a childhood disease or injury does not provide the initial 'trauma' which prompts a shamanic vision, the 'natural wound' of menstruation possibly will. In their words:

For the menstruation is an instinctive process: a natural wound, which heals naturally – and it energizes at the very deepest level all the humanly tinged natural processes of the body: we have seen how radical the physiological process is. Now our natural language for instinctive processes, things which happen accurately, or themselves – is that of the animals and plants; the natural living world outside us. It is hardly surprising then, if our awareness of these processes within, especially at the period, takes animal form. Jung has noted that a characteristic dream during an illness is that of a visit by helpful animals, or by animal-headed people. This is a sign that the healing processes are operating... So the woman who is developing techniques of reverie or dream-recall of approaching her unknown country in her periods must not be surprised if she encounters, as in the fairy tales, speaking animals, or a man with a beast's head... (*The Wise Wound*, pp 116-7)

In my own studies of Aboriginal culture, I found the significance of dreams in the relations of the body repeatedly confirmed. For instance, in Ojibway legends, "Kitche Manitou (the Great Spirit) beheld a vision," and understood that the vision had to be brought into being: for that reason, he created the world. When he created the plants and animals and human beings, he bestowed special gifts upon each of them, and "man had the greatest gift – the power to dream" (Johnston, *Ojibway Heritage*, pp 12-13). Some Aboriginal traditions assert the shamanism and magic performed by male hunters and warriors was originally a women's activity, which men learned, borrowed, or stole from women. For example, Mircea Eliade wrote that among the Selknam people of Tierra Del Fuego:

... the puberty initiation was long ago transformed into a secret ceremony reserved exclusively for men. An origin myth tells that in the beginning – under the leadership of Kra, Moon Woman and powerful sorceress – women terrorized men because they knew how to change themselves into 'spirits'; that is, knew the arts of making and using masks. But one day Kran, the Sun Man, discovered the women's secret and told it to the men. Infuriated, they killed all the women except little girls, and since then they have organized secret ceremonies, with masks and dramatic rituals... (Eliade, *Rites and Symbols of Initiation*, pp 29-30)

Nor is shamanism the only spiritual practice apparently rooted in women's experiences of their own bodies. Shuttle and Redgrove describe mediaeval European witchcraft as "the natural craft of the woman" and "the subjective experience of the menstrual cycle." Witchcraft, as they portray it, has to do with "the natural crafts of midwifery, hypnotism, healing, dowsing, dream-study and sexually fulfillment" (*The Wise Wound*, p 198). These activities, they say, are especially aided by the menstru-ation-induced changes in a woman's emotional and mental life. The horned demon-lover that witches were said to worship is the aforementioned *animus* who visits women in their dreams. Other magical capabilities ascribed to witches are, in the view of the authors, borne of men's fears of what menstruating women might be capable of.

I'm not trying to suggest that all women are (or should be) shaman or witches. My reason for exploring this experience is to draw attention to the way that different bodies have different spiritual, relational, and experiential possibilities. But aside from the gender dynamic, the relationship between our corporeal health and our dreams is a very interesting spiritual relationship in its own right. And men can have such a relationship with their dreams too. A conversation with a dream-being is a conversation with your own body, and with the various multifaceted parts of the self; and this conversation can empower and heal. For this purpose, it may be helpful to try and converse with dream-beings as if they are autonomous people, to trust and not to fear them, and to listen and consider carefully what they have to say. (Carl Jung prescribed this as a therapeutic technique.) Shuttle and Redgrove found that women who develop a relationship with their own cycles, who observe them seriously and fearlessly, and with the aid of their dreams, soon experience fewer symptoms of pre-menstrual tension, and less physical pain. She may also benefit from an increase in artistic or creative initiative, an increase in personal confidence and self-esteem, and an increase in the libido. The evidence they offer for the truth of this proposition is that as a working hypothesis for therapeutic purposes, *it works* (*Ibid*, p 119).

The differences between men's and women's bodies suggest other differences in men's and women's spiritual experiences. I have a friend who lectures in anthropology and women's studies at the University of Ottawa, and I asked her about those differences. Is there such a thing as a female religious experience? She described how, as a girl, she attended a Christian boarding school run by nuns, and she described a little of what the experience of religion was like for her when only the women came to chapel, and when a male priest also attended.

There was a huge difference when the nuns were alone with the female students in the chapel, and when the priest was there. When it was just the nuns and the students, and I was there one weekend when I was the only student there and I attended chapel with them, the singing, the songs, the prayers, even just the quiet, the silence, was deep and very – well think of a mole-hair shawl. Or butterscotch. Or warm milk. It had that feeling to it, of great honesty and depth and comfort and sanctuary. When the priest would show up, and he was a perfectly ordinary, good person, he didn't stand on ceremony or anything. But everything became guarded.

58

Everything became by the rules. Everything became the way they had to be, should be. So that there was a kind of nervousness. And that was very interesting; I didn't put my finger on it until I did my thesis work [many years later]. I realised that when they were alone, it came from the heart, and when they were with the priest, it was according to the rules. I've seen similar things happen with pagan women, when it is just women, and when there are men there. When it's just women, they'll dare anything... (L. DuFresne, 2010.)

Thus there may be ways of being-in-the-world which are distinct to the sexes, not only bodily but also socially. But we must be careful here. If there are diverse ways to inhabit and celebrate the body, so there are also diverse ways to oppress the body. As Dr. DuFresne reminded me,

Like it or not, women's bodies are more permeable to others. Just by the way they're constructed. And we are socialized to guard ourselves, to keep ourselves private, to keep ourselves somehow closed off... The body is the ground of being, but it is also where the war is fought. It is very much [a question of] who owns a woman's body? And if she doesn't, why doesn't she? (*Ibid*)

If I understand Dr. DuFresne's words correctly, the war that she speaks of is the way people enforce on each other some model of what it means to be, to look, to speak, and to behave male or female. In this way, misercorpism oppresses women differently than men. The concepts of 'race' and 'gender' are *socially* constructed (and sometimes politically constructed). Not that there are no physical or biological differences between the races and the sexes. But the significance of those differences, and especially the way those differences figure into someone's evaluation of another person's worthiness for respect, is social and not biological. The 'fight', then, is the process of defining those significances, as well as defining *who gets to define* them, and also the various ways of enforcing them. Feminist philosopher Sandra Lee Bartky observed that "we are born male or female, but not masculine or feminine. Femininity is an artifice, an achievement..." She then examined several "disciplinary practices" which aim to produce a recognizably feminine body: dieting, avoiding eye-contact, smiling more often, holding one's arms close to the body, keeping hands folded on the lap while seated, wearing makeup and jewelry and fashionable clothes when in public, chemically treating the skin so that it looks and feels soft. As Bartky explains, there is no organized conspiracy of men against women here: this is something ordinary people do to each other, and women sometimes do to other women. "The disciplinary power that inscribes femininity in the female body is everywhere and it is nowhere; the disciplinarian is everyone and yet no one in particular. Women regarded as overweight, for example, report that they are regularly admonished to diet, sometimes by people they scarcely know."[27]

In the area of reproductive rights, the fight is perhaps most obvious. Various countries legislate what a pregnant woman may or may not do with her body, when the life or health of her unborn child might be affected. The laws in some countries permit doctors to intervene in a woman's body for the sake of the fetus without the woman's consent. In 1987, a court in Washington DC, USA, ordered a woman who was terminally ill with cancer to undergo a caesarean section to save the life of her unborn child, against her own wishes and the wishes of her husband and family.[28] A court of appeal eventually vacated the original decision. There have also been cases of women jailed for doing things that might harm their fetuses, such as taking drugs.

In the spirituality of the body, what matters is not whether a body is of one size or another. Nor does it matter that a body has some disposition or potential inherited from its genes, which other bodies do not inherit. *What matters is whether your way of being in the world embodies life-affirming values,* like courage, generosity, friendship. It may be true that that most men have as much as 30% more muscle tissue than women. But this says nothing about whether women's sports are more interesting, competitive, or enjoyable than men's sports. Women's brains appear to be biologically structured for sociability and relationship-building, more so than men's brains. A scientific study found that female brains have a 17% larger language center than male brains.[29] But this says nothing about whether one gender can think and reason better than another. Moreover other researchers are finding that all the differences between male and female brains come from socialization and not genetics. Researcher Lise Eliot, a scientist at the Chicago Medical School, said:

> Yes, boys and girls, men and women, are different. But most of those differences are far smaller than the Men Are from Mars, Women Are from Venus stereotypes suggest. Nor are the reasoning, speaking, computing, emphasizing, navigating and other cognitive differences fixed in the genetic architecture of our brains. All such skills are learned and neuroplasticity – the modifications of neurons and their connections in response experience – trumps hard-wiring every time.[30]

Another researcher in the field emphasized that the 'innate differences' school of thought is dangerous: "All sorts of ridiculous conclusions about very important issues are then made. Already sexism disguised in neuroscientific finery is changing the way children are taught."[31]

I therefore classify all racism and sexism under the heading of misercorpism. They are prejudices which affirm the goodness of only *some* kinds of bodies (such as white male bodies), and deny the goodness of other bodies, for arbitrary reasons. A body which is inhabited in a virtuous way, by which I mean a body that expresses life-affirming qualities in its motions and habits, is a body I'd like to call a spiritual body, made by its possessor into a work of art. And it simply doesn't matter if that body is male or female, Caucasian, African, Asian, or Aboriginal.

Nakedness

Loving your own body means caring for and treating the body with respect. This can obviously mean eating, resting, cleaning, dressing, exercising, and sexually enjoying your body, with concern for your health, fitness, and pleasure. Medical scientists found that thirty minutes of exercise three times a week was more effective at treating clinical depression then Zoloft. After ten months, "participants in the exercise group exhibited lower rates of depression (30%) than participants in the medication (52%) and combined groups (55%)."[32] The same study also found that exercise prevented the patients from relapsing back into depression far more effectively than drugs. James Blumenthal, one of the lead researchers in the team said, "For each 50-minute increment of exercise, there was an accompanying 50 percent reduction in relapse risk. Findings from these studies indicate that a modest exercise program is an effective and robust treatment for patients with major depression. And if these motivated patients continue with their exercise, they have a much better chance of not seeing their depression return."[33] Exercise need not be strenuous: even thirty minutes of ordinary walking, every day, is enough to stave off the worst.

But many people who do these things regularly and with care nonetheless have very poor *knowledge* of their own bodies. Some, for instance, do not look at themselves while bathing, or while changing clothes. Yet it seems to me that a spiritual life must involve self-knowledge, and self-knowledge must involve knowledge of one's own body. It can be important, perhaps, to examine one's own body from time to time, not simply nor only for the sake of health and hygiene, but also for the sake of learning its contours, shapes, and dimensions.

Consider the story of "The Descent of Inanna". This is one of a series of stories about the Sumerian goddess Inanna, and it begins just after she established herself as the queen of heaven and earth. Her attention was then drawn to the underworld: "from the Great Above she opened her ear to the Great Below." When Inanna arrived at the first of the seven gates and demanded entry, the gatekeeper went too Erishkegal, queen of the underworld and Inanna's sister, to find out what to do. Erishkegal said that Inanna may enter but only if she first removes all her accoutrements.

When she entered the first gate,
From her head, the *shugurra*, the crown of the steppe, was removed.

Inanna asked:

"What is this?
She was told:
"Quiet, Inanna, the ways of the underworld are perfect.
They may not be questioned."[34]

At the second gate Inanna gave up her necklace of lapis lazuli; at the third, another necklace; at the fourth, her armored breastplate; at the fifth, her gold ring; at the sixth, her measuring rod and line. In each case, she protests, and the guardian tells her that "the ways of the underworld are perfect." At the seventh and last gate, the guardian removes her royal robe, leaving her fully naked.

This story can serve as an excellent model for an exercise in self-examination. Find a full-length mirror. It must be large enough that you can see yourself reflected in it, in good detail, from the top of your head all the way to your toes. Set up the mirror in a private room with good lighting. Look at yourself, up and down. Then, just as Inanna had to do, remove one of your articles, for instance a ring, necklace, or wrist-watches. If your hair is typically tied up in a band or a clip, or even just a ponytail, unbind it and let it fall loose. If you are in the habit of wearing makeup, wash it off too. If possible, remove studs and piercings. Some people have emotional difficulty removing wedding bands, for instance, or religious symbols held on chains around the neck. But these objects impose certain external associations or meanings on the body. They thus distract from the task of examining the body *directly*, and seeing it for what it actually is, for its own sake, in its own presence. Once you have put all these things away, look at yourself in the mirror again.

Next, remove an article of clothing, just as Inanna removed her breast-plate and royal robe. Again, go to the mirror and ask yourself diagnostic questions of identity such as: When I look in the mirror, who looks back? How does it feel to be without the article that you just removed? Without it, who or what remains?

Remove another article of clothing and repeat the cycle, until all of your clothes are gone. I do mean *all* your clothes. Again, the point of the exercise is to gently lay aside anything that covers of hides the body, or which attaches to the body a significance which it does not inherently possess. Some people find nudity deeply distressing. Certain accessories such as jewelry, watches, expensive and stylish clothes, and the like, are indicators of class membership and wealth, and many people have bound their sense of identity to such things. For such people, to set aside the signs of wealth and class is to set aside a large part of their personal identities. Others don't like to look at themselves because they don't like what they see: they think they are too fat, for instance, or they are revolted by the stretch marks of child-birthing or the wrinkles of old age. Even when bathing, they avert their eyes from their own bodies. For her part, Inanna faced a tribunal of sorts as well. When all her clothes and ornaments were finally removed, she was ushered into Erishkegal's presence. The judges of the underworld "passed judgment against her," killed her, and hung her body on a meat hook.

Yet after she was judged and found wanting, Inanna returned to life. The other gods send messengers to dance and sing for Erishkegal, empathize with her loneliness and misery, and coax her back to happiness. In gratitude, Erishkegal agrees to send Inanna's lifeless body back to the world of the living, where the gods awaken her again. Thus if you are one of those people who would judge your own body negatively, now is an excellent time to face and explore these feelings, and to try and discern why they arise. Look at every part of yourself, one part at a time, from your toes and fingers to your breast and head. Use an entire hour or more for this purpose if you need to. Looking in the mirror, who looks back? How does it feel to be without anything covering you at all? And without any clothes to cover you, who or what remains? I have found that when these questions are raised while clad only in the sky, so to speak, the answers tend to be illuminating, and surprising.

2

Landscapes

The relations of mind and body, so important to the good life, seem to suggest or to lead to the relations of the environment in which the body lives. For it is obvious that a body needs air, water, sunshine, food, space to move and grow, and so on. Indeed, all of the body's powers and functions exist in relation to its environment. In every moment the body takes in one mass of energy and matter, transforms it internally for its own purposes, and then discharges some of it back to the world again. That is what we do by eating, drinking, and breathing. There is no separating the body from these relations without stunting its growth, denying it the full development of its potentials, or putting it to death. It is perhaps less obvious, but no less significant, that many of the organic functions necessary for life take place outside the body itself: the purification of air and water in an ecosystem, for instance. Thus there is no such thing as a body that is lacking in nothing for the completion of its existence, unless it is a corpse. Thus the relations of mind and body are carried beyond the body itself and into the lands, seas, skies, and elements of the world.

Anthropologists have found that in the history of religion, one of the most consistent themes is the 'worship', so to speak, of the things of the natural world. Julius Caesar said of Iron Age Germans: "The only beings they recognize as gods are things that they can see, and by which they are obviously benefited, such as Sun, Moon, and Fire; the other gods they have never even heard of."[35] This is perhaps unsurprising information: but what might be very surprising is how late into the Christianization of Europe this theme in religious life persisted. A 9th century text called the

Ecclesiastical canons of King Edgar says:

> We enjoin, that every priest zealously promote Christianity, and totally extinguish every heathenism; and forbid well worshippings, and necromancies, and divinations, and enchantments, and man worshippings, and vain practices which are carried on with various spells, and with 'frith-splots', and with Elders, and also with various other trees, and with stones, and with many various delusions, with which men do much of what they should not do.
>
> (Cited in Murray, *The Witch-Cult in Western Europe*, pp 22-3)

King Edgar also ordered that "on feast days heathen songs and devil's games be abstained from." Two centuries later, it seems that some people were still worshipping things in the natural world, for *The Laws of King Cnut* say:

> We earnestly forbid every heathenism: heathenism is that men worship idols, that is, that they worship heathen gods, and the sun or the moon, fire or rivers, water-wells or stones, or forest trees of any kind; or love witchcraft, or promote *morth-work* [ancestor-worship] in any wise. (*Ibid*, p 23)

Yet the landscapes of the earth outside of our cities, which we all depend on for life, are also seen by some as fearful places. For many centuries human communities existed like islands of safety in a sea of the unknown: surrounded by unexplored or barely explored forests, deserts, mountains, ice fields, or seas. Such places might be full of monsters. Some of our rituals, therefore, are not rituals of thanksgiving, nor of requesting boons from friendly deities, but are of *propitiation*, in which the petitioner asks a malevolent spirit to leave the community alone. Fear, as much as wonder and magic, may accompany the unknown landscape.

Even today, with the entire land surface of the earth meticu-lously mapped, some people still experience fear of the world outside the city and town. The Director General of England's National Trust, for instance, observed that:

> There is evidence that people who are brought up in big cities are scared and see the countryside as a place full of unfamiliar and unexpected things. It's becoming this great unknown, alien place. If you've grown up in the inner city, you're used to a place where there's lots going on, where there's lots of buildings, lots of light. The countryside is quiet and dark – not having that same geography can be frightening for people... Whether through pressures of time or physical access, as a nation we seem to be increasingly disconnected from the fabric of the country. Today's generation runs the risk of being terrified of the countryside.[36]

It therefore seems appropriate that the next set of relations to discuss are the relations of the landscapes of the earth. Here I shall describe three special kinds of environmental relations. Each is distinct from the others, and yet none exclude the others: indeed I think it likely that everyone is involved in all three of them, all the time. Different people might emphasize them in different ways. Yet they are all invariably part of our lives.

The Circle of Life

Perhaps the theory of environmental relations with the greatest prestige today is the one described by the science of environ-mental biology. Here we learn that every life form on Earth is in various ways supporting, interacting with, reliant upon, and involved in the existence of every other life form on Earth. In most cases that involvement is very distant and indirect. But that involvement remains inextricably part of any creature's way of being in the world. It may be useful to think of this relation as a global stream of biodynamic energy. This energy enters the earth from the sun, and is gathered by the cells of plants and microbes. It then streams from one life form to another through the food chain, through symbiosis and symbiogenesis, and reproduction. Some of this energy is sent back into the soil, as animals and plants die and their bodies decay into the earth. There it is gathered again by plants, mosses, fungi, and various micro-organisms. The energy may lie in a potential state for many millennia before being recaptured by another organism. The petroleum we burn in our cars, for instance, is the energy of the sun captured in the cells of plants and animals that lived, died, and decayed many millions of years ago. Eventually, some of the energy of the circle of life radiates back into space in the form of infrared light. Organic co-operation reaches across the whole planet. The microbiologist Lynn Margulis, co-inventor of the Gaia Hypothesis, wrote that co-operation and not competition is the more dominant activity of life on earth. In her words, "the tendency of 'independent' life is to bind together and re-emerge into a new wholeness at a higher, larger level of organization."[37]

People in cities have much the same relation to the environment. They still depend upon the air, water, and food of the earth in order to live. Indeed cities can appear to be living things in their own right: they pull in resources and produce waste, just as individual organisms do. Lewis Thomas once wrote that ant colonies "are so much like human beings as to be an embarrassment. They farm fungi, raise aphids as livestock, launch armies for wars, use chemical sprays to alarm and confuse their enemies, capture slaves... They exchange infor-mation ceaselessly. They do everything but watch television."[38] In that respect, humanity's cities are just as much a part of the world as are fields and forests. Although it may not seem obvious, the reverse is also true: the rest of the world is just as much a part of the city and the life of its people as are its streets, buildings, and built infrastructure. It is now commonly understood in the social sciences that a city occupies more land than is inside its boundaries. A city is also defined by its 'ecological footprint', the land area required to feed its inhabitants, supply its industrial and commercial activities with energy and raw materials, and receive its waste. The idea of the 'ecological footprint' for cities was initially put forward by environmental economists M. Wackernagel and W. Rees. It is an analysis tool for government agencies and local authorities for use in planning the sustainable development strategies required by various domestic laws and international agreements.[39] The World Wildlife Federation defines it concisely as follows:

The footprint expresses the land area that is required to feed, provide resources, produce energy, assimilate waste, and to reabsorb its CO_2 output from fossil fuels through photosynthesis. This approach uses land as its 'currency', and provides a notional figure for the land area required, wherever and however located on the planet, that is necessary to support an individual, a community or a nation's population at its present standard of living.[40]

This ecological footprint of a city is almost always very much larger than the land occupied by the roads and buildings. It can also overlap the footprint of other cities. For instance the ecological footprint of London, England, is nearly 50 million acres, or approximately the size of the whole of Britain. Herbert Girardet, professor of environmental planning at Middlesex University, put this figure into perspective this way: "Although [London] contains only 12 per cent of Britain's population, it requires an area equivalent to all the country's productive land to service it – though this extends to the wheat prairies of Kansas, the tea gardens of Assam, the copper mines of Zambia and other far-flung places."[41]

This mode of relation to the world, that of a great circle of life, is now well-known. It has been popularized by films like *Fern Gully* (1992), *The Lion King* (1994), *Pocahontas* (1995), and *Avatar* (2009). There are also schools of philosophical thought which emphasize the global inter-connectedness of life, such as Deep Ecology. This understanding of life on earth has often been used as a major premise in the argument that people ought to show moral respect to the earth. Most friends and informants who I spoke to about their relations with the land knew of it. They also knew of the problems that can arise from a city's pollution and from excessive resource demand. So they described how they try to 'live lightly on the land'. By this they meant they recycle and compost as much of their household waste as possible, shop at local stores instead of big-box chain stores, carry things in reusable shopping bags, and reduce their household electricity consumption. One friend emphasized the importance of making fewer 'impulse' purchases of toys, junk food, household goods, and other things that they don't really need. I'm completely in favor of such practices, and I urge you, my friend, to do likewise. But as an answer my initial question about environmental relationships, this was not quite what I was looking for.

Knowledge

For the second means of relating to the environment, let's go to Ireland, and to a chain of hills in the midlands called the Loughcrew Range. On top of the center hill, called Sliabh na Caillí, ancient people built a great artificial mound, with an interior chamber and passage facing due east. The light of the morning sunrise can enter the mound and strike the stone at the far end for only a few days a year, on either side of the equinoxes. On equinox day itself the light of the sun directly targets an engraving on the rear wall, depicting of a circle with eight lines radiating from the center. Researchers have interpreted this engraving as a sun-wheel: for just as there are eight lines in the picture, so there are eight special stations of the sun: two equinoxes, two solstices, and four 'cross-quarter' days. The passage mound on Sliabh na Caillí is a kind of clock, or sundial, and its builders almost certainly used it as one. Similar passage mounds exist all over Ireland and Britain, measuring the solstices, equinoxes, and the movements of the sun and moon. And the Loughcrew Range sports numerous other similar features. The Mound of the Hostages, on the top of the Hill of Tara, is pointed to the cross-quarter sunrise on Imbolc (early February) and Samhain (early November). The mound of Knowth, part of the Boyne Valley complex in county Meath, Ireland, has two passages, one aligned east and one west, for the sunrise and sunset on both vernal and autumnal equinoxes. Newgrange, just a kilometer away, is aligned to the midwinter solstice sunrise. And the hill of Dowth, another kilometer further on, may have been aligned to the Midwinter solstice sunset (but the original entrance was sealed off by archaeologists, so now we'll never know). Maes Howe, on the Scottish island of Orkney, is aligned like Newgrange to the midwinter solstice sunrise. The mound of Fourknocks (from the Irish *fuar knocka*, for 'cold hill'), in northern county Dublin, Ireland, is pointed 17 degrees east of north, and never sees the sun; but the 17 degree angle is found in other monuments and is thought to be related to a constellation of stars. Nor are these alignments limited to mounds. Neolithic stone circles were also designed with similar alignments. The most famous is England's Stonehenge, which has numerous solar alignments, the most dramatic of which is the alignment of the midsummer morning sun.

The relationship with the world embodied in monuments like these is not a relationship based on bioenergetic exchange, like the Circle of Life. Rather, these monuments embody a relationship with the environment based on *knowledge*. To build these monuments, the Neolithic architects would have had to observe the world very patiently and carefully over a very long time. They would have had to measure the movement of the sun in its course throughout the day for many years, and compare its position to the landmarks on the earth. The site of each monument would have been carefully selected for its access to the rising and setting places of the sun. They also chose sites with the right relation to other nearby landmarks, like the peaks of nearby hills, or the valleys between the hills. Once a site was chosen, each stone in the monument would have to be positioned with great care. The builder likely experimented with wooden poles for a while, which is not hard to do, although it is time-consuming. By placing a single tall pole in the center of an empty field, and by measuring its shadows every day, the solstices and equinoxes can be determined quite precisely. Many years would have been needed, not just because bad weather might prevent a measurement on a critical day. But many measurements over many years are needed to reach the greatest accuracy. Then, when the builder was satisfied, the poles can be replaced with a more permanent structure of a more enduring material, like stone. These stones could then be carved, painted, and decorated: and the art carved on them attests to an under-standing of the cosmos that is both scientific and artistic. There are whorls and spirals representing the movement of the sun, crescents representing the moon, zigzags and waves which both resemble and also count the stations along the path made by the highest angle of the sun and moon in its course through the year. These diagrams also relate to the play of light and shadow cast by the sun and moon at various moments on the eight-fold solar calendar. Relations of narrative mythology, we could say, begin with the sun and moon and stars.

European monuments are not the only stone calendars in the world, and they are not even the world's oldest. So let us travel next to southern Alberta, Canada, to a five thousand year old site called the Majorville Medicine Wheel, also known as Canada's Stonehenge. Here we find a huge stone cairn at the center of a circle of stones, with twenty-eight lines of stones radiating from the center to the circumference. Four of those lines correspond to the four cardinal points on the compass, and their ends are encircled with another ring of stones. The center of the circle and various smaller cairns and rings along the edge of the circle align with the rising and setting places of the sun at the solstices and equinoxes. Indeed the monument, seen from above, strongly resembles the rock art of the megalithic monuments of Britain and Ireland. (This should not be surprising, since the astronomical facts measured by the circle are the same for the whole world.) The prairies of Canada, and the adjacent American states, hold hundreds of medicine wheels like the one at Majorville. The best known wheel in America is at Bighorn, Wyoming. But the circle at Majorville is by far the largest. Recent research has discovered that it is only the center of an astronomical complex covering around twenty-six square kilometers.

The practical importance of the knowledge embodied in these monuments is fairly obvious. A community has to know when to plant the crops, when to harvest them, when to expect seasonal weather to change, when to expect the return of migrating animals. Even so, the relationship with the landscape and cosmos embodied by these monuments is more than just practical. Aboriginal writer N. Scott Momaday explained it as follows:

When I first went there [to Jemez Pueblo, New Mexico, USA], to live, the cacique, or chief, of the Pueblos was a venerable old man with long, gray hair and bright, deep-set eyes. He was entirely dignified and imposing – and rather formidable in the eyes of a boy. He excited my imagination a good deal. I was told that this old man kept the calendar of the tribe, that each morning he stood on a certain spot of ground near the center of the town and watched to see where the sun appeared on the skyline. By means of this solar calendar did he know and announce to his people when it was time to plant, to harvest, to perform this or that ceremony. This image of him in my mind's eye – the old man gazing each morning after the ranging sun – came to represent for me the epitome of that real harmony between man and the land that signifies the Indian world. (Momaday, "A First American's View", *National Geographic*, 1:50, July 1976, p 15)

Momaday's story shows us a living man doing what the medicine wheels and passage mounds do. By standing at that place, and deploying the special knowledge he possessed, the man was able to perceive his landscape as a *meaningful* landscape. It became for him and his people a landscape that could be *read* almost like a book, and intimately *known*. Stone circles like the one at Majorville help people to know their world by replicating the patterns of the world in their monuments. To know the world is to understand it, possibly to predict or to control it, and certainly to cease fearing it. But most of all to know the world is to *internalize* its contours and patterns in your mind. This internalization contributes to a feeling of belonging.

Perceptual Intelligence

I discovered something in a book by Rupert Ross, who was an Assistant Crown Attorney in northern Ontario for many years. He wrote of his attempt to understand the Aboriginal worldview, in order to better serve the mostly Aboriginal communities where he was assigned. Here is how he introduced his understanding of the Aboriginal way of thinking about the Earth.

The hunter-gatherer did his shopping in the natural world. As already noted, his success depended upon his ability to accurately read the innumerable variables which each season, day and hour presented. Those variables, however, presented patterns which, over time and with great attention, one could learn to recognize. Reading those patterns to determine when 'the time was right' was the essential life skill, and it constituted, in my view, a very specialized form of thought.[42]

The complexity of this form of thought cannot be under-empha-sized. Not only was the hunter-gatherer examining all the environmental variables this way. He was also considering these factors in relation to an average of 120 local species of edible wild plants and animals per community.[43] Ross described how he himself developed this form of thought while working as a fishing guide in northern Ontario, many years before becoming a lawyer. At the beginning of each day, just before heading out on the lake, he would stand at the dockside for a while and get a 'feel' for the day:

> I made mental notes about such things as wind speed and direction, cloud cover, temperature... the quality of the light, the humidity, the sense of disturbance-building or distur-bance-waning... In truth I simply cannot list all of the things that were finally incorporated into this 'feel' for the day. I don't believe that they ever came to my conscious attention, but they were noticed all the same.[44]

Ross would then use this collected information and "super-impose it mentally" on each of the places in the lake where he could take his fishing tour guests. He would then imagine what each place might be like, and then he would compare the reality upon arrival with his expectations. As he got better at it, he was able to predict conditions at those places more and more accurately. It gradually began to feel to him as if he was not just imagining those places, but "experiencing them in advance." The final step, which he said was hardest to explain, involved ascer-taining which of the fishing spots seemed to 'attract' him, or 'draw' him to it. In his words:

> I can make this step intelligible only by thinking of my dock

image of a particular spot as a transparency of sorts, with all the variables sketched opaquely on its surface. Then similar images of past days at the same spot are slid under it. What I look for, of course, is correspondence between what I anticipate and what I recall.[45]

Ross also stated that this was an *intellectual* exercise, as it involved observations, calculations, and predictions. "What was taking place was, without doubt, a very complex and compacted form of reasoning. We are tempted, however, to deny it that status."[46] It might not look like intellectual reasoning, because, as he says, much of it happens slightly beneath the level of the conscious mind, and because the conclusions appear with an emotional content. The result of all this calculation is a feeling of being drawn to a particular place. When the calculus produced a match between the expectations of what a fishing-spot would be like, and memories of past success at that spot when conditions were the same, then he would think to himself, "I have a hunch," or "This spot feels right today." The vocabulary used here is that of interior emotional experience. But it is a form of intellectual reasoning nonetheless. Ross concluded by saying, "I believe it was this sort of mental process that guided the choices of the hunter-gatherer. His central daily, unending preoccupation was with this one mental task: accurate prediction."[47] This would certainly have been of great importance in the lives of ancient people: the accuracy of the predictions would determine whether you ate anything that day, or whether you starved.

I think that Ross has described the best phenomenological account of what it means to be involved in a relationship with the environment. I call this a *phenomenological* account in part to distinguish it from the biodynamic account described earlier, in which relationships are established through the food chain. Ross' account is phenomenological because it is rooted in the activity of our senses, and the activity of the mind interpreting and drawing conclusions from the information provided by the senses. Ross called this process "pattern thought". But for reasons that I hope will be clear in the next few chapters, I would like to call it *perceptual intelligence*. I think that perceptual intelligence is the human organism's primary instrument for learning about the world, and an essential part of every human relationship with anything.

Some people might claim that their relationship to the earth and the environment is an emotional bond, and some may prefer to describe it as a psychic or magical awareness. Yet I think Ross is right to describe it as a form of intellectual reasoning. For the 'feelings' he described emerged from the work of a highly developed faculty for mathematical and scientific calculation, at work in the whole body. It makes observations and formulates hypotheses as surely as any scientist in a laboratory. This perceptual intelligence probably looks like an emotional or psychic event because it happens beneath the notice of consciousness and it uses the sensory apparatus of the whole body. Thus we do not experience its operations in the same way that we experience, for example, communication via spoken or written language. Even the skin and internal organs are involved, as they can measure things like temperature, air pressure, air quality, and electrostatic charge. Scientists at the University of British Columbia recently found that the brain processes sound not only through the ears, but also through the skin. Participants in the experiment were asked to listen to various aspirated syllables like 'pa' and 'ta', through a recording device. The participants reported hearing different sounds when the syllable was accompanied by a barely perceptible puff of air against their hands or necks.[48] Perceptual intelligence does not appear at first glance to be the kind of mathematical reasoning that one learns in a university course on logic. But it is a form of intelligence nonetheless. Indeed I suspect that what most people ordinarily call 'intuition', 'instinct', 'gut feelings', or even 'psychic awareness', is actually the intelligence of the body, rationally observing its environment, and communicating its predictions to the brain. A spoken or written language is not involved, and no numbers are being manipulated on a balance sheet, but it doesn't follow that something other than reason is at work.

Furthermore, I think that this experience is not distinct to Aboriginal people: I think we all have it. All of us have the physiological and intellectual ability to notice all the subtle signs by which things reveal to us what they are. And if we are patient and keenly observant enough, and if we take the time to practice, we can get to know things this way so well that we can feel deeply connected to them, profoundly involved in their existence, and, in other words, *related* to them. This kind of relationship may well have interesting health benefits for people. Japanese scientists found that people who gazed on forest scenery for twenty minutes produced 13.4% less salivary cortisol, a stress hormone. Forests also helped reduce fluctuations in heartbeat and blood pressure. As these findings became more widely known, local governments in Japan started to promote 'forest therapy' for stressed-out industrial workers (Akemi Nakamura, "'Forest Therapy' taking root" *The Japan Times Online*, 2 May 2008).

But having said that, let us be clear about what the environmental relation via perceptual intelligence really requires for success. If I'm right that perceptual intelligence is the medium for our environmental relations, it follows that you cannot simply walk into a forest at random, sit on a stump at its geographic center, breathe deeply, 'visualize peace', and find yourself suddenly fully 'connected' to everything around you. Similarly, meditating on imagined trees will not do much to help build and sustain a relationship with a non-imaginary forest. Relationships with landscapes are built with patience, memory, experience, habit, practical purpose, and with long familiarity. Obviously one can, and should, visit the countryside as often as possible, even if one does not have a practical purpose like fishing or hunting to take you there. But one cannot 'commune' with the whole of the Earth after only an hour. You *might* establish a relationship with a certain field or hill or river-length after visiting it for an hour, every day, for a whole year. But that would also depend on how often, and how intensely, and for what purpose, your faculty of perceptual intelligence was engaged.

Ethical values are involved in perceptual intelligence too. Habits of mind like perceptiveness, alertness, inquisitiveness, patience, and attention become values here, since the capacity for perceptual intelligence seems to depend on these habits for success. This is a practical principle, not a theoretical one. To put it simply: if you find it useful and ethically desirable to be related to something, you will also find it useful and ethically desirable to learn the habits that make the relationship work. Those useful habits thus become values, albeit of an indirect or instrumental kind. But aside from this practical aspect: perceptual intelligence, as a means of relating to the environment, both requires and also generates certain inherent or intrinsic values, especially deep feelings of care and love. These values can motivate you to attend more closely to what is happening around you. Yet they can also *emerge from* the relationship. An exercise of perceptual intelligence can lead people to feel closer to places, drawn to them, and involved in their activities. This closeness can inspire people to protect those places, and to protect cultural traditions and customs associated with them.

Aboriginal people almost always emphasize the values of respect and care when speaking of the spiritual significance of the earth. They will use the language of family relationship: the earth is humanity's spiritual mother. One need not look far to find good examples of this way of thinking. A man named Bedagi, or Big Thunder, told a researcher that: "The Great Spirit is our father, but the Earth is our mother. She nourishes us, that which we put into the ground she returns to us, and healing plants she gives us likewise."[49] Chief Luther Standing Bear described the Lakota's attitude toward the Earth as follows:

> The Lakota was a true naturist – a lover of nature. He loved the earth and all things of the earth, the attachment growing with age. The old people came literally to love the soil and they sat or reclined on the ground with a feeling of being close to a mothering power...[50]

This idea is nearly universal among Aboriginal people all over the world. In my own exploration of Aboriginal ideas and culture so far, I have never seen an exception.

Nor are Aboriginal cultures the only places where we can find perceptual intelligence at work. Consider as another example *The Shadowy Waters*, in which The Poet describes the seven forests of Coole Park, in county Galway, Ireland. The first few lines go like this:

> I walked among the seven woods of Coole,
> Shan-Walla, where a willow-bordered pond
> Gathers the wild duck from the winter dawn;
> Shady Kyle-dortha; sunnier Kyle-na-no,
> Where many hundred squirrels are as happy
> As though they had been hidden by green boughs
> Where old age cannot find them; Pairc-na-lee,
> Where hazel and ash and privet blind the path;
> Dim Pairc-na-carraig, where the wild bees fling
> Their sudden fragrances on the green air:
> Dim Pairc-na-taraiv, where enchanted eyes
> Have seen immortal, mild, and proud shadows walk;
> Dim Inchy Wood, that hides badger and fox
> And marten-cat, and borders that old wood
> Wise Biddy Early called the wicked wood:

Seven odours, seven murmurs, seven woods.[51]

I visited Coole Park several times, and felt I understood why he was inspired to write some of his best poetry there. Coole Park is magically beautiful. If you read this poem while walking the seven woods, you will soon discover that there are no fields or boundaries between them. There are a few low stone walls where farm boundaries used to be, but they do not bar the movements of wildlife or visitors. A photographer in an airplane would look down and see just one forest, not seven. On the ground, tourist plaques installed by the Office of Public Works show you where the boundaries are. In Yeats' time, when the property was the private demesne of Lady Augusta Gregory, there were no such plaques. Yeats learned the character of each of the woods by walking in them for many years, and considering carefully what he saw. His whole sensory being surely grew aware to the changes of flora and fauna, and to the subtleties of winds, sounds, scents, and sunlight, even if only barely consciously. His whole mind and body was constantly assessing them, comparing them, and mapping them. Thus he was able to *know* the seven odors and seven murmurs of the seven woods; and he shared this knowledge with us in the form of the most wonderful poetry and prose. I think that is surely the same kind of perceptual intelligence which Rupert Ross described.

Some might feel that this explanation of Yeats' poem is too mechanistic, and strips away some of its mystery and magic. Certainly, as a philosopher, part of my purpose is to *de-mystify* the world: to render it intelligible, familiar, and our own. But I think that perceptual intelligence, as a means of relating to the world, is itself magical. The idea that the body is a comprehensive sensory organism is a highly magical idea, and I think it opens up more enchantment in the world than any metaphysical and occult speculations can do. In the next sacred relationship, we'll explore another part of that magic, and hopefully we'll see why relationships based on perceptual intelligence are actually *more* full of wonder than those which are based on a so-called 'psychic' awareness. But first:

A Note about Global Warming

I've studied the scientific evidence for and against global warming for many years at a very advanced level. I wrote my Ph.D dissertation on the topic. I find that the weight of evidence overwhelmingly favors the conclusion that industrial pollution *is* causing severe damage to the ecosystem of our planet. I'm convinced that the damage to the world ecosystem is changing the world into a much less livable place for human beings. I am also convinced that resource depletion is real. It appears that the vast majority of climate scientists agree. The scientific evidence of global warming is becoming more and more obvious now, such that a few high-profile skeptics, such as economist Bjorn Lomborg, are beginning to change their minds.[52] I have also found that among scientists who disagree, what primarily concerns them is not the environment. What primarily concerns them is the economy and the body politic. Historian Naomi Oreskes studied climate change skeptics and found that almost all of them assume that efforts to prevent global warming will concentrate power in the hands of the state, or in the hands of international bodies like the United Nations. They fear that efforts to prevent global warming will harm people's economic and political freedoms. "The sceptics [of global warming] thought, if you give up economic freedom, it will lead to losing political freedom."[53] In my own research I found a similar situation. Although global warming skeptics do look at the scientific facts, they are not primarily driven by those facts. Instead, they are primarily driven by fear. In particular, they fear that if the economic changes needed to halt global warming were implemented, then the economy might have to be reorganized into a more socialist shape. Stephen Harper, before he became

Prime Minister of Canada, expressed this fear when he described the Kyoto Accord as "essentially a socialist scheme to suck money out of wealth-producing nations."[54] Other skeptics of climate change are afraid that environmentalism, as a movement, threatens Christianity. A group of American evangelical Christians produced a video series called *Resisting the Green Dragon*, which asserted the paranoid claim that the environmental stewardship movement "is striving to put America, and the world, under its destructive control."[55] A declaration by an evangelical group called the Cornwall Alliance called on Christians to do absolutely nothing to prevent global warming and climate change. Its argument asserted that the earth's climate is self-regulating (which is true), that the current warming trend is normal and natural (which is false), and that green energy initiatives are a "regressive tax" (which brings us back to economics again).[56]

These fears are completely unfounded. But the dangers of global warming and climate change are very real and serious. A certain amount of environmental activism, then, may be an important part of a sound relationship to the land.

3

Animals

The closer you study the historical roots of religion, the more animals you find. The oldest known religious structure in the world, for instance, was discovered in 1994 at Göbekli Tepe, a hilltop in eastern Turkey, just at the north end of the Fertile Crescent. It holds around 50 monumental T-shaped pillar stones arranged in circles. It is also 11,500 years old: making it older by centuries than the Pyramids, Stonehenge, and apparently older than the invention of settled agriculture and animal husbandry. Of interest here is the fact that its pillars are covered in carved representations of animals. Some, like the wild boar, are probably animals that the builders hunted. Some, like the lions and foxes, may have been animals admired or feared for their physical qualities. And some, like the spiders, scorpions, and vultures, may have been included here because of the assistance they provided in disposing the bodies of the dead.[57]

If you want to go back further in the history of religion, you have to go underground, into the caves that Paleolithic people decorated with their enigmatic paintings. The first such cave to be discovered was at Altamira, in northern Spain. There you can find handprints, geometric designs such as checkerboard patterns and rows of dots. But most of all, you find hundreds of animals. For a long time anthropologists believed that animal images had to do with shamanism, and in particular with hunting. They might have laid offerings of food or made prayers to the image, and thus 'summoned' the actual animal that the image represented. Many Paleolithic hunting scenes depict the animals stuck full of spears: perhaps they 'rehearsed' the hunt by 'killing' the image, in order to ensure a successful kill of the actual animal. The most recent theory, advanced by South African anthropologist David Lewis-Williams, is that the cave artists drew what they saw in their minds during mild trance states, induced by the extreme sensory depravation of the caves. This theory explains why the animals that feature in the caves were not, in fact, the animals the artists were eating, as proven by the excavations of nearby Paleolithic midden heaps. It also explains the geometric shapes which do not represent anything in nature at all. The Paleolithic artists were painting the things that they knew from hallucinations. They probably thought they were seeing into a supernatural otherworld, and communicating with spirits. And in those magical otherworldly visions, what did they see? Geometric shapes, lines, spirals, rows of dots, and lots and lots of animals.

Ancestors and Totems

Within the family cluster of shamanistic ideas is the idea that people are actually descended from animals. Folklorist James Frazer noted in *The Golden Bough* that on the island of Wetar, near New Guinea, "people believe themselves variously descended from wild pigs, serpents, crocodiles, turtles, dogs, and eels; a man may not eat an animal of the kind from which he is descended; if he does so, he will become a leper, and go mad."[58] This idea is called 'totemism', and refers to the belief that the progenitors of human life and culture were the culture's most important animals, whether the animal is relied upon for food, or for labor in the fields, or for war, or is simply admired for other reasons. Thus the idea that humanity is descended from animals is far older than Charles Darwin!

Basil Johnston, an Ontario folklorist and member of the Ojibway Nation, explained that the totem is not only a divine ancestor. It is also a source of personal purpose and social belonging. Among his people, there were five totems originally, each representing one of five basic social functions: leadership, defense, sustenance, learning, and healing. Other totems were added later: in his book he listed 29 of them. But each still served one of these five general social functions (cf Johnston, *Ojibway Heritage*, p 60.) Johnston further explains the original meaning of the word *totem*:

> The evidence is strong that the term 'dodaem' comes from the same root as do 'dodum' and 'dodosh'. 'Dodum' means to do or fulfill, while 'dodosh' literally means breast, that from which milk, or food, or sustenance is drawn. Dodaem may mean "that from which I draw my purpose, meaning, and being."
> (Johnston, *Ojibway Heritage*, p 61)

To be born into the family of a certain totem meant that one could find a place in society and a meaningful role to play. The child would be encouraged to contribute to society in a manner consistent with the role of his or her totem. Of course, one's totemic 'role' in society was not a rigid assignment over which a person had no choice. If someone was uninterested in the role given to her by her totem, or not particularly talented at it, then she could do something else.

Other than the temple complex at Göbekli, the oldest religion in the world for which definite artifacts, monuments, and written documents exist is Egyptian polytheism. Interestingly, this religion featured numerous deities who are only partially human. They walk upright as we do, and (usually) have the same kind of arms and legs, but many of them have the heads of animals, and sometimes other animal features too. "Apart from a handful of deities such as Isis and Osiris," says Rotherham, "the Egyptian pantheon was adorned with goddesses and gods of animal likeness."[59] Rotherham looked briefly at some of the better known Egyptian deities to make his point. Hathor, a goddess of family life and motherhood, is depicted as a cow.

Sebek, who represents the skills of warriors, has a crocodile's head. Bast, who protects people from diseases and is also responsible for the sexual fertility of animals and people, has the head of a lion, although in later depictions she has the head of a cat. To Rotherham's list we could add the deities of early Vedic Hinduism, the religion which produced the world's very oldest written religious texts. Many of the Hindu deities also have animal features: Hanuman, who is a monkey; Ganesha, who has the head of an elephant; Garuda, who is a bird-man. Of the ten canonical avatars of Brahma, the first four are animals: *Matsya*, the fish; *Kurma*, the tortoise, *Varaha*, the boar; *Narasimha*, who is half man and half lion. Other human-shaped deities have special associations with animals. Shiva, for instance, sits on a tiger skin, and wears a tiger skin as a tunic, with a living snake around his waist serving as a belt. All the Vedic gods are associated with a special animal which sits at the foot of their thrones, or which pulls their chariots. Among West African indigenous religious traditions, one of the most popular spiritual beings is a spider called Anansi. And in China, Lao Tzu, the founder of Taoism, is normally depicted riding atop his water buffalo.

Those who are descended from Caucasian Europeans, like me, might think there is nothing like this in Europe's ancient history. But in fact there is. One of the oldest religious traditions in Europe, the religion of the Scandinavian and Germanic people, which today is called Asatru, also associates the gods with animals this way. Thor's chariot is pulled by two goats. Odin has two ravens perched on his shoulders. Freyja wears a cloak made of falcon feathers and rides in a chariot pulled by two great cats. Some Greek gods have similar animal-totemic associations. Zeus has his all-seeing eagle, and he also transforms himself into various animals to seduce his paramours. Athena has her owl, Nike has bird's wings, Pan has the feet and legs of a mountain goat. Similar evidence exists for the Celtic nations. Irish mythology includes a story called "Cat Heads and Dog Heads", which starts when nine of the members of the Fianna were traveling the length of Ireland, "looking for a pup they wanted." Somewhere along their travels they saw a great plain in which three armies were mustered: "Cat-headed one army was, and the one alongside of it was Dog-headed, and the men of the third army were White-backed" (Lady Gregory, *Gods and Fighting Men*, p 214). It seems likely that this story refers to three tribes, one which held the cat as its primordial ancestor, one which revered the dog that way, and a third which honored some animal with a white back (I suspect it was a species of fish). They therefore made their war-costumes and armor in the likeness of those animals. Nora Chadwick wrote that the most frequently appearing totemic or deified animals in the Celtic world are the bull, the boar, the horse, various water-birds, and the stag. "There can be little doubt that certain animals – and these would include birds – were sacred to the Celts. The dedication to Tarvos Trigaranus and the very name Epona alone suggest this." (Chadwick, *The Celts*, p 154)

In the Irish kingdom of Ulster, the ceremony of inaugurating a new king was witnessed by a 12th century Christian priest named Geraldus Cambrensis (Gerald of Wales), as follows:

> There is in the northern and farther part of Ulster, namely in Kenelcunill, a certain people which is accustomed to appoint its king with a rite altogether outlandish and abominable. When the whole people of that land has been gathered together in one place, a white mare is brought forward into the middle of the assembly. He who is to be inaugurated, not as a chief, but as a beast, not as a king, but as an outlaw, has bestial intercourse with her before all, professing himself to be a beast also. The mare is then killed immediately, cut up in pieces, and boiled in water. A bath is prepared for the man afterwards in the same water. He sits in the bath surrounded by all his people, and all, he and they, eat of the meat of the

mare, which is brought to them. He quaffs and drinks of the broth in which he is bathed, not in any cup, or using his hand, but just dipping his mouth into it round about him. When this unrighteous rite has been carried out, his kingship and dominion have been conferred. (Gerald of Wales, *History and topography of Ireland*, ed John J. O'Meara (London: Penguin, 1982), p 110)

The ceremony is Iron Age political theatre, of course, and probably embellished by Gerald in order to both frighten and entertain his readers. His disapproving judgment is certainly stamped all over his description. But the ritual is powerful, even if only as theatre, because the white mare, in the mythology of the Irish Celts and that of other European Celtic people, was closely associated with the goddess of the sovereignty of the land. Sovereignty goddesses like Mórrigan, Epona, Rhiannon, and Rigantona are all associated with horses, in their symbols and their stories. It's easy to speculate why the Celts chose the horse as their totem of leadership. A horse is tall and swift and strong. It can carry you over long distances further and faster than you can walk, and over shorter stretches further and faster than you can run. In either case the horse represents freedom, much the same way that cars, motorcycles, and aircraft do today; movement through space is an ancient natural symbol for freedom of both body and mind. You can also use your horse to pull wagonloads of goods to distant markets, or to carry warriors into battle. Thus if you can breed, train, ride, and handle horses, then you can wield political power. Of course the best way to take on the power of a horse is to 'be' one: and in this kingship ceremony described by Gerald of Wales, that is exactly what the candidate for kingship did. In this way, the human tribe, embodied in the person of its king, ritually confirms its relationship with the land and the goddess, who symbolizes power and freedom, and is embodied by the horse. A similar ritual is known among the Hindu people where it is called the *Ashvamedha* ceremony. And like the Celtic ritual observed by Gerald of Wales, the *Ashvamedha* normally involves a horse.

Another animal that the Celts associated with sovereignty was the bull. One story tells us that the kingship of Ireland was foretold by a prophetic Druid who ate the meat and broth of a ritually sacrificed bull. Here's the story itself from the earliest literary reference:

> This is how they did the bull-feast (*tarb-feis*) – a white bull was killed and one man consumed his fill of the meat and of its soup, and he slept after that meal, and a charm of truth was sung by four Druids over him, and it would be revealed to him then in a vision the identity of the man to be made king, as to his form and his appearance and the nature of the actions he would do. (Dillon, Myles, *Serglige Con Culainn*, (Dublin, 1953), p 9)

In other versions of the story, the seer also sleeps beneath the hides of the same bull who was sacrificed at the beginning of the ritual. The bull symbolizes strength and virility all over the ancient Celtic world (and beyond), again for reasons that are easy to guess. For instance, the Celts used their cattle as a measure of economic position. One who owned cattle would also need sufficient land to graze them, dogs to help herd them, hired workers to help handle them, and so on. You could also eat your cattle: so the larger your herd, the more secure your prospects for survival. The Celts exchanged herds of cattle like money, to pay debts, seal contracts, and pay fines for criminal offences. Landlords 'lent' cattle to their clients, and in return the clients had to pay the landlord a food-rent and provide various other services. It is therefore perhaps no surprise that the bull should feature so prominently in this account of an attempt to magically identify a future tribal king.

It is noteworthy that in both stories, that of the horse and of the bull, the animal is ritually killed. Prof. Rotherham explains that in animal sacrifice customs of various cultures, the participants do not regard the sacrificed animal as dead and gone. Rather they treat the animal as transferred in spirit to those who partake of its flesh (cf Rotherham, *Ibid*, pp 181-3). Although we know fairly little of the actual teachings of the ancient Celtic Druids, one teaching which we do know of is the belief in the immortality of the soul, its capacity to take on other forms, and to migrate into new bodies after death (cf Piggot, *The Druids*, pp 113-4). The transferal of an animal's spirit from its sacrificed body to the body of a newly inaugurated king, and from there to all who partake of the broth, seems to me fully consistent with what we know of the Druidic doctrine of the immortal soul. The same can be said of the bull-feast. The spirit of the bull is transferred to the person who takes its meat, and that spirit reveals itself to him or her in the dream which follows. Note that there are two ritual actions here which establish the magic: the killing of the animal is only one of them. The use of the animal's meat and broth in a feast is the other, and perhaps the more significant act. But I shall have more to say about that in the following studies.

After a Celtic king was so inaugurated, it was believed that his character and his decisions would be reflected in the condition of his territory. A just king would preside over a peaceful and prosperous land, whereas an unjust king would be rebelled against by the very earth itself. Plagues, crop failures, lightning strikes, and even military defeat would ruin his reign. This teaching also exemplifies a strong notion of relationship between the human community and the landscape that the people call home.

This relationship is also particularly visible in certain traditions and customs, some of them hundreds of years old or more, in which people dress themselves as animals. In *The Golden Bough*, James Frazer also described various societies in which young men and women would be initiated into adulthood by undergoing a ritual dramatization of death and resurrection. The identification with animals and the spiritual connection to an animal-ancestor featured prominently in the rituals Frazer studied. The youth would be taken by adults dressed in the skins, furs, and masks of animals, and kept away from his family and community for a time. It might be a few days, or it might be an entire year. Somewhere in this period, a ritual takes place in which the adults dramatize the death of the youth. He is poked or beaten with sticks, imitating murder, or he is walled up in a shallow cave, imitating burial. Then he is put through a series of paces which dramatically represent a passage through the Otherworld. There he meets with the ancestors and the gods (again adult members of his tribe in costume). Various proverbs and wisdom teachings are imparted to him. Meanwhile back at home, his family may host a funeral in his honor and may even mourn him as if actually dead. When he returns, he has taken on a new identity. He has died as a child and been reborn as a adult, with the soul of his ancestral animal dwelling within him. Thereafter he calls himself a rabbit, or a bear, or a magpie, or whatever animal it was. He treats those animals as his family members. On certain special occasions he dresses himself in a costume resembling that animal, made from the furs or feathers of the animal. If he should die by the tooth and claw of his own animal, his people would certainly lament the loss. Yet they would also view the manner of his passing as meaningful, even fitting, and therefore easier to accept.

Frazer asserted that this process is universal, in its wider symbolic pattern, and that only the local details are unique to different times and places. As he says:

> With good right, therefore, does he call himself a Bear or a Wolf, etc., according to his totem; and with good right does he treat the bears or the wolves, etc., as his brethren, since in

these animals are lodged the souls of himself and his kindred.[60]

Animal costuming customs are not limited to rites of passage into adulthood, and not limited to ancient or Aboriginal cultures. It seems to have persisted in Europe for quite some time after the advent of Christianity, which tended to frown on such practices. For instance, In the region of Haithabu, northern Germany, archaeologists discovered several leather masks resembling the faces of animals. These masks, dating from the 10th century and surprisingly well preserved, would probably have been worn by hunters in the days or hours before going on a hunt, to help the hunter to *identify* with the animal that he was about to chase. Like the cave paintings described earlier, this too may have been to help procure a successful hunt using magic. But even so, this is a magic spell that the hunter casts not upon the animal he seeks. Rather, he casts his spell upon himself. He doesn't just summon the animal to himself: he *becomes* the animal. As 'late' as the year 690 CE, Archbishop Theodore of Canterbury wrote the following about people who dress up in the skins and costumes of animals:

> If anyone at the kalends of January goes about as a stag or a bull; that is making himself into a wild animal and dressing in the skin of a herd animal, and putting on the head of beasts; those who in such wise transform themselves into the appearance of a wild animal, penance for three years because this is devilish. (Archbishop Theodore of Canterbury, *Liber Poenitentialis*, 690 AD.)

One can presume that the custom was widespread and popular because someone as prestigious as the Archbishop found it worthy of his attention (and his condemnation!). But I don't think that statements like these can serve as evidence of a continuous and organized survival of paganism, as scholars like Margaret Murray once believed. I think they can serve as evidence of a feeling of kinship with the animal world which began in pagan times, and which survived the Christianization of Europe. Ordinary people simply continued to do in private the things which they found useful, empowering, or just plain fun, even while in public they had accepted the doctrines of Christian faith.

Consider as a contemporary example, the Bulgarian festival of Kukeri, which takes place in the early spring of every year, even to this day. Participants dress themselves in the skins and masks of animals, as well as other characters, and they decorate their costumes in colorful ribbons, tassels, beads, and small copper bells. Many of these costumes are very large, and are perhaps better described as giant puppets. Participants march, dance, and cavort through their town, followed by drummers and musicians and other dancers in traditional folk costumes. The traditional purpose of the Kukeri is to frighten off any unfriendly or evil spirits that might prevent the onset of springtime, or interfere with the fertility of the crops. Participants today understand the science of agriculture, and know that the spring will arrive anyway without the ritual. But the festival persists because it is a way of demonstrating national and cultural identity. And like the animal costuming customs of 7th century Britain, I've no doubt that Kukeri is a lot of fun.

Finally, although perhaps most significantly, humanity's relationship with the animals of the world can also be a relationship of helpers and friends. Aboriginal traditions exemplify this relationship best, and for an example I shall turn to the traditions of the land where I was born: the land of the Algonquin Ojibway. The Ojibway creation story tells of the first human being created by the Great Spirit, a woman called 'the Sky-Woman', the progenitor of the human race. The first of her children had 'opposite natures', so they fought and killed each

95

other. The animals, sensing Sky-woman's despondency, came forward to console her. The whole world was an ocean at that time, so a great turtle swam up from the depths and gave her his back to rest upon. A muskrat brought up soil from the bottom, which Sky-woman used to create an island on the turtle's back. There she gave birth to new children, who lived peacefully and happily together, and the animals promised to continue to serve and to help them. As Basil Johnston tells the story: "In the first year, the animal beings nourished and nurtured the infants and the spirit woman. For all their needs the spirit woman and her children depended upon the care and goodwill of the animals." (Johnston, *Ojibway Heritage*, p 16) The dog, however, felt he had the least useful of powers, being not as fast as the fox, nor as strong as the wolf, nor a good swimmer, and so forth.

> Less gifted than his brothers, the dog had nothing to offer. He could not serve. Nevertheless he felt constrained to do something. In his despondency, he pledged to give his love. Others could serve according to their natures and capacities: he to his. Consequently, the dog settled down by the side of the bed in which the sleeping infants lay, alternately sitting or lying down. He gazed into their eyes, placed his head near their feet, or played to amuse them. The babies smiled. From that time on the dog never left the side of man.
>
> (Johnston, *Ojibway Heritage*, p 16)

Now that I am a dog owner myself, I appreciate that passage more and more. My dog makes about a dozen different sounds, barks, yips, and whines, to let me know exactly what is on her mind. She also knows what I'm thinking, by observing my head and eye movements, hand gestures, and the tone of my voice when I give her orders or call her name. She snuggles near me when I'm in a low mood, and she plays with me when I'm feeling excited about something. And I felt very surprised at how quickly

I warmed to her and began to love her, especially when she started to cry a little each time I stepped out my door in the morning to go to work.

Johnston wrote that the animals served humanity in three main ways. First, animals were sources of food. Second, they were sources of information about the environment and the future: Ojibway tradition attributes a certain amount of magical prescience to some animals. But animals also respond to various facts about the environment, especially the movements of other animals, by their behavior in the wild. A scout or a hunter who knows how to read that behavior could claim to be listening to, or learning from, the animals. Third, the animals represented images of character: for example, the crane represented leadership and eloquence; the loon, fidelity; the beaver, resourcefulness; and the whitefish, abundance. Literary and folkloric evidence suggests that people in all kinds of societies around the world, from mediaeval Europe to feudal Japan and China, also attributed human qualities to the animals of their worlds.

Why do you find so many animals in the history of religion? Professor Roland Rotherham explained that ancient people "chose the nature around them to reflect their belief world. The animals, birds, reptiles, insects, and other beings were used because they were part of the natural world they worked with, and their symbolism was used in order to make the incomprehensible comprehensible."[61] In this study, I have here described totemic animal ancestors, the transfer of animal spirits into human bodies, and the friendship of the helper animals. But these are only a few of the many ways that people have used the animals and plants of their own environment to represent, to symbolize, or even to embody religious ideas. From these observations, we could draw a philosophical principle like this one. Humanity does not emerge from some prehistoric state of grace. We are not fallen angels struggling to regain a lost perfection. That proposition, I'm convinced, is misercorpism. The reality is that we emerge into the world as animals. We share 'one skin' with animals, to use the phrase many Aboriginal cultures use to denote our kinship with all living things on Earth. We might believe that our spiritual project is to transcend this condition, overcome our 'base' animal nature, and become fully human. Then we proceed to overcome our humanity and become fully divine. But even if this is true, it is as animals that such a project begins. We do not begin as angels, nor even as fallen angels. We begin on the most practical plane, as beings of flesh and bone. We find our intelligence first of all in our eyes, ears, hands, and feet. Only later do we find it in our minds and hearts and souls. This argument might not be as rigorous as some philosophers would prefer, given that its main premises come from a mixed bag of cultural traditions and practical activities, rather than from categorical propositions. But I think that in a general way, these relationships do seem to presuppose the idea that humanity is but one animal among many.

Hunters

Johnston also emphasized that in the Ojibway world view, animals are "living beings entitled to life and existence. But for men to live, the animal beings had to die." (*Ibid*, p 55) In the Aboriginal point of view, this is an essential moral dilemma at the heart of human survival. As the Ojibway creation story continues, some of the animals eventually feel exploited and taken for granted by man. They convene a great meeting to decide what to do about it. (The dog, by the way, snuck off to warn the humans about the meeting, but was caught and punished by the other animals for it.) The animals eventually decided not to help humanity as much as they used to, and to go and live in some other part of the world. The Ojibway people went in search of them. Guided by an owl, they went north, and found a herd of deer, moose, and caribou, protected by a flock of crows. They fought the crows to rescue the herd, but were defeated: moreover, the deer, moose, and caribou told the Ojibway that they did not want to be 'rescued'. Then the chief of the human tribe and the chief of the deer had a little negotiation. The animals agreed to return to the Ojibway lands, but in return, the chief of the deer made man promise to treat the animals better. "Honour and respect our beings, in life and in death. Do what you have not done before. Cease doing what offends our spirits." (*Ibid*, p 57) On one level this story explains how life changed for the people when their game animals left on their seasonal migrations. But on another, it explains how Aboriginal people addressed the dilemma of killing for survival. Hunters would still go out and hunt, but with full awareness of the inescapable moral tragedy of doing so. They therefore undertook the hunt with great respect for the animals. They killed only the males, and spared the females, the young, and mated pairs. They thanked every animal they killed, prayed to it, honored it, and used every part of its body, wasting nothing. Even fish bones could not be dropped back into the water (*Ibid*, p 58). One finds this respect for the animals in nearly every Aboriginal culture in the world.

I wanted to know if these ancient ways to relate to animals are still part of the consciousness of my own people. I therefore sought out friends of mine whose livelihoods were connected to animals, and I started with hunters. Hunting is certainly a demanding exercise. In ancient times, a hunter would have had to learn extraordinary skills in hand-eye coordination, depth perception, speed, and stealth. Such skills would be necessary to follow an animal across a landscape without alerting it, and to strike it with one's spear or arrow at exactly the right spot for a quick and mostly painless death. But aside from the technical talents necessary for successful hunting, what else might be involved? I asked a few hunters among my friends if they feel a relationship with the animals they hunt. One of them said, "The most important relationship I am involved in is that between myself and the land, understanding that I view the animals as being as much a part of that land as any tree or river." I also asked him why he hunts, and his answer elaborated on this relationship:

> When seated quietly, waiting for the first sign of an approaching deer, you have time to meditate and contemplate, yet still be very connected to the place where you are, a remote and more primal place than most of us typically enjoy in our daily lives. Hunting offers a direct connection to the land, a connection that cannot be experienced by a mere walk in the woods. When one is hunting the air has another more substantial feel to it. The land comes into sharper view and broken vegetation or the subtle disturbance in the leaves on the forest floor becomes loaded with meaning. All this is due to the act of hunting, the hunter becomes tied through the earth to the animal they pursue whether the animal is in their sight, hidden or not even there. (J. Phoenix, 2009)

I think this is an example of the perceptual intelligence which Rupert Ross described, in his account of his relationship with the lake. The hunter carefully examines the landscape as he moves through it. He notices every sound made by birds, insects, and the wind; he notices every bend in the undergrowth, and every rustling tree branch; he observes the smell of the air. An experienced hunter can look on a landscape and know almost instantly what animals have passed by the area, and how recently, even if there are no obvious signs such as footprints or dung heaps. He looks on the grass and the leaves and sees if they are folded over, for instance, and how far they have folded themselves back to normal. She sees that if certain species of grass, fern, or tree is close by, then she must also be close to a stream or a river, or close to certain animals that like to use those plants for food or shelter. The hunter also looks for what is *not* there. As one conservation hunter taught me:

> I can follow various birds of prey, at a distance, even on cloudy days, by watching the negative space. I know what kind of insects that bird eats, and if I see none of them around, it's probably because they are all in hiding. Their predator has just passed by.
>
> (N. Bertrand, 2009)

I also learned that a hunter carefully attends to what the other animals around him are doing. If he or she is hunting from horseback, or with a pack of beagles, for instance, he looks at the things which catch their attention. The helper animals can often hear and smell things that humans cannot. So by watching which way their ears perk up, and which way they follow their noses, the hunter can calculate the likely direction and proximity of whatever prey he is chasing. The hunter also observes the behavior of birds, rodents, and other wildlife around her. One conservation hunter told me that she is especially attentive to the ravens:

> The ravens are important to hunters. If you go into the wild and you are hunting, you will move your head in a certain way, and dart your eyes in a certain way, and the ravens will see that. They will know that you are not just passing through, but actually searching for the game. They will fly ahead of you, and show you where the deer is. If the deer is on the ground and it looks like it's still alive, they will circle in the air above it. If the deer isn't moving and looks like it might be dead, they perch on the trees above, and call to you. In return they want some of the meat for themselves. (N. Bertrand, 2009)

This may look like instinctual and non-rational knowledge. The person who has this knowledge may certainly feel as if it comes from 'the gut', or from 'a hunch', or even from a spiritual and supernatural source. The apparent fact that animals have it too also suggests that it is a kind of instinct. But I think it is actually a form of highly subtle and advanced intelligence, at work not only in the mind and body of the hunter, but also in the minds and bodies of the helping animals too. For the hunter's mind puts all of these signs together to create a mental map of where the animal he is chasing is most likely to have gone. Then when the map is complete, he might 'feel' something compelling him to explore in one direction or another. It may be experienced like an emotional sensation, or a magical pull. But it is actually an intellectual awareness in which everything you can see and hear is profoundly 'loaded with meaning'.

Another hunter I spoke with pointed out the difference between walking in the woods as a tourist, and walking in the same woods as a hunter. "In the first case, you are simply observing the forest. You've entered the forest to enjoy the beauty of it. As a hunter you're participating. You there to enjoy the beauty, but also to kill something and take it home, and eat it. You are part of the food chain there. If you're just a tourist, you're not." (J. Phoenix, 2009) Another hunter related to me a similar idea: she said to me that while hunting, the presence of non-hunting people in the same landscape can be disturbing. This is not just because non-hunters might accidentally startle the animals and mess up their trails. Nor is it just because another person's presence can disturb the work of gathering the perceptual information necessary for hunting. Rather, it's because hunting is also a state of mind. "I'm not in a human headspace," she said. "I hunt; I become part of the land, part of the animal world. I am not myself. I don't like being pulled back into the human world again before I decide I'm ready." (Name withheld by request.) She described an occasion when, while moving through a forest, a pair of pleasure hikers approached on a nearby trail. So she bent low, under the cover of some bushes, like any other animal trying to avoid human detection. It appears that some contemporary hunters do continue the tradition of 'becoming' an animal, in spirit, as part of their activity.

Companions and Pets

We should also examine our relationship with our companion animals, which is also very complex. We breed animals for specific purposes, and we train them from a very young age for the job we will want them to do. It surprised me to learn how little time is needed to accomplish this. Russian geneticist Dmitri Belyaev conducted a 40-year long experiment to determine how long it would take to selectively breed a wild animal to produce a domesticated, sociable animal. His major thesis was that early people may have selectively bred their animals not for size or shape, nor for being strong or fast, but rather for a single behavioral quality: namely, friendliness to humans. He also hypothesized that other changes in their shapes, sizes, and basic morphology emerged as a side effect of breeding for the single intention of producing a tame animal.[62] Beginning with a group of silver foxes, he tested them for aggressiveness and for submissiveness to humans, once each month until they were seven or eight months old. Then he allowed only the tamest of the animals to reproduce. Here is how Belyaev's successors described the results:

Forty years and 45,000 foxes after Belyaev began, our experiment has achieved... a unique population of 100 foxes (at latest count), each of them the product of between 30 and 35 generations of selection. They are unusual animals, docile, eager to please and unmistakably domesticated. When tested in groups in an enclosure, pups compete for attention, snarling fiercely at one another as they seek the favor of their human handler. Over the years several of our domesticated foxes have escaped from the fur farm for days. All of them returned. Probably they would have been unable to survive in the wild. (Lyudmila N. Trut, "Early Canid Domestication: The Farm Fox Experiment", *American Scientist*, Vol 87, March-April 1999, pp 163-4)

Within only four generations, Belyaev had his first fully domesticated, socialized foxes; within thirty generations, he had over a hundred of them. They were eager to please; they licked people's faces and hands gleefully; they allowed themselves to be petted and hand-fed; they competed with each other for human attention. Their 'window of bonding', that is, the time from when the animal first opens its eyes to the time when it first starts to fear the unknown, was much longer, allowing more time for it to become involved in human social relationships. They also physically resembled dogs more than their predecessors had. In the eighth to tenth generation, they gained a star-shaped pattern on the face, floppy ears (in the wild, only elephants have floppy ears), and rolled tails. After around 20 generations, they had shorter legs, and their jaws had underbites or overbites (*Ibid*, p 164). At the end of the experiment, 70 to 80 percent of the foxes in Belyaev's colony were fully domesticated. The experiment shows that our ancient human predecessors could have bred companion animals for themselves within a very short amount of time: perhaps within one human lifetime.

I think that this is significant not only scientifically, but also philosophically. For Belyaev's discovery introduces another way to understand the philosophical and spiritual significance of relationships. His experiment is evidence that *relationships configure our very identities*, even at the genetic level. Our companion animals are what they are because of the relationship with them that our ancestors created.

Alas, there are ways in which the ancient bond between humankind and the other animals can also break down. For instance, animals that are factory-farmed for food are usually kept in deplorable, unsanitary conditions. 97% of all eggs produced in the United States come from hens kept in battery cages for their whole lives, unable to walk anywhere, with an average floor area of 7 by 7 inches per bird.[63] Feedlot cattle, where the meat for your fast-food hamburger comes from, live in pens with hundreds, sometimes thousands, of animals, again with hardly enough space to walk. They stand knee-deep in their own excrement, and they eat hormone-laden corn mixed with waste fat, meat, and gristle from the slaughterhouses.[64]

Furthermore, people often take in pets and companion animals only to neglect them when the responsibilities of caring for them become inconvenient. Think of the old dog who is sent to the backyard, perhaps tied by a chain to a brick or a post, and no longer walked or played with. If they get underfoot, they might be shouted at, or even kicked around. Perhaps the most extreme case of breakdown in the ancient bond between humankind and the companion animals is the puppy mill: essentially a factory for mass-producing the largest number of puppies at the lowest cost, for sale to pet stores. Little or no attention is given to the care and health of the puppies. The sole purpose for the operation is to make money, and therefore the dogs are treated as mere commodities. They are systematically abused, through both violence and neglect, for their whole lives. A friend of mine who has been involved in rescuing dogs from puppy mills described them as follows:

When a bitch is in heat she is chased down and pulled out of her pen and then shoved into another pen with an equally mistreated male. These dogs might be related to each other, but chances are the mill owner doesn't remember or care about such things. If the male is too big or rough for the girl and he hurts her, if the female turns nasty during the mating and bites the male, they are kicked or water is dumped on them. If the male is lucky, he may receive treatment for his bite. If the female is lucky, she will receive an extra portion of food after being bred. They are fed the cheapest possible dog food along with little more than slop or scraps. They may have a cow or pig carcass tossed into their pen every now and then. They are often fed just enough to stay alive, becoming emaciated, especially the males. The females, because they are pregnant much of their lives, may be fed large quantities of cheap dog kibble, along with cow brains or pig hearts and gods knows what else. However, with a complete lack of exercise and being overbred they often become dangerously obese. (J. Cox, 2009)

A sheriff's report of a raid on a puppy mill in Illinois said that, "Puppies had broken bones, internal organ problems and were infected with fleas and mites. One dog had injuries that will likely require amputations of a limb." (Patrycja Malinowska, "Rescue Alert: Over 50 dogs seized from alleged puppy mill" *The Examiner*, 12 February, 2010) The Ontario SPCA described the condition of 125 dogs rescued from a mill near Waterford, Ontario, in 2003: "They were emaciated, filthy, severely matted and feces encrusted, infested with parasites and suffering various medical problems. Sadly, two had to be euthanized because they were too sick to humanely treat." (*OSPCA Newshound*, Vol 6 Iss 1, June 2003)

There are various community organizations which receive animals rescued by the authorities from mills and from abusive homes, and which transports them to new families. When I moved to Ottawa in the spring of 2009, I stayed for a while with a family who fostered rescued Great Pyrenees dogs. One particular dog we took in had a kill order on his head, because he had bitten an emergency services worker. This is normal territory-defense behavior, as just about anyone who understands dog psychology will tell you. But the law requires that a dog which bites a human out of malice must be put down. When we brought him to the house, we found him a loving, happy, playful, and friendly animal. We saw no evidence of the problems of which we had been warned. We were only fostering him, not keeping him, so we had him for only a little more than a week until a new home had been found for him. I got to like him a lot, and at one time my partner and I volunteered to take him ourselves if another home could not be found. Later on, however, at his new home, he bit two other people in the space of a few days. We who had fostered him for even that short time were very upset when we heard the news that he was put down anyway. The dog described to us in the accounts of the biting simply wasn't anything like the dog we knew and loved who we fostered: the behavior was very different. That, however, is what fostering a rescued dog often entails. If you agree to foster a rescued dog, you will be opening your home to a traumatized and psychologically damaged animal, who almost certainly has a variety of unpredictable anxieties and fears, and may panic or attack or cower in fear for no obvious reason. But it will almost always give affection in return for affection, and will pull your heartstrings in every way.

Animal shelters and humane societies with 'no kill' policies might not help save a rescued animal's life. For instance, in late 2009 the City of Toronto Police laid criminal charges for animal cruelty on five directors of the Toronto Humane Society. The animals kept there were so badly diseased and malnourished that putting them down would arguably have been profoundly merciful. The report said that the building was "absolutely disease infested," and "one officer recalled a cat whose skin came off in his hands when the officer lifted the cat up." ("Humane Society Officials charged with cruelty" *CBC News*, online edition, 26 November 2009) I've been informed from reliable sources that other animal shelters which do have kill policies are so overwhelmed with dogs and cats, that any animals that arrive there are put down within as little as three days. They simply do not have the funds, the space, the personnel, or the food, to house any more. Moreover, people often drop off their animals there for frivolous reasons: the dog isn't a puppy anymore, or it barks too much, or is too much 'trouble' to look after. Animals have thus become not only consumer commodities, but also *disposable* consumer commodities.

When our relations with our companion animals are sound and healthy, they can run very deep. As an example of this, and as a final thought for this study, consider how animals can have the same feelings of affection and loyalty for us as we can do for them. A friend recounted to me the story of how her dog, a blue heeler named Crash, protected her from a violent ex-boyfriend at great risk to itself.

> Once, when my relationship with [a certain ex-boyfriend] was reaching its end, he had a severe diabetic episode and he went crazy (as happens sometimes). I walked through the door, coming home from work, and he was screaming at the top of his lungs. He rushed me. As I tried to open the door and back out, Crash leapt out of nowhere, and put herself between me and him. She snarled and barked at him. He didn't stop. He kicked her in the ribs, sending her flying to my feet. She hit hard and I screamed "Oh gods!" but he was still coming at us, angrier than ever, hollering that he was going to "kill that f****** dog." (J. Cox, 2009)

My friend managed to escape the house because the protective instinct of her dog gave her the extra few seconds she needed to reach her vehicle before her attacker did. This protective instinct appeared because she raised her dog from puppyhood, trained and disciplined her, took care of her, loved and played with her, and kept close to her for her whole life. In return, her dog loved her strongly enough to put itself in danger to protect her. As she concluded her story: "that kind of selfless loyalty is what makes an animal a 'familiar'."

4

The Kitchen

The relationships in the mind and body, and in the landscapes around you, intersect with human relationships in various places, but perhaps most intensely in the kitchen.

But before reading any more of this chapter, take a moment to think about your last few meals. Did you get the food from a drive-through window, and eat it in your car? Did you eat it from a plate on your lap while watching television? Did you eat it straight from the pot you cooked it in? Did you just heat up a package of processed frozen food in a microwave? How much of it was whole food, and how much was a processed artificial product? Did you take any vitamin or nutrient supplement pills with it? Were there any ingredients listed on the package that you couldn't pronounce? Did you gobble it down as quickly as possible? If there were leftovers, did you throw them away? Did you eat alone?

Finally, could you answer 'yes' to as few as four of those ten questions concerning the last ten meals that you ate? If so, then you are probably depriving yourself of one of the most important sacred relationships in all of human life. We all owe our lives to food – of that there is no question. Yet we also owe much of the quality and the character of our lives to all the relationships that happen in our kitchens. By 'the kitchen' here I mean more than just a room in the house. I also refer to everything in that room: the knives, bowls, cutting boards, pots, pans, ovens, pantries, and equipment. And I refer to the animals, plants, waters, and other edible materials that we actually consume. And most of all, 'the kitchen' also means the people with whom and for whom we prepare food, and with whom we eat it. These relationships are centered in the kitchen, but they often begin far away: in farmer's fields where crops and livestock are raised, in deep oceans where fish are caught, and in the high atmosphere, with the wind and rain. The most complete account of the things which are necessary for food to appear on your table would ultimately encompass every ecosystem in the whole of the earth. It may also reach beyond our planet, to the light and heat generously provided by the sun.

From Survival to Culture

Up to about 150 years ago, the majority of people in every human society on earth were involved directly or indirectly in the production of food. Some estimate that up to 90% of the population of pre-modern Europe was involved in food production or distribution. The mediaeval European diet consisted mainly in grain crops milled into bread, various root vegetables, wild nuts and berries that could be scavenged in the forests, lots of fish, and lots of meat. For sweets they had fruit, berries, and honey. All meat was from free-range animals, whether hunted or farmed, and aside from hay and grass for winter feed no one planted crops to be fed exclusively to animals. This made most animals very lean, and their meat contained three times as much protein as fat. Farm animals today, fed on scientifically designed diets, inoculated with hormones, and kept in small constraining corrals, often have three times as much fat as protein.[65] The kind of food people ate depended on the seasons, as different foods became available at different times of year. This also meant that the poor had to endure an annual cycle of scarcity and abundance. The hungriest month of the year was July, as grain reserves from the previous year would be almost completely gone, yet the harvest was still another month ahead. In mediaeval England this period was known as 'the hungry gap'. Rich people could pay for the food they wanted, even as scarcity drove up the prices of basic staples like bread. But the poor had to scavenge the fields and hedgerows for herbs and nuts, and could only make bread from beans, peas, and coarse grains like rye.

In August, when the first loaves of bread could be made from the first good grains of the year, the whole community pitched into the harvest effort, and then held great celebrations. Agricultural festivals are excellent ways that a community affirms the ethical desirability of life, because they *celebrate* the availability of food, which is like celebrating the fact that we are surviving. In a modern society, most of our food is produced with the use of machines and chemicals, and a lot of it is imported from other parts of the world. Just about any kind of food you might want is available in a local supermarket at any time of year, whether it is in season locally, or whether it could even grow locally at all. We no longer deal with an annual cycle of scarcity and abundance. So we may not be fully able to appreciate the desperate importance that was once attributed to the successful planting in the spring and harvest in the fall. Nor do we celebrate harvest festivals with the same gusto: our community's survival no longer depends on the annual cycle.

A special philosophical understanding can be discerned in our food when we consider the human relations involved. Indeed I shall be bold here and say that at least two fundamental moral principles are inherently bound into the sharing and distribution of food. We have already seen the first one: to eat means to survive. We all know what happens when we go without food for too long. To share food with someone, that is, to share with someone the means of survival, is to implicitly affirm that person's right to live. And to deny food to someone is to implicitly deny that person's right to live. Or, to be a little less strict, to deny someone a share of your food is to put that person's right to live into question. You could deny that you are the one responsible for that person's survival: perhaps other people should take care of him, or perhaps he should take care of himself. You can also doubt or deny someone's right to live by poisoning the food, to harm or kill him. You can use food to snub someone, for instance by serving good food to one guest and bland food to another, or by offering someone food that you know he cannot eat. Think of the banquet scene in the film *Indiana Jones and the Temple of Doom*.

The recipient of the food also implicitly affirms various moral values: trust, for instance. If you are about to eat something that you have not prepared yourself, you have to trust that the person serving you is not about to poison you. By accepting an offering of food, you can also implicitly judge its quality: by accepting it, you show that you find it worthy. Similarly, if someone important to you serves something truly horrid, you might eat it anyway, again to show your esteem for that person. By declining it, you can make other, less flattering social judgments about the food itself or the person who offered it. As a summary observation, Margaret Visser, professor of classics at the University of Toronto, wrote: "Food can be shared, abstained from, used as a weapon or as proof of prestige, stolen, or given away; it is therefore a test of moral values as well."[66]

In all of these realizations, we can discern at least two primary 'patients' of ethics: the person with whom we share food, and the person with whom we do not share food. Related to these are two variations: the person whose offering of food we accept, and the person whose offering of food we decline. These will lead us to the moral categories of the 'friend' and the 'not-friend' (or the 'stranger'). The affirmation that someone is or is not your friend appears in the way that we prepare and serve (or do not serve) our food. I shall have more to say about this in the next two studies. Here, all that needs to be said is that the sharing of food enacts a basic moral proposition: the affirmation of another person's right to live. The denial of food may thus enact a denial of responsibility for that person's survival.

But this does not say everything. For if the right to mere

survival was all that we implicitly affirm by serving food, that affirmation can be accomplished by serving someone nothing but water and chemically synthesized vitamin supplements. But we obviously serve each other much more: we serve chicken cacciatore, and veal parmigiana, and marinated barbecued beef. We prepare and serve each other food intended primarily for pleasure: chocolate, for instance. We have created elaborate and wonderfully enjoyable traditions for food *celebration*. I think this leads to a second basic moral proposition, as I shall here attempt to explain.

On one level, food preparation requires a little bit of talent. Sometimes even the simplest foods require some advanced technical skill. Consider that which the poet Louis Bromfield called "the king of the table": bread. Although it has few ingredients, it can be surprisingly difficult to make. The ingredients must be mixed in a precise ratio to each other, and the dough baked at a precise temperature. If anything is amiss, the end result will be something resembling a hockey puck. Modern countertop bread making machines make the process easier. But imagine how much painstaking trial-and-error was required to invent bread in the first place, many centuries ago, using hand-ground grains and a wood-fired stone oven. Extraordinary perceptual intelligence would have been required. The ingredients need to be mixed and kneaded together until the consistency of the dough was just right. The baker would have ascertained this not only by sight, but also by touch, as he pushed his fingers through it. Once the dough was in the oven, for instance, the baker would have to be perpetually conscious of the smell of the bread as it baked, as well as the smell of the fire, and how much time had passed, and quite a list of other conditions too. He didn't have a thermometer to know when the oven reached the right temperature, nor had he a clock to know that the right time to remove the finished bread had arrived. He had to use his eyes, ears, nose, and ultimately his mind. (Mediaeval people sometimes kept time while cooking by counting recitations of the Lord's Prayer.) Furthermore bread is a remarkably diverse food, and similar observations about attention to subtlety also apply here. Bread can be made from numerous kinds of grain: wheat is only the most common kind in a supermarket today, but it can be made from coarser grains like barley and rye, or it can be made from rice or even from acorns. Spices, nuts, fruit, and other ingredients can be added to the dough, to change the flavor. And it can be kneaded into any kind of shape the baker wants. Thus artistic considerations are possible, perhaps necessary. Bread can be served as a delivery device for other foods, like cheese, or olive oil. It can be sweetened with sugars and chocolates and fruit and that way served on its own as a desert: in which case we call it cake. Or we can serve it as a light snack, in the form of cookies, or as a cocktail party favor, in the form of crackers. And it comes in a liquid form, called beer! Similar observations about the skills and subtleties that go into preparing bread can be made about other noble foods: wine, cheese, olive oil, tea, coffee, beer, chocolate, meat, fish, and maple syrup.

I think these observations point the way to a spiritual dimension. Food, and everything involved in the production, preparation, and presentation of food, feeds more than just our bodies. The relationships that center in the kitchen reflect the climate we live in, the techniques of farming that we use, and the importance of the quality of our food, and in turn the importance of the people with whom we share all these things. The spiritual dimension of food is the dimension at which the relationships of the kitchen not only configure who we are, but also affirm *the goodness and the beauty of embodied life on earth*. If we ate only to survive then we could eat the same bland and boring thing every day. But we clearly do more than that. We also serve food to *enjoy life*. We eat to live: we eat *well* to live well. The ancient Greek philosophers had a name for this 'living well': *eudaimonia*, meaning happiness, flourishing, blessedness, or translated almost literally, 'a good or desirable fortune or destiny'. And it seems to me that this notion of *eudaimonia* is a more significant ethical category than mere survival. Indeed I suspect that the invention of the kitchen table did more for civilization than the invention of the wheel.

Someone who eats in fast-food joints most days of the week, or who eats breakfast each day in his car while driving to work, has one kind of 'relation' with food. Someone who cooks most of his own meals almost from scratch almost every day, and eats them at a table with his family, has another. The former person probably doesn't find that his food is a medium of his social relationships: he probably sees it instead as something like 'refueling'. (And people do use the language of machine-function to describe their relation to food.) Our relationship with food becomes a sacred relationship when we transform the bare biological necessity for material sustenance, the need to eat, into an important cultural and artistic event that affirms the goodness and the beauty of being alive.

The Soul in the Kitchen

Some spiritual traditions give special significance to the kitchen precisely to help people discern the sacred in the relationships that center themselves there. For example, in the Mevlevi Order, a community of Sufis established by Jalaludin Rumi, initiations take place in the kitchen. There is also a designated area for new students to sit and study the culinary practices of their teachers. Certain ritual gestures are required for anyone entering or leaving a kitchen in a Mevlevi community: Celaleddin Celebi, a descendant of Rumi, wrote that:

There is a 'Soul' in the kitchen that nobody wishes to disturb. For this reason people only entered the kitchen if it was for something important. They would approach the door in silence, salute with a gesture of the head, gently sound the door knocker, say, "With Your Leave Holy Dervishes, Hu." If the door was opened, slowly explain what they desired to the person who answered the door and never enter without the permission of the senior dervish on duty, or without being invited in. Once they entered they would carry out their business immediately and then walk out of the door backward, saluting with their heads.[67]

It is possible that this ritual etiquette emerged from the fact that kitchens are busy workplaces, and if it gets too crowded then no one will be able to get much done. Anyone who has worked in a kitchen at a campground or a restaurant, for instance, knows this. Yet this description of the etiquette for entering and leaving a Sufi kitchen strongly resembles the etiquette for entering and leaving a temple. The conspicuous gestures of respect, and so on, serve to emphasize the sacredness of the kitchen. Similarly, the etiquette for setting the table, for eating, and for finishing also served this purpose. For instance, everyone at the Sufi table ate from a single large communal dish, and ate in silence. If someone wanted water during the meal, he requested it with a gesture, and everyone would pause their own eating while he drank, so that he would not end up with a lesser share of the communal dish. The meal ended when the most senior person at the table finished with a prayer of thanks.

What is the 'soul' in the kitchen, which Celaleddin says no one wishes to disturb? Perhaps that soul has to do with the way that the production and sharing of food creates relationships and bonds between people and each other, and the natural world, which in their greatest extension can create a sense of global environmental unity. Here, as an example, is a passage from the *Taittiriya Upanishad*:

From food, verily, all creatures are produced,
Whatever [creatures] dwell on the earth

Moreover by food, in truth, they live.
Moreover into it also they finally pass.
For truly, food is the chief of beings;
Therefore it is called a panacea [all-healing].
Verily, they all obtain food
Who worship *Brahman* as food.
For truly, food is the chief of all beings;
Therefore it is called a panacea.
From food created things are born.
By food, when born, do they grow up.
It both is eaten and it eats things.
Because of that it is called food.
Verily, other than and within that one that consists of the essence of food is the self that consists of breath. By that this is filled. This, verily, has the form of a person...[68]

Although this example is rather far removed from the Islamic tradition of the Mevlevi community, it expresses a principle which may help further explain the philosophical significance of food. Here the unknown author of the text seems to claim that food is a medium of global unity: 'everything is food'. This may sound a little strange to Western-trained ears. The metaphor (which is only partly a metaphor) of eating and being eaten represents the movement of matter and energy from one life to another, and a transformation of one form of life into another form of life. Imagine a small child, who is shown a cow grazing in a field, and who then says, "Look, our food is eating the grass! Does that mean when we eat the cow, we eat the grass too?" Well, indirectly, the answer is yes.

The ceremony of sharing food is one of the most basic and universal rituals of human culture the world over. Ancient people affirmed it when they sacrificed bulls and other prestigious animals to their gods. Christians affirm it when they re-enact the Last Supper, recalling Jesus' words, "This is my body, this is my blood." Hindus affirm it when they offer rice, vegetable oil, milk, honey, and *ghee* (butter-fat) to sacrificial fires and to statues of the gods. Jews affirm it with the *kosher* laws that describe which animals can be eaten, and under what conditions. Muslims affirm it by fasting from dawn to dusk during the month of Ramadan. Wiccans affirm it when they bless the cakes and ale, dipping the athamé into the chalice or touching it to the paten plate from which the wine and the bread-cakes are passed around. And all eight festivals on the Wiccan religious calendar are based on environmental observations, either directly or indirectly related to agriculture. The Celtic spring festival of Beltaine, for instance, celebrates the planting of crops in the fields, and the herding of the sheep, goats, and cattle from their winter corrals to their summer highland pastures. These activities, important for survival, were further sanctified with magical and religious actions in order to ensure success. The cattle, for instance, were driven between two blessed bonfires, to protect them from injuries and diseases and malevolent magic in the coming year. Young couples would magically empower the fields by making love in them. (It's also likely that Beltaine sexual customs came about because the young men were about to herd their animals to the summer pastures, and would not see their girlfriends again until the fall.) In summary, the ancient ritual of sharing food affirms the goodness of bodily life, which is the goodness of being in the world. The ceremony renders one of the most basic of our bodily needs into a means of approaching and responding to the immensity of the Earth, the provider of our food. It also opens the door to the immensity of other people, with whom we produce and share our food.

To recognize the soul of the kitchen, it is minimally necessary to respect the food itself. The award-winning French chef Régis Marcon included in his recipe book a 27-page discussion of food-philosophy, in which he described what respecting food should mean to us. In his thinking, respect for food involves two main considerations. The first is waste avoidance. He says:

> Once, while working a gala presentation in Los Angeles, I was outraged to see mountains of food destined for the garbage bin. I was disgusted by the frantic accumulation of food for the purpose of surreal and almost morbid bingeing. The amount of waste was terrifying. Back in Saint-André, my mother would work magic with leftovers. She lived courageously, from hand to mouth. The journey from my parent's house to Los Angeles seemed long. In our home, waste was forbidden. My mother had to feed seven children, who responded well enough under the circumstances, and learned to finish their bread and mop up their ragout. The imprints of my upbringing still mark my everyday existence, several decades later. I constantly monitor the storeroom and manage the foodstuffs as strictly as any bank account.[69]

Part of the reason for the strict monitoring of the contents of the food store is of course practical: he notes that food should not be left in cold storage for more than 24 hours. Although Marcon doesn't mention it, I suspect that a sense of justice is also in play. It could be inferred from his discussion that good food *deserves* to be eaten, and should not be thrown out for no reason. I suspect a principle of self-respect is also in play here. A habit of wastefulness is a sign of a lack of care for the things that make up one's world, and a lack of appreciation for the work that goes into making the things of our world useful and delightful to us.

A second consideration described by Marcon involves not limiting yourself to a small number of food sources and ingredients. This is not just a matter of waste-avoidance. It is also about finding something wonderful about everything and anything we can eat, whatever it may be, and wherever you may find it. Marcon says a good chef does not limit himself to what he calls the 'luxury foods', but rather he considers all the materials in his environment as possible contributors to his kitchen. A good chef, he says, "benefits greatly by taking an interest in the humble and familiar foodstuffs, ennobling them through this rare, deferential treatment."[70] He also explains that one should not always go for the prestigious cut of meat while ignoring the rest of the animal. In his words, "Preferential selection only has meaning, for me if it includes a broad range of choices. At Saint-Bonnet-le-Froid, we prepare the whole pigeon, rabbit, and lamb, for example. After all, a book cannot be truly appreciated on the basis of a few brief extracts."[71] His remarks here reminded me of the Aboriginal custom of respecting their hunt animals by using every part of the animal.

A friend of mine is the lead chef at a restaurant, and she told me how her primary relationship as a chef is with the people who come to eat at her table.

> Yes, I appreciate the artistry of ingredients and flavours. But it's most of all the people in my restaurant, especially the regulars. People live such routine lives, where they go to work and do the same paperwork job, then they go to the gym, and we have to keep the hamster on the wheel running! But if I can make for them a dinner that they know is especially made for them, it interrupts the pointless routine a little bit. I also get to know the people: there's the guy who doesn't like carrots, and there's the guy who likes extra mushrooms on his steak, and there's the guy who only likes asparagus. When they come into my restaurant, I try to remember facts like that about them and I can prepare a dinner that is just for them. They appreciate knowing that they didn't have to remind me about their preferences. (K. Weiler, 2009)

My informant here is a professional chef. But you don't have to be a professional to explore your own relationship with your food, and with the people with whom you share your food. An obvious way to do so is to host a dinner party. You can probably find reasons to have a dinner party once a month: life milestones like birthdays and anniversaries, cultural occasions like Robbie Burns Day, religious holidays like Samhain or Easter. On those occasions, decorate the table with tablecloths, candles, flowers, and placemats. Before the feast begins propose a toast, or recite a blessing, or describe some reason why the day deserves celebration.

A Note about Wine

It may amuse you to learn that in some traditions, the particular food which receives the most prestige is alcohol. The Roman historian Tacitus reported that among the Germans, "Drinking bouts lasting all day and all night are not considered in any way disgraceful… they often make a feast an occasion for discussing such affairs as the ending of feuds, the arrangement of marriage alliances, the adoption of chiefs, even questions of peace or war. At no other time, they think, is the heart so open to sincere feelings or so quick to warm to noble sentiments."[72] Tacitus also noted that important decisions made while drunk would be examined afresh on a subsequent day when everyone was sober again. Scholar Michael Enright explained why alcohol was the food of choice here. In European Iron Age Heroic societies, the only people you can truly trust are the members of your own blood-related family, your kinsmen. But at the heroic feast, alcohol can serve as a substitute for blood. In Enright's words:

> … communal drinking, which had the purpose of creating fictive kinship, must also be viewed as having some of the aspects of a cultic act. It aimed at creating a non-natural bond of loyalty, and liquor was used because liquor was the medium through which one achieved ecstasy and thus communion with the supernatural. (Enright, *Lady with the Mead Cup*, p 17)

Nor is European pagan society the only society in which alcohol plays an important social role. In early Hebrew society, certain kinds of religious thanksgiving celebrations could not proceed without wine. Thus when Noah's Ark finally found dry land, the first plant that the harried captain put into the earth was the grape. Finding land gave him cause to celebrate and to give thanks to God – and by planting a grapevine, he signaled to his family that he was already preparing the thanksgiving dinner. (It is perhaps no accident that the word 'feast' refers to a meal as well as a religious holiday. In Catholicism, a 'feast day' is the anniversary of the death of a Catholic saint. But I digress.) The feast of Passover is one such Jewish holiday that requires wine. And that was the very festival which Jesus and his friends were celebrating when he proclaimed that the wine being served was his own blood. He asked his friends to share bread and drink wine in his memory. I am certain that Jesus drank wine at the Last Supper because it is scientifically impossible that he drank mere grape juice. The moment a grapes is pressed, the wild yeast on the skin enters the juice and the process of fermentation begins immediately. The process of preventing fermentation – pasteurization – was not invented until 1864.

Fermentation is an ancient symbol for the process of growing into wisdom and maturity, and drunkenness is also an ancient symbol of ecstasy and enlightenment. Examples from sacred literature, East and West, are easy to find. Here's an example from *The Rubáiyát of Omar Khayyám*:

> And lately by the Tavern door agape,
>   Came stealing through the dusk an Angel shape:
> Bearing a vessel on his shoulder; and
>   He bid me taste of it; and 'twas – the Grape![73]

A poem by the Sufi philosopher-poet Jalaludin Rumi often used wine and drunkenness as a metaphor of the experience of the presence of the divine:

> God has given us a dark wine so potent that,
> Drinking it, we leave the two worlds…

And since that is the case, Rumi reminds us to choose not just any wine, but only the best:

> Every object, every being
> Is a jar full of delight.
> Be a connoisseur
> And taste with caution.
> Any wine will get you high.
> Judge like a king, and choose the purest.
> The ones unadulterated with fear,
> Or some urgency about 'what's needed'.
> Drink the wine that moves you,
> As a camel moves when it's been untied
> And is just ambling about.[74]

Today most people don't imagine that alcohol represents anything quite as lofty as communion with God. But we do find people creating and improving upon their friendships by drinking together. We drink to watch sporting events, to entertain a 'date', to discuss philosophical matters at academic conferences, to toast newlyweds or college graduates, and even to close business deals. Like a scaled-down version of the heroic feast, the drink is a shared cultural experience that creates relations with others.

Of course, alcohol also loosens inhibitions and impairs judgment. An estimated 2% of Canadian adults over the age of 35 are dependent on alcohol, but for Canadians from 20-24 years old the figure rises to 8.6%.[75] Certainly, alcohol did nothing to help create friendship between the Aboriginal people of Turtle Island,

and the first European colonists. Indeed in that context, alcohol was used as a weapon. Tacitus observed that the Roman traders used wine this way to subdue the Germans: "If you indulge their intemperance by plying them with as much drink as they desire, they will easily be conquered by this besetting weakness as by force of arms."[76] Values like temperance (which does *not* mean abstinence) may have a place here. But let me address another social and moral problem related to food, which I think is just as serious, if not more so.

Food and Social Justice

Today, machine and chemical intensive farming and a global market have reduced the danger of famines by making our food production processes more routine. We are no less dependent on nature than ever in the past. But modern farming methods and the global market have reduced our awareness of that dependency, and our awareness of our relations with the people who produce our food for us. If you are eating a vegetable out-of-season, and imported from a faraway place, for instance, it is almost certain that the crop was harvested by slaves. Workers in the tomato growing industry in Florida, for instance, are paid about 45 cents per bucket, and can make around $50 on a good day. But from this income their employers deduct the costs of lodging, food, beer, even water. They have no choice in these deductions. If it rains, or there is too much dew, they cannot work, and cannot pay these charges. The workers end up incurring debts faster than their ability to pay them off. At nights they are locked in boxes and trucks, unable to leave. If they take breaks, or get ill, complain about working conditions, demand to see their account with the company, or declare the intention to leave, they are severely beaten.[77] In 2008, six farm operators in Florida were handed criminal convictions for imprisoning more than a dozen people. Prosecuting attorney Doug Molloy called it "slavery, plain and simple."[78] Thus, I'm sorry to say, you cannot easily avoid becoming complicit in food-related cruelty by eating a strictly vegetarian diet.

You also might be missing the fullness of your relationship with your food through no fault of your own. You might be one of the estimated 1.02 *billion* people in the world, right now, who have no food at all, or no access to even minimally decent food.[79] Even in prosperous countries like America, people live in areas where the only readily available food is fast food and junk food, bought from small convenience stores and from retail chains. The nearest supermarket where fresh produce could be found might be up to an hour's drive away. And if you are on welfare, or working a very poorly paying job, you probably can't afford to buy fresh whole food anyway. The year 2008 saw the beginning of a disastrous world wide food shortage, which still exists at the time I write these words. In less than a year, the international market price of wheat rose 130%, soya 87% and rice 74%. There were riots in 61 countries. Some, such as the protests in Dhaka, Bangladesh, were attended by 10,000 people. Violent food riots in Mozambique that year caused the deaths of seven people, two of them children. The government of Vietnam had to ban harvesting machines from driving on public roads at night, in order to prevent raiders from harvesting other people's rice crops.

A variety of causes are involved. The rising cost of petroleum also raises the cost of running the tractors and other machines involved in production, and raises the cost of transporting the produce from the farms to the processing plants, distribution centers, and even small local markets. The United States, and several other Western countries, dedicated millions of acres of farmland to producing ethanol and biofuels, thus reducing their food exports. Climate change and global warming caused more droughts and more floods, ruining harvests around the world. In 2010 widespread wildfires in Russia and a nationwide flood in Pakistan destroyed most of the grain harvests in both countries, further contributing to world hunger and to rising food prices.

The total population of the world is also growing. The most populous countries like India and China are becoming wealthy enough to demand more foods, and more varieties of food, including more expensive varieties. Each of these factors cause scarcities which raise the prices of the most basic food staples beyond most poor people's ability to pay.[80]

Yet an unacknowledged primary cause of the food shortage is the fact that world food prices are not governed by supply and demand anymore: they are governed by capital commodity speculators. These forces create unpredictable price spikes for basic staples: a 40% increase in the price of wheat in July 2010 alone; a 20% increase in the price of barley in just one week.[81] These rising prices are not benefiting farmers: an economist at Cornell University found that the main beneficiaries of the higher prices were the contractors and international commodities brokers.[82]

Genetically modified crops, promoted as being more bountiful and more resistant to insects and diseases, and therefore a solution to world hunger, have turned out in many cases to worsen the problem. Canadian government researchers found evidence that genetically modified food causes various health problems. But the public is not allowed to know whether they are eating GM food or not: international trade rules make it illegal to identify foods as genetically modified on the store labels. Lobbyists for GM food corporations called it 'discriminating against the process of production'.[83] Farmers in poor parts of the world, to whom GM seeds are marketed most aggressively, find that GM seeds cost 100 times more than seeds for natural varieties. They are told that they will save money in the long run because they will not need any pesticides, and the crops will grow in greater abundance. However, the GM crops have turned out to be just as vulnerable as ever to certain parasites, especially bollworms. Some strains require twice as much water as their natural counterparts. And farmers often went deep into debt to pay for the seeds, and lost everything when droughts and parasite invasions destroyed their harvests. Furthermore farmers cannot recover seeds for the next season from their failed crops, as farmers have done for thousands of years, because most GM varieties contain a 'terminator' gene which prevents the plants from producing fertile seeds. This compels the debt-laden farmers to buy more seed from the company each year, and to go further into debt. In 2008 an estimated 125,000 farmers in India, burdened by insurmountable debts, took their own lives by drinking agricultural insecticide – an intensely painful way to die. In Maharashtra province that year, the suicide rate among farmers was around 1,000 people per month.[84]

There is also a biodiversity factor: we rely on too few crops now, and we don't properly account for the role of other plants, insects, animals, and environmental factors. Gonzalo Oviedo, a senior advisor on social policy with IUCN (formerly the World Conservation Union), warned that reduced biodiversity makes farmland less productive, and more vulnerable to blights and droughts and other dangers. Here are his words:

The past 50 years have seen massive expansion of agriculture, with food production more than doubling in order to meet demand. But it has left us with 60% of all ecosystem services degraded, accelerated species extinction, and huge loss in genetic diversity. Currently, four plant species – wheat, maize, rice and potato – provide more than half of the plant-based calories in the human diet, while about a dozen animal species provide 90% of animal protein consumed globally. We have already lost three-quarters of the genetic diversity of agricultural crops. As the agricultural frontier has expanded, those farmers previously dependent on a more diverse source of livelihood have converted to cash crops. As traditional varieties and breeds die out, so too do the traditional knowledge and practices of local farmers. Those same practices could now be critical in adapting to climate change. The focus on agricultural commodities rather than on food production to meet the basic needs of people has undermined diversity and self-reliance, and left farmers vulnerable to volatile markets, political instability and environmental change. Increased food production in some parts of the world has been at the expense of natural and semi-natural ecosystems that provide us greater long-term security.[85]

Oviedo also states that landscapes with greater species diversity, in terms of plants, insects, microbes, and animals, are more agriculturally productive than landscapes with less diversity. Where farmers rely on synthetic chemicals to enrich the soil with nutrients and to kill parasitic insects, landscapes are less productive. And in the oceans, "areas with a higher number of conserved species generate more fish for humans to catch and eat."[86] But I think his most important point is his distinction between agricultural commodities and food production. It is consistent with the idea that food is not just a delivery-vehicle for chemical nutrients. *Food is a social and cultural event.* Food is aesthetics, language, environmental awareness and involvement, planting and harvesting, caring for plants and for animals, and planning for the future. It involves mindfulness of rainfall, climate, the movements of insects and birds and other wildlife. It involves cultural traditions of cooking, presentation, and eating. And it involves thanking everything and everyone that make food possible. As Aboriginal poet Chief Dan George said,

We all wander through life
United by the bond of creation
And become brothers
Through gratitude.
We have much to be thankful for.

Let each of us
Talk to the same Supreme Being
In his own way.
A man who cannot give thanks
For the food he eats
Walks without the blessings of nature.[87]

For reasons like these, it seems abundantly clear to me that the relations involved in the way we eat deserve an important place at the table of our sacred relations. There is a lot that you can do – probably more than you think you can do, and probably more than you are already doing – to affirm the sacredness of your kitchen, and promote food justice. This can be true even if you have very little money, and the quality of food available to you is poor. The first thing you can do may seem obvious: *learn to cook*. If you take one hour away from your television-watching time each day, you may suddenly find you have enough time to learn to cook. There are literally hundreds of books and videos that can help you here. Cooking classes may also be available through local community colleges, restaurants, and food co-operatives. Here are a few things you can do on a weekly or daily basis.

- Join an organic food supply club, or a food retail co-op.
- Shop at food co-ops and farmer's markets, and buy as much of your food as you can from local producers.
- Get to know the people from whom you buy your food.
- Grow herbs in flower pots, window boxes, and hanging baskets right in your own home.
- Placing an image or a figurine of a deity, saint, or spiritual figure of importance to you on or near your oven as you cook. Bring it to the table for special occasion meals.
- Donate to local food banks.
- Cut down the amount of junk food that you consume.
- Do not buy food that you suspect may have come from

farms or plantations that employ slaves.

- Do not buy meat which you suspect came from a factory farm.
- Make your largest meal at roughly the same time every day.
- Encourage others in your household to eat with you, at the same time, and (unless there are serious food allergies) to eat the same meal with you.
- Collaborate with the shopping, preparation, and washing up.
- While eating, put away all your electronic devices, including your mobile phones, pagers, game players and music players. Keep your attention on your food, and on the people immediately around you.

When you stop treating food just as a source of 'fuel' and start treating it as a medium for affirming the desirability of life, many benefits will follow. Almost certainly, your physical and mental health will improve. And, of course, you may get to know and better appreciate the people around you. The habit of a good dinner will contribute enormously to the quality of your life.

5

Families

A family gathering around the kitchen table for a meal is probably the first social event most of us experience in life on earth. It is in the family where we see most easily that our lives are shaped and configured by our relationships with others. Each human being is already the product of the relationship between his or her parents, even if their relation with each other was short-lived. We also receive from parents, possibly before birth, a gift which configures our identities for the rest of our lives: a name. Furthermore, from the moment you are conceived you have grandparents as well as parents, and you may also already have siblings, aunts, uncles, and cousins. You cannot choose these people: they are already a part of your life from the moment you are conceived. Thus the relationships of the family are in some sense 'given' to us, already part of what it is to be alive on earth. The temporal priority of the family configures the very structure of our language. For when we speak of our 'relatives', we all know we are speaking of our blood kin, and not of other associates.

The notion of family solidarity, and the care of parents especially in their old age, is an ancient religious idea. The fourth of the Ten Commandments, for instance, calls for parents to be honored. The Koran has a similar requirement: "Whether one or both of them attain old age in thy life, say not to them a word of contempt, nor repel them, but address them in terms of honor." (The Night Journey, 17:23) Filial piety, the near-worshipful respect paid by children to parents, is perhaps the most important of values in Confucian society. In one passage from *The Book of Mencius*, the relationship of parent and child seems to be the highest of the Five Relations:

> There are five things which in common practice are considered unfilial. The first is laziness in the use of one's body, without attending to the support and care of one's parents. The second is chess-playing and fondness for wine, without attending to the support and care of one's parents. The third is love of things and money and being exclusively attached to one's wife and children, without attending to the support and care of one's parents. The fourth is following the desires of one's eyes and ears, thus bringing his parents to disgrace. And the fifth is being fond of bravery, fighting, and quarrelling, thus endangering one's parents.[88]

This passage describes five kinds of vices: sloth, gluttony, greed, intemperateness, and recklessness. Yet the wrongness of these five habits is explained in every case by the harm it can cause to one's parents. We can infer that Mencius felt that filial piety was an ethical requirement of the highest order.

Although the idea of family solidarity is old and well established, we should ask: does the temporal priority of the family confer upon the family *moral* priority? What is the basis of family loyalty? And if we should care about our families, should we care about them more than we care about others?

Blood and History

Some people believe that family solidarity is an intrinsic duty. You should be loyal to the people in your kin group, so this way of thinking goes, just because they are the people in your kin group. In this way of thinking, it matters very much that the people in your family are related to you by blood. I think the force of this argument lies in the fact that one's genetic inheritance is a benefit of a very distinct kind: it makes you who you are. The egg and seed from my parents formed the first cells of my body. I am similarly blood-related to my siblings, who share the same parents, and to my cousins, who share the same grandparents. My parents are blood-related to their own siblings, my aunts and uncles, for having the same parents. And they, in turn, are similarly blood-related to their own cousins, as they share the same grandparents. My relationship with all of these people takes the form of a line of connectivity through time and space, like a knotted rope, or a long chain. Along every station on this line, each person receives a genetic code from parents who received it, in turn, from their parents, who in their own turn received it from their parents, and so on. The line of genetic inheritance gives each of us the set of natural predispositions, possibilities and limitations which make us who we are. Indeed the importance of this relation is so great that other relations in our lives are modeled after it. Teachers, Elders, leaders, and even the gods become like parents; students, young people, a leader's supporters, and a god's worshippers become like children. Notice that the most important prayer in Christianity begins with the words, 'Our Father'.

In this way of thinking about family solidarity, it matters a great deal that everyone on the same line has the same, or very nearly the same, genetic origin. This broad notion of natural similarity, of common origins, produces a sense of someone's being 'one of ours' or 'one of us'. To put it simply, your family receives your loyalty because you are all in some sense part of the same club. This notion of membership is a powerful force in most people's moral psychology. Perhaps the reason for this is not just biological, but also metaphysical. The line of one's blood kinship and genetic inheritance can go as far back in time as you wish to measure. It connects you to the foundation of your nation, language, or culture. It connects you to the gods themselves. For as various sources attest, the gods were the progenitors of ancient tribes and noble dynasties. An Irish text called the *Lebor Gabála Éireann*: "...every princely family that is in Ireland, save the

Eoganacht, is of the seed of Nuadu Airgetlám."[89] Julius Caesar (who claimed to be descended from the goddess Venus) observed the following about the Celts of the continent: "The Gauls claim all to be descended from Father Dis, declaring that this is the tradition preserved by the Druids."[90] Similarly, an Icelandic text called the *Prose Edda* states that Odin was originally a Trojan, and a descendant of Priam, and that he traveled north at the behest of a prophetess. On the way he and his people had many adventures, and "wherever they went on their travels, tales of their splendour were told, making them seem more like gods than men." When Odin reached Norway, "he placed his son in power. This son was named Saeming, and Norway's kings, as well as its jarls and other important men of the kingdom, trace their descent to him..."[91]

Now that we possess scientific knowledge of the origins of humanity, for instance using mitochondrial DNA, we can trace the line of our origins back the first human beings to walk the earth. Genealogy is thus not only a study of one's ancestors: it is also a study of time, and the origin of things. Studying one's genealogy imparts the sense of belonging to some part of the world and to some part of history, and thus the sense of *rootedness in reality*. Knowing your ancestors can be a large part of knowing yourself.

Some people feel they can live without that sense of rootedness. A friend of mine has a Scottish-born mother but doesn't feel any special sense of being Scottish at all. Being a champion video-game player is more important to him. But there is another dimension of family loyalty that also leads him, and perhaps others like him who don't care about genealogy, to care about his family anyway. We receive from our families more than a genetic origin. We also receive from our family lines a language, a nationality, a culture, a folklore, a set of moral and political values, perhaps a religion, and certainly a general worldview. As the Aboriginal poet Chief Dan George wrote:

The wisdom and eloquence of my father
I passed on to my children,
So they too acquired faith,
Courage, generosity, and understanding,
And knowledge in the proper way of living.[92]

Clearly, parents do more than just give birth to children. Parents also feed, clothe, house, educate, protect, discipline, comfort, entertain, and love their children, and do all the things involved in raising them to adulthood. Parents teach us to walk and to speak: arguably the two most important qualities of being human. We might receive symbols of group identity and tribal membership from our parents, such as a tradition of heraldry, a coat of arms. Some people inherit professions and occupations: a family business, or a hereditary trade. Upper class children might inherit titles of nobility, and the lordship of lands. Of all material things we receive from the family line, perhaps the most interesting are *heirlooms*: objects that may have little or no market value, but which feature prominently in the life and the story of an ancestor. My own father received from his father a large collection of old vinyl records of traditional Irish music. One of my students at the college where I teach, as another example, came to class one day wearing his grandfather's dog tags from the Second World War. A friend of mine who is a professional chef told me:

> I have a pastry board which used to belong to my grand-mother. Sometimes when I'm using it, I think of how many breads and pastries were made on this board, and how many other women used it. (K. Weiler, 2009)

Sometimes an heirloom may be important not just to one family, but to a whole community or a nation. Among the Aboriginal people of the prairies and plains of western North America, religiously important objects called *sacred bundles* are passed from one keeper to another, usually (although not always) along ancestral lines.

Parents might continue to serve and help their children like this well into the child's adulthood. A study published in the Journal of Marriage and Family found that 76% of adults aged 18 to 33 received some kind of domestic assistance from their parents, most of it in laundry services, each month. 79% of the same group received money from their parents each month, and 93% got a check-in chat with their parents almost every week. The study also found that this was a lot more support than what parents gave their adult children in the previous generation.[93] Usually parents bestow on their children a material inheritance, defined very precisely in a legal last will and testament. This might be a sum of money, or a house, or other valuables. We may receive some or all of these things whether we are born into a 'traditional' nuclear family, a single-parent family, a mixed or blended family, or even a non-traditional family: a gay couple with adopted children, for instance.

Let it be added here that siblings also contribute to this cultural, pedagogical, and material bounty. Unless you are a single child, some of your best childhood friends were probably your own sisters and brothers. You went to the same school, explored in the same neighborhood, attended the same church, played with (and fought over) the same toys. But unlike other neighborhood friends, you and your siblings also ate at the same table every day, and slept under the same roof every night. When you were very little indeed, you and a brother or sister might have been washed in the same bathtub (or laundry sink!) at the same time. Younger siblings may have worn an older sibling's hand-me-down clothes. As you grow up together you might love each other and hate each other in equal measure. There might be aggression, resentment, and frustration, as one sibling compares himself to the other, or competes for the attention of friends, parents, and other adults. Yet in sibling rivalry, we still find that 'blood is thicker than water'. For when a sibling has problems with non-siblings, for instance if she is being harassed or bullied by other kids in the school playground, then you come to her rescue anyway. Siblings also sometimes cover for each other against the enquiries of their own parents. You might keep a window unlocked so that your younger sister can be out with her boyfriend later at night, and still get back into bed before Mom and Dad notice she is gone. Bonds of solidarity are formed very early in life, through the way siblings (and sometimes also cousins and other relations) live together, stick up for each other, protect each other, and even partly define themselves in terms of their relations to each other. The solidarity between siblings can remain powerful later in life. Most adults I know turn to their adult siblings first when they need to move to a new house, or when they need someone to feed their pets for a weekend. The bonds between siblings can sometimes grow stronger when one gets married or starts having her own children. Most women will turn to their sisters first when planning a wedding. When your own children appear, your siblings become uncles and aunts, and can be almost as involved in their lives as you are, for instance as babysitters, playmates, and educators. And their children can become playmates for yours.

The basis of family loyalty can be stated fairly clearly now. We receive from our families a complex inheritance which shapes us as people in the earliest and most formative stages of our lives. This inheritance is a gift of such enormous value that perhaps nothing could ever repay it. Therefore, children owe their parents (siblings, aunts, uncles, grandparents, cousins, etc) their solidarity and loyalty. The argument here depends on an economic way of looking at things. The respect children owe parents is based on nothing more profound than a trade imbalance, an un-repayable debt. And to some, this economic view may seem too banal. Some may prefer the view that parents and children should love each other unconditionally, and not on the basis of an implied contract. Perhaps the answer is in the unique combination of the genetic and the cultural inheritances that families bestow on each new generation. For we are united in our families by two forces, blood and history. We are part of the same club if we received the same inheritance of culture, knowledge, material wealth, *and* genetic identity, from the same parents, grandparents, and forefathers. The differences here are matters of emphasis, not of essence. Thus where one is lacking, the other can supplement; and where both are present together, the sense of belonging can become very strong indeed.

Tribalism

The trouble with family solidarity, as a social value, is that it can imply that the members of your kin group are the only people you are obliged to care about. You might trade or share things with people who are not your kin. But you might just as soon lie to them, steal from them, or kill them, if that will help you get what you want. And if you could get away with it, you might not consider it an ethical issue one way or the other. Their moral standing might not be as important to you as the moral standing of your kin. But when one of your kin has been lied to, cheated, stolen from, or murdered, your kinship with the victim would compel you to help her take revenge on the offender and his family. Strong feelings of 'the family honor', which in one context lends to human life an important sense of meaning, in another context lends to human life an ugly justification for violence. This kind of justice is called *Lex Talionis*, 'the law of retaliation'; it is also called the Blood Feud. It appears in Heroic literature, for instance in the *Iliad*, where it is one of the most important forces driving the plot. A scene in book 6 shows the Achaean hero Menelaus about to show mercy to a Trojan fighter, and accept his offer of a ransom for his life. But Agamemnon rushes up and shouts:

So soft, dear brother. Why?
Why such concern for enemies? I suppose you got
Such tender loving care at home from the Trojans.
I would to god not one of them could escape
His sudden plunging death beneath our hands!
No baby boy still in his mother's belly,
Not even he escape – all Illum blotted out,
No tears for their lives, no markers for their graves! (*Iliad* 6:63-
70)

Lex Talionis appears in several places in the Old Testament, for instance in Leviticus:

And he that kills any man shall surely be put to death. And he that kills a beast shall make it good; beast for beast. And if a man cause a blemish in his neighbor; as he hath done, so shall it be done to him; Breach for breach, eye for eye, tooth for tooth: as he hath caused a blemish in a man, so shall it be done to him again. And he that kills a beast, he shall restore it: and he that kills a man, he shall be put to death. (Leviticus 24:17-21)

The book of Numbers says that Lex Talionis must be carried out by the victim: "The avenger of blood shall put the murderer to death; when the avenger comes upon the murderer, the avenger shall put the murderer to death." (Numbers 35:19) Blood vengeance seems to have been one of the central social problems of pre-Muslim Arabia, which Mohammed's new religious movement was designed to counter. Thus, although eye-for-an-eye justice does appear in the Koran (cf 5:45-47), the text also gives offended parties the chance to forgo retaliation as a form of charity. Lex Talionis was criticized by Jesus, who suggested that it is better to 'turn the other cheek'. (Matthew 5:38-42, and Luke 6:27-36).

The principle of tribal solidarity can also produce unsolvable moral conflicts, for instance when someone harms a member of his own kin group. In such circumstances, there is no way to restore the loss of honor, and no way to mitigate the shame. The Irish hero Cú Chulainn was trapped by various circumstances into killing a kinsmen of his, not once but *twice*. One was his own son, who he did not know was his son until after dealing the death-blow. When he learned the truth, he became so aggrieved by his actions that his brothers-in-arms feared for their safety. A Druid was summoned to create the illusion of an army emerging from the sea, for Cú Chulainn to fight instead. The other kinsman he killed was his foster-brother Ferdiad, who was summoned to fight as Maeve of Cruachan's champion. And after killing Ferdiad, Cú Chulainn became so overwhelmed with grief that he collapsed on the earth and refused to fight at all, not even to defend himself from his enemies. His divine father, the god Lugh Lamhfada, had to stand over him and protect him.

One way to address the problem of the blood feud is to note that your tribe has very hazy boundaries, and might include a lot more people than you first believe. Under some circumstances you might be willing to treat third cousins twice removed as part of the club. Under other circumstances, you might extend your loyalty only as far as your own parents and siblings. But the closer you look at your genetic roots, the more and more people you find sharing your genetic inheritance. The mitochondrial DNA that everyone receives from her mother passes almost entirely unchanged down the female line. Similarly, the Y chromosome that every man receives from his father passes almost intact down the male line. Both of these lines go back in time as far back as you can measure. I've already mentioned that genealogy has a metaphysical dimension, that reaches through time and space. What I'm adding here is that the further back in time you trace your genealogy, the more of humanity becomes part of your tribe. Therefore, the circle of people to whom you should feel a sense of family connectivity can be very large indeed. Could it some day include the whole of humanity?

The hope that we can answer in the affirmative is called 'the expanding circle'. The idea is partly a claim about history, and partly a claim about morality. It observes historically that over time the circle of those who posses moral standing, and thus deserve respect, grows over time to include more people. Thus in the beginning, the circle may include one's nearest extended family and nearest geographical neighbors, but exclude people from other tribes or villages, people who spoke different languages, people sold into slavery or captured as prisoners of war. Then over time, people invent higher-order 'tribes', so to include more people in the circle of those who deserve one's loyalty and respect. Some are religious tribes like churches and spiritual communities, and include everyone who has the same faith, or everyone committed to the same god. Others are civic tribes like towns, cities, and nations, and include everyone who lives under the same governing power. Religions, nations, and other higher-order human groupings give people something in common with each other such that they can think themselves part of a larger quasi-family. That can be true even if that family has millions of members, otherwise distinct from each other in time, geography, language, and culture. The Koran, for example, makes all Muslims in the world, whatever their language or culture or homeland, into one *Ummah*, one community or nation, saying: "You are the best nation produced [as an example] for mankind. You enjoin what is right and forbid what is wrong, and believe in Allah." (3:110). The idea of the expanding circle also sometimes includes the moral claim that the circle should continue to expand. Thus in the year 1791, Thomas More published the first part of *The Rights of Man*, in which he described how all civil rights are rooted in natural rights, "which appertain to man in right of his existence" no matter their nationality or ethnicity or religion. Thus the circle expanded to include all human beings. In 1823, Jeremy Bentham included a footnote in the second edition of his *Principles of Morals and Legislation* in which he suggested that the circle could grow to include animals. His main argument: "The question is not, Can they reason?, nor, Can they talk?, but, Can they suffer?" Thus the circle expanded to include all animals capable of feeling pain. In 1949 the American forestry professor Aldo Leopold argued that the circle should expand again to include landscapes and environments. As he wrote in *A Sand County Almanac:* "... a land ethic changes the role of *Homo Sapiens* from conqueror of the land-community to plain member and citizen of it." Thus the circle expanded again to include plants and inorganic matter.

Although I have some confidence in the idea of the expanding circle, I am unsure of how complete an answer it can be to the fear-labyrinth of tribalism. I suspect that by itself, the expanding circle is not enough. Loyalty and solidarity with one's tribe can be expressed as competition, antagonism, and hate for another tribe. It can promise peace and freedom and love to those who join, while also promising war and death on those who choose not to join. What is more: expanding the size of the group is no guarantee that the group itself will remain internally coherent and peaceful. Religious groups fracture along differing lines of doctrine, ritual practice, ecclesiastical authority, or visionary experience. Nations may also split into factions and fight civil wars against themselves over any number of domestic issues. Nothing is more toxic and destructive in human life than the idea that only you and your tribe possess the truth. A national group might claim to be exceptional among nations with a manifest destiny to fulfill. An ethnic group might claim to be a superior race. A religious group might claim to possess the special favor of God. On the basis of such claims, the members may think themselves always in the right, and never in the wrong, no matter what they do, and no matter who they harm, oppress, or kill. And they may prefer to fight and destroy the people of other circles, or assimilate them by force, instead of grow their circles together. Therefore, I find that the notion of the expanding circle, while powerful, is not enough by itself to help reduce fear among strangers, and bring us to a more peaceful world.

Human morality does not rest on group membership alone. It also rests on direct personal interactions, face to face, hand to hand, voice to ear. We are more moved by the sight of a person suffering, than the story of some faraway person's suffering, even if the situation is otherwise exactly the same. Rather than just investigate ways to expand the circle, we also need to investigate ways to deal with people who dwell outside the circle. We need to figure out what to do about strangers, and what to do about the fear that strangers can often create. To that end, I shall soon discuss guests, friends, loving couples, Elders, and those who we meet in the public sphere. But before going there, we should have a look at:

Dysfunctional Families

Although I count family loyalty and love as an important part of the worthwhile life, I'm well aware that many families are not very loyal nor very loving to each other. Studies have shown, for instance, that one-quarter of all women in America have experienced domestic violence at least once in their lifetimes.[94] Further, another study found that nearly three-fourths of all Americans claimed to personally know a woman who was violently abused by her husband or boyfriend in the last twelve months.[95] I have several friends who, when they were children, were physically and psychologically abused by their parents. They described to me horrific stories of fathers (usually) and mothers (often) traumatizing their children with verbal abuse, psychological manipulations, beatings, confinement, and with other acts too horrible for me to print in this book. I asked some of them what might have been going on in their parents' minds. I was told that the abusive parent is simply and straightforwardly unable to do wrong in his own eyes. He (the abusive parent) always saw the suffering he inflicted upon others as fair, deserved, and just. He never saw the ways in which he contributed to his own problems. For whatever problem the abusive parent was experiencing, there was always someone else to blame, and therefore always someone else to punish. (It was at this stage in the research for my book that I began to conceive of the fear-labyrinth, as a theory of why people do such things.)

Furthermore these friends told me that as child-victims they would invent rationalizations in their minds which made the experience tolerable: 'at least I'm not dead', or 'at least he doesn't hit my child', or 'at least he's not like this every day'. They also were unable to see an escape route, or else it took them many years to see one. Therefore they continued to accept the abuse and did little or nothing to change it, for many years, sometimes well into adulthood.

I suspect that the abusive parents described by my informants here knew of no other way to see their will taking hold of the world. They perhaps knew no other way to assert their self-worth than by inflicting suffering upon others. The terror and submission in the eyes of a victim is a consequence of the abuser's actions that the abuser himself can visibly see. Thus someone who causes suffering to others knows himself to be powerful, dominant, able to have an effect on the world, and therefore knows himself to be something-that-is-not-nothing. He does what he does in order to assert a specific identity: he believes himself to be in some way superior, and he needs to continually confirm that he is who he believes himself to be. The most obvious way to assert and maintain that sense of superiority is to constantly put others down, whether through verbal abuse, physical abuse, neglect, shame, humiliation. Less obvious ways to abuse someone, although they are forms of abuse nonetheless, include isolating someone from her family and friends, and restricting access to domestic resources such as bank accounts or telephones. And since the point of such abuse is to assert superiority, the abuse would often be inflicted on someone weaker, someone less likely to retaliate, such as a child. I was reminded of the Marxist proverb, "Crap always rolls downhill."

Yet this strategy for affirming the worth of one's life is always self-contradicted by the way that person's actions affect his own life. Many people who have abusive and violent habits are utterly unable to face themselves. They might see what their actions do to others, but they can't or won't see what their actions do to themselves. They might see what they do, but *they almost never see what they become because of what they do*. My friends and informants observed that the abusive parent's way of relating to his terrorized children never gave him any happiness. The abusive parent was always frustrated, angry, aggrieved, and generally *miserable* with his life. He created an environment of fear around him, out of some displaced sense of entitlement or justice, and then he became trapped in it. It seems to me that the avoidance of that kind of contradiction is an ethical necessity.

Instead of facing himself, the habitual abuser creates elaborate rationalizations to justify himself. For instance, he might claim the right to punish others for even the smallest inconveniences. He says things like "You made me angry", instead of saying, "I am angry." Or, he might blame his actions on the alcohol that he is addicted to, without doing anything to treat his addiction. Abusive parents may have lived through a worse situation when they were children themselves. Therefore they may say that what they do is justified because it is an improvement over what was done to them when they were children. The parent who traumatizes his child with psychological manipulation and verbal abuse thinks himself 'better' than his own parent who deployed leather belts, horse whips, and burning cigarettes. But this kind of justification for abuse is clearly a rhetorical deception.

The assertion of the desirability of life, to be fully ethical, must be accompanied by honest and genuine self-knowledge. This kind of knowledge takes courage, especially when there is a wide difference between the way you imagine yourself and the way you actually are. You may have to face shame, or loss of pride, or loss of power. You may have to make uncomfortable changes in your habits. It is for this reason that I have no patience for psycho-therapy programs that require nothing more than the repetition of mantras, or the acceptance of yourself 'as you are'. A malefactor should *not* accept himself just as he is. He must *face* the loneliness and the isolation he feels, and the fear he creates in others around him. Then he must do something to change his way of being in the world. A family can affirm life by helping him, and giving him as much encouragement and compassion as they can (without compromising their own safety, of course). A consistent and heroic demonstration of the goodness and beauty of life is often a powerful catalyst in an abusive person's process of healing and change. For it demonstrates that there are other ways of being in the world, and that those alternatives are better, and that they work.

Passages

Probably the most practical of activities which families can do to demonstrate the importance of their shared blood and history is celebrate rites of passage together. These are the occasions when we undergo a more-or-less definite transition from one stage of life to another. Those occasions might not be singular moments: it might take a few weeks or a few months to begin, or even realize that the transition is in progress; then it may take weeks or months again for it to finish. Rituals of passage, of course, take place over a single day or a short span of days. The ritual is not the transition, but it can become part of the transition, and for social purposes it can be the most important part. For convenience's sake, I shall use the names for these passages which come from my own spiritual tradition, although I'm aware the other traditions use different names, and may recognize more passages than these. I shall speak of each only briefly, as the broad picture is more important here than the many hundreds of fine details.

- *Naming*: Birth is the obvious first passage for everyone. It is honored by a Naming ceremony of some sort, in which the child's parents or an Elder announce to the community what the child's name will be. The parents may also call upon various people to help educate, protect, and help the child into adulthood.

- *First Blood / First Watch*: Sometime during or near the child's twelfth year, the child receives some of the signs, benefits, and responsibilities of early adulthood. For girls, this is called the First Blood ceremony, which takes place shortly after the first menstruation. In the Celtic tradition, the sign of entry into adulthood was the gift of a sword or weapon, symbolizing strength, self-reliance, and courage. For boys, then, the passage is called the First Watch, representing the first time the child is assigned overnight guard duty. Although the ancient sources do not attest it, I think it well to also give a chalice, as a symbol of less 'macho' but equally important qualities like reason, generosity, and gentleness.

- *Coming of Age*: A second coming of age ceremony is sometimes offered when the youth turns twenty-one, or when he or she finishes third-level education (whichever comes first). At this time the young woman or man is acknowledged as a full adult, with all of the benefits and responsibilities that come with it.

- *Handfasting*: This is a marriage ceremony, in which the private love of two people becomes public, and wedding vows are exchanged. A local Elder or other notable person binds the couple's hands together with a cord or thin rope, to symbolize the joining of their lives.

- *The Trimesters*: A woman's pregnancy is celebrated three times, at the end of the third, sixth, and ninth month. These celebrations are for women only, and often double as baby showers!

- *Elderhood*: In this ceremony, a deserving person is acknowledged as a community's Elder. It is a kind of lifetime achievement award, in recognition of many years of service, leadership, generosity and knowledge. Thus it is not offered to just anyone. Women, however, may be offered a separate passage celebration called *Croning*, in acknowledgement of having reached menopause.

- *Last Days*: A person nearing his or her death might request a ceremony to mark his or her last and most final passage, and to say goodbye. Prayers are offered for the healing of whatever condition is threatening the person's life, or for the easing of pain as he or she dies, 'whichever the gods have decided must be'. Sometimes a few final parting words are exchanged, a few of the dying person's possessions are distributed, and a few last requests carried out. Given that the celebration of Last Days can be a very emotional occasion, and can unexpectedly become Last Hours (or Minutes), it is extremely private, and often secret. Only a small group of carefully selected friends and family attend.

- *Memorial*: After someone has died, a more open gathering commemorates the departed person's life with storytelling, and prayer for the spirit of the departed person's well-being in the Otherworld and the next life.

Each of these passages are acknowledged with feasting, music, gift-giving, storytelling, and celebration. I'd like to share a little custom, derived loosely from the Catholic Baptismal Candle, but which has taken on its own use and meaning in my tradition. At a child's Naming ceremony, one of the gifts given to the child is a Birth Candle. Normally a parent or grandparent gives this candle, and it is lit for the first time during the Naming ceremony itself. Thereafter, it is lit only during her passages. A handfasting couple are given a Marriage Candle, which they light together from their own Birth Candles. And the child's Birth Candle is lit from this Marriage Candle at her Naming and First Watch / First Blood, or else from one (or both) of her parent's Birth Candles. It is lit for the last time during the person's Memorial, then extinguished for the last time, and buried or burned with the body, or otherwise disposed in a dignified way. This item, and the flame which is transferred from one person's Birth Candle to another, is a tangible sign of the blood and history which brings a family together.

6

Guests and Hosts

When people in my spiritual tradition part and say goodbye, sometimes they also promise to meet again by saying: "You're always welcome at my fire." A friend told me that the phrase dates back to pioneer times in Saskatchewan and Alberta, when European settlers came to the region and established permanent farms and homesteads. Alberta has some of the most severe and unpredictable winter storms in the world, because of its position just on the edge of the western mountains, and its flat prairie all the way to the Arctic. In pioneer times, if someone knocked on your door during one of those storms, you would let him in, no matter who he was. You did this because if you turned him out again, frostbite and hypothermia would almost certainly kill him. Thus some of my earlier comments concerning the ethical significance of sharing food also applies to hospitality. In a climate where a person denied hospitality runs a significant risk of injury or death, the act of welcoming the stranger into one's home can serve as an implicit affirmation of that person's right to live.

This affirmation may not be so easy to see today. We do not normally meet strangers at our doorsteps anymore, unless the stranger is selling something. Rather, we meet new people in public places or shared semi-public places: a social gathering at someone else's house, or a workplace, or a market. We assume that a stranger who knocks on your door has other options: hotels, guest houses, traveler's hostels, bed & breakfast inns, possibly even homeless shelters. Thus you probably don't feel under an obligation to let a stranger into your house. Many people today also assume that a stranger knocking on your door has hostile intentions. Certainly, a woman at home alone has good reason to keep her door shut against the stranger. But there is an important spiritual relationship between a host and any person she does invite into her home as a guest. Historically, this relationship is governed by customs which serve to reduce the distrust and the fear that can exist between strangers. These customs tend to arise in climates where those who lack shelter run a great risk of starvation, or injury, or death. Mongols, Arabs, north Africans, and the First Nations of the American Southwest all have ancient traditions of hospitality owing to the harshness of the desert. Similarly, the hospitality of Scandinavian and Baltic countries and of the Inuit people owes much to the severe cold of the winter. Celtic hospitality appeared because of the treacherous bogs and fens that once covered the Celtic lands, the natural and supernatural perils of the mists, the bitterly cold wind and rains of winter, and the unruly roughness of the sea.

When you invite someone into your home, and shelter him from these dangers, sometimes you do more than implicitly affirm his right to live. You also start the process of creating a relationship with him. It is worth exploring how this relationship develops. Although it is often only temporary, it is a step in the creation of more substantial and longer-lasting relations like friendship.

Strangers at the Door

When the stranger first appears, he is an unknown figure, a source of mystery, and perhaps also danger. You do not yet know what his intentions are. Those inclined to be suspicious may worry that he has come to cause mischief or harm. The stranger at the door may have his own reasons to feel trepidation too. The host, because he is at home, surrounded by his own possessions and his own friends and family, starts off with the upper hand. So the stranger at the door does not know whether he will be welcomed in, or sent away again, or even held as a prisoner.

Many people find guest-hood deeply uncomfortable, because they are away from home, in strange surroundings. Perhaps they are unsure of the rules of courtesy and etiquette in the house, and perhaps unsure of whether there are any such rules. Some people even feel stress and humiliation when accepting the generosity of others. Because fear, stress, and an imbalance of power is built into the situation, many cultures have created social rituals and routines designed to help strangers communicate peaceful intentions to each other. A simple one such as a handshake and a formulaic greeting ("Hi, how are you?" "I'm fine, how are you?" "Fine, thanks. Lovely weather, eh?") is often enough to do exactly that. The handshake establishes each participant as 'safe', non-threatening, agreeable. It shows that one's hand is not carrying a weapon. Other cultures have more elaborate rituals. In mediaeval Irish culture, for instance, etiquette requires a guest entering a home to say, "God save all here!" In response, everyone within the house answers, "God save you kindly." Sometimes the greeting invokes a litany of saints and apostles too. Friends and family members would normally enter a home in this way; so a stranger who announces himself in the same way demonstrates that he knows the custom, and is willing to act accordingly. Those inside, by responding in the expected way, acknowledge the stranger's overture, and demonstrate their own trustworthiness. Among the Dogon people of Mali, in west Africa, the formulaic greeting is even more elaborate. A journalist described the exchange as follows:

First man:	Let's go in the morning.
Second man:	Indeed. Did you pass the night?
First man:	I did.
Second man:	Did your menfolk pass the night?
First man:	They did. Are you in peace?
Second man:	In peace.
First man:	Are your menfolk in peace?

Second man:	In peace.
First man:	Is your wife in peace?
Second man:	In peace.
First man:	Are you not ill?
Second man:	There is no evil.[96]

The exchange then happens all over again with the other person leading the questioning. Exchanges like these, as routine and banal as they may seem, help strangers feel a little more comfortable in each other's presence. A slight aura of danger may yet remain: one side of the exchange might be trying to deceive the other. But once the stranger becomes your guest, in accord with the local customs, then *the presumption is shifted from suspicion to trust.* He is a stranger when you first hear his knock on your door, but as soon as you invite him to cross your threshold and make him into your guest, his moral standing changes. Margaret Visser, a Canadian professor of classics, observed that:

A guest is an outsider who has been ritually 'domesticated', made temporarily part of the host's *domus*, or house. He is given food, offered gestures of affability, and sometimes presented with gifts on his departure – for he must be free to leave. There may be genuine interest in him and delight in his company. But underlying the performance is the formal and primary aim of 'disarming' him, of forestalling any likelihood of violence or resentment. (Visser, *The Gift of Thanks*, p 28)

This process of precluding violence, dispelling fear, and creating trust between strangers dwells at the very heart of ethics.

A scene near the beginning of the story of Beowulf illustrates how the process was done in the Iron Age. When Beowulf first arrives at the court of King Hrothgar, the king first welcomes him warmly. But then a warrior named Unferth steps up and accuses

Beowulf of being an inept hero because he once lost a simple swimming race. Unferth is King Hrothgar's *thyle*, a kind of spokesperson for the king whose job is to challenge newcomers in precisely this way. Beowulf counters that he lost the race because he had to fight a swarm of sea monsters on the way. Then he accuses Unferth of being an ignoble hero, because he never heard a tale featuring Unferth performing similar deeds. (cf *Beowulf*, VIII: 506-581) The idea here is not to deny that some incident took place, but to put the best possible interpretation on it. This dialogue may seem very confrontational to us, but in fact it is a highly stylized ritualistic exchange. And it has a name: it was called a *flything*. Its purpose is to establish the worthiness of the stranger, and to test how he responds to conflict and competition. (Thus it is not the case that trickster-like characters in mythology cause trouble for the sake of causing trouble. But I digress.) We see this kind of exchange in Tolkien's novel, *The Two Towers*, where Grima Worm-Tongue acts as a kind of *thyle* in the court of King Théoden of Rohan. Grima challenges Gandalf by questioning Gandalf's worthiness to advise the king in matters of war. Of course, Grima is also spying for Saruman, so there's more going on there.

Beowulf is greeted next by Hrothgar's wife Wealtheow. She enters the hall and presents a cup brimming full of mead to Hrothgar, the chieftain, for him to drink. Then she brought the cup to everyone else in the hall, each in their turn, until she came to Beowulf:

> She greeted him well, gave thanks to God,
> That she might expect help against crimes
> From any man. He accepted the cup,
> Battle-fierce warrior, from Wealtheow's hand,
> Then made a speech, eager for combat –
> Beowulf spoke, Ecgtheow's son:
> "I made up my mind, when I set out to sea,

boarded our ship with my band of men,
That I would entirely fulfill the desire
Of the Danish nation or else fall slaughtered,
In the grip of the foe. Tonight I will do
A heroic deed, or else I will serve
My last day of life here in this mead-hall."
(Beowulf, VIII: 625-638)

Superficially, the lady's job is to serve mead to all the guests at the feast. But she too is part of the ritual 'domestication' drama happening here. Her kindness is the exact counterpart to Unferth's hostility: indeed she and Unferth effectively put Beowulf through a good-cop-bad-cop interrogation. By offering Beowulf a cup of mead, she was also testing his capacity for politeness, decorum, and etiquette. Beowulf demonstrates that he knows the etiquette by accepting the cup and then making an oath to protect the people from the monster Grendel, possibly at the cost of his own life. This oath serves as his expression of trust-worthiness, and of his desire to join with the group. The ritual 'domestication' thus accomplished, Hrothgar then assigns to Beowulf a place to sit. Interestingly, the place the king assigned was between his sons, suggesting that Hrothgar now thought of Beowulf as a foster-son and a kinsman. Later in the poem, we find that Hrothgar is considering Beowulf as his successor.

This scene from Beowulf is perhaps the very best description of the Germanic hospitality ritual. Its purpose, as Enright explained, is to give Hrothgar and the other members of his retinue a chance to assess Beowulf's merit, and so to decide what to do about him. By observing how Beowulf handles himself when addressed by the thyle and by the lady, the chieftain can decide how far a newly arrived stranger can be trusted, and whether he can be welcomed into the group.

The challenge, provocation, seating and service of the visitor are all ways of drawing him out and thereby assessing and appraising an intrusive influence. His [the arriving stranger's] performance can be enjoyed by all while simultaneously providing time and a tool of judgment to the leader and *seniores* of the retinue who may then develop some preliminary lines of policy based on the level of the visitor's skills and connections. These episodes of the poem are not mere literary embellishments but are unique testimony to an actual contemporary survival strategy. (Enright, *Lady with a Mead Cup*, p 181)

Unferth's overt hostility is perhaps the most obvious element of this process. But Queen Wealtheow's role is more significant because it is more subtle. She is the one who restores the peace and civility which the *thyle* disturbs. A troublemaker or a chaos-instigator is always followed by the peacemaker. She also tests the visiting hero to discern whether he knows the local etiquette, and whether he can behave with the required politeness and dignity. Furthermore, the original audience for this story may also have understood Wealtheow not just as the queen, but also as the warband's priestess and seer. The woman who trained the Irish hero Cú Chulainn to be a warrior was also consulted as a seer. Cú Chulainn was advised to ask three boons from her: "thoroughness in his training, a dowry for his marriage, and tidings of his future – for Scáthach was also a prophetess."[97] Tacitus wrote that the Germans "believe that there resides in women an element of holiness and a gift of prophesy; and so do not scorn to ask their advice, or lightly disregard their replies. In the reign of the emperor Vespasian we saw Veleda long honored by many Germans as a divinity…" (Tacitus, *Germania*, §8) On the basis of Tacitus' observation, among others, Enright claimed that Wealtheow "is the prophetess of the warband," and therefore she is "peculiarly qualified to proclaim kingship and provoke oaths, to witness them and in some way to 'bear' them." (Enright, *Lady with a Mead Cup*, p 182) Thus when Beowulf accepted her cup, he probably understood that she was offering him a psychological and social commitment. She was giving him a chance to bind his destiny to that of Hrothgar's warband. Hence, again, the ritualistic form of the oath he makes at that moment: to perform the heroic deed he described, or die trying. Enright observed that a visitor in this situation would probably feel profoundly disadvantaged. However, if he had been educated properly, he would know what to expect, and how to behave, and indeed how to manipulate the situation to his advantage. "A talented man can do much with this opportunity; an inferior one can do less. But that is exactly what the greeting ritual is meant to elicit, an understanding of the talents, temper and intentions of the stranger." (Enright, *Ibid*, p 182)

The English words *guest* and *host* emerge from a common etymological origin: the Indo-European root word *ghostis*, which referred to the overall 'event' of hospitality. The host has a role assigned to him by *ghostis*, and so does the guest, and when all people fulfill the requirements of their assigned roles, *hospitality* is achieved. *Ghostis* also gives us familiar English words like *hospital*, and *hospice*, originally referring to places of rest and entertainment, and which now refer to institutions for the care of the sick and elderly. The original function of the hospital is today preserved in the word *hotel*. Furthermore, *ghostis* also gives us the word *hostile*, the word for an outsider (and hence a potential enemy!), and *hostage*, originally a person given to the care of an enemy in order to preserve a peace agreement. *Hospitality* is thus the transformation of a *hostile* stranger (or a *host* of hostile men) into a *guest*. Similarly, enacting the customs of *ghostis* assures a *guest* that he is not a *hostage*, given to the care of an enemy against his will; nor is he an *oiste*: an old French word, from the Latin *hostia*, referring to a person prepared for ritual sacrifice! It is perhaps curiously appropriate, then, that Catholics use the word *host* for the Eucharist: the god who invites his followers to a ritual supper, and who offers them his own body to eat (cf Visser, *Ibid*, p 28; and Shipley, *Dictionary of Word Origins*, pp 183-4).

These primary moral categories, derived from the virtue of hospitality, can be stated in the form of a moral proposition: 'This man is a guest, therefore he should be treated as a guest should be treated'. Perhaps this principle arises just because the householder doesn't want to be responsible via negligence for whatever harms the stranger may come to after he is turned away. Yet part of the virtue of hospitality stems not from the rights or entitlements of the other person. It has to do with the more general virtue of generosity, of which hospitality is a species.

Bearing Gifts

Consider the 'societies of the gift', as 18th and 19th century European explorers called some of the communities they encountered in Polynesia, Africa, and the Arctic. In those societies, people feel themselves under a general obligation to give whenever asked to give, and to share almost everything that they have. There was no point in stealing anything. Such communities are small enough that everyone knew each other, and everyone knew what belonged to who. And if you wanted something, you could just ask for it: no one could refuse you without incurring great dishonor. Moreover, the system had a built-in mechanism for dealing with the miserly person who takes more than he gives, and who does as little work as possible. According to Harris, if the community suffers a twist of bad luck, such as a crop failure, an unsuccessful hunting expedition, a long period of bad weather or a disease outbreak, the local shaman will accuse the local freeloader of being a witch or a malevolent sorcerer (Harris, *Our Kind*, p 355).

In a society of the gift, a hunter returning home with a fresh kill would divide up the meat as equally as possible among his family members, friends, and neighbors. He might eat some of the more perishable innards at the kill site, such as the liver, but otherwise he makes his own portion the same size as everyone else's. At least one portion, also of equal size, is given to the gods as a thanksgiving sacrifice: they, too, get their share. Why does the hunter do this? One explanation is that the hunter calculates his self-interest. He reasons that by giving a share of his kill today, he is sure to get a share of someone else's kill tomorrow. Anthropologists have found that this is a widespread and probably ancient custom. Marvin Harris wrote that in a tribe or band sized society:

> People gave with the expectation of taking and took with the expectation of giving. Since chance played a great role in the capture of animals, collection of wild foodstuffs, and the success of rudimentary forms of agriculture, the individual who had the luck of the catch on one day needed a handout on the next. So the best way for them to provide for their inevitable rainy day was to be generous. (Harris, *Our Kind*, p 344-5)

Margaret Visser seems to confirm this point of view:

> 'Open-handedness' of this kind is what we call 'hospitality'. It is offered by hosts to guests – by those at home, who are expected to give to those who are away from home (and by definition 'foreigners' to the hosts), and who *therefore* receive. They receive because they are in need, and also for the same reason that the Inuit seal hunter gave most of his meat away: because one day the host himself might be traveling and need assistance either from his guest or from somebody else who keeps the rules of courtesy. (Visser, *The Gift of Thanks*, p 27)

Yet people in 'societies of the gift' always endeavored to preserve the appearance of *not* being a calculating, self-interested giver

(*Ibid*, p 345). Indeed, in this context it can be extremely rude to say 'thank you'. People in gift-giving cultures prefer to think of generosity as a duty, rather than as a free act of spontaneous kindness. Giving a gift, so this way of thinking goes, "...can also cause resentment. One carries around a need to pay somebody else back: where the duty is strongly felt, it can seem like a menace." (*Ibid*, p 30) Gift-giving can dominate and subordinate the recipient. But no one wants to be subordinated: people want to feel respected as an equal. One way around this is to never give 'gifts', but instead to give that which your social and moral duty obliges you to give – but (perhaps paradoxically) to fulfill that moral duty freely and spontaneously. An Inuit informant told the anthropologist Peter Freuchen: "You must not thank for your meat; it is your right to get parts. In this country, nobody wishes to be dependent on others. Therefore, there is nobody who gives or gets gifts, for thereby you become dependent. With gifts you make slaves..." (cited in Visser, *The Gift of Thanks*, pp 30-1).

The Host

The hospitality of an Iron Age householder seems to be where Western civilization obtained its notion of moral goodness. Indeed, among the Heroic societies of Europe, hospitality and generosity seem to be among the very highest of moral and social values, perhaps second only to honor. The Greek word for hospitality is *xenia*, which is a curious mix of the words *xenos*, for a stranger, a foreigner, or an outsider, and *philia*, for friendship and love. A host is thus someone who treats strangers and outsiders as friends. Several scenes in Homer's *Iliad* illustrate this. In the opening scenes, Achilles is ravenously angry with King Agamemnon, because the king kept a certain captured slave-girl which Achilles claimed for himself. Achilles therefore refuses to join the fight against Troy. So Agamemnon sends Odysseus, Ajax, Phoenix, and two heralds to plead his case on his behalf.

Although they come at the behest of Agamemnon, Achilles receives them warmly, since they are some of his best friends. He says to his friend Patroclus, who acts here as part of Achilles' household:

> Come, a bigger winebowl, son of Menoetius, set it here.
> Mix stronger wine. A cup for the hands of each guest –
> Here beneath my roof are the men I love the most.
> (*Iliad* 10.237-9)

Thus we have an early example of what was expected of an early Greek householder, even in his home-away-from-home. More interestingly, however, is a later scene which shows that *xenia*, Greek hospitality, could be extended to enemies. Priam, the king of Troy and father of Achilles' sworn enemy Hector, whom Achilles had killed that afternoon, visited Achilles to plead for the return of Hector's dead body.

> The majestic King of Troy slipped past the rest
> And kneeling down beside Achilles, clasped his knees
> And kissed his hands, those terrible, man-killing hands
> That had slaughtered Priam's many sons in battle.
> (*Iliad* 24.559-562)

All the onlookers were impressed by Priam's audacity, yet also tense. Achilles now had a chance to kill the King of Troy and end the war right then and there. But he did not. Instead, he acknowledged Priam as his guest, and treated him accordingly. A man presenting himself to you as a guest in your home is to be treated as a guest, even if he is otherwise your enemy. (It probably helped that Priam appealed to Achilles' love for his own deceased father, and compared those feelings to his own feelings as the grieving father of a dead son. Tribal loyalties also run deep in this kind of culture!) After Priam's 'deposition', Achilles offered

Priam a chair to sit in – an essential act in the hospitality customs of a Heroic society. Priam declined the seat, saying that all he wants is Hector's body returned. Priam's rejection of Achilles' gesture of hospitality is a snub, and Achilles warns him:

> So don't anger me now. Don't stir my raging heart still more.
> Or under my own roof I may not spare your life, old man –
> Suppliant that you are – may break the laws of Zeus!
> (*Iliad* 24.667-9)

Achilles' final remark here strikes me as theological: it suggests that the hospitality customs of his people have a divine origin, a point repeated a few lines later in the text as well. In Greek society at the time, a transgression of the requirements of hospitality was a very serious offence, and could instigate violence. Indeed the whole story of the *Iliad* begins with just such a transgression. It begins when a retinue of people from the city of Troy are guests at a feast in the hall of King Menelaus of Mycenaean Sparta. The head of the Trojan delegation, Paris, son of King Priam of Troy, broke the rules of *xenia* in a most dramatic fashion by abducting Helen, the wife of his host. The offended Greeks probably felt themselves duty-bound by the laws of Zeus to avenge the transgression by sacking the city of Troy.

Nor are these hospitality customs limited to the Greeks. The Roman observer Tacitus, writing in the second century CE, observed the Iron Age Germanic people's disposition for generosity:

> No nation indulges more freely in feasting and entertaining than the German. It is accounted a sin to turn any man away from your door. The host welcomes his guest with the best meal that his means allow. When he has finished entertaining him, the host undertakes a fresh role: he accompanies the guest to the nearest house where further hospitality can be

had. It makes no difference that they come uninvited; they are welcomed just as warmly. No distinction is ever made between acquaintance and stranger as far as the right to hospitality is concerned. As the guest takes his leave, it is customary to let him have anything he asks for; and the host, with as little hesitation, will ask for a gift in return. They take delight in presents, but they expect no repayment for giving them and feel no obligation in receiving them. (Tacitus, *Germanica*, 21, pp 119-20)

Note how Tacitus observes that gift-giving among Iron Age Germans is never intended to incur *obligatory* reciprocity. I suspect that gift recipients nonetheless felt some obligation to return the favor anyway. The situation may have been very much like that which obtains in some Aboriginal societies, where gift-giving is never described as gift-giving, lest the feeling of obligation weigh upon a recipient's mind. But that aside, this notion of unselfish hospitality has a very important place in Heroic society. It is tightly involved in the Heroic society's understanding of goodness, and its understanding of the psychological constitution of a good person. As researcher Stephen Pollington observed:

... the Germanic notion of 'goodness' involved a willingness to share resources; it was, however, an outward, public rather than an inward, private quality, and involved public recognition of worth as part of its reward. A 'good man' in this early Iron Age society was one who acted in a practical, utilitarian way to preserve the society and to promote its aims. This 'good man' was a man of means, a leader or prominent member of his social group, economically independent and dominant in his settlement...[98]

Yet this notion of goodness was not necessarily egalitarian: and the best place to see its inequality is in the seating arrangements. In the feasting hall of an Anglo-Saxon chieftain, the seating plan was organized very carefully. The *hlaford* (lord) and the *hlafdige* (lady) sat on chairs mounted on a raised dais called the High Seat. At his foot sat a *thyle*: in the story of *Beowulf*, this is Unferth's position. Next to the *thyle* sat a *byrele*, cupbearer, responsible for ensuring that no one runs out of drink. In *Beowulf*, Queen Wealtheow is both *hlafdige* and *byrele* at the same time. In front of the high seat and in the center of the hall was the hearth, which may have had some food warming on it, but was used primarily for heat and light. To the left and right of the high seat was a bench for the *dugud*, the warriors and guests who had most recently earned honor. On the other side of the hearth ran another parallel bench for the *geogud*, younger or less prestigious warriors (*Ibid*, pp 66-7). In this way, not only material goods like food could be distributed at a feast: one can distribute social goods such as honor and prestige. Generally, the closer you sat to the host of the feast, the better your position. As Visser says:

> Eating together is a sign of friendship and equality, and yet people have always used the positioning of the 'companions' as an expression of the power of each in relationship to the others. Hierarchical seating arrangements make up one of the most intricate aspects of protocol, for placing guests at a table is a deeply political act. Where dinners are *not* ranked, a political, or social and religious, statement is just as surely being made.[99]

Interestingly, the very notion of a hierarchical division among people seated at a dinner table also emerges from ancient food distribution customs. The modern English word for a Lord comes from an Old English term, *hlaford*, itself derived from *hlaf weard*, meaning 'loaf keeper'. The idea is that the lord is the person responsible for managing the tribe's food stores (cf

Pollington, *The Mead Hall*, p 182). One can infer from that observation that the lord is the person with the power of life and death over his followers, which he exercises when he decides whether to feed or to starve them.

Celtic feasting halls were round, not rectangular, but apparently no less hierarchical. The Roman observer Posidonius recorded the seating arrangement at a feast among the Celtic Gauls:

> Whenever the Celts hold a feast, they sit in a circle with the most powerful man at the center, like the chorus leader in a Greek play. His power may be because of his bravery in war, noble birth, or simply his wealth. Next to him sits the host of the feast, followed in order on both sides by the other guests in descending rank. Behind each guest stands his shield bearer, while the lesser warriors sit apart in their own circle.[100]

The chieftain had a high seat of his own, and his wife sat on her own high seat on the chieftain's left side. On his right sat another high seat for the person deemed by the chieftain to be the best warrior present. This person was also given a special cut of meat from the animal, called the Hero's Portion (which was probably the haunches, but we don't know for sure). Various Celtic tales include boasting competitions in which the guests compete for the right to claim the Hero's Portion. So obsessed was the average Celtic warrior with honor and prestige that the boasting competitions sometimes ended with fist-fights.

In the stories of Britain's King Arthur, we see a mediaeval version of Iron Age culture in the castle of Camelot. Like a Celtic feasting hall, Arthur' table is round, so that all who are seated there could think themselves equals. Nonetheless this egalitarian table had at least one seat more prestigious than the rest: the Siege Perilous, the chair set aside by Merlin for whichever knight successfully locates the Holy Grail. So the story goes. Recently, archaeologists turned up evidence that the round table was not a piece of furniture but actually a building. It is likely to have been a round structure built on the remains of a Roman amphitheatre, near Chester, England, where the discoveries match the earliest descriptions of Arthur's court. This round amphitheatre could have held up to a thousand people: and the researchers believed the nobles sat in a front row, and the lesser subjects sat on stone benches around the circumference (Martin Evans, "Historians locate King Arthur's Round Table" *London Daily Telegraph* (online edition), 11 July 2010). The ranking of guests at a dinner party seems to be as old as recorded history, and it is certainly still with us. Think for example of the decisions concerning who can sit at 'the head table' at a wedding banquet. I've also seen children compete for the right to sit closest to the parent they loved best, or closest to the child whose birthday is being celebrated, and so on.

The Celts also embedded the virtue of hospitality into their laws. In the early Irish laws, for instance, the obligations and entitlements of the *bruigu*, the hospitaller or hostel-owner, are described in some detail. A law text called the *Uraicecht Becc* said that the hospitaller could not refuse anyone, nor refuse that person's retinue of followers and supporters, and the *bruigu* also "does not keep an account against any person however often he comes" (cited in Kelly, *A Guide to Early Irish Law*, p 36). A hospitaller had to have certain resources available at all times, such as a cauldron full of food, a warm fire, a lamp in the guest bedroom, and a clean bed. As the *Uraicecht Becc* says, "He is not a *bruigu* who is not a possessor of a hundredfold wealth" (*Ibid*, p 37). It would seem that most hospitallers had to have a second job in order to be wealthy enough to meet the requirements. A successful *bruigu* could have a legal standing on par with a landlord. Indeed a particularly wealthy and respected one could become an *ollamh bruigu*, equal in rank with a chief poet or a lesser king.

A ninth century Irish wisdom-text describes the responsibilities of a person who runs a hostel, or a feasting hall, as follows:

"O grandson of Conn, O Cormac," said Carbre, "what are the dues of a chief and of an ale-house?"
    "Not hard to tell," said Cormac.
    "Good behavior around a good chief,
    Lights to lamps,
    Exerting oneself for the company,
    Settling seats,
    Liberality of dispensers,
    A nimble hand at distributing,
    Attentive service,
    To love one's lord,
    Music in moderation,
    Short story-telling,
    A joyous countenance,
    Welcome to companies,
    Silence during a recital,
    Harmonious choruses–
Those are the dues of a chief and of an ale-house," said Cormac to Carbre.
    (*Teosca Cormac*, § 4)

The fourth line there, 'settling seats', suggests that the bruigu has to know how to settle arguments about the seating arrangement at the dinner table. This passage also suggests that in addition to food and drink and lighting, the bruigu has to have prepared entertainment: music and storytellers at least. And the second-to-last item on the list, 'silence during a recital', suggests that he also had to be able to exercise a little bit of control over his guests. When I lived in Ireland, there were several traditional music pubs I attended where the barman would order the patrons to quiet themselves and listen silently to a solo singer. Foreign tourists who continued to talk or make noise during the performance were angrily shushed by the barman and other patrons. Someone who disturbed the performance of 'a royal call'[101] risked being ushered out of the building.

The story of the first satire ever recited in Ireland also gives us an insight into what can befall a host who doesn't meet his obligations. A poet named Corpre arrived at the house of King Bres, looking for a place to stay for a short while.

> And it is how he was treated, he was put in a little dark narrow house where there was no fire, or furniture, or bed; and for a feast three small cakes, and they dry, were brought to him on a little dish. When he rose up on the morrow he was no way thankful and as he was going across the green, it is what he said: "Without food ready on a dish; without milk enough for a calf to grow on; without shelter, without light in the darkness of night; without enough to pay a story-teller; may that be the prosperity of Bres". (Gregory, *Gods and Fighting Men*, p 34)

In some versions of the story, the satire caused Bres sufficient loss of honor (and also caused him to break out in skin blemishes!) that he lost the kingship right then and there. In other versions, Bres loses his good luck for a while, and because of that he is eventually compelled to abdicate the throne. But the average Celtic hospitaller may have felt himself in an almost impossible position: his obligation to guests appeared to have no limit. Several stories in Irish mythology describe famous poets, or the sons of kings, and their followers, staying at a hostel for months on end, reducing the frustrated host to poverty. Yet the hospitaller couldn't refuse his guests: in old Irish law a *bruigu* who refuses hospitality is immediately no longer a *bruigu*, and loses much of his honor-price.

The custom of Celtic hospitality may have lasted a very long time into the modern era. We see an instance of it in Shakespeare's *Macbeth*, for instance. Early in the play, Macbeth is talked into killing King Duncan, in order to take the crown for himself. But before doing so, he expresses some deeply-felt cognitive dissonance:

> He's here in double trust:
> First, as I am his kinsman and his subject,
> Strong both against the deed; then, as his host,
> Who should against his murderer shut the door,
> Not bear the knife myself.
> (Macbeth, 1.VII.12-16)

This leads me to the next part of the moral discourse. What of the person who you turn away from your door? The basic principle 'This man is my guest, he should be treated as a guest' has a corresponding opposite: 'This other man is not a guest; therefore he is not treated as one treats a guest; he is treated some other way'. To deny someone your hospitality can amount to a denial of moral responsibility for that person's well-being. In some climates, where an unsheltered person risks death by exposure to the elements, that denial could be a serious moral problem of its own. Of course, it does not follow from this principle that you are always obliged to invite everyone you meet to dinner every day! This responsibility can belong to a spectrum of intensity: it is strong when the risk is great; less strong at other times. It may also depend upon the person's ability to give: the wealthy incur the responsibility more than the poor. Another Irish story called *Manannan's Three Calls to Cormac* ends with a teaching concerning hospitality and generosity, imparted to the young Cormac by the god Manannan:

"And the Riders you saw thatching the house," he said, "are

the men of arts and poets, and all that look for a fortune in Ireland, putting together cattle and riches. For when they go out, all that they leave in their houses goes to nothing, and so they go on for ever."

"And the man you saw kindling the fire," he said, "is a young lord that is more liberal than he can afford, and every one else is served while he is getting the feast ready, and every one else profiting by it."

(Gregory, *Gods and Fighting Men*, p 110)

This teaching concerns the nature of generosity and the distribution of wealth. This is an important lesson for Cormac, as he was about to become king, and therefore responsible for economic distribution. Specifically, I think this story speaks of the wrongness of being both too miserly *and* too generous. One can be too greedy, as for instance when your efforts to gain more wealth dominate your whole way of being in the world. Rich people often find that the more things they own, the more precautions they must take for the maintenance and security of what they own. In other words, the more stuff you own, the more your stuff starts to own you. Thus you can lose the enjoyment of the things you worked so hard to gain. One can also be too generous, and thus undermine yourself in another way: a person cannot take care of others if she cannot take care of herself.

Note that the person who is not your guest, and thus is not treated as a guest, is not necessarily your enemy. Someone who you are meeting for the first time, and know nothing about, and therefore have no reason to love or hate, is neither a friend nor a foe. If he was your enemy, you would at least know a few things about him: enough to give you reason to hate him. But as he is an unknown quantity, he is a stranger. And as a stranger, he is both a potential friend and a potential enemy. Those inclined to be trusting tend to assume that the stranger means well; those inclined to be worried and fearful tend to assume that the stranger means to do harm. Thus even in first glances, we start to sort out what to expect from the people we meet, how to treat them, and how to respond to their presence. But in general, it seems to me that the act of offering hospitality to the stranger implicitly re-classifies the stranger into the category of the guest. I view that transformation of the stranger's moral standing as a highly significant moment. Indeed it may be related to the more fundamental transformation of someone's moral standing from an object in the world, to a person.

The Guest

I've been dwelling on the requirements of hosts here. But the guest in this situation had obligations too. The Koran, for instance, requires people to make a kind of announcement of their good intentions when they enter another's house: "O believers, do not enter houses not your own without first announcing your presence and invoking peace upon their occupants." (*Koran* 24:2) Another of Carbre's questions in *The Instructions of King Cormac* is: "What were your habits when you were a lad?" To this, Cormac says, "I was mild in the mead-hall." (*Teosca Cormac* § 7) The text as a whole describes the importance of preserving one's honor and treating others with respect. Those teachings can certainly apply to the way a guest should treat his host, and also treat other guests. But even without the precedent of a Celtic literary reference, it seems logically consistent that the overall situation of *ghostis* assigns ethical obligations not just to the host, but also to the guest. It takes a certain understanding, a certain disposition, even a certain talent, to be a good guest. These obligations help ease any fears that the hosts may have about an unknown person in their home. Margaret Visser says that as a guest you must "accept your host's intentions, be seen to receive them passively and admiringly, and do not attempt to advise your host, order his family about, or criticize him. Look pleased by his kindness." (*Ibid*, p 29) The guest receives the host's gift of hospitality, but he knows not to exploit or exhaust his host. The good guest knows that his presence, even if welcomed, incurs various costs and troubles for the hosts. If the guest was initially a stranger, one of those troubles is fear. The good guest therefore does things to reduce the fear. He is respectful, amiable, modest in his requests, and even helpful. He knows what things he can, and cannot, ask for. A guest should also be stimulating company for his hosts. He contributes to the occasion in his own way: storytelling, for instance. In mediaeval and early modern Irish culture, a recently arrived guest usually 'brings the news'. He describes any events that happened in the world which might be of interest or concern to his hosts, or in which he was somehow personally involved. He does this almost immediately after he is offered his tea and his seat: he might even do this before he is asked his name.

Some hosts feel that guests honor them: the guest's presence implicitly judges the host's hospitality as worthy and good. But for this to be true, a guest must be an honorable guest, one whose presence is enjoyable, and whose judgment of the host's worthiness is genuinely valuable. Unless the hospitality customs of one's culture are particularly stringent (as in the case of the Celtic *bruigu* laws noted earlier), a guest who doesn't act in the expected manner can be asked to leave. Thus even after the ritual exchange of peaceful intentions has been performed, the host retains a certain veto-power over the whole situation.

The guest has two final obligations. One is to depart before he exhausts his welcome. A strophe of the *Havaml* affirms this:

The tactful guest will take his leave,
Early, not linger long;
He starts to stink who outstays his welcome
In a hall that is not his own. (§ 38)

The *Iliad* also includes an instance of this item of etiquette. When the embassy from Agamemnon to Achilles has concluded, Achilles "... gave Patroclus a sharp glance, a quiet nod / to pile the bedding deep for Phoenix now / a sign to the rest to think of leaving quickly." (*Iliad* 9.756-9)

The other obligation on a guest is to ensure, when he leaves, that the good will between him and his host remains. Therefore the guest must offer to return the favor: he must invite the host to his house some day, where he shall be the host, and the host shall be the guest, and the circumstance of *ghostis* shall be achieved between them again.

For a summary comment: let it be noted here that all kinds of social principles can be affirmed, or withdrawn, through the way people extend (or do not extend) hospitality. When we give and receive gifts, we also give and receive respect, prestige, loyalty, honor, even dominance and superiority. Sometimes people give gifts not to be generous, but to be powerful. Aristotle's "Great Soul", for instance, "is fond of conferring benefits, but ashamed to receive them, because the former is a mark of superiority and the latter of inferiority." (*NE* 3.iv.24) Such a person gives in order to establish himself in the position of the provider, and to reduce the recipient down to the position of the dependent. The gift-giver may also wish to put the recipient in debt. Or he may wish to snub someone by bestowing gifts on someone else. At the same time, the recipient is in a position to give things to the giver in return: at the very least his thanks. But someone could decline gift, in order to demonstrate that he has no need of the giver's help, and thus subordinate the would-be giver! And if the host offered his hospitality from a genuine feeling of care and generosity, and not out of a desire to dominate, then to decline the gift is to insult him. Furthermore, in some circumstances, a gift-giver could actually subordinate himself, not elevate himself, by his generosity. In traditional Chinese society, for instance, gifts usually flow from people of lower status to people of higher status: the landlords and administrators had to be 'kept sweet', or placated. Even after the Communist revolution in China, when landlords were replaced by politically appointed cadres, local peasants would give gifts to their new superiors. Those people, in turn, were busily giving gifts to their own superiors in the hierarchy of the communist party. The situation was reasonably similar for tenant farmers in Europe who, until the early twentieth century, had to stock the pantries of their landlords with a share of what their labors on the land produced. (This, by the way, is the origin of paying rent.) But in that situation there is no question of the gift-giver subordinating the gift-receiver. The gift-receiver, for instance, may be in a position to retaliate if he does not receive. A subject of the Duke of Savoy once described the situation by saying, "We are not so much offended with the Duke for what he takes from us, as thankful for what he leaves us." (Cited in Visser, *The Gift of Thanks*, p 114)

Although full of paradoxes and contradictions, a consistent theme in any cultural tradition is the way in which gift-giving expresses social, moral, and sometimes political values. The nature and the direction of the flow of gifts within a community is a sign of the character of that community. Obviously gift-giving and hospitality has a utilitarian dimension: people act generously in order to benefit others. But like all virtues, generosity and hospitality also emerge from the character of the people involved, and from their pursuit of some conception of the good life. A hospitable person shares his home and his food with others because he is the sort of person who habitually acts that way. The stranger's entitlement to hospitality (or the absence of that entitlement) is in this sense less important than the extent to which the host considers generosity part of his identity. Thus the moral proposition that I started with might be phrased this way: 'I am a generous person, therefore I make the stranger my guest, and I treat him as a guest should be treated.'

The Sumbel

Someone keen to establish himself as a good and honorable man in a European Iron Age society would build a special hall as part of his home. In the hall he would frequently host a special kind of dinner party called the *sumbel*. This was a cultural event of the greatest importance: not only did the host share food, drink, material treasures, and other gifts with his guests, but he also distributed immaterial social goods such as honor and prestige. Guests at the *sumbel* would also make elaborate displays of their own worth and power, for instance by pledging their loyalty to their lord and to the other guests, swearing to protect or assist them in some future adventure, possibly at the cost of their own lives. Researcher Stephen Pollington described a traditional sumbel, as follows:

> At the *sumbel*, warriors drank alcoholic drinks, probably from the lord's collection of drinking-horns, goblets or glass beakers. The lady of the household took the mead-cup to each person in turn, beginning with the lord himself and passing in a strictly hierarchical order among the nobles, the older men (*dugud*) and then the youths (*geogud*). The lady spoke flattering or consoling words to the menfolk and it may have been her duty to promote goodwill among those present. There was then an exchange of words: the warriors individually stood before the lord, who thanked them for their past deeds and handed out the valuable gifts (*madmas* or *madmas*) which recognised their high status; they in turn spoke the *beot*, a kind of boast or promise to perform some feat, such as to slay such-and-such a foe of the people, or less specifically to stand beside their lord and never flinch from his protection, though their lives depended on it. By means of such exchanges the bonds of friendship, loyalty, and inter-dependence were reinforced. Small wonder that those who failed their companions were reviled.[102]

In the summer of 2009 I was invited to attend a *sumbel*, hosted by the chief of a modern-day Druidic grove located near Ottawa, Canada. More than forty guests assembled at a campsite, around nightfall. A ring of oil torches illuminated the space. An honor guard was posted outside the circle, mainly to prevent passing pedestrians (and the occasional car) from accidentally walking right into the center of the circle. As the guests arrived, they placed their camping chairs in a circle and chatted among themselves. Eventually, the host stood up, held aloft a drinking horn full of mead, and declared, "The sumbel is now begun." (This is a fine example of what philosophers call a speech-act.)

The horn, we were told, would go round the circle clockwise three times. The first time that it came around, each person was invited to honor one of the gods, whichever they wished. Yet there was no obligation to do so. Those who didn't want to say much were permitted to simply say, "To the gods!" or "To the mighty ones!" or something like that, as they poured a drop of the mead on the earth as an offering. Taken together, the gods that people chose to honor were a fairly eclectic bunch: most people named Nordic deities, but some honored gods from Ireland, Greece, Egypt, Sumeria and Mesopotamia, and from Aboriginal traditions. A locally well-known Irish-Canadian Druid honored, "The gods of my people," without naming them. And in fine Celtic form he proceeded to tell part of the tale of one particular goddess, again without mentioning Her name. In the Celtic tradition, one does not simply invoke a god without telling the story of that god. Yet you don't mention your gods' names in mixed company because the names are holy. Besides, there might be an enemy hiding in the bushes and you wouldn't want him invoking your own gods against you. Ritual invocations and oaths to Celtic gods also thereby served an educational function; and at any rate, you want to be sure of exactly which god you are invoking. Thus this particular sumbel, although mainly modeled on the Germanic and Scandinavian model, was a curiously multicultural event.

For the second circuit of the mead-horn, we were invited to honor an ancestor, or a hero, or a recently deceased person. Again, there was no particular obligation to do so. Yet the previous round had made most people a little more comfortable with each other, and so more people were willing to share intimate personal feelings. Tears flowed as several described their grief for the loss of parents and close family members. The aforementioned Druid named his male family line back to four generations: again, in the Celtic custom, one identifies oneself not just with one's name but also with part of the story of one's blood and history. He ended the lineage with his great grandfather, who was "... the son of a man whose name I do not know." For a hero to honor, one person described his mother's uncle, who in his retirement personally ferried a plane-load of food and medicine to Haiti, once a year, every year, for thirty years. Stories of ordinary people's heroism can be inspiring: they show what our possibilities are, even with few individual resources.

For the third circuit, we were invited to do one (or more) of three things: a toast, a boast, or an oath. This third circuit seems to have been the highlight of the event. Earlier that afternoon several people described to me how oath-taking at a sumbel had changed their lives for the better. Many people in this third round boasted of having successfully completed the oaths they made at a previous sumbel, and also toasted others who fulfilled their oaths. Oath-fulfillers then enjoyed a well-deserved round of cheering from the circle. Our host impressed upon us the understanding that whatever oath we might make, the gods would witness it, and that they would help us to succeed as well as hold us to its completion. 'Good wyrd' (a good fate, or a good 'luckiness') would follow whoever successfully fulfilled his or her oath, and 'ill wyrd' would follow whoever failed. Those making an oath were also asked to describe a forfeit he would have to accept if the oath was unfulfilled within a certain timeline. This forfeit normally took the form of a requirement to do something embarrassing or unpleasant, or to give up some activity that the oath-maker enjoyed for an appropriate length of time. Oath-makers could suggest their own forfeits, although those forfeits could be modified or rejected if people in the group found it to be too harsh or too light. An oath could also be rejected, if the group thought it too difficult, or too easy. Everyone could contribute to the decision to accept or modify an oath and a forfeit, and most people did, even if only making an agreeable or disagreeable sound in response to something that another person suggested. But in practice oaths and forfeits were accepted when the most respected people in the circle had reached a consensus among themselves, which seemed very natural.

Again, in the third round, no one was obliged or duty-bound to say or do anything. All contributions to the sumbel were voluntary. But the inspiration of the private disclosures of the previous round, the mead that had been consumed slowly over the evening, the stories of successful oaths, and perhaps a little bit of good-natured peer pressure, probably motivated a few people to stand and make the most impressive oath they could. As acts of individual 'grandstanding', the oath-taking, toasting, and boasting of the sumbel was curiously community-oriented. A successful oath-fulfiller could gain well-deserved individual praise, but only for having done something that his peers agreed was worthy, and which benefited others. Then the whole community could celebrate and share in an individual's accomplishment. These are the kinds of things that bring people together, reduce fear and create trust between them, and give them reasons to care about each other. These are among the things that create shared adventures and shared life experiences between people, which is the basis of the next sacred relationship to study.

7

Friends

When you invite the stranger into you home, and share food and conversation with him, then he becomes your guest. The customs of *xenia* and *ghostis* give people reasons to trust each other as a first principle of their association. Yet those customs are but the first moves in a larger moral drama, like the first notes in the overture of a longer musical score. The imbalance of power between guest and host is never perfectly equalized. This is not because equality is impossible, but because *equality changes the nature of the relationship*. Similarly, when you invite the guest not just into your home, but also into your heart and mind, he becomes more than a guest. When you offer him not just a share of your food but also a share of your life, he becomes your friend.

A Relationship for Its Own Sake

What, then, is friendship? One of the earliest and most often cited philosophical definitions of friendship is the one provided by Aristotle, in his book *The Nicomachean Ethics*.

> The perfect form of friendship is that between the good, and those who resemble each other in virtue. For these friends wish each alike the other's good in respect of their goodness, and they are good in themselves, but it is those who wish the good of their friends for their friends' sake that are friends in the fullest sense, since they love each other for themselves and not accidentally (*NE* 1156b10).

A similar understanding of friendship was also echoed by Confucius, who in complete isolation from Aristotle hit upon a very similar idea:

> There are three kinds of friendship which are beneficial and three kinds which are harmful. Friendship with the upright, with the truthful, and with the well-informed is beneficial. Friendship with those who flatter, with those who are meek and those who compromise with principles, and with those who talk cleverly is harmful. (*Analects* 16:4)

These are perhaps long-winded ways to say that the true friend loves you *because of who you are*, completely, and unconditionally. This may help explain why, as mentioned earlier, one of the primary features of friendship is equality. If someone made a detailed economic accounting of the goods and services exchanged between two friends, perhaps the result would demonstrate that one gave more than the other. Yet the point of friendship is also to *not* make such an account. Friends benefit each other without a concern for being benefited in return. Elsewhere in the text Aristotle adds that the friend is "a second self". His deeds and virtues resemble your own, and his happiness is just as important to you as your own (*NE* 8.iii.6). The Aboriginal poet Chief Dan George possibly meant something like this when he wrote: "Friendship lives in every heart."[103] Similarly, Confucius recommends that you should "have no friends who are not as good as yourself." (*Analects* 1:8) And this is perhaps part of why Aristotle wrote that "if men are friends, there is no need of justice between them." (*NE* 8.i.4) This is not because friends lack a sense of fairness, for obviously friendship does entail such a sense. ("The highest form of justice seems to have an element of friendly feeling in it." *NE* 8.i.14) Rather, I think Aristotle's meaning is more like this. The kind of problems that are the concern of justice – problems like undeserved harms or uncompensated burdens – ideally never arise between friends. The friend who seeks only to gain an advantage for himself by associating with you is not a true friend, but only a "friend of utility" (*NE* 8.iii.1) or as we would say today, 'a fair-weather friend'. This seems to me a very astute observation. We all know what it is to be abandoned by someone who seemed like a friend until you had to ask for a favor from him.

Yet that conclusion introduces a curious philosophical problem. On the one hand, we should affirm (as Aristotle did) that true friends love each other because of who they are, and not for the sake of gaining a material reward from each other. Yet we clearly do benefit materially from our friends. We sometimes receive gifts from the friend. We reasonably expect that friends will help each other when in need. And if nothing else, we gain pleasure from their presence. But there's the rub. Do we love our friends for our friend's sake, that is, do we love them intrinsically? Or do we love them for the sake of the pleasure and the usefulness they give us, that is, instrumentally? If the latter is true, even the pleasure of the friend's presence might count as a benefit we gain from him, and so perhaps we do not love him for his own sake after all. This objection to Aristotle's classic definition of friendship and others like it have been raised by various philosophers over the centuries. To choose a 20th century example, philosopher George Nakhnikian wrote that to love someone because of his "admirable character traits" is still "transactional". To love someone "undemandingly" means that there can be "no thought of expected returns and no requirement that the person loved be a good human being."[104] In other words: according to Nakhnikian, if we love someone because there is something about him that we find loveable, then we do not actually love him for his own sake. Instead, we love him for the reward of pleasure that his lovable qualities gives us. But if we truly did love someone for his own sake, we could expect *nothing* back from him – not even pleasure. Further, if we truly loved him for who he is, we could not expect him to be other than he is – even if he is a scoundrel. Thus Aristotle's 'true' friendship apparently collapses back into a friendship of expediency.

I think the idea that friends love each other for their own sake is still worth defending. And I think the objection I've described here, that even 'true' friends are mere opportunists for their own pleasure, can be overcome. For one thing, friendship obviously involves mutual benefits. But friendship also assumes, perhaps counterfactually, that imbalances in giving and taking are small and unimportant, and easily overlooked. It's not that friends shouldn't talk about their problems, nor that they cannot get angry with each other if they have reason to do so. But that they shouldn't allow imbalances in giving and taking to reach the point where their friendship could be threatened. Still, friendship is not, at its heart, a matter of trade and exchange. And we should not allow the language of economics to dominate its definition, lest we miss an important dimension of the relationship which economics cannot describe. Perhaps a little bit of intellectual archaeology, digging up the cultural and logical origin of friendship, may help here.

Sources of Friendship

How are friends made? We have already seen one method: communal eating and drinking. Yet this is perhaps an instance of a more general theme: friendship is created by shared life experience. To witness the same event together, such as the entertainment and camaraderie of a dinner party, is to share a life experience. Think of how people who attend a particularly exciting sports match, or an excellent theatrical performance, or even a grisly car accident on the road, can more easily approach nearby strangers to talk about what they just saw. The shared event makes strangers less strange to each other, even if only for a few hours.

To *do* something may be better than to witness something. In the literature of Heroic Europe, the best kind of deed to do together is military adventure. Achilles and Patroclus are perhaps the best known, and most analysed, pair of fighting friends in all European literature. Yet they are not the only friends in the *Iliad*. Late one night, King Nestor of Pylos proposed a reconnaissance mission into the Trojan camp. Diomedes agreed to undertake the mission, but asked for someone to come with him:

> If another comrade would escort me, though,
> There'd be more comfort in it, confidence too.
> When two work side-by-side, one or the other
> Spots the opening first if a kill's at hand.
> When one looks out for himself, alert but alone,
> His reach is shorter – his sly moves miss the mark.
> (*Iliad* 10.261-6)

Diomedes' speech here asserts the idea that friends together can do more than individuals can. Yet the text also suggests not only that friendship makes military success more likely; it also suggests that military adventure *creates* friendship between co-adventurers. There is a kind of constructive circle here between friendship and adventure. Odysseus agrees to go with Diomedes on his mission, and the two perform various acts of sabotage behind enemy lines, including the theft of a team of purebred war horses. When they returned to their own camp, Odysseus "drove the purebred team / with a rough exultant laugh as comrades cheered / crowding in his wake." (*Iliad* 10.658-9). Think here of a hurling team bringing home the Liam McCarthy Cup, and parading with it on a fire truck through the streets of town, cheered on by the people. After that triumphant return to camp, Odysseus and Diomedes,

> Wading into the sea, washed off the crusted sweat
> From shins and necks and thighs. And once the surf
> had scoured the thick caked sweat from their limbs

and the two fighters cooled, their hearts revived
and into the polished tubs they climbed and bathed.
And rinsing off, their sleek skin with an olive oil rub,
They sat down to their meal and dipping up their cups
From an overflowing bowl, they poured them forth –
Honeyed, mellow wine to the great goddess Athena.
(*Iliad* 10.661-670)

These lines which close off the scene beautifully depict two friends at ease in each other's presence after hard work together. It's easy to imagine them washing each other down in the sea, then toasting each other's bravery as they gave their thanks to the goddess.

Let's turn now to a non-military example of shared 'adventure'. In the spring of 2009, two close friends of mine bought a 100-acre disused trailer park. They then assembled a team of people, myself among them, to turn the property into a working campground again. Plumbing and electric wiring was fixed at individual campsites and several outbuildings. A new fire-pit was dug, and a burm raised around it to contain the sound of the fifty drummers who would play there by night. A riverfront beach was cleared of weeds and rubbish. Fallen branches and dead trees in seventy acres of pine forest were removed to a man-made hedgerow, which would serve as habitat for birds and small animals. A timber-frame stage was made. An artificial pond was dug. A children's playground was repainted and repaired. Outbuildings were cleaned and upgraded to make them wheelchair accessible. One of the outbuildings was lifted from its foundation and moved a hundred meters. Roads and paths were cleared. Almost a hundred people donated many thousands of labor hours and thousands of dollars to make the campground ready for public use again. For my part, I worked with the various field crews and building crews, and made a comprehensive inventory of everything on the site. I also ran the carpentry shop for a while, and built furniture for the outbuildings.

Why did all those people volunteer themselves for so much time and work and trouble? We were regular attendees of a cultural festival which was set to move to the site we were developing, only thirteen months after it was purchased. The festival, and to the culture it embodied, certainly underscored the work: it gave us something in common to believe in. From morning to evening every day, we worked in the fields, in the woods, in the workshops and sheds, in the kitchens and in the river waters, to be ready for the festival. We were busy and purposeful, but never hurried or rushed. For this was a labor of love. Then from evening to late at night we gathered around a fire to tell stories, share food and drink, recite poems, sing songs, make even more grandiose plans, to play with the children and the dogs, and to rest. This combination of sharing work by day and sharing culture at night produced in many of us a great sense of belonging to each other and to the land. As one of the team leaders said, "This is old magic." New friendships were created this way, and existing ones strengthened.

The transformation of the land was a team effort. We all relied on each other, not just to do our jobs, but also to encourage each other to do them well. No one wanted to be a slacker. Some of the most important decisions were made by the couple who bought the land: it could thus be said that our tribe had two chieftains. Yet the 'vision' for what the campground and the festival should be was a shared vision. Or perhaps it would be better to call it a shared 'multi-vision', for just about everyone could contribute to it, and everyone could see in the site something from his own dreams. Of course, the discussions over the nightly fires rendered some ideas more agreeable or prevalent than others. The opinions of those who had been part of the festival since its beginning twenty-one years earlier also tended to carry more weight than the opinions of younger or less knowledgeable people. This too seemed very natural, and reminded me of the way Aboriginal people treat their Elders. We faced a few problems on the way. Some critical materials were in short supply, and some of our equipment broke down at inconvenient times. We also had a few injuries, for instance one of the volunteers fell from a tree and broke three ribs. But otherwise, our shared purpose, shared labor by day, shared leisure at night, produced in us a shared identity. People began to say we were building not just a campground, but a community.

One day, while walking around the site just to explore it and get to know it, one of the leaders discovered a long slab of stone, about a meter wide and perhaps three meters long. I remember watching his face light up as he brushed off the pine needles with his shoe. "This is the perfect Orkney Island style standing stone!" he said. So in the following spring, during a smaller-scale event on the site, a team of people prepared a place to raise the stone up. All the festival goers were invited to turn a shovelful of earth from the hole, giving everyone a chance to contribute. Numerous people also placed offerings in the hole, to be buried with the stone. Some whispered little wishes into their offerings first. Then the stone was levered and wrestled into position, tipped upright, and straightened; and then we backfilled the hole again. About an hour later, we held a stone blessing ceremony. Everyone took a turn to cover their palms in red ochre, and then plant a hand-print on the stone. This gave the stone an identity: it is not just any stone, but *our* stone. I felt somehow as if in relation to the ancient Neolithic people who raised standing stones on their own lands, and who painted their handprints onto cliff sides and cave walls. History bore down on us – but not as a weight. It felt more like a river, or a wind, carrying us into a magical time.

Shared life experiences and shared activities, like these, can create relations between people in which the parties obviously benefit from each other, and at the same time grow to love each other for their own sake. In the Homeric story of Diomedes and Odysseus, no sharp distinction can be seen between instrumental and intrinsic friendship. The two men love each other as friends *and* benefit from each other's help as they scout the Trojan camp. As my own friends and I built Raven's Knoll, we helped and benefited each other in numerous practical ways *and* intrinsically enjoyed doing it together. Through doing things for the festival which a year before many of us thought would not happen for decades, many of us discovered a great sense of belonging to each other. When the project began, some of the people were only vague acquaintances. Indeed some found certain others on the team rather annoying. But by the middle of the summer, they were drinking from the same horn.

What these stories show, I hope, is that the intrinsic value of the friend *emerges from* the practical things that you and your friend do together, and from the ways you benefit each other. Thus the aforementioned objection, that if you benefit from a friend then you do not love him intrinsically, is (in cases like these) a false dilemma.

But this does not explore all of the meaning of friendship. I'd like to look at one more dimension of friendship which I hope will put that objection to bed at last. Here it may be useful to explain a concept which I have so far only alluded to: symbiotic identity. In its simplest terms, symbiotic identity is the idea that a decisive part of who you are stems from the relationships in which you are involved. Obviously one's own autonomous choices are decisive as well, but even those choices are embedded in a social environment, full of relationships. It is with others, because of others, for others, against others, in response or in reaction to others, in competition or co-operation with others, in hope of avoiding others, in solidarity with others, and so on, that we make the choices which eventually define who we are. These others may be anonymous, such as the one who passes you by on a busy street, and who nods in greeting or turns away from you, and thereby passes a silent judgment upon you. But they may also be others who you have known your whole life.

Symbiotic Identity

Your identity, to be simple about it, is your answer to the question "Who are you?". Your identity can be personal and individual, as when you answer the question with facts that are very particular to you. It can also be social, as when you say you are a member of a certain family, community, religion, or nation. But the more completely you answer the question, the more you find the influence of other people. Suppose you are at a party and a mutual acquaintance introduces you to someone new. The first thing you do is describe a few facts: your name, your occupation, your hometown, for example. From there, you might recount how you happened to get an invitation to the party, or a funny thing that happened to you and the mutual friend who brought you. The other person tells similar stories. If the two of you like what you hear of each other's stories, you continue to tell more stories, and you go deeper into each other's background. It's through storytelling like this, in the rush and banter of everyday life, that we introduce and reveal our lives to others. For your identity, your answer to the question "Who are you?" is not just the uniqueness of your name, or your face, or your fingerprints. It is also the uniqueness of your biography and your history. As observed by philosopher Barbara Hardy: "... we dream in narrative, daydream in narrative, remember, anticipate, hope, despair, believe, doubt, plan, revise, criticize, construct, gossip, learn, hate and love by narrative." (Hardy 1968 p 5) Philosopher Paul Ricoeur, going one step further, observed that we find our very identities in the stories that we tell:

Our own existence cannot be separated from the account we can give of ourselves. It is in telling our own stories that we give ourselves an identity. We recognize ourselves in the stories we tell about ourselves. It makes little difference whether these stories are true or false, fiction as well as verifiable history provides us with an identity.[105]

The relevance of biography to one's relationships is as follows. When you tell the story of your life, you also inevitably tell part of the story of other people's lives too. You also tell stories about your neighbors, work colleagues, family members, schoolmates, strangers in city parks, and any number of other people who played a role in the story of your life, however small. Your friends are the people whose life stories are irreplaceably intertwined with yours, perhaps more so than anyone else's stories excepting your parents and siblings. If you are a good friend to someone, over a long time, then you cannot tell the story of your life without also telling part of the story of your friend's life. Similarly, his or her life story cannot be told without also telling part of your story. Contemporary philosopher Alasdair MacIntyre reflected on this point when he wrote:

> ... we are never more (and sometimes less) than the co-authors of our own narratives. Only in fantasy do we live what story we please... We enter upon a stage which we did not design and we find ourselves a part of an action that was not of our own making. Each of us being a main character in his own drama plays subordinate parts in the dramas of others, and each drama constrains the others.[106]

The story of the funny thing that happened on the bus this morning could have involved anyone: you might not even know the names of the other people involved. But the story involved other people nonetheless. The story of how you and a friend backpacked across Europe for a summer must involve the friend who came with you. Stories of one's childhood are also good examples here. The story of how you grew up must involve those with whom you grew up. It includes your parents, your sisters and brothers, your neighbors, your schoolmates, your teachers, maybe even the owner of a local candy store, and any number of other people whose life story intersects with yours.

It may be objected that no two people's life story is ever exactly the same, and indeed part of the function of narrative is to differentiate you from other people. This is true. Yet if you have a long-time friend, with whom you shared the most important adventures and experiences in your life, then your story and hers will intersect each other so deeply that they become impossible to separate from each other. This does not make the two of you the same person: there are still two people present, and two stories told. But it is the case that your story and your friend's story must be told together, and cannot be told apart from each other lest the story remain incomplete, or even unintelligible.

It may be objected, further, that your life story could overlap like this with an enemy. This person might be a competitive colleague at your workplace, who sabotages your efforts in order to put himself ahead. It might be a schoolyard bully who humiliated and roughed you up as often as he could. It might be a former spouse who makes your divorce as expensive and as frustrating as possible. In cases like these, the overlap of narrative can be used as a kind of diagnostic tool. When you find that someone is turning the story of your life into the script of a horror film, it is probably time to change your life. You may not be able to control what that other person does; but you can avoid the choices which would trap you in a vicious circle of mutual hate and fear. The other person, by tying his life story to yours through antagonism and hatred, is almost certainly trapping himself in a labyrinth of fear. You don't have to be trapped there with him.

Obviously, the role of friendship in your identity is not all-or-nothing: there is a scale of intensity here. On one end of the spectrum, a friend can be an acquaintance whose presence you enjoy, but you almost never think about when he is away. On the other end, a friend can be a lifelong and loving companion whose presence informs your very identity in the way I have just described. The non-friend can also exist on a scale of values, from the totally anonymous stranger, to the acquaintance you are polite to but would rather not see again, to the enemy who you may wish to actively harm (and whose story also, curiously, informs your identity). In this way, the friend is the person who you love for his own sake, with a love that is not contradicted by the benefit you may gain from his presence. For the primary benefit you gain from him is an intrinsic rather than instrumental good. It is the part of your biography which he wrote with you, and which remains with you as an irreducible, irreplaceable part of who you are.

8

Sex and Loving Couples

We have now seen how friendship begins, first of all in gift-exchanges and in guest-host associations. We have seen how it grows to include shared life adventures, and shared storytelling, in a way that figures into your personal identity. There is a further stage, at which you invite your friend not only into your life, but also into some very privileged and private areas of your life: your physical sexual intimacy and your love.

Almost every religious tradition in the world affirms the sacredness of a loving sexual relationship between a man and woman, who are married to each other, and who also desire to produce a child together. The usual reason behind this affirmation is that monogamous heterosexual sex fulfills a primary divine commandment, such as "Be fruitful and multiply" (Genesis 9:7). Therefore sexual lovemaking is a religious activity. On that point there is virtually no significant disagreement anywhere in the world: indeed, on that point, there is rather little more that needs to be said. Because of this near-universal understanding of the sacredness of the monogamous heterosexual relationship, most societies in the world find ways to support it, economically and politically. Married couples can normally benefit from various tax incentives, for example.

But after that, there is enormous disagreement and conflict. Does the sacredness of sex imply that people should have more of it, or less of it? Is sex permissible for pleasure alone, when the couple does not intend to conceive a child? What about cross-dressers, homosexuals, and lesbians? What about people who decide to never marry? Why all the fuss about polyamory, prostitution, and even masturbation? Should some kinds of sex be forbidden, such as sado-masochism, or bestiality, or even costume-play and masking? What is to be done with people who have the 'forbidden' kind of sex anyway, or who have sex with a forbidden person? Should gay marriages or polygamous arrangements receive the same legal rights as monogamous marriages? Should 'those people' even be allowed to hold hands in public places? Should unmarried people of the opposite sex be allowed to socialize with each other in public places without supervision? Should they even be allowed to speak to each other – indeed, should women be allowed to show their faces in public, or should they be compelled to wear a veil? (Or a burka, or a niqab, or – you get the idea.)

Because of questions like these, there is probably no other part of human life that has served as a battleground more than the area of sex and sexuality. And when I say that human sexuality is a religious *battleground*, I mean this quite literally. Religious people have been willing to inflict terrible violence on their neighbors, family members, and married partners for even the mere *suspicion* of sexual misconduct. Those punishments range on a very wide spectrum, from malicious gossip and verbal abuse to physical assaults and murders. Why is sex and sexuality of such specifically religious interest? The answer has to do with our earliest ideas of the nature of the sacred.

Tales of the First Lovers

According to one influential way of thinking, the sacred is that which has a precedent in the story of the creation of the world. Mircea Eliade, the great scholar of mythology, reached this theory after examining numerous classical, heroic, and Aboriginal religious ideas around the world. In his understanding, the sacred is whatever re-enacts or re-joins us to the events of mythic time, especially the event of the creation of the world. In his best known work, *The Myth of the Eternal Return*, he says that every ritual has a precedent in the story of the creation of the world or in the story of the foundation of the culture or the nation. Here are his own words on the matter:

> All religious acts are held to have been founded by gods, civilizing heroes, or mythical ancestors... Not only do rituals have their mythical model but any human act whatever acquires its effectiveness to the extent to which it exactly *repeats* an act performed at the beginning of time by a god, a hero, or an ancestor... In fact the sacred year ceaselessly repeats the Creation: man is contemporary with the cosmogony and with the anthropogony because ritual projects him into the mythical epoch of the beginning. A bacchant, through his orgiastic rites, imitates the drama of the suffering of Dionysus; an Orphic, through his initiation ceremonial, repeats the original gestures of Orpheus.
>
> (Eliade, *The Myth of the Eternal Return*, p 22)

In Eliade's account of the sacred, the repetition of the creation story has the effect of bringing the mythical past into the present, making the present co-incident with the original event of creation, and placing the ritual participants in that original event. As he says,

> Insofar as an act (or an object) acquires a certain reality through the repetition of certain paradigmatic gestures, and acquires it through that alone, there is an implicit abolition of profane time, of duration, of 'history'; and he who reproduces the exemplary gesture thus finds himself transported into the mythical epoch in which its revelation took place.
>
> (Eliade, *The Myth of the Eternal Return*, p 35)

Similarly, anthropologist Wade Davis, in his recent account of some of the world's last remaining uncontacted or barely-contacted indigenous people, described the Aboriginal view of the purpose of humanity as follows:

> The entire purpose of humanity is not to improve anything. It is to engage in the ritual and ceremonial activities deemed to be essential for the maintenance of the world precisely as it was at the moment of creation.
>
> (Davis, *The Wayfinders*, Anansi Press, 2009)

And this claim also appears in religious scripture itself. Here are two examples from the Upanishads, the holy writings of Hinduism. "We must do what the gods did, in the beginning." (*Satapatha Brahmana*, VIII.2.1.4) "Thus the gods did; thus men do." (*Taittiriya Brahmana*, I.5.9.4) These two short quotes suggest that the sacred is that which repeats or imitates something that one of the gods did, 'in the beginning'.

What does this have to do with sexuality? The answer is that *sexual lovemaking almost always counts as one of those exemplary events*, performed by the gods at the beginning of things. Marriage customs, and sexual play in general, is often explained as, and planned specifically to be, a re-enactment the marriage and the love of two gods, who may themselves represent or embody two primordial elements of the world. Or if the first sex is not between two gods, then it will be between two mythic human beings, possibly the very first human beings: Adam and Eve, for instance. "Marriage rites too have a divine model," says Eliade, "and human marriage reproduces the hierogamy, more especially the union of heaven and earth." (*Ibid*, p 23)

The idea of the sacred marriage seems to have been important to my ancestors, the Celts. We have already seen one example of it in Gerald of Wales' account of the inauguration of the kings of a certain northern Ireland tribe. Another Celtic example appears in the Irish story called the *Caith Maigh Tuireadh*. In that story, the goddess Ériu was gazing out to sea in quiet contemplation, when a beautiful ship came to shore. In the ship was a beautiful man –

the text describes his handsome appearance and rich apparel in great detail – who approached her and said, "Shall I have an hour of lovemaking with you?" Ériu rebuffs him by saying, "I certainly have not made a tryst [a formal courtship] with you." The smooth-talker replies, "Come without the trysting!" And so she did. The text suggests that the affair was consensual, even loving, since she laments his departure afterwards. He also gives her a token ring by which she may identify him again in the future. (E. Gray, trans, *Caith Maigh Tuireadh*, § 16-18).

One way to understand this story, as the Iron Age audience would likely have understood it, is that the story represents a sexual meeting between two primordial deities, one who represents or embodies the earth, and the other who represents the human tribe. Their lovemaking restores fertility to landscapes and people. As archaeologist Barry Cunliffe observed:

> The end of the old year and the beginning of the new was marked by the greatest of the ceremonies, Samhain, held on 1st November. For the Celts it was a time between the two years and as such was dangerous: the spirits of the dead could roam free. It was on this occasion that the male god Dagda and the female goddess, usually Morrigan, came together, and through their intercourse the well-being of the tribe and fertility of all their enterprises were assured. In some versions of the myth the goddess, now an old hag, was revitalised by the union and became young and beautiful once more.
>
> (Cunliffe, *The Ancient Celts*, (OUP 1997) p 205 [187])

The Celtic "Great Marriage" is also attested by a variety of other Celtic scholars, such as Nora Chadwick and Dáithí Ó h-Ógaín. Some historians, such as Ronald Hutton, have cast doubt upon whether Samhain was the time of year in which the magical nuptials took place. According to Hutton, the midwinter solstice was the more likely day. But whatever the season, the idea itself is powerful: ancient people explained environmental phenomena in terms of a human sexual and loving relationship. The inference may seem a fairly obvious one to a people who don't have the same scientific and biological knowledge that we do. They observed that human children come from the sexual lovemaking of their parents. They also surely observed the same for their domesticated animals. From that observation they imagined that the new growth of plants, flowers, trees, wild animals, and every other form of life in their environment perhaps followed from a similar event. Thus they created fabulous mythologies to describe that event, and projected those mythologies onto the history and geography of their world.

As another example: in the post-holes of Nordic longhouses, archaeologists often find little gold tokens, about the size and shape of your thumbnail. On them has been stamped the image of a man and a woman in sexual embrace. As described by researcher Stephen Pollington,

> These foils show a consistent image: a man and woman embracing, thought to be an icon of the divine pair Freyr and his wife Gerd. Freyr is strongly associated with fertility, wealth, and sexual love. The implication appears to be that these are amulets designed to promote fecundity, well-being, health and harmony in the household. (Stephen Pollington, *The Mead Hall*, (Frithgarth, Norfolk, UK: Anglo-Saxon Books, 2003) p 115)

Thus some archaeological evidence suggests that the building of houses and the establishment of human relationships required some kind of ritual or magical return to the beginning. And at that beginning, we find human love.

The Temple of Ishtar

Herodotus, the 'Father of History', gave a lot of space to the customs of sex and marriage in his 5th century BCE account of the history of Greek civilization. For he was concerned not only with military and political events: he was also concerned with social and cultural influences too. And it seems he gave special attention to marriage and courtship customs. If there was a strange marriage custom among some people he was studying, he mentioned it. For instance he described a Persian custom in which women of marriageable age are sold at auction to prospective suitors by their fathers. He also includes a snide remark about how the plain-looking or disabled women were offered with a dowry, instead of a bride-price, and given to the man who would accept the smallest sum: this he called "an admirable practice." (Herodotus, *The Histories*, p 121) Herodotus describes of the worship of the Arcadian goat-legged god Pan, and includes a mention of a woman who, in honor of the god, permitted herself to be 'tupped' by a goat, while a crowd of onlookers watched. Herodotus called this "a most surprising incident." (p 148) But the best known and perhaps most prurient part of his text is his description of the worship of the love goddess in Babylon. It seems that there was a certain temple where a woman of marriageable age had to go, and remain, until a man came and had sex with her. Here is the full description of the custom from Herodotus' text.

There is one custom amongst these people [the Babylonians] which is wholly shameful: every woman who is a native of the country must once in her life go and sit in the temple of Aphrodite and there give herself to a strange man. Many of the rich women, who are too proud to mix with the rest, drive to the temple in covered carriages with a whole host of servants following behind, and there wait; most, however, sit in the precinct of the temple with a band of plaited string round their heads – and a great crowd they are, what with some sitting there, others arriving, others going away – and through them all gangways are marked off running in every direction for the men to pass along and make their choice. Once a woman has taken her seat she is not allowed to go home until a man has thrown a silver coin into her lap and taken her outside to lie with her. As he throws the coin, the man has to say, "In the name of Mylitta" – that being the Assyrian name for Aphrodite. The value of the coin is of no consequence; once thrown it becomes sacred, and the law forbids that it should ever be refused. The woman has no privilege of choice – she must go with the first man who throws her the money. When she has lain with him, her duty to the goddess is discharged and she may go home, after which it will be impossible to seduce her by any offer, however large. Tall, handsome women soon manage to get home again, but the ugly ones stay a long time before they can fulfill the condition which the law demands, some of them, indeed, as much as three or four years. There is a custom similar to this in parts of Cyprus.

(Herodotus, *The Histories*, trans A. de Sélincourt (Penguin 1954) pp 121-2)

Herodotus appears to have thought this custom quite scandalous, although he thought it worthy of inclusion in his *Histories* anyway. Perhaps he thought it would both amuse and disturb his readers. But in the light of Eliade's observation that the purpose of ritual is to re-enact mythology, we may understand it like this. The sex temple of Babylon was the stage of a ritual re-enactment of a central event in Babylonian mythology. It is likely that the event being re-enacted was part of the story of the goddess Inanna. In that story, her brother, the sun god Utu, observes that the flax in the fields is ready for harvesting and for cloth production. She asks him who will harvest it, spin it, warp and weave it, and bleach it, and to each question Utu says he will do it. When she asks the last question, "Brother, after you have brought my bridal sheet to me, who will go to bed with me?" Utu replies that her husband will share the bridal sheet with her, and that her husband will be the shepherd Dumuzi. At first Inanna rejects the match, complaining that he is too 'low born'. But Dumuzi reasons with her, and invites her to sit down and talk it over. The text then makes the interesting statement that: "The word they had spoken was a word of desire. From the starting of the quarrel came the lovers' desire".[107] We do not know what the word of desire actually was, although (for my part) I suspect it was her name. But whatever it was, Inanna loved him for it. The story then passes into a description of their sexual concourse, both elegantly poetic and hotly erotic.

> At the king's lap stood the rising cedar.
> Plants grew high by their side.
> Grains grew high by their side.
> Gardens flourished luxuriantly.
> (*Ibid*, p 35)

The king's 'rising cedar' is an undisguised sexual metaphor, as I'm sure the reader can see. Yet the plants, grains and gardens mentioned here probably allude to the return of earthly fertility in the springtime, brought on by the lovemaking of the divine couple. James Frazer, who in *The Golden Bough* studied this story, observed that a divine couple who fertilize the earth with their lovemaking is a nearly universal theme in religion and magic.

> If we survey the whole of the evidence on this subject... we may conclude that a great Mother Goddess, the personification of all the reproductive energies of nature, was worshipped under different names but with a substantial similarity of myth and ritual by many peoples of Western Asia; that associated with her was a lover, or rather a series of lovers, divine yet mortal, with whom she mated year by year,

their commerce being deemed essential to the propagation of animals and plants, each in their several kind; and further, that the fabulous union of the divine pair was simulated and, as it were, multiplied on earth by the real, though temporary, union of the human sexes at the sanctuary of the goddess for the sake of thereby ensuring the fruitfulness of the ground and the increase of man and beast.

(Frazer, *The Golden Bough*, (New York USA: Simon & Shuster / Touchstone, 1996) p 385)

It seems that ancient people had their own way of saying "Love makes the world go round"!

Frazer also studied Herodotus' account of the sex temple of Babylon, and said of it that "Whatever its motive, the practice was clearly regarded, not as an orgy of lust, but as a solemn religious duty performed in the service of that great Mother Goddess of Western Asia whose name varied, while her type remained constant, from place to place." (*Ibid*, p 384). I am not sure the occasion was so 'solemn'. I find it easier to imagine a temple courtyard full of shouts, arguments, tears, orgasms, pleas, laughter, insults, giggles, screams – any of the sounds you might expect to hear from people having or wanting all that sex. It is also likely that many of the people there, both men and women, didn't want to be there, and that not all of the sex was consented to. And Frazer also repeated Herodotus' cold joke about how the unattractive women waited for years.

Some scholars claim that the historical reality of pagan sexual indulgence was probably not quite as Frazer and Herodotus describe it. According to Jonathan Kirsch, for instance: "Rituals of sacred sex, if they took place at all, probably consisted of a single act of sacred intercourse by a priest and a priestess on a holy day or at a moment of crisis such as a plague, drought or famine." (Kirsch, *God Against the Gods*, p 42) Moreover, classical pagans could be just as prudish as the Christians who followed them. In the year 186 BCE, for instance, the senators of Rome ordered an end to the festival of Bacchanalia, with its heavy drinking and its indulgent sexuality, because they thought it was a "depraved foreign superstition." (*Ibid*, p 43) It was also, I'm sure, a public health nightmare!

The Garden of Eden

All this may seem very strange and silly to most modern people. After all, we have better scientific knowledge now, and we know that ritual sex does not cause the sun to rise nor the crops to grow. Upon the advent of monotheism, did things improve? The early prophets of Judaism, for instance, seemed to have been horrified by sexuality in any form other than within a lawful marriage. The law of Moses, for instance, prescribes death for anyone who commits adultery, homosexuality, and bestiality (Leviticus 20:10-15). The prophet Ezekiel warned that God will destroy the entire nation of Israel, by delivering it to the hands of enemy nations, because of the adulterers and prostitutes among them (cf Ezekiel 16:25-41). Jesus himself says that one commits adultery just by *thinking about* sleeping with someone who is not your marriage partner (Matthew 5:28). In *City of God*, Christian theologian Augustine says that God punished mankind for Adam's disobedience by inflicting upon him the frustration of erectile dysfunction! It's worth digressing to examine the argument he makes, since the Doctrine of Original Sin is perhaps the most important teaching of all Christianity. Without it, other Christian teachings, such as those related to salvation and redemption, make no sense. I'm including some lengthy quotations here because most commercially available editions of the *City of God* are abridged editions, which exclude these important steps in Augustine's argument.

Augustine's first observation is that sexual pleasure, as a source of happiness, is unsustainable and self-defeating because:

... the lovers of these carnal delights themselves cannot have this emotion at their will, either in nuptial conjunctions, or wicked impurities. The motion will be sometimes importunate against the will, and sometimes immovable when it is desired, and being fervent in the mind, yet will be frozen in the body.

(*City of God*, Bk 14, Ch 16)

In other words: there are times when a man just can't get it up whenever he wants. So the man who thinks that the good life is full of sex will sometimes find his body not co-operating with him. This is a straightforward and obvious observation, from which Augustine draws the following conclusion:

... the insubordination of these members, and their defiance of the will, are the clear testimony of the punishment of man's first sin. And it was fitting that this should appear specially in those parts by which is generated that nature which has been altered for the worse by that first and great sin – that sin from whose evil connection no one can escape, unless God's grace expiate in him individually that which was perpetrated to the destruction of all in common, when all were in one man, and which was avenged by God's justice." (*City of God*, Bk 14, Ch 20)

In other words, according to Augustine, the fact that the body does not always co-operate with a sexually aroused person's desires *is evidence that* God punished humanity for the sin of Adam. This is the moment of the argument which I think is a plain *non sequitur*. But Augustine does not stop here. Indeed a few chapters later he repeats the argument using a series of rhetorical questions:

Do we now move our feet and hands when we will to do the

things we would by means of these members? Do we meet with no resistance in them, but perceive that they are ready servants of the will, both in our own case and in that of others, and especially of artisans employed in mechanical operations, by which the weakness and clumsiness of nature become, through industrious exercise, wonderfully dexterous? And shall we not believe that, like as all those members obediently serve the will, so also should the members have discharged the function of generation, though lust, the award of disobedience, had been awanting? (Augustine, *City of God*, Bk 14, Ch 23)

And in the next chapter, Augustine speculates that while Adam and Eve still lived in Paradise, Adam could probably have controlled his penis the same way he controlled his arms and legs.

Seeing, then, that even in this mortal and miserable life the body serves some men by many remarkable movements and moods beyond the ordinary course of nature, what reason is there for doubting that, before man was involved by his sin in this weak and corruptible condition, his members might have served his will for the propagation of offspring without lust? (Augustine, *City of God*, Bk 14, Ch 24)

How the history of Christianity would have been different if Augustine had a supply of Viagra!

But to be fair, Augustine did not choose this major premise by accident. In his mind there is a certain elegance and symmetry to God's justice. Man who disobeys god is disobeyed in turn by his own body. "Man has been given over to himself because he abandoned God, while he sought to be self-satisfying; and disobeying God, he could not obey even himself. Hence it is that he is involved in the obvious misery of being unable to live as he wishes." (Augustine, *City of God*, Bk 14, Ch 24) It is also true that Augustine was writing while the Roman empire was in the process of falling down. The great light of civilization and reason which Rome stood for was swiftly being extinguished by internal corruption and external military attack. Refugees from the sacking of Rome by the Visigoths in the year 410 BCE were arriving in the north African town of Hippo, where Augustine was bishop, even as he was writing his text. Indeed the very first chapters of the book criticize the pagan Romans for claiming that the cause of the sacking was the abandonment of the pagan Roman gods. Augustine probably wanted to console and comfort the Christians in his care, and to offer them an indestructible city in heaven to replace the swiftly collapsing city of men. Still, as I read Augustine's words directly, taking them at face value, I cannot help but feel as if the cornerstone of the city of God, the doctrine of original sin, is not made of rock, but of clay.

It is also possible that Augustine was responding to the sexual libertinism of some forms of classical Roman paganism. Various passages imply that he thought the decadent sinfulness of the people helped cause Rome to fall. It seems that the early Christian fundamentalists, perhaps remembering cases of *hieros gamos* they had heard of or seen, could not imagine what a woman might be doing in a pagan temple unless she was a harlot.

Still, certain segments of modern society continue to be informed by the same anti-sex prejudice that stems from Augustine and the early monotheists. The government of the United States, for instance, spent billions of taxpayer dollars on chastity education programs to teach high school students the merits of sexual abstinence before marriage. Alas, this hugely expensive program demonstrably did not work. The average age of first sexual contact for teens who had, and who did not have, the chastity education turned out to be exactly the same: 14.9 years. The other sexual habits of both groups, including the average number of sexual partners, also turned out to be the same.[108] Another study found that the average age of first sexual experimentation for Evangelical Protestant teens was 16.3 years; for Catholic and mainline Protestant teens the average was 16.7; Jewish teens, 17.5, and Mormon teens 18.0. The same study also reported that teens who had taken a chastity pledge were also less likely to use contraceptives, since their first sexual contact was less likely to be planned and prepared for. Therefore, those who take the pledge are more likely to have an unplanned or unwanted child at an early age.[109] Another study reported that 95% of Americans of any age or religion had sex at least once before they were married.[110]

We have a kind of spectrum here. At one end is the temple of Ishtar in Babylon, characterized by sexual liberty (and likely also sexual oppression) in the name of religion. At the other is the puritanical misercorpism of the Old Testament prophets and the doctrine of Original Sin. Neither of these poles on the spectrum strikes me as very enlightening. Yet there *is* something magical about sex and sexuality. And it should be possible to reclaim the idea that in sexuality we find something of the sacred.

Selfhood and Ecstasy

We've seen that one of the reasons why sexuality has its place in religion is because of its place in a creation story. Both the rampant promiscuity of the Temple of Ishtar, and the puritanical chastity of Original Sin, are justified by a creation story. We have two different creation stories here, of course: one appears in the Biblical book of Genesis, and the other comes from Babylonian and Sumerian mythology. I don't think the solution is just to pick which creation story is 'better' than the other. I think we need to ask the deeper question: What is it about sexuality that merits its inclusion in any creation story? I think there are five elements in particular.

First, sexuality is the biological process by which our species reproduces itself. Your very existence on earth follows from, among other things, the sexual relationship of your parents. (I know that no one wants to imagine their own parents having sex, but there it is.) They, in their turn, were created in the sexual play of their own parents, and so on, all the way back as far as you want to count. Sex happened at every link in the chain of blood and history that connects you to the beginning of things, whatever you understand that beginning to be. Sex and the conception of children is the means by which organic life renews itself, triumphs over death, and confers upon itself a practical immortality. These observations may be sufficient by themselves to explain the appearance of sex in a creation story; but there is more.

Second, sex is clearly not just intercourse and procreation. It is also the *desire* for sex, and the many (sometimes surprising) things that can awaken that desire within us. You might desire to submit to your partner and lose yourself in her, or you might desire to dominate and possess her and to own her completely. You might seek a perfect union with your lover as part of a perfect couple. You might desire 'I-know-not-what', except that you know it is found in your lover's mysterious and beautiful body, so surprisingly similar and different to your own. As with other desires, sexual desire is so often full of problems. Often it overwhelms people. Kings ransom their kingdoms, rich men squander their riches, and good and rational people do strange and reckless things. Yet even with its power to overwhelm other interests, sexual desire often cannot be satisfied. We can't have sex whenever we want, or with whomever we want. This is not just because some men have trouble 'getting it up', especially after having consumed too much alcohol. It's also a matter of never having *enough*, because the desire has no limit. You might go to fetish clubs and burlesque shows, use aphrodisiacs, play erotic foreplay games and have numerous partners, and yet still find yourself unsatisfied and wanting more. The whole labyrinth of desire, so accurately described by Hindus and Buddhists as a major source of suffering, makes its appearance here. Yet even in frustration, sexual desire leads us to something about ourselves which I think real and true, as we shall see in its next element.

Third, in relation to desire, sex is also flirting, courting, and foreplay, and the things we do to *demonstrate* sexual identity, availability, and desire. It is a fleeting touch on the hand or the face, the click of a woman's high-heeled footstep, and sweet nothings whispered in the ear. In all these things we may find a fascinating phenomenology of reality and illusion. You want to bring home a partner, and so you want to appear *desirable* to others. You also want to be desired on your own terms. But what terms are those? You might wish you were stronger, wealthier, smarter, more dashing and daring, more witty, more confident, more adventurous, more *interesting*, than you normally are. And you may want to be desired by others *as if you are* that much more interesting person. Therefore, with carefully chosen clothes, adornments, accessories, words, gestures, and postures, and so on, you may present to others a carefully constructed illusion, a fantasy. You become an actor playing a role in a theatrical production instead of an authentic self. This is an ancient game. Even the Neanderthals, in Paleolithic times, wore makeup![111] And yet this role you are playing is still 'you'; for you are the author and the costume designer and the director of this drama. Even as you pretend to be other than you are, you always remain yourself; the pretense you project reflects one's feelings and wishes and dreams. In this sense you might feel *more* authentically yourself when you play the game, rather than less. The way you see yourself, how you wish to be seen, what you desire, who you desire, and how you want to be desired by others, are very important parts of who you are. These desires reach to the highest and deepest importance, since we stake the integrity and health of our own bodies as the field of play.

The sexual game is also a field of apprehension and fear. It is the fear of going lonely tonight, of being thought undesirable, or even laughable. It is the fear of unwanted pregnancies, of sexual diseases, or of causing pain to third parties (for instance, in adultery). The power dynamics of sexual 'play' may create the fear of sexual violence. And there is also the risk of creating around oneself a fantasy world, and the fear that reality may some day cause that world to collapse. Some might try to make themselves desirable by cutting their appearance from a cloth of lies, whether big or small. Think of the woman who never leaves her house without makeup. Think of the man who tries to impress someone by saying he owns a factory, when in fact he is merely a line-worker there. Think of the man who rents an expensive car to impress a lady he likes, and tells her the car is his own. Perhaps these people 'score' more often that way. But like any lie, more lies soon need to be created to protect the original ones from exposure to reality. The woman wakes herself in the morning before her man wakes, so that she can make herself up without him seeing what she really looks like. The man at the factory needs his colleagues to play along with his story of being the owner. The man with the car needs to explain why that car hasn't been parked in his garage for a month. And those new lies will eventually need protection by more lies. Soon the liar finds himself trapped in a labyrinth of illusions. As those illusions have become part of his life, integrated into his relationships, and his sense of identity, so in turn he grows to fear losing them. Thus he builds himself into a complicated labyrinth of fear. But in the next element of the sacredness of sexuality, we may find a way to escape.

Fourth, sex is an occasion in which people open and reveal themselves to each other. We have sex facing each other: unlike every other animal on earth, except for some primates, we can look at each other and make eye contact in the midst of sex. We also (usually) have sex while naked, so your partner sees your body undisguised, in its totality, and for what it actually is, whether clean and smooth, or scarred and blemished. Yet to reveal yourself in your entirety this way is also to reveal yourself in your vulnerability. Your partner has a chance to harm you, for instance by injuring your genitalia or by transmitting a disease; she also has a chance to judge you. Thus some people feel they need to keep a protective façade in place, even during intercourse. Fetish clothes, or role-playing games, often serve this purpose. I once knew someone who owned a collection of Venetian carnival masks, and wouldn't have sex unless she was wearing one of them. She didn't want her face to be seen. (Erotic arousal revolves around what is visible and what is hidden, and when and how something is revealed or not revealed.) Yet it is surely when we reveal ourselves in our nakedness and vulnerability, exposed to the possibility of harm or judgment, that we trust most completely. Trust is risky: trust can be rejected, betrayed, or exploited. Yet trust cannot trap you in a labyrinth of fear. Moreover, in sexual intimacy your partner is open and vulnerable to you in the same way that you are to her. You are in the same position to see, to harm, or to judge her as she is to you. In mutually revealing yourselves to each other in your nakedness and vulnerability, sexual partners have a chance to liberate each other from fear. I am vulnerable to her, as I show her who I am, and yet she does not harm me; and I see her vulnerability, as she shows me who she is, and yet I have no will to harm her. This creates trust between people, which opens the way to the immensity of human love.

Sex thereby becomes a place in human life where the care of the self necessarily turns you toward others. It is the thing we do for our own needs which we cannot do by ourselves, because it is the place where you cannot have your own liberation from fear, nor your own experience of love, unless your partner shares it with you.

Fifth, and finally, sex is ecstasy. When we orgasm, bodily pleasure overtakes the heart and mind: all façades are thrown away, all other interests and cares are forgotten, even if only for a few seconds. The whole of one's being is consumed by this single and wonderful experience. (This is obviously why we desire it so much.) No other activity in human life, except eating and drinking, engages all five of our bodily senses in the same action and the same pleasure, all at once. It is here that sex writers speak of an experience 'beyond words', which for some people reaches the spiritual; it is with the language of sexual ecstasy that mystics often speak of the experience of God. Consider, as an example, St. Teresa of Avila's description of her spiritual epiphany:

> I saw in his hand a long spear of gold, and at the iron's point there seemed to be a little fire. He appeared to me to be thrusting it at times into my heart, and to pierce my very entrails; when he drew it out, he seemed to draw them out also, and to leave me all on fire with a great love of God. The pain was so great that it made me moan; and yet so surpassing was the sweetness of this excessive pain that I could not wish to be rid of it. The soul is satisfied now with nothing less than God. The pain is not bodily, but spiritual; though the body has a share in it, even a large one. It is a caressing of love so sweet which now takes place between the soul and God, that I pray God of his goodness to make him experience it who may think that I am lying. During the days that this lasted I went about as if beside myself. I wished to see or speak with no one, but only to cherish my pain, which was to me a greater bliss than all created things could give me.[112]

A better description of an orgasm you will probably never find in religious literature. The artist Gianlorenzo Bernini, in his famous masterwork of marble sculpture *The Ecstasy of St Teresa*, certainly didn't miss the meaning of Teresa's words here. The face of the saint expresses an agonizingly sexual bliss; the arrow held by the vaguely androgynous angel is pointed at her vagina, not her heart. Of course, one must be careful not to read too much into the correspondence between sexual ecstasy and spiritual bliss. Christian ecstatic saints like Teresa, John of the Cross, and Bonaventure knew perfectly well how to distinguish sexual feelings from other physical feelings in their spiritual experiences. And they tended not to describe the highest and most complete spiritual experiences in sexual terms. Teresa herself in the passage just now quoted specifies clearly that the experience she had was spiritual and not simply physical. But I do think it is the case that sexual ecstasy and spiritual bliss intertwine with each other. Both are totalizing experiences; both are animated by a totalizing desire; and under the right circumstances both may aid the other in the pursuit of their own kind of enlightenment.

We have reviewed the place of sex in the line of one's blood and history, in the triumph of life over death, in the expression of identity, in the freeing of the mind from fear, and in the ecstasy of spiritual feelings. So we have five preliminary reasons why sexuality deserves its place in the creation stories of humanity. But alas, even here, there are still ways to fall into a labyrinth of fear. Some people worry that intercourse may be painful. Some young men personally known to me (believe this or not) fear that a woman's vagina may have teeth! Some people simply fear being physically and emotionally vulnerable. Desiring a sexual encounter with every cell in their bodies, yet terrified of actually having one, such people may vent their frustrations in other areas of their lives. Think of the woman who flirts with almost everyone around her, and enjoys spreading sexually charged gossip, but runs away at the first sign that one of her boyfriends might be a nice guy. Think of the man who campaigns vigorously against legalizing gay marriage, or who starts fistfights with gay men in public places, but who secretly uses homosexual pornography when he masturbates. A recent scientific study showed that homophobic men often do have hidden homoerotic desires, and are more likely to have those desires than non-homophobic men.[113] Some people fear the ecstasy of orgasm itself: they fear the loss of control, and the takeover of the mind by the body. That fear may help explain the misercorpism in many religious traditions. In the throes of sexual ecstasy, there is no ignoring that you are a bodily being, and that you are an animal. But your priest might teach you that you are a spiritual being, whose true essence is an immaterial soul that survives death and lives forever. And your philosopher might teach you that only your mind can contemplate the truth of things, and that only when freed from the distractions and limitations of bodily life can the mind be fully enlightened. But sex has a special place here since sexual pleasure brings ecstasy and thus brings its own (rival) experience of the sacred. The question thus arises: Which is the highest and deepest truth about your existence: that you are a body, or that you are a soul?

But the question is a false dilemma. We do not have to choose one *or* the other, especially given that the body is as expressive as we have seen in an earlier study. The answers to the highest and deepest questions concerning human sexuality dwell in the Temple of Ishtar, *and* in the Garden of Eden.

9

Elders

Elderly people in our society are often invisible. They live in retirement homes, or gated 'adult lifestyle' communities, or in nursing homes and hospitals, segregated from the rest of society. Aside from a few venerable news anchors, and a few semi-retired actors, there are almost no high profile seniors in the mass media. When we pass older people on the street we ignore them, or we bark at them to get out of the way. But the relation between the young and the old is important, and worth exploring. Let me begin with a story of how I encountered this relationship in a culture both near and far from my own.

In the spring and summer of 2006 I worked as a contract researcher for the branch of the government of Canada responsible for peacekeeping and policing in the First Nations. Prior to that occasion, I had very little real personal contact with Native people. Whenever Aboriginal people make the news, it is almost always bad news. My supervisor gave me a list of the names of a few Elders that I could try to reach, and by contacting local Native Friendship centers and health centers I managed to find a few more. I was also taught that one doesn't just walk up to an Elder and start badgering him or her with questions. A specific protocol must be followed: a short and simple ritual involving the presentation of a gift of tobacco in a cloth pouch. The night before my first interview, I bought a few packets of rolling tobacco and made a few pouches to give to the Elders I was set to speak to that week.

The first Elder I was scheduled to meet was from the Cree Nation of northern Ontario. My first impression of him happened before I met the man himself. I had an appointment

215

with him at ten o'clock one weekday morning, but I entered the Native Friendship Centre about half an hour early. I had the grandiose idea that I would stand on the front steps to await his arrival, and welcome him inside. When I arrived a young man was near the door, and I asked him for some help finding the room where the meeting was to take place. When I told him the name of the Elder I was going to meet, he stood up a little straighter, and smiled a little more. Thus the presence of an Elder was already apparent, even before I met him in person. The young man's response to the mention of the name taught me that an Elder is someone who receives a quality of respect above and beyond the standard respect everyone already owes to each other.

I was directed to a boardroom near the front door, where I waited. Around ten to the hour, a tall dark man came in and said, "You Doctor Myers?" I said yes. The man then nodded and left. I suddenly realized that this was the man I had come there to see. I also realized the absurdity and the arrogance of the idea of welcoming him at the door of what is really *his* territory. I quickly gathered my notebook and followed him to the Elder's Lodge, a room in the center dedicated for the use of Elders. I started to introduce myself and describe the nature of my research. He politely interrupted me, and asked if I had any tobacco. I had just made my second mistake: the tobacco should have been offered first. So I produced the tobacco offering in the little red cloth pouch and handed it to him. This was now my third mistake. The tobacco is to be offered to the Elder in a particular way. I explained that I knew very little about First Nations culture, and that he was the first Elder I was to speak with for the project. He was very patient with me. He produced a small pouch of sage which he put into a seashell, and lit it. He smudged himself with the smoke of the sage, and invited me to do the same, which I did. He placed the unwrapped bundle of tobacco in front of him, where it stayed for the duration of our interview.

My expectation, originally, was that meeting an Elder would be like meeting a university professor, which is a context that as a young academic I understand very well. But quickly I discovered that this is not the case. There is no question of an applicant controlling the situation, or negotiating to get what he wants. The space belongs to the Elder. It is my job to meet *his* expectations, and not his job to meet mine. This, I quickly learned, is part of what it means to respect an Elder.

An Elder of the Algonquian Nation, who I met later that same week, described to me the proper protocol with which to approach an Elder when one has a question or a favor to ask. First the tobacco must be offered in the left hand, and offered in such a way that the Elder can decline it if he should so choose. The tobacco must be tied into a little cloth pouch, which must be one of the four sacred colors of the medicine wheel: black, white, yellow, or red. I was also told that part of the reason for the offering of the tobacco was not just the matter of the applicant providing a gift, in return for the service. The Elder who agrees to receive your gift shows, by his act of receiving it, that he is committing himself to helping you for a little while. It is often also appropriate to offer another gift at the end of the session: a thank-you card at the very least. It is appropriate to put some cash in that thank-you card too (and among the people I worked with, the usual amount was $200). All of these actions are expressions of respect, on multiple levels: respect for the Elder as a person, respect for the knowledge he or she possesses, respect for tradition and culture; respect for the Great Spirit who dwells both in the Elder and in the person asking for the Elder's help.

Carriers of the Sacred

Who are the Elders? What do they do which entitles them to this quality of respect? There are several answers. In the time before contact with Europeans, the Elders acted as social and political decision-makers. Anthropologist J. Noon wrote that:

The tribal government consisted of a council made up of the clan chiefs, the matriarchs and the Pine Tree chiefs, who represented the warriors. Mention is also made of a council of Elders whose decision in tribal matters was final over the deliberations of the other tribal bodies. The procedure for arriving at a decision... was first, a meeting of the women of the clan, then the chiefs and matriarchs counseled together, next, a secret session of the Elders, followed by a public mass meeting after which the decision given by the Elders was accepted.[114]

While the secrecy of the Elders' circle may seem undemocratic, law professor John Borrows compared it to the secrecy that covers cabinet meetings in democratic governments. "Just as cabinet discussions in a Parliamentary democracy may be privileged, some Indigenous legal procedures can be analogously limited."[115] The Elders deliberated in secret apparently to be able to speak their minds to each other freely. Similarly, folklorist Basil Johnston wrote that in the case of the Ojibway, Elders not only acted as an advisory body for the community's leaders, but that they also acted like a leadership selection committee:

By custom, the Elders invited a man of their choice and offered him the Pipe of Peace. Acceptance of the pipe signified acceptance of leadership, its smoking a solemn undertaking... In the exercise of leadership, a leader did not act upon his own initiative. In matters that concerned the community he was expected to seek and rely upon the guidance of a council consisting of the leading men and women in the community. These were frequently the Elders.[116]

One might still ask here what entitles a person to be respected as an Elder, and what entitles a person to be involved in these decision-making councils. The most important reason is that the

Elders have a lifetime accumulation of cultural and traditional knowledge and wisdom. It also seemed important that the holders of this knowledge be unassuming about it. "I only know a little," one Elder told me. The impression I got from this statement is that his knowledge, while comprehensive, is 'only a little' when compared to the totality of all human knowledge. He made a comparison to my own specialized knowledge of philosophy: I may have great knowledge of that field, but that's 'only a little', compared to the sum of all that there is to know. An Elder, it can be affirmed, is one who possesses a great store of cultural knowledge, but he is not normally inclined to boast about it. A little bit of modesty, or perhaps it is better to say unpretentiousness, seemed to be a necessary quality.

Most of my informants emphasized that an Elder is usually involved in a teaching relationship with various people, mostly with young people. I spoke about this with the associate director of the First Nations House of Learning at the University of British Columbia. She taught me that: "Elders are an integral part of the building of significant relationships." In her view, it is not quite enough for the person to be a holder of knowledge. He or she must also be involved in a teaching or sharing relationship of some kind. As she taught me:

What is an Elder? A relationship between yourself and one who has knowledge they're willing to share. Elder-hood is recognised in the relationship between the knowledge-holder and the person they are sharing it with. So there could be a person who is an Elder for some but not others. One must find the right kind of Elder for the purpose at hand. (M. MacIvor, 2007)

Many sources I consulted said that an Elder plays the role of the teacher particularly in relation to children. Having accumulated the lifetime of experience and cultural knowledge, Elders then

219

see themselves as bearing a sacred responsibility to pass that knowledge and experience on to the next generation. Here are two examples. Chief Dan George wrote of an experience he had with his own father, when he was a boy. He recounts how his father taught him the importance of respect for the earth and its living things:

> I remember, as a little boy, fishing with him up Indian River and I can still see him as the sun rose above the mountain top in the early morning... I can see him standing by the water's edge with his arms raised above his head while he softy moaned, "Thank you, thank you." It left a deep impression on my young mind. And I shall never forget his disappointment when once he caught me gaffing for fish just for the fun of it. "My Son," he said, "the Great Spirit gave you those fish to be your brothers, to feed you when you are hungry. You must respect them. You must not kill them just for the fun of it."[117]

Later in his life, when he became an Elder himself, Chief George began to think deeply about the children around him, and to care for them a great deal, and to see in them hope for the future. "The only thing the world really needs is for every child to grow up in happiness."[118] It is perhaps noteworthy, in this respect, that Handsome Lake, the Iroquois prophet, declared it wrong to discipline children with corporeal punishment, and declared that kindness to children must extend beyond the circle of one's own offspring. "To adopt orphans," for instance, "and bring them up in virtuous ways, is pleasing to the Great Spirit."[119]

It may be tempting to think of Elders as 'service providers'. Certainly, some of the things that Elders themselves told me suggested this very interpretation. Elder T.L. said: "What Elders do, is we care for our people." But I think that 'teacher' is a better interpretation than 'service provider'. The notion of a service provider need not imply that any direct personal relationship is involved. It isn't necessary to be friends with your gas station attendant or your bank teller. But the notion of a *teacher* certainly could have that implication. In White Canadian society people sometimes develop personal respect for teachers at their primary schools or high schools, as well as their sports coaches, priests or clergypeople, music instructors, and other adults in their life. When I was a child and a teenager, I had that kind of personal respect for J. Purdy, my karate sensei, and for P. Chataway, who was very elderly when I knew her, who founded my local community theatre. I also had that feeling for my grandparents on my mother's side, who lived in a forest and made maple syrup. From people like these, we learn things which are unrelated to the school curriculum, but these things often remain important and inspirational for the rest of our lives. Teaching, as Aboriginal people understand the term, necessarily implies a direct personal relationship. The Elder you are speaking to might be your grandfather, or otherwise blood-related to you. But he may also be addressed as 'Grandfather' by everyone in the community. (I used to refer to Mrs. Chataway as "Gran", just as her blood-related grandchildren did.) The respect which the Elder is accorded is expressed with the vocabulary of family intimacy. In the Aboriginal worldview, there must be a mutual and spiritual respect involved between the teacher and the student, between the Elder and the person who is seeking the Elder's knowledge.

Some of the knowledge that an Elder possesses is personal and experiential in character, rather than 'traditional'. Someone can be acknowledged as an Elder because he or she overcame enormous personal hardships, survived various forms of trauma or suffering, and came out the other side as an honorable person. If he or she learns to stop drinking or gambling, or if he or she learns to control anger and violence, or overcome the traumas he or she experienced in a residential school, and, most importantly, *is able to teach others to do the same*, then he or she is likely to be regarded as an Elder. Such people become valuable to the community as role models. They are admired for their perseverance, their strength of will, their fortitude, and for other qualities which are seen as necessary for the healing process. *Their presence alone shows others who are still grappling with the effects of trauma that healing is possible.* The honoring of role models is a powerful value for Aboriginal people: and of all role models, the Elders are the most esteemed.

Having said that, one informant taught me that someone could be an Elder even if in other ways he is not a very good role model:

> … what matters is that he knows stuff. A young person might be sent to spend time with an Elder, and he might not want to do it because the Elder is also a drinker, or has a bad temper. But he has the cultural knowledge.

Thus, Elders don't have to be perfect. They might have the same personal problems that anybody else has. There is no question of holding Elders up to absolutely impossible moral standards. Nonetheless, I think it can be safely generalized that Elders, as role models, are people who may be admired for the way that they have healed, or are continuing to heal, the wounds in their bodies, minds, hearts, and spirits. They are therefore valued in their communities for the way they can assist others in their own healing processes.

This final point leads me to a discussion of how someone's standing as an Elder requires the acknowledgement of a community. The surest sign that someone is *not* an Elder is that he claims to be one and demands to be treated like one. Many of the Elders I spoke with told me, several times, "I don't call myself an Elder." The first time an Elder said this to me, I thought he was trying to deny being an Elder. But he explained that it is other people who acknowledge him as such. A First Nations Elder becomes such by the acknowledgement of his community. It is simply not given to anyone to declare himself an Elder: indeed, if someone did declare himself to be an Elder, he would be seen as an attention-seeking egotist. As one Elder taught me, "No one sets out to become an Elder from the beginning." And with a laugh he added, "Especially if they knew how much work they would have to do!" Almost all the people I spoke with were very clear on the point that there is no such thing as a self-proclaimed Elder. The acknowledgement from the community is absolutely vital. Elder T.L. said, "There is no such thing as an Elder certificate. And Eldership is something no one craves. It's not a career path." No offence is taken against someone who doesn't recognize him as an Elder. But he also implied that people should be able to recognize their Elders. At the very least, "we've got to give respect where respect is due."

How, then, does someone become an Elder? How is the community acknowledgement obtained? One of them said:

> You sit at the feet of your Elders and learn from them and learn from them, starting when you are young, and continuing maybe for twenty or thirty years. Then people start to notice that you know stuff. Word gets around. Then one day someone offers you a tobacco pouch and asks you a question. (Elder T.L., 2006)

The process, it seems, is quite spontaneous and organic. There are few formalities and no institutionalized criteria, and yet there is a system which works.

Finally, yet perhaps most importantly, Elders in Aboriginal communities have a sacred and a spiritual function. It's hard to describe exactly what it is. When I first saw Elder D.R., we were in the lobby of an Aboriginal-focused public health clinic in Ottawa. I did not know at the time that he was the Elder I was going to meet. Yet somehow I knew that he was a person of importance. My attention was drawn to him immediately. He was unperturbed by the noise and the busy pace of the clinic. Rather, he was calm, composed, unpretentious; he gave me the impression of a man at peace with himself and his surroundings, no matter what those surroundings may be. When he moved to the stairs to find the room where the "Tea and Bannock with the Elders" event was to take place, I suddenly felt motivated to hold the door open for him. If by chance I happened to be ahead of him then I might have done so anyway, since it is a polite thing to do. But on that occasion I suddenly felt as if there was an extra significance in the act, and so I moved quickly to be in the right place to do it. When he was speaking to the group, it was very easy for me to imagine that there was something or someone speaking through him; something powerful, wise, and loving. I felt this way in the presence of the other Elders I interviewed as well. Another Elder taught me that this is part of how some Elders themselves understand their relationship to the Creator. "In part, it's not me speaking, it's Him, it's Her", he said, and he gestured to the sky.

As already mentioned, the most significant difference between Aboriginal values and those of Europeans, or European-descended cultures like Canada, is the spiritual dimension. Elders are people with special responsibilities for the spiritual part of Aboriginal culture and life. They are not exactly like priests or shaman or magicians. I'd like to say instead that they are 'carriers of the sacred'. The 'sacred' which they 'carry' can take many forms: traditions, objects or artifacts, traditional teachings, or even social responsibilities. In particular, Elders carry the sacred in their person, their knowledge, their presence and their character. They express it through the voice, they reveal it through the gaze. A person who, by word or deed or by his general character, appears to embody the presence of the Creator somewhat more visibly and tangibly than other people, is likely to be considered an Elder.

Most of the time Elders also carry material artifacts of religious significance such as those already described: eagle feathers, peace pipes, sacred bundles. But it is important to note that in Aboriginal society, no one 'owns' these objects. They are said to belong to the Creator, and to the community. Therefore, an Elder would normally say that she 'carries' the feather, or that she is its 'custodian':

I do not carry the feather, I do not carry the peace pipe, I do not carry the drum. The feather carries me, the pipe carries me, the drum carries me. They belong to the whole community. And so I take care of them, as a mark of respect to the whole community. (Elder D.R., 2007)

Elder L. explained to me that such objects sometimes function as outward signs of someone's Elder-hood. But they can also be used to sort out who really is an Elder from who is not. An Elder might be given these treasures by other people in the community. The Blackfoot have special ceremonies called 'transfer rites' in which responsibility for a sacred bundle is passed from one carrier to another.[120] Alternatively, the Elder may have made the object himself, in response to a dream, or a significant life-changing event. In either case, the person has to be able to account for his custodianship of the object. In Elder L.'s words:

A pipe carrier, or one who carries a feather, or a sacred bundle, has to be able to tell the story of how he got it. This is part of an Elder's 'quality control'. They may be asked at any time how they got it. Or they can volunteer the info: "There's a funny story of how I got this pipe… "

Mainstream 'Western' society does not have the same attitude toward Elders. For one thing, we do not usually call them 'Elders'; rather, we call them 'senior citizens', or (rather uncharitably), 'old people'. We also do not take care of them in quite the same way. We expect that they will have made preparations for their own old age, for instance by investing in pensions or in retirement plans. And we put them away in separate retirement facilities or in hospitals. People often respect and wish to care for their own aging parents and grandparents. But they may not have the same feeling for other people's aging parents and grand-parents. There is simply nothing in modern Western society that corresponds neatly or closely to the Aboriginal idea of an Elder. The idea of a community-acknowledged Elder, and the respect due to Elders, may be something that modernity could learn from the Aboriginal worldview.

Signs of Respect

If there is someone in your community that you regard as an Elder, treat him or her with great respect. Don't interrupt them when they speak; don't jump the queue in front of them; don't speak poorly about them behind their backs. Of course I don't mean that they should be treated with the deference of royalty. But I do think they need to be treated with a special consider-ation.

Here are a few other points to consider. Don't feel yourself under an obligation to call someone a Elder, just because other people do, nor even just because the person happens to be old. It is up to everyone on their own, and with the advice of those whose opinions they respect, to call someone an Elder, or not, as they judge appropriate. In this way, the scale of values may be flexible, meeting the needs of each local area.

If you seek the advice, the help, or the services of a Elder, for more than just a casual question or two in a setting like a pub, it may be useful to present your request in a formal and recog-nizable way, with deep respect, and with gift-giving. Although it may seem contrived, it may be very useful if the request for the Elder's help included a formal statement of some kind. You might

226

offer a flask of mead to your local gothi, or a pouch of acorns and some whiskey to your local Druid, and say, "Dear (name), I seek your help as an Elder..." In that way, that everyone knows exactly what is going on and there are no doubts that a sacred activity is in progress.

The request should be presented in such a way that the Elder can decline the request without making the petitioner feel snubbed or brushed off. After all, these are people, not gods, and if they have a headache that day, then they should be able to gently refuse the gift. The Elder could suggest a future time, or another person better qualified to answer the petitioner's question, or briefly explain the reason he is unable to help at that time.

If you feel that whatever service or help the Elder provided was beneficial, and of excellent quality, you should offer another gift, perhaps a few hours or a few days later. I think the second gift can be a sum of money, the amount to be determined by local precedents, the petitioner's ability to pay, and his or her assessment of how good a job the Elder did. (I used to give $200.) But I am also happy with the thought that it could be a material service too. Why not make dinner for her that night, or weed her garden?

Finally, I think it most important, above almost all other criteria, that the word Elder should designate someone who does this kind of community-building work consistently, effectively, and in accord with the very highest standards of excellence, over the space of a long lifetime.

10

Dwelling Places

As a child, in my free hours after school, or on weekends when I had no responsibilities, I would ride my bicycle all over every street in my village. Perhaps this is because I had many brothers and sisters, and therefore could not find true privacy in the house. But it's also true that I wanted to explore the village everywhere, and claim it as my own. My family moved to the village a week before my ninth birthday. By the time I was ten, I knew the streets by the shape of the cracks and potholes. I knew the houses by the friendly and unfriendly dogs that would bark at my passing. I knew the bushes where wild raspberries grew. In the winter I knew the shapes of the snow drifts, and the best toboggan hills, and I knew spring was coming when the cedar trees threw off the snow that covered their boughs. There was a conservation area to the west of the village. It started at the place where the Grand River cut a deep gorge through the limestone, eighty feet deep, and it went on forever. I knew this terrain as intimately as I knew the streets and tracks and parks of the village itself. I knew the sinkholes and shallow caves where I could hide, together with a stash of pebbles to throw at passing tourists. I knew how to race through the trees at top speed without crashing into the crags and steppes. I knew the overlooks and plateaus where I could watch the beaten paths, unseen. I invented names for those places, and stories of battles and romances and escapes from danger that happened there. And I had a regular route that took me to each one, in its sequence, like a sentry on guard. These were my sacred places, and this was my land.

Something about this knowledge struck me as *spiritual*, even before I knew the meaning of the word. I attended a good Catholic school, and I went to church on Sundays. I made a good show of being devout, since I knew it would please the adults around me. I suppose I believed in God, but that belief was never on the front of my mind. I was never popular among my class-mates, yet most of the time that did not trouble me. I had no interest in most of the things that interested them. Indeed I was one of the runts of the playground. In this way I lived in the school and the church and the family home like everyone else. But I also lived in my forest, among cedar trees and limestone cliffs, and stars in the clear night sky.

The Elora Gorge Conservation Area is where I made the first intellectual and emotional discoveries which deserve to be called 'spiritual'. What made the landscape spiritual was not something supernatural: I was not seeing visions or experiencing trance states. Nor was there something new every time I explored it. Moreover, the forest was not untouched by civilization. Paved roads, water wells, stone walls, campsites with electric hook-ups, and other signs of human management could be found every-where. Some of the landmarks of my route included a ruined stone factory, a ruined mill race, and a hand-pumped water well. (That well, by the way, has been filled in, and an unspiritual pressurized tap in a concrete base was installed nearby to replace it. I'm annoyed.)

Yet I think that I knew, somewhere in my childhood mind, that when I raced through the trees on the riverside at full speed, or when I scaled the cliffs of the gorge without any safety harnesses, or did any number of reckless and dangerous things with no thought of injury or death – on those days I knew that I was *strong*. What is more – when I set out and ran my regular path from one secret place to the next, and saw that all was in order, I was most truly *myself*.

Going Home

Your home is the place where you live. This definition is surely true, but also not especially enlightening: it prompts the question, what does it mean to live somewhere? And what is the nature of the relation you have with your home? A simple answer might go like this: to live somewhere means to make a certain place into the setting, the stage, the supporting backdrop of one's life. Notice that I have used the language of theatre and story-telling here. In the discussion of friendship we saw that you cannot tell the story of your life without also telling part of the story of other people's lives. That overlapping of people's stories serves as one of the ways people relate to each other. The same principle also appears in the story of one's home. You cannot tell the story of your life without also describing the hills, trees, rivers, rocks, houses, shops, and other features of your environment. The brief story of my childhood, presented a moment ago, intertwines with the story of the village and countryside where I grew up. The places of my youth appear in the story of my youth almost like characters in their own right. Indeed the places of my youth *configure my story*. For had I lived elsewhere as a child, I would have done different things, played different games, followed different adventures. Thus I would have had a different life, and become a different person. My identity is symbiotically intertwined with my landscape in the same way that it intertwines with other people's life stories.

Landscapes have stories, just as people do. Colm Moloney, the director of an archaeology company in Ireland, told a journalist that he became interested in archaeology because, "My own childhood revolved around my dad, who spent a lot of his time walking his greyhounds (and his children) around the landscape of east Cork. Every hill, river, nook and cranny had a story attached to it and he told them so well it was captivating."[121] Through landscapes, stories relate me to other people whose life stories also involve the same landscape. Some part of my story, then, is common with other children who attended the same school, or who lived on the same street as my house, even if my personal association with them was vague and fleeting. Furthermore, that relation can extend through time, not only bringing me closer to my contemporaries, but also to my predecessors. For instance, it can include the small group of Hurons fleeing the Iroquois Wars, who hid a sacred wampum belt in a nearby cave. It can include the 19th century British sea captain who built a grain mill which still stands to this day (and is now a posh hotel). I can visit my grandparent's ancestral farm and learn of their stories; similarly, I can visit heritage monuments, historic landmarks, ancient battlefields, and see the history of my nation written on the environment. My home, then, is the place where I can read a story on the landscape which is in some sense *my* story.

To live somewhere also means to *inhabit* that place. We speak of animals and their *habitats*; we speak of one territory on earth as *inhabited* and another as *uninhabited*. The word *inhabit* comes to English from the Old French words *enhabiter*, meaning 'to live somewhere', or 'to dwell somewhere', as well as the words *abit*, and *habit*, a condition or appearance. It also comes from the Latin words *habitus* and *habere*, meaning 'to have, to possess'. The English language also gets the word *habit* from these sources. A habit is like a way of having or holding oneself; a quality of one's character; a way of thinking, feeling, and moving. It is also a kind of constancy or integrity with these things, which makes them familiar and recognizable over time. In simpler terms, a habit is a way of being in the world. To *in-habit* some place is to have *habits* formed *in* that place (or in-formed by that place). It is to have a *habit* of being there, and to be *habituated* to it. It is to 'have' that place as your own, not just as a possession, but as part of your way of being in the world. (And if the place you inhabit is a hole in the ground, you are a *holbytian* – or in Tolkien's English, a *hobbit!*)

How does this happen? Following a job opportunity, a romantic interest, a school program, or a bit of wanderlust, you might move to a new city, new locality, or new country, and decide to settle there. But you do not inhabit a new place instantly. You ease into it, by walking its hills and valleys, beating its bounds, and learning its ways over time. Your senses grasp hundreds and maybe thousands of subtle details, most of them beneath your conscious notice. You do this for months, or better yet for years, until by means of perceptual intelligence you learn its character as intimately as you know the character of your own body. It might be a relatively small space, such as one's house and yard, one's workplace, and the roads between them. It might be a large space, such as an entire city neighborhood, or an entire mountain valley. But whatever the size, your home is the place to which, through your perceptual intelligence, you have become intimate and familiar, and finally habituated.

We have two ways to understand the relation to the home now: one through storytelling, another through habit-forming with perceptual intelligence. Both, I think, contribute constructively to each other. However, as the philosopher Martin Heidegger observed, our lives play out in many kinds of places, and not all of which are 'home' in a strict sense.

> Bridges and hangars, stadiums and power stations are buildings but not dwellings... The truck driver is at home on the highway, but he does not have his lodgings there; the working woman is at home in the spinning mill, but does not have her dwelling place there; the chief engineer is at home in the power station, but he does not dwell there.[122]

Notice how Heidegger introduces a distinction between the places we inhabit, and the place where we 'dwell'. His discussion of the meaning of 'dwelling' is rather obscure, but I think it points to an understanding of what it is to belong somewhere. If I understand Heidegger correctly, he is saying that our 'home' includes anywhere that our lives play out, from private lodgings to the public buildings and places of work. But the dwelling place has been 'spared' and 'safeguarded' from the busy-ness of the workplace. It serves as a refuge of peace and freedom from such things.

> To dwell, to be set at peace, means to remain at peace within the free, the preserve, the free sphere that safeguards each thing in its essence. The fundamental character of dwelling is this sparing. It pervades dwelling in its whole range. That range reveals itself to us as soon as we recall that human being consists in dwelling and, indeed, dwelling in the sense of the stay of mortals on the earth.[123]

So, the peace and the freedom of dwelling is not set only in the negative sense of being saved *from* something. For "real sparing is something positive" and "saving does not only snatch something from a danger. To save properly means to set something free in its own essence."[124] But what, exactly, has been set free? This leads Heidegger to a short discussion of "the Fourfold".

The idea of the Fourfold is that there are only four sacred things in all the world. This may seem an unusual thesis: some may want to say that there is only one sacred thing in the world (such as God), or that there is an infinite number of sacred things (sacred books, sacred water wells, sacred mountains, churches and cathedrals, etc). But Heidegger says that all sacred things are actually variations of only four primary, elemental themes. The first element of the Fourfold is the earth, which is "the serving bearer, blossoming and fruiting, spreading out in rock and water, rising up into plant and animal." The second element is the sky, "the vaulting path of the sun, the course of the changing moon, the wandering glitter of the stars, the year's seasons and their changes, the light and dusk of day, the gloom and glow of night, the clemency or inclemency of the weather... " The third element is the divinities, "the beckoning messengers of the godhead." And the fourth constituent of the fourfold are the mortals, "those who are capable of death *as* death."[125] The place where we dwell, Heidegger says, is the place where these things are gathered together into a simple oneness, safeguarded and free. "Mortals dwell in the way they safeguard the fourfold in its essential unfolding."[126]

Let us summarize our exploration so far. To dwell, to have a home, to belong somewhere, means three things. One is that you have a story which intertwines your identity with a landscape and perhaps with a history. Another is that you have habits of character formed in part by the work of your perceptual intelligence in relation to a certain landscape or neighbourhood. And third, dwelling means remaining with the immensities of earth and sky, divinity and humanity, where they are 'spared' from the toil, drudgery, and fear of the everyday struggle for existence. In those places, we may face the immensities freely, we may safely let them be what they are, and we may remain at peace with them. Such places, I hope you agree, are worthy of the name *sacred places*.

An important implication here is that dwelling is something we have to learn. Mere living, mere existing: that just happens anyway. But dwelling 'dwells' above and beyond existence and survival. Dwelling involves thriving, prospering, flourishing. And that's not something we automatically do. It's something we have to deliberately strive for. Thus after his discussion of dwelling, Heidegger turns to a long discussion of building, architecture, and urban planning. Dwelling places are not just found: they are also *created*.

As one may expect, some logical problems still remain. For not everyone has the same story about their home, nor does everyone have a chance to grasp their surroundings with their perceptual intelligence and make them their own. Someone who is the child of military parents, for instance, may have moved around too much to become rooted somewhere, as I was in my town. Some people, when they become adults, have a job in one city, a house in another city, and a girlfriend or boyfriend in a third city, and parents in a fourth. German sociologist Knut Petzold called this "multi-locality", and observed that it is becoming more common. An associate of mine who works for an international organic farming aid agency moves regularly between two Canadian cities and also Freetown, Sierra Leone. I asked him which of those locations was 'home' to him. He said, "I think I'm beyond that now." But nothing I have said so far requires that someone have only one home.

A second objection may run as follows. One can have intimate knowledge of a certain landscape, and yet wish with all one's heart to be elsewhere. Someone might have lived in the same town her whole life, and yet feel profoundly trapped in it. The town might offer too few economic opportunities, for instance. Or the people of her family, or church, or minor league sports team, or whatever, might pressure her into staying against her wishes. Think of Luke Skywalker, near the beginning of *Star Wars: A New Hope,* watching the two suns of his planet setting. To know something may not be to love it: to know it may be to despise it all the more perfectly. Against this objection, it may be observed that one's home and sacred ground may indeed be elsewhere, and you will have to adventure the world to find it, or create it.

It is perhaps only when deprived of a home that the importance of having a home becomes most apparent. A report published in 2007 showed that 150,000 people in Canada (out of 33 million) are effectively homeless, and a further 1.7 million people have "housing affordability issues."[127] The argument that most homeless people chose to be homeless is simply not true. Most of the time, people are driven to homelessness by the combination of low paying jobs and high rental prices.[128] A similar situation exists for home ownership: if income does not keep up with the cost of mortgages, a serious housing crisis can become inevitable. In Canada, between 2002 and 2007, the cost of buying a house grew twice as fast as the average income of a homeowner.[129]

Whole nations can also be deprived of a homeland, when for instance a colonial power uses its laws and its armed forces to push an indigenous population off of its traditional territory. The Highland Clearances come to mind as an example, as well as the one-sided treaties that pushed Aboriginal people of North America into reserves. Here are the words of Wetatonmi, sister-in-law of Chief Joseph Nez Perce, on the night of the loss of the Battle of the Nez Perce in September 1877, and the tribe's forced removal to a reservation in Idaho.

It was lonesome, the leaving, husband dead, friends buried or held prisoners. I felt that I was leaving all that I had, but I did not cry. You know how you feel when you lose kindred and friends through sickness – death. You do not care if you die. With us it was worse. Strong men, well women and little children killed and buried. They had not done wrong to be so killed. We had only asked to be left in our own homes, the homes of our ancestors. Our going was with heavy hearts, broken spirits. But we would be free... all lost, we walked silently on into the wintry nights.[130]

To be separated from your home is also to be separated from the story of your life and your people, from the environment where your way of being in the world makes sense, and from your meeting place with the sacred immensities of the world. This does more than increase the risk of starvation, or criminal victimization. It also demoralizes and demeans people. To be without a home, to be forcibly separated from your home, is to be separated from part of who you are. That some may be able to move on and create new homes does not diminish the tragedy and sorrow of losing one's home. It is a loss that strikes at your dignity and pride.

Thus in 1903, when the Mojave-Apache people were restored to their traditional lands after a forced exile of more than 25 years, they had a festive dance in honor of those who made their return possible, and they sang: "We have our homes, we are men again."[131]

Urban Landscapes

From landscapes, hunting grounds, kitchens, and the forest around my village, the discussion has perhaps privileged rural and small town life. What about urban life? In the year 1990, more than 50% of the world's population lived in cities. The city has now become humanity's primary habitat. Indeed the largest migration of human beings ever in the history of the world is in progress right now: the migration of the people of China from their countrysides to their cities. Civilization itself probably needs cities. No other kind of human gathering provides the concentration of people, ideas, labor, wealth, and political power that a civilization needs for its growth and expression. To understand how we relate to cities, let's look at how perceptual intelligence functions in one. An urban environment is certainly different from a 'natural' one. In forests, farm fields, and wild lands, the sounds of the world come from animals, insects, waters, winds, and sometimes fires. The smells come from animals, trees, flowers, and soils. In a modern urban environment, almost all the sounds of the world come from machines: power tools, construction equipment, trains, aircraft, buses, and cars. Loud music blares from stereos and loudspeakers in bars, houses, storefronts, and (again) from cars. Thousands or even millions of car engines create a constant low-frequency drone which can never be escaped from, not even in large parks. But if you are like almost all but the poorest city dwellers, then you probably hear very few of these machines, because you are wearing a personal music player. (And that device is, after all, another machine!) In a city, the smells come from synthetic sources, such as asphalt and concrete, engine exhaust, and the chemicals that people put in their hair. The exception to that list is probably the rank of uncollected garbage. Everywhere you see posters, billboards, traffic lights, and mass market advertising. All of these messages in the visual field implicitly deliver *commands*: they tell you how to spend your money; they tell you what to do. Similarly, while surfing the Internet your visual field is veritably bombarded by numerous short intense bursts of information, sometimes simultaneously: status updates on social networking websites, blog entries, RSS feed items, photographs, videos, animations, news flashes, instant messaging service posts, pop-up windows, and of course more advertising.

Each sight, smell, and sound is an event that the mind has to process, even if only briefly, to ascertain whether it is relevant to what you are doing, or whether it might be a threat to your safety. This contributes to making people stressed, exhausted, headache-prone, and even physically ill. A loud 'bang', for instance, might be a car engine backfiring, a heavy object falling, a gun shot, a door slam, or a sound effect from a television or radio show. You might think you are accustomed to these busy sights and sounds, and that you don't see or hear them anymore. But in fact you do, and your mind has to devote a little slice of its time to identifying and ignoring each piece of irrelevant information that comes in. In a city, there is almost nowhere for your mind to rest; almost nowhere that you can have your own thoughts. Public parks and gardens can help the mind 'recover', and can contribute to people's overall good health. Scientists at the University of Glasgow, Scotland, recently found that urban green spaces improve people's physical health and vitality. They compared

238

mortality records and income data to the availability of urban green spaces like parks, sports fields, and river corridors. They found that people living far from a green space had almost double the rates of circulatory diseases, heart diseases, and stroke, than those who lived close to a green space. They also found that the health of poor people who had access to green space was much closer to that of the middle-class and the rich.[132]

I was glad to know these facts, but they were not quite what I was looking for. So I spoke with gardeners, herbalists, and horti-culturalists. I was curious to know if perceptual intelligence is involved in their work. One friend, who works as the manager of a nursery, said:

Most people start with getting out of bed and heading for coffee. Me, I start by getting out of bed, opening the blinds and gazing at my gardens, and yes, even in the cold Canadian winters, that is how I start my mornings; then I go get my coffee. When it is warm enough to go outside, I go out into my gardens and walk the perimeters, clockwise, sipping my coffee and talking to all my green friends that are growing and flowering on my small piece of the planet. That is my sense of peace. I start and end every day that way, in my gardens. (A. Taylor, 2009)

Taylor's daily practice probably does contribute to the development of a perceptual intelligence relationship with her own garden. On one occasion when I visited her home, she spotted from across the yard the signs of aphids invading her hops. She told me that she could have sprayed the hops with a soap spray, which wouldn't harm the plant and would be perfectly safe for the soil. But she decided against it, because "if I have an aphid problem, then Hamilton [her city] has an aphid problem. So I decided to import five hundred ladybugs from B.C., the natural aphid predators, so that way my solution is good for my plants and good for Hamilton." (A. Taylor, 2009).

Another friend of mine is an artist in Montréal, Québec, who makes guerilla gardens. Just in case you don't know, a guerilla garden is a garden planted in a public space, on public property, with or without the permission of municipal officials. In a newspaper report she said she created a guerrilla garden on a small piece of abandoned industrial land in order to "add a flash of colorful beauty in an otherwise neglected spot for sheer 'visual pleasure'," and also "to show city officials that people really do care about this meadow, no matter how derelict it has become."[133] So at my earliest opportunity I traveled to Montréal to help her plant bergamot seeds in her garden, and learn more about why she was doing it. One of the things that she emphasized was the connection to people and to local community which she was hoping to establish. As she told me:

My background is in painting and performance art. My work is thus a constant navigation between the work and its effect on people. The garden helps create situations with people. It is in part a reclaiming of the commons. Not even a public park can be used for gardening. But this field is an unmanaged, uncultured space that belongs to everyone. It's a true commons... I wanted a space that is active creatively, and an aesthetic that demonstrates care of the land. When people see a sign like this garden that other people care about the space, then you feel connected, and you feel good about the city. (E.R. Michaud, July 2008)

This seemed to me an important idea: this remark suggests that her reasoning was guided by a desire to assert presence to anyone who passes by, and to prompt a response from people. It thereby encourages people to establish relationships with their landscape and with each other. Furthermore, as the garden is also the work of an ensemble of people, it is already accomplishing this goal. Indeed it would be more accurate to say the garden asserts a collaborative presence: 'We are here'. To those who might otherwise ignore the field, the garden shows that local people care about it and love it. That can be a heart-warming thought.

Among those she hoped would hear that assertion of presence are land developers and city planners, since the field in which she planted the garden is one of the last undeveloped meadows in Montreal. She therefore designed it in the shape of a Roerich symbol: three filled-in red circles, arranged in an upright triangle relative to each other, and enclosed by the outline of a fourth red circle. This symbol was invented in 1935 by Nicholas Roerich, a Russian artist and peace activist. He wanted to hang it on banners or paint it on the roofs of culturally important buildings like museums and concert halls and churches. The idea was that bomber crews during the war could quickly identify, and *not* destroy, the buildings with the symbol on it. Michaud told me that she wanted to make the same kind of statement for urban green spaces:

I decided to design the garden in the shape of a Roerich symbol to represent the idea that urban green spaces are just as important to culture as buildings are. And that public greens spaces are under threat sometimes: not by bombers, but by developers and city planners. (E.R. Michaud, 2008)

Other values were implied in her choice of what plants to sow: she selected indigenous plants which would attract local birds and insects, resist droughts in the summer, and would likely thrive despite the toxins in the soil (the meadow was once a rail yard). In this way the garden also asserted specific cultural and moral values: the goodness and desirability of shared public green spaces.

But there is one other part of a city which is usually not a green space – in fact it is almost *never* a green space – and yet can be vital for the flourishing of a community. Let us turn to a discussion of that part of the city now.

Public Service and The Agora

In *The Politics*, Aristotle wrote that the purpose of a city is to create the environment that best supports human *eudaimonia*, flourishing and happiness.

> … as our object is to find the *best* constitution, and that means the one whereby a state will be best ordered, and since we call that state best ordered in which the possibilities of happiness are greatest, it is clear that we must keep constantly in mind what happiness is. (*The Politics* 1332a6)

It is worth exploring Aristotle's portrait of the ideal city: it shows he apparently thought that the eco-physical world stands in an important relation to the flourishing of the members of a *polis*. As Aristotle describes it, an ideal city should be easy to access from both land and sea, and it should be easy to get raw materials and other goods into the city. It should be easy to survey the territory controlled by the state, for instance to see if the city is being invaded, and the army should be able to defend it easily. The site of the city should be chosen with consideration for the health of the citizens, for instance it should be sheltered from cold winter winds. Half of the territory controlled by the city should be privately owned and the other half communally owned. Half of the communally owned land should "support the public service of the gods"; this apparently means to use it for the location of temples and religious festivals, otherwise to leave it alone, as land that 'belongs to the gods'. The other half should "meet the expenses of the communal feeding." (*The Politics*, 1130a13)

Aristotle's claim that the function of a city is to provide the environment best suited for human flourishing reminded me of things said to me over the years by people who work in the public service. As I live in the capital city of my country, many of my local friends are government workers, and I asked a few of them what they thought were the most important relationships in their professions. Many spoke of the direct recipients of the services they provide, and of their importance. but almost all of them also spoke of the nation as a whole. Many have told me, over the years, that they pursued their careers in government service because they believe in the importance of building culture and community, or protecting people, or empowering people. Someone who works for a private enterprise can have such a goal too. But nearly all the public servants I spoke to felt that the private sector was too narrow, too limiting for them. As one policy analyst said to me,

> I want to work for Canada, not for some shareholder. I want to work for something that belongs to everyone. I want to help put into place the things people need to live free and decent lives. (Name withheld by request.)

To Aristotle's physical description of the ideal *polis*, we could add a social description, and populate our city with policemen, firemen, mail carriers, garbage collectors, food safety inspectors, and bus drivers, just as a few examples. These services are ways that a community gets organized to take care of itself; the professionals who provide these services contribute to the flourishing of its members. Some of those services can be absolutely essential. In May of the year 2000, for instance, the Ontario provincial government cut the budget to water safety inspections, which led to the water supply in the town of Walkerton being contaminated with E.coli bacteria. Seven people died, and 2,500 became seriously ill.

There can, of course, be more than one model of what a flourishing community looks like, and these models might compete with each other. Recall Michaud's comment about how urban planners sometimes threaten a city's green spaces, instead of protect them. But that does not refute the basic thesis here. A city is, among other things, a great negotiation between differing conceptions of the good life, played out through the way land is built upon, laws are enacted and enforced, money is exchanged, and so on. I think it fair to say that the people who help a city to flourish are people involved in a sacred relationship with a whole community, and in some sense with civilization itself. It is a relationship which contributes something, whether large or small, to the good life for everyone involved. This can run from the most visible and best paid public servant, such as a politician, to the ordinary local volunteer who gets no money and very little publicity for what she does, but still cares about her city.

To return to Aristotle: I think he would agree with the addition of a social dimension to his description of the ideal *polis*. For he also describes the features of the *agora*, the center of the town and its most important public meeting place, and he describes some of the things that should happen there. The *agora* has to be close to, but distinct from, other parts of the city. For instance, it should look down on the marketplace. No economic transactions are allowed in the *agora*, as it is meant exclusively for leisure and for publicly debating the governance of the city. Farmers and tradespeople are not even allowed to enter it unless summoned by the civil authorities, apparently because their livelihoods are too strongly rooted in material production and practical affairs (*The Politics*, 1331a30). This picture of the ideal urban environment is ethically significant because it is intimately connected with an idea of what constitutes the worthwhile life. It describes how we should arrange ourselves in the environment to maximize the possibilities for human flourishing.

Like Aristotle, I also believe that an agora is necessary for the flourishing of the people and culture of a city. We today might use Internet-based social media for mass communication, debate, entertainment, and for mobilizing people's support for public causes. But the public square has served this purpose in human life for nearly three millennia. Governments have used public squares to demonstrate their power, for instance with monumental architecture, mass rallies, parades, and the rituals of inaugurating new leaders. Populist movements have also used public squares to make their wishes known and their power visible. Think of the thousands who came to the National Mall in Washington, USA, to hear Martin Luther King, Jr. speak of his dream. Think of the thousands of people who occupied Independence Square in Kiev, Ukraine, in 2004, to protest a corrupt election. Think also of the thousands who occupied Tahrir Square, in Cairo, Pearl Square in Bahrain, or Kasbah Square in Tunis, to demand the removal of their dictators. People still need to be able to see and hear each other, and gather in public, face-to-face, to do great things together. Thus even with whole populations 'wired' to the new electronic media, nothing replaces the immediacy and power of the public square.

Of course, things do not always turn out well for the people: think of Tiananmen Square, in Beijing, in 1989, for example. Similarly, Place de la Concorde, in Paris, was the site where French revolutionaries beheaded around 1,300 people, including King Louis XVI. But these examples do not diminish the importance of a universally-accessible public domain for a community's arts, music, and language, for political action and democracy, and for culture. It is very significant, I think, that the very first thing to be placed on the United Nations list of the Masterpieces of the Oral and Intangible Heritage of Humanity was a public square: Djamaa el-Fna Square, in Marrakesh, Morocco. Its importance emerged as a stage for traditional storytellers, musicians, and craftsmen. But in the ten centuries since it was built it has been used for just about everything that has ever been important in Moroccan culture. The UNESCO description of the square says:

A cultural crossroads, local people as well as visitors use it as a central meeting place. They come for entertainment and trading – even medical treatment. Here they find storytelling, acrobatics, musical recitals, comic acts and stunts, dancing, animal shows, snake-charming, glass and fire-eating. The square also hosts fortune-telling, astrology, numerology, one-hole miniature golf, and preaching. Even dental, traditional herb medicine and henna tattoo businesses are established here. Trading includes fruit, bread, water-carrying and the rental of lanterns during the dark evenings.[134]

At night the square fills with tables, chairs, and food stalls, and becomes the world's largest outdoor restaurant.

In the public square people can see and be seen by each other: they can be *present* to each other in a way that does not happen online. This seeing and being seen, in public, while doing whatever one is doing, becomes critical for a community's social integration. Any public or semi-public space can accomplish this: from the street between your home and your workplace or school, to the restaurant, café, library, or sports arena where you can meet others, see and be seen by them, and participate in public life. Yet I think that an agora has a certain special relationship with this understanding of the public commons. It is an area in the city with an almost Aristotelian purpose: it is specifically reserved for the activities which are useful and necessary for an interesting and enjoyable social life. It is a flexible, multi-purpose public space reserved (or 'spared', as Heidegger would say) for face-to-face cultural and political inter-action. Richard Rogers, the well-known architect, described this in a small but important text on urban planning called *Cities for a Small Planet*: "Safe and inclusive public space, in all its forms from grand to intimate, is critical for social integration and cohesion. Democracy finds its physical expression in the open-minded spaces of the public realm, in the quality of its street life."

To this he added that the space by itself must be protected and supported by important civic and political values.

> Human rights create the freedom of the public space. Without them the public domain is a sham – think of events in Tiananmen Square. The free expression in urban space of a citizen's rights creates the experience of freedom and helps to protect and nurture those rights. The Greek agora constituted just such a special expression of social rights, albeit the rights of an exclusive class. The physical and intellectual accessibility of the public domain is a litmus test of society's values: inclusive and thriving public spaces foster tolerance and radical thought. It is no accident that under Fascist or similarly repressive regimes the city is segregated and specifically designed to overwhelm the individual. Sharing public spaces breaks down prejudice and forces us to acknowledge common responsibilities. It binds communities.[135]

With these comments in mind, we could 'update' Aristotle's description of the agora. Here are my suggestions.

- The buildings and main features that surround the agora should be made of materials which can be worked by hand or with simple machines, such as brick, clay, timber, and stone. In this way the agora can be a showcase of a city's local art, culture, and talent.
- It should display some of the city's best architecture, and its most important public monuments.
- The most prominent buildings that front on the agora should be public works, such as city council halls, libraries, court houses, armories, museums, train stations, transit hubs, and post offices.
- Private or commercial buildings in the agora should be locally and independently owned and operated, must

represent local arts and culture, and must support the local economy. Thus it may include restaurants, cafés, art galleries, concert halls, theatres, churches, sports facilities, bookstores, bakeries, cheese mongers, butcher shops, and craftsman's workshops.

- The agora should be pedestrian-only. Cars should not be able to enter it, except during limited hours in the early morning so that shops and businesses can re-supply. Facilities for cars, such as parking lots, may be located nearby, but must be out of sight.
- The agora should be close to a local farmer's and artisan's market in one direction, close to a green space of comparable size in another direction, and close to residential and corporate or commercial areas in other directions. Adjacent streets can have mixed residential / commercial buildings.
- It should include comfortable public seating for the elderly and for people with disabilities.
- It must be able to accommodate small-scale encounters such as Speaker's corners, casual vending areas, busking and street performing, as well as larger-scale events such as concerts, political rallies, and festivals.
- If space permits, it should include an *axis mundi*: a 'center of the world'. The axis mundi is a feature representing a community's relationship with the immensities of earth and sky, history, mythology, and time. It could be a fountain, a grand tree, a war memorial or cenotaph, a clock tower, a perpetual flame, a flagpole, an obelisk or decorated pillar, or a statue commemorating an important historical person or event.

A public space with these features might be a purpose-designed open space in the downtown core of a city, such as the great squares mentioned earlier. Or, it could be a series of downtown streets that have been closed to vehicle traffic, such as the Shop street corridor of Galway, Ireland, Toronto's Distillery District, or the Sparks Street Mall of Ottawa, Canada. Most old European cities have made their older, mediaeval centers pedestrian-only, since those streets and courtyards are often too narrow for car traffic anyway. (There are other reasons to banish cars from the agora. Cars are too noisy, they pollute the air, they obstruct the view, they take up space that should be given to people, and they make the space too dangerous to walk in.) There's also no reason why a city must have only one agora. A large city might have one or two great squares serving the whole city, and a number of smaller ones serving local neighborhoods. Towns and cities which do not have an agora can create one easily enough, if the people and the city council have enough political will. Existing streets can be closed to car traffic. Asphalt can be ripped up and replaced with paving bricks or cobblestones. Derelict buildings can be pulled down and replaced with new open spaces, or transformed into multipurpose open courtyards. Civic ordinances and zoning by-laws can be adjusted accordingly. A flourishing culture, as much as an individual, needs a home: the agora of a town or city is that home.

11

Arts, Crafts and Artisans

All our relationships involve people seeing and hearing each other, talking to each other, doing things together, and so on. Yet these relations are also assisted by material goods: the food in our kitchens, and the layout of our homes, as we have seen. Let us add books, musical instruments, clothing, furniture, and works of art. And let us add the tools that we use to make these things, and the workshops where they are made. Let us consider carpenters, potters, stonemasons, tailors, fiber-artists, needle-workers, glass blowers and jewel-smiths, and any other maker of useful and comely things. We relate to others with our material culture, as much as we do by seeing, hearing, touching, and speaking to them. And the kind of material culture that surrounds you will influence, and to some extent configure, your human relations.

Before reading on, take a moment to look around your home. No matter where you are in the world, and no matter your affluence or poverty, it is likely that most your furniture, clothes, kitchen wares, and so on, were machine manufactured from synthetic materials. Industrialization has been with us for around 200 years now, and it may be difficult to imagine life without it. So we should ask: how do we relate to our material culture, and how do those relations inform our human relations?

Craftsmanship and Pride
Bobby Watt is a stonemason, originally from Scotland but now based in Ottawa, Canada. He and his crew were hired to restore some very prestigious buildings, including the Legislature of Ontario, the Washington Monument, and the Centre Block of the

Canadian Parliament. A journalist asked him why he chose his line of work. "It really is love of the past, of timelessness. The thought that you're doing something that's going to be there long after you've gone."[136] He then quoted a few lines from *The Seven Lamps of Architecture* by John Ruskin. A trip to my local library turned up the whole quote, as follows:

> Every human action gains in honour, in grace, in all true magnificence, by its regard for things that are to come... Therefore when we build, let us think that we build forever. Let it not be for present delight, nor for present use alone; let it be such work as our descendants will thank us for; and let us think, as we lay stone on stone, that a time is to come when those stones will be held sacred because our hands have touched them, and that men will say, as they look upon the labour and wrought substance of them, 'See! This our father did for us.'[137]

Alastair Simms started his apprenticeship as a cooper (that's a traditional barrel maker) when he was 16 years old. In November of 1983 he 'came out' as a full journeyman cooper, with an initiatory welcome: "I was rolled around the cooperage in a 54-gallon cask known as a hogshead. Stale beer, wood shavings and soot had been poured in as well. After a trip around the yard I was handed my indentures, which made me a journeyman cooper."[138] The occasion must have been a lot of fun, with the other journeymen and the masters laughing along, remembering how it happened to them. Almost thirty years later, he is the very last master cooper in England. Although his material is wood and not stone, nonetheless his work puts him into a similar relationship with time. He uses tools handed down to him from previous coopers. For instance he has a topping plane which, on the basis of the initials carved into it by previous owners, he estimates to be 130 years old. The barrels themselves (and casks and firkins and hogsheads) may also be inherited: damaged or rotting barrels can be disassembled and remade into smaller casks. As he explained to a journalist: "So you're looking at somewhere between 190 and 215 years of life out of that timber. We've got this chuck-away culture we should get away from."[139]

A friend of mine who builds timber-frame houses described how he places his signature somewhere on the frame of every house he makes. Here he explained why:

My bind rune insignia is something that has evolved over time. My father has a symbol he used of his initials which he used as a mason. When I got interested in things Norse, I created a bind rune which is a combination of my initials and it is also the shape of a house. I like to put it somewhere on the frame that isn't too obvious. It is normal that few people know who built a place, so this is my attempt at a little immortality. (D. Rolfe, 2011)

When I asked him about the most important relationship involved in his work, he said:

It would easy for me to say the most significant relationship is with the wood itself. I love trees. I have been asked how I can be a tree hugger and build with wood. I feel I'm obligated to do the best I can with what the tree gives me... a few years ago I built a horse stable for a client, and one day he asked me how long did I think it would last. I told him that after about 75 or 100 years when all the regular construction had rotted and fallen away, somebody will come along and use the timber frame in a new building. (D. Rolfe, 2011)

Notice the connection, in these stories, between a craftsman's pride, the efficient use of materials (something we also saw in our relations with food), and future generations.

I asked most informants about the values that figure into their work. A mechanical engineer from England told me that a good engineer needs patience and more patience, because "without patience, you'd abandon every project," and because: "The best aspect is 'getting it right'. It's not just getting the solution, it's getting an elegant solution. There is a difference between a machine and a contraption." He also said that he knows that he has cut the metal properly when it "sings". I asked him what he meant by this, and he said, "The singing thing is impossible to explain. No one taught me, it came with time and practice. I rely upon it and it seldom lets me down." (A Poore, 2010) Mr. Poore's remark here made me think of Rupert Ross' remarks about somehow 'just knowing' where to take his fishing tour guests. Perceptual Intelligence, it would seem, has a place in an artisan's workshop too. I asked a blacksmith what he thought was the most important thing in his workshop. Not knowing much about blacksmithing, I thought he would say his hammer, since it is the tool that he handles the most, and which serves as the extension of his arm. Instead, he said that the most important thing is the fire.

> The fire is the center. An inadequate fire is worse than no fire at all. It has to be just right. I have to be thinking about the fire the whole time, and it's a process. I have to be thinking four or five steps ahead. Second is my anvil. Third is the hammer. Without those three things, you can't do anything. (Helmut, 2008)

When I asked him if he had a relationship with the fire, he said:

> Yes, it's a relationship. When my back was turned and one of the apprentices was working, I could tell by the sound of the hammer on the metal, and by the sound and the smell of the fire, whether it was the kind of fire it needed to be. I could tell

whether it was hot enough, and whether the coal had too many impurities. (Helmut, 2008)

It seems to me that Helmut was describing perceptual intelligence. Many years of practice and familiarity with his working environment inculcated in his mind a sense of what things should look, sound, and smell like when they are as they should be. This sense would alert him whenever his actual situation differs from that understanding, in even a small way. Similarly, the cooper watches the horse-drawn wagons delivering beer in his casks to a nearby pub, and he says: "They're like your children so you look at them and you think, 'Ya they're looking good.' Or sometimes you look at them and you think: 'I must catch that one when it comes back. It could do with some tender loving care.'" [140]

As I asked other questions to other informants, it soon appeared that an artisan's sense of perceptual intelligence also tells him when he had achieved excellence. I found this in almost everyone I spoke to. When I asked a friend who is a needle-worker how she knows when she has done a good job she said: "I'm not sure really. There's either this sense of satisfaction or there isn't. A little birdy says to me: *That'll do*." (L. Keane, 2011) I think the feeling of pride, described earlier in terms of time and future generations, is also a function of perceptual intelligence. It is the feeling one experiences when one's perceptual intelligence reports to you that the job is done well. Both craftsman and client can detect excellence in this way: for instance, as D. Rolfe said, "I have gotten many compliments for my work over the years, but I think my favorite one is when somebody walks in, looks up, and doesn't say a thing!"

Some perceptual intelligence regarding people and social relations are also important here. D. Rolfe, the timber-frame house builder, said:

I enjoy working with the dynamic of the many different people involved with a project. Everything from keeping employees motivated and inspired, keeping subcontractors in line, convincing building inspectors, and most importantly creating what the client is imagining. I think being able to manipulate people (in a positive sense) is probably my most valuable tool. Understanding my own, and other peoples, capabilities and using all talents to their fullest and most importantly, making sure everyone is enjoying themselves. (D. Rolfe, 2011)

Similarly, a friend of mine who is a luthier (a maker of stringed musical instruments) told me that he likes to make every one of his instruments unique. He might make two or three in the same pattern, but never more than that, and even instruments made from the same pattern will have different ornamentation. He sells his instruments, but he does not sell them to just anyone. Here in his own words is his reason why.

I have a look at the buyer for a while, and watch him as he tries out one of my guitars. I need to hear some of his repertoire, and hear his style. This is so that I can decide which of my guitars is best for him. But I also need to study how he treats his instrument. I need to see if he keeps it clean, handles it gently. I will refuse to sell a guitar to someone who doesn't treat it with respect.
(B. MacDonald, 2009)

My mechanical engineer friend told me a wonderful story about what happens when a group of capable engineers are not fully trusted by their employers.

Long ago and far away, there was an aircraft company that guarded its tools fiercely. It kept its expensive tools in a huge metal cage which was transported around the factory to where it was most needed. During the dark hours, when the human soul reaches its lowest ebb, say between 3-5 am, this store of wonders was unguarded and unmanned. To keep our spirits up, burglary was essential. After all, we had been assured by the 'Powers that Be' that forced entry was IMPOS-SIBLE. Impossible. We liked the sound of that. For the first assault, an overhead crane was employed to raise the entire cage 10 feet from the floor. It was then a simple matter to saunter in and purloin the golden tools of the great Satan. In reply, they bolted the cage to the ground. Right over a large channel cut into the floor through which electrical cables and utilities ran. A slim and nimble person could lift the covers from the culvert on the outside, worm his way under the perimeter wire, lift the covers on the inside and have free rein of this Aladdin's cave, then, carefully replacing the covers, exit the way he came in. For a long while this sufficed. Then the less sinuous members of the party, feeling left out, indulged in an orgy of lock picking, culminating in the complete stripping of aforesaid stores. By now boredom had set in. Every member of the party had more tools than you could backpack on a mule train – indeed, more stores than there were in the stores. The grand finale was to gently lower an engineer on an overhead crane to the top of the tool store, with a pair of wire cutters. He cut out the perfect silhouette of a falling man in the wire mesh roof, removing the man-shaped silhouette and taking – nothing. After all, there were other games to play. The moral? Beware of informing an engineer of any impossibility, lest he feel obliged to test the theory. (A. Poore, 2010)

I am reliably informed by Mr. Poore's wife that most of the engineers in the story were new to the job, and that Mr. Poore was helping to train them. With an exercise like the one he described here, it's clear he was teaching them more than just the rote facts about engineering. He was also teaching them to be creative, playfully rebellious, and when it is right to be proud of themselves.

And finally, a number of informants described to me how they do what they do because their projects have 'lives of their own'. The will to create something dwells deep in their minds and lives. This will may take hold of them due to dissatisfaction with the way things are done by others. As D. Rolfe said, "After working for many years in the construction industry I became bored of the dumbed-down way modern construction is done." But the will to create may also manifest in their feelings as a force in its own right. Some informants said that they don't feel fully happy unless they have a project to work on. Here is how that feeling was described by a friend of mine who is an artist:

I do art because I seem to have to. It's usually an exorcism, of sorts, of something that won't leave my head until I get it out somehow. Doing art is one of the best ways to get it out. Once it is out, I think of each piece as being like a turtle egg. I can produce the piece, I can prepare the immediate environment for it much as a turtle manipulates the sand into a nest, and then it is on its own. If it communicates at all is up to how the piece fits in with the world as the world continues to change around it. Not at all like raising a child, it is releasing the little turtle off into the wild to make it's own way out there. (N. Bertrand, 2011)

Alienated Labor

I am not the first philosopher to suggest that interrupted relations with our material culture prevent people from fully flourishing. At the risk of alienating a few readers, let me briefly visit the Marxist concept of 'alienated labor'. Think of it this way. Imagine any of the artists and craftspeople already interviewed here, producing a piece of work that he or she is proud of. Now imagine that someone else bought the materials, paid the artisan for his or her time, and otherwise contributed nothing, but then told others that he made the work, and not the craftsman who contributed the actual labor effort. This interruption is called alienated labor.

Marx's idea was that industrialization, the process of using factory machines to mass-produce most of a society's material goods, oppresses people because it separates people from things that they should be connected to. First and foremost, the industrial worker is separated from the products of his own labor. He uses machines to make things instead of hand tools, and thus he is partially disconnected from the materials and from the production process. But more importantly, he does not own the machines he uses, nor does he own the finished products he makes. As soon as his product is made, the capitalist investor, who rents the worker's labor, takes it away and sells it. The capitalist investor makes the profit; the industrial worker receives only a wage, and it may or may not be a fair wage. (And normally the wage is offered on a take-it-or-leave-it basis; the worker can't negotiate his own price.) Most importantly, the industrial worker is disconnected from other industrial workers. He can't share his tools nor teach his skills with others in a natural way, since they might be proprietary to the employer. Indeed may even be discouraged from *talking* to other workers – lest they commit a mortal sin against capitalism, and form a union! Here are Marx's own words on the matter, in an essay published in 1844.

What, then, constitutes the alienation of labor? First, the fact that labor is *external* to the worker, i.e. it does not belong to his essential being; that in his work, therefore, he does not affirm himself but denies himself, dos not feel content but unhappy, does not develop freely his physical and mental energy but mortifies his body and ruins his mind. The worker therefore only feels himself outside of his work, and in his work feels outside himself. He is at home when he is not working, and when he is not working he is not at home. His labor is therefore not voluntary, but coerced; it is *forced labor*. It is therefore not the satisfaction of a need; it is merely a *means* to satisfy needs external to it. Its alien character emerges clearly in the fact that as soon as no physical or other compulsion exists, labor is shunned like the plague. External labor, labor in which man alienates himself, is a labor of self-sacrifice, of mortification. Lastly, the external character of labor for the worker appears in the fact that it is not his own, but someone else's, that it does not belong to him, that in it he belongs, not to himself, but to another.[141]

I'm well aware that introducing Marxist ideas will strike many readers as troublesome, to say the least. While teaching business ethics at a major Canadian university, I learned that the fastest way to annoy two hundred marketing and managements students was to mention Karl Marx by name. I'm also aware that Marx himself thought that religion is but another tool by which a ruling class can oppress a working class. So contemporary Marxists might not be all that thrilled with my use of his work in a book like this one. But I wish to draw attention to the simple (Marxist) idea that when your relationship to your own labor is interrupted, your own humanity is also interrupted. Your labor, which is your ability to work, to think, to create things, and to make changes in your material surroundings, is a very large part of who you are. My needle-worker friend, for instance, described how she finds spiritual expression in knitting and crochet work:

There is a lot of joy for me in the process of having a creative idea and bringing it to fruition or seeing how it turns out differently from what I imagined, but at the same time it's the microcosm of it all that brings peace to my soul. There are days that I would like to throw whatever I'm working on into the fire and be done with it, but even if I did, you know, the world would keep turning. It is a way that I can channel all of my frustration or energy into something that I can create and destroy without having any impact whatsoever on anyone else in the world (unless, of course, I choose that to be otherwise)... Being a needle worker has taught me how to quiet my mind, facilitating my ability to meditate. It has given me an outlet for creative energies, tapping into the unlimited energies of the Universe. It has given me a canvas on which to paint good wishes and intentions to be given as a blessing to the project's intended recipient. It is a vehicle for magick, if I want it to be... (L. Keane, 2011)

The materials you work with, as this example shows, can form a partnership with you in your search for the highest and deepest things. And the products of your labor can be part of that relationship as well. They can serve as gifts to share with each other, or as signs and symbols for speaking to each other of the highest and deepest things. Now imagine how you would feel if someone took that away from you. You would lose a way of expressing yourself, a way of making your own changes in the world, a way of communicating with others, and a way of *being in the world*. Hence you would lose a way of being human, and a way of being who you are. Marx believed that alienation was inevitably part of the capitalist system. He believed that even if a contract between a worker and an employer is entered in good faith, the situation would still be alienating for the worker. For my part, I try to be hopeful. Fair and just relations between workers and employers might reduce the dehumanization effect that workers feel, equalize each party's power, and help preserve everyone's humanity. But there is another dimension to the problem, and to explore it, I must turn to the next major relationship in this grand tour of the sacred.

12

The Market

Whenever I travel to a country or a town I've never visited before, I often try to visit a local farmer's market. The character and identity, the climate, the history, and the culture of a people is often most clearly visible in the locally produced market goods: food, clothes, furniture, children's toys, decorative things, and handicrafts of all kinds. I enjoy the smell and the color of the displays, and the voices of vendors and hawkers calling out to their customers. At one farmer's market in a city in southern Ontario where I lived for a year, I got to know some of the vendors by name, and something of their lives too. The cheese monger who I regularly visited had around a hundred species of cheese available, most of which he produced himself. One day I asked him to recommend a cheese that could be served on its own at a dinner party. He gave me a block of Havarti spiced with sun-dried tomato, and a wedge of Appenzeller. The latter I had never heard of before. From then on, whenever I went to market, I asked him to recommend something to me. Another vendor sometimes gave me subtle signals, not seen by other less regular customers, to let me know if the bread I picked out was getting old and stale. If it was, I'd put it back and get another one. When the other customers were out of earshot, she said to me: "The good ones get sold to the regulars, and the stale ones get sold to the tourists who visit a farmer's market once in a blue moon and don't know what they are doing."

I don't wish to give the impression that all vendors at farmer's markets treat all their regulars this way. It took over a year to earn the rapport with the vendors that I just described. Even so, there were still a few vendors I visited each week with whom I barely exchanged any words at all. But it does seem true that in a local market, the relationships among people and their material culture can flourish in a way that they cannot do in a commercial supermarket. The anthropologist Marvin Harris wrote, "Giving and taking, or exchange, is the glue that holds human societies together".[142] Sophisticated systems of co-operation emerge as exchange becomes bonding, friendship, and eventually political alliance. Consider, for instance, food as a basic commodity that we all need. Hunting, gathering, planting and harvesting, cooking and preparation, and so on, all require group effort. They therefore also require ways for people to trade with each other. For millennia, it has been the case that to share food is also to share time and labor, agricultural land, and living space, and this sharing of material goods calls for communication, co-operation and friendship, and ultimately for the holding-in-common of ideas and values. In ancient Irish Celtic society, for instance, people were housed, clothed, and fed by an economic system of redistributive exchange and barter. Food and other valuable material goods would be collected by a wealthy tribe or clan leader, and then distributed again to everyone in a lavish feast called the *tarb-feis*. This event was also an occasion for political debate, religious ceremony, and for storytelling and music. These feasts would last for days or even weeks. They are the setting for some of Irish mythology's most well-known and funniest tales. Other cultures had similar customs, such as the *potlatch* ceremony of native tribes along Canada's west coast. The contemporary farmer's market is similar: it too is a venue for musicians and performers (we call them buskers when we find them in public places), and for charity fundraising drives, military recruiters, political campaigners, and almost any kind of cultural phenomena that you can think of. Most of all, it is a venue for *talking*. People talk to the vendors and to other customers about everything: the quality of products, the news, the weather, jokes, gossip, even the events in their personal lives and in the lives of their families. In this way they get to know each other: perhaps only superficially at first, but over time, more deeply.

Harris claims that this process began in the societies of our ancient proto-human ancestors of Paleolithic times and earlier. They probably traded sex, food, and grooming services the way modern chimpanzees and other primates do. Trading these things prepared them for group life, and forced the development of memory, attention, and intelligence. Once our ancestors' lives became governed more by language and culture than by genetic evolution, then long-term relationships could be formalized. We could keep accounts of our transactions, and also exchange material goods and services in return for immaterial rewards like 'status' and 'prestige'. Harris says,

> ...once cultural takeoff had been passed, exchange relation-ships could evolve rapidly into different kinds of economic transactions: gift exchange, barter, trade, redistribution, taxation, and eventually buying and selling, salaries, and wages. And to this day it is exchange that binds people into friendships and marriages, creates families, communities, and higher order political and corporate bodies.[143]

A modern business, according to Harris, is a product of this process. It takes informal relations of material exchange and turns them into formal commitments with legal status, such as firms, contracts, enterprises, and corporations. This helps everyone involved be clear about what to expect from each other, and helps us deal with people who are otherwise anonymous strangers. It also clarifies what is to be done about people who don't hold up their side of a bargain.

Having said all that, the economic ties between people should be taken in their proper context. Some of our most important relationships, such as the bonds of love and friendship, nationality and citizenship, family life, and the like, are *not* primarily economic relationships. Economic ties strengthen them sometimes: for we also believe, for instance, that friendship is shallow and false if the friends are not willing to share their toys with each other. We can expect that our friends will help us in times of need, and we expect that we will have to help them in their need. But a society in which all human relations are reduced to material transactions would be a horrible place to live. Respect and prestige would be connected to wealth instead of to honor and integrity. People would be more calculating, and less loving. And the rich would probably rule the world, whether personally qualified to do so or not.

Distinguishing Local from Global Markets

Much of what I have said here about the benefits and joys of the market applies only to a local community market, and not to the global capitalist market. These two kinds of market are very different from each other. In the community market the money-investor is the direct producer; in the global market, it is an unrelated shareholder. The products for sale in a community market are usually foods and handicrafts, for which there is a natural need. In the global market, the product can be anything at all, even if there is no natural need for it, and even if the product is hazardous to human health – cigarettes, for instance. In the global market, the demand for superfluous products can be artificially stimulated with advertising. But in a local market, there are few superfluous products to be seen, if there are any at all. And the nature of the advertising is very different. The relation between seller and buyer is face-to-face in the community market; you get your product information face-to-face, and you can sometimes haggle the price face-to-face. In the global market, that relation is nearly non-existent. The kind of rapport I had with some of the vendors at my local farmer's market simply cannot be replicated in a national chain supermarket, not even in theory. The worker who made the product lives far from the point of sale, perhaps in a foreign country, as does the manager who fixes the price. And product information comes from the mass media, especially from advertising, again managed by faraway anonymous people. In a community market, the sign above the vendor's table or the storefront door is custom-made, and perhaps even handmade. Above the entrance to a corporate franchise outlet, the sign conforms to a fixed brand-logo standard. The labor needed to produce the goods of the community market comes from those who own and sell the products on offer, and their friends and family members. In the global market, the work is done by machines and by unrelated workers, who the management can dismiss and replace almost at will (even if the workers have the protection of a union). The community market meets in public places like neighborhood shops, or even in the public streets. The global market sells its wares in private-property installations, like shopping malls and industrial estates, under the surveillance of closed-circuit television cameras, security guards, and detectives. The products you buy in a local market are packaged in recyclable bags and wrappings. Almost all the cheese and meat I buy in an Ontario farmer's market, for instance, gets wrapped in a plain reddish-brown paper, locally produced for the purpose. Commercial products in the global market come in machine-manufactured packages of synthetic materials such as plastic, all stamped with the corporate logo. Finally, the *sounds* you hear are different in the two kinds of markets. In a global market store, you hear prerecorded music on public address systems, and sometimes announcements for special offers or for price-checks at the cashier station. Other customers' voices are sharper, more demanding, even ruder. In a local market, the music comes from live performers busking, and people's voices are more polite. At the same time, vendors are not under a corporate requirement to always be nice to all customers, and they happily tell off the belligerent ones!

The list can go on, but I trust that the point is clear. In every significant point of difference, that local community market presupposes face-to-face human relationships between people, accompanied but not limited by the material goods and services being traded. The global market, by contrast, systematically excludes the face-to-face relationship, except where mediated by institutions, and persons acting as agents of an institution. The kinds of relationships that can happen in a local market are almost entirely impossible in a global market.

A primary difference, I think, between the local community market and the global market has to do with the role of profit. The profits of a community market are collected mainly by the producer himself and his associates, redistributed to his family and friends, and most of it is spent locally. Profits from sales in the global market are returned to distant unrelated stockholders, and are spent by them and by the corporate head office. In the local market, profit is only one of the goals that people aim for. There is also friendship, health, community, and culture, and the goods for sale are instruments for the affirmation of these values. In the global market, profit is the only incentive, and the only value. Other values like sustainability and growth potential may feature in the strategic plan of a corporation, but they are valued only insofar as they promote increasing profit. An investor might be motivated by several interests: humanitarianism, for instance, if he believes that the enterprise provides a necessary and beneficial public service. But he won't run his business into the ground in order to continue providing it. He might sponsor a public good such as an environmental reclaiming project, if he believes in the environmental cause. But he also gains some publicity for his business that way, as well as a significant tax write-off. On the whole it is profit which drives the corporate investor, and not culture.

The Financial Crash of 2008

We live in a global capitalist market. It is the system that houses, clothes, feeds, employs, and enriches us. Those who doubt the perfection of the capitalist system, or who call its profit incentive into question, are always pushed to the side, ignored, laughed at, or rejected. If they persist in their questions and doubts, they may be attacked: labeled as 'communists', or even as 'traitors'. The most virulent and hateful of attacks are always directed at those who pose a threat to the highest and deepest of our beliefs. And yet the real mavericks of society are not those who aggressively defend the status-quo, but rather those who aggressively question it, often at great personal risk. So at the risk of losing all my friends, and maybe most readers of this book, let us examine the extent to which the global financial collapse of 2008 follows the logic of the labyrinth of fear.

In that year, several of the world's most important stock exchanges crashed. The price of petroleum, the most important strategic resource in the world, had become unsustainably high, and forced the prices of other goods to rise. Yet wages and salaries did not rise with the rising cost of living. At the same time, unscrupulous money lenders in the United States, encouraged by a lack of market regulation, sold 'sub-prime' mortgages to low income people. One company, First Alliance, spent millions of dollars annually to target people who had defaulted on other loans, or who were late with their taxes, in order to sell them a sub-prime second mortgage.[144] Eventually other companies jumped on the bandwagon, and few paid attention to the risks. But as more and more borrowers became unable to pay their new mortgages, and unable to pay the hidden fees, more and more people defaulted. The lenders found themselves unable to repay their own creditors. Then other sectors that depend on the financial sector were affected, such as manufacturing and international trade. Some of the world's oldest and most stable banks and corporations went bankrupt.

Lehman Brothers Bank, for instance, declared insolvency on 15th September 2008, and soon afterward ceased to exist. The World Bank later reported that the demand from rich countries for the products of poor countries dropped to its lowest point in 80 years.[145] There was a 63% rise in mortgage foreclosures in the United States in 2008: more than a million homes were lost, and the foreclosure process was initiated on two million more.[146] Homeowners across America put their house keys into their mail-slots and simply walked away, often leaving behind computers, cars, and plasma televisions. 3.6 million American jobs were lost from December 2007 until the end of 2008.[147] In only one month, June of 2009, just as most economic indicators were beginning to recover, another 467,000 Americans lost their jobs.[148] By the end of 2009, the poverty rate rose to 14.3% of the total population, or 43.6 million people: the highest it had been in more than half a century.[149] It is March of 2011 as I write these words, and all the signs of economic recovery I have seen so far have been superficial, and few.

In the situation leading up to the sub-prime mortgage crisis, every element of a free market was in place. Material resources were allocated efficiently, government regulation was drastically scaled back, taxes were reduced, consumer demand was measured and met, and competent investors were profitably rewarded. Yet the result was not a prosperous society for everyone: the result was a planet-wide economic collapse. The very structure of the capitalist system allows an investor to withdraw more money from the economy as profit for himself than he deposits in the economy as investment. The system remains stable so long as the total investment money deposited by everyone in the game outweighs the total profit that everyone withdraws. But this stability never lasts long. Economic growth always inevitably runs up against the limits of reality. These include the limits of non-renewable resources, and the limits to an ecosystem's ability to renew itself and absorb pollution and waste. Another such limit of reality is the willingness of poor people to tolerate their poverty, as we saw in Tunisia, Egypt and Libya in February of 2011. In the case of America's sub-prime mortgage crisis, the limits to growth were the productive economy's ability to support non-productive financial speculation, and the ability of poor people to pay their debts. When limits to growth like these become apparent, investors fear the loss of their profits. So they start withdrawing more profit from the system than they deposit as investment, in a race to squeeze as much profit as possible before the limit is reached. The result is a credit crisis which, depending on how large the bubble was when it burst, can bankrupt a sovereign nation. These crisis events are not accidents or flukes. In the words of Nouriel Roubini, professor of economics at New York University, "crises are part of capitalism's DNA. They are not the exception but rather the rule. Many elements vital to capitalism, like innovation and risk taking, also trigger frequent collapse. And what we just went through could get much worse in the future."[150] Thus in the credit crisis of 2008, we can clearly see the operations of the labyrinth of fear. Investors did what they thought was in their interest, with very little government regulation or interference, but produced a situation that made millions of people suffer.

After Lehman Brothers Bank declared bankruptcy on 15th September 2008, the crisis was unignorable. A number of people with great personal stake in the capitalist system began tentatively admitting its flaws. Alan Greenspan, former chairman of the US Federal Reserve bank, admitted that the free market cannot police itself. When asked by a US Congressman, "Do you feel that your ideology pushed you to make decisions that you wish you had not made?" Greenspan answered, "Yes, I've found a flaw. I don't know how significant or permanent it is. But I've been very distressed by that fact." When asked if he was wrong about his support for de-regulation of the lending market, he said, "Partially".[1521] Mervyn King, governor of the Bank of England, later blamed the banks for exploiting "gullible or unsuspecting" customers.[1532]

Religious literature is filled with condemnations of profiteering. The prophet Isaiah, for instance, invokes of God's judgment upon those who "grind the faces of the poor" (Isaiah 3:15). In China, the sage Confucius taught that: "The superior man understands righteousness; the inferior man understands profit."[155] Jesus Christ told a questioner that: "It is hard for a rich man to enter the Kingdom of Heaven... it is easier for a camel to go through the eye of a needle than for a rich man to enter the kingdom of God." (Matthew 19:23-4) Similarly, he taught that God's blessing is bestowed not on the rich, but on the poor (Luke 6:20). Poverty can obviously be an impediment to happiness, but wealth is not necessarily an asset. Indeed wealth can create new problems, such as an insatiable drive to acquire yet more wealth. But wealth is clearly not the same as happiness: once your basic needs for survival, comfort, and dignity are met, and perhaps a few minor vices can be had, owning more will not necessarily make you happier. If you tie your sense of self-worth to your wealth, and then lose your wealth, you will lose your sense of self worth too. This truth seemed grimly symbolized in April of 2009, when David Kellermann, the Acting Chief Financial Officer of Freddie Mac, one of America's largest mortgage lending corporations, committed suicide.[156]

If you wish to engage in business as a whole human being, then the community market is the model to follow. A businessperson is at the same time a human being, a member of a family and a community, a citizen of his country, and a living and breathing part of the world. Therefore the normal rules of human morality still apply to him: he cannot escape them by claiming, "It's nothing personal, it's strictly business." A businessperson's decisions, then, must take moral considerations into account. That is, it must take into account the respect we owe to others and the empathy we (ought to) feel for them. A businessperson can choose to sell goods and services which fill genuine human needs, produce them in ways that do not unduly exploit workers and suppliers, and charge a fair price to buyers. He can choose not to psychologically manipulate people with advertising. He can choose to eliminate as much as possible any harmful side effects his industry is likely to cause to civil society or the environment. This may mean that when self-interest and profitability come into conflict with other considerations, self-interest and profitability may have to give way. But this too should not be surprising. Doing the right thing can sometimes be costly and hard, and this is true of business just as it is true of friendship and love and all of our other relationships.

13

Soldiers and Warriors

Having built our community and populated it with families, neighbors, artists, craftspeople, and other relations, it seems appropriate to think about how to protect it. On a national scale, we often find that a nation's identity and pride and history is very often bound up with its military. Its most important civic holidays, its revered heroes, its monuments and commemorative structures, and its relation with other communities, are often the products of its wars and battles. This can be true even if the decisive battles were lost and the wars were humiliating defeats. For this reason I turn next to the relations of soldiers and warriors.

Ancient Warriors

The Greek philosopher Posidonius, as he traveled the world to learn about different cultures and customs, attended a warrior's feast in Celtic Gaul. Halfway through the evening, he saw two men stand up to test each other's swordsmanship skills, after one jokingly boasted that he was a better fighter than the other. Posidonius related the story like this:

> ... the Celts often engage in single combat at their feasts. This usually begins as a friendly contest with the warriors striking each other in good fun. But sometimes blood is spilled, tempers get out of control, and the two combatants will try to kill each other, unless their friends step in and separate them.[157]

In Celtic Gaul, losing even a play-fight among friends might entail a loss of prestige and honor. The 'friendly' play-fighting that Posidonius observed became more serious and dangerous with each blow landed. Eventually, one of them was killed.

The instinct for honor in this kind of situation assumes that honor is won through competition, and assumes that second place is the same as last place. The ancient Celtic warrior could not stand humiliation. Yet the notion of honor in these societies was very complex and could also manifest itself as loyalty to one's friends, and to one's lord, and a willingness to die to protect them. We have already seen some of this ethic in the discussion of friendship, and of respect for Elders. It is likely that the two warriors who Posidonius observed in the bar brawl had been friends their whole lives and had risked their necks to protect each other many times. Yet honour also made them unable to tolerate a threat to their pride or reputation.

Another view of the Iron Age 'warrior path' can be found in an Irish wisdom-text in which Fionn MacCumhall advises a younger unpopular member of his retinue. Here Lady Gregory's poeticized translation of the whole speech.

If you have a mind to be a good champion, be quiet in a great man's house, be surly in the narrow pass. Do not beat your hound without cause; do not bring a charge against your wife without having knowledge of her guilt; do not hurt a fool in fighting, for he is without his wits. Do not find fault with high-up persons; do not stand up to take part in a quarrel; have no dealings with a bad man or a foolish man. Let two-thirds of your gentleness be showed to women and to little children that are creeping on the floor, and to men of learning that make the poems, and do not be rough with the common people. Do not give your reverence to all; do not be ready to have one bed with your companions. Do not threaten or speak big words, for it is a shameful thing to speak stiffly unless you can carry it out afterwards. Do not forsake your lord so long as you live; do not give up any man that puts himself under your protection for all the treasures of the world. Do not speak against others to their lord, that is not work for a good man. Do not be a bearer of lying stories, or a tale-bearer that is always chattering. Do not be talking too much; do not find fault hastily; however brave you may be, do not raise factions against you. Do not be going into drinking-houses, or finding fault with old men; do not meddle with low people; this is right conduct I am telling you. Do not refuse to share your meat; do not have a niggard [a greedy person] for a friend; do not force yourself on a great man or give him occasion to speak against you. Hold fast to your arms till the hard fight is well ended. Do not give up your opportunity, but with that follow after gentleness.[158]

MacCumhall's advice here is generally practical and straight-forward. It is certainly a product of its age, for instance it presupposes certain class divisions (the 'low people', the 'high-up people', etc). Yet as you can see, it emphasizes fair play, respect for non-warriors, generosity, loyalty, and the preservation of one's dignity. Significantly, it ends with a non-violent moral value: gentleness.

We've seen how friendship, in Bronze Age and Iron Age warrior societies, is often created by shared military adventure. The literature of such societies emphasizes the importance of friendship perhaps because you rely on your friends to protect you in battle. Friendship can be a matter of life-or-death. We should look at the Iron Age warband for a while, as it seems to be the most important social organization in a warrior society, and tightly involved with tribal affiliation and blood kinship. As Pollington observed:

The smallest military unit above the individual warrior was the 'warband', possibly represented in Old English by the term *werod*, derived from the verb *werian*, 'defend, protect' and denoting a group of men which stands together for mutual protection. The usual number for such a group is between six and ten men (platoon strength, in modern terms) – any less and they are ineffective, any more and they will not cohere as a unit. It may be presumed that the men of the *werod* knew each other well, trained together, lived, ate and slept together when on campaign and were sworn to mutual protection.

(Pollington, *The English Warrior*, p 81)

The loyalty of a *werod* members to each other was very strong: Pollington observes that the members owed personal allegiance to their chieftain before their own families (*Ibid*, pp 83-4).

Companionship and loyalty among fighters in a warband can be found elsewhere too. Among mediaeval knights, loyalty to each other seems also to have been reinforced by arranging the fighting teams such that everyone has different yet mutually complimenting skills. Historian Franco Cardini described how this worked in mediaeval codes of chivalry:

The *Song of Roland* offers a first important model of the codification of the *ritterliches Tugendsystem* – the chivalric system of ethics. It turns around the two poles of *prouesse* (valor) and *sagesse* (wisdom), or the particular variety of wisdom sharpened by experience usually expressed in terms of prudence. The terms are complimentary; when they are both present and in harmony, the result is *mesure*, controlled equilibrium. The valiant knight who is not wise is a madman; the wise man who cannot show proof of valor is vile.

(Cardini, cited in Le Goff, *Medieval Callings*, trans. L. Cochrane (U of Chicago Press, 1990) p. 81)

While this idea of chivalry appealed greatly to the mediaeval fighting man, very few people would possess both qualities at the same level of excellence. Thus very few people would attain *mesure* on their own. But the solution to this problem was fairly straightforward. An individual knight might not achieve *mesure* on his own, but a team of knights banded together could. Thus, a knight who was courageous but perhaps not too bright would be matched with a knight who was a little more thoughtful, if not as physically strong. As Cardini explained: "The perfect knight was less an individual than he was the result of what Cicero, St. Bernard, and Ailred of Rievaulx all defined as *amor socialis*, which coincided with the *notitia contubernii*, group spirit or *esprit de corps*." He also added that this principle of *esprit de corps* is "both the innermost and the most obvious meaning of the image of two knights on one horse on the seal of the Order of Templars." (Ibid. pg. 81-2) Two knights could be assigned together because of the way their different skills complemented each other. As they worked together, they would (presumably) grow to trust and to respect each other. A 'bond of brotherhood' would emerge.

It's not well-known, but there is an English martial arts tradition as well. In the sixteenth century, teachers of English martial arts were organized by a body called The Company of Maisters of the Science of Defence. In many ways this body acted like a trade guild: setting standards for excellence and professionalism, and also preventing non-members from teaching (to preserve its own members' employment). They also apparently ran friendly inter-club tournaments. The Company of Maisters did not make the legal status of a full trade guild due to various historical circumstances which need not be mentioned here. But some of its teachings on the social and personal importance of the martial arts were preserved in the letters that Maisters wrote to their students and to each other. One teacher known only by the name of 'Silver', for example, wrote that the martial arts not only benefited people in terms of self-protection, but also in terms of their physical and mental health:

The Noble Science of Defence is to be preferred next to Divinity: for as Divinity preserveth the soul from hell and the devil, so doth the Noble Science defend the body from wounds and slaughter. And moreover the exercising of weapons putteth away aches, griefs, and diseases, it increaseth strength, and sharpens the wits, it giveth a perfect Judgement, it expelleth melancholy, choleric, and evil conceits, it keepeth a man in breath, perfect health, and long life.

Like many Oriental martial arts, the English Science of Defence also taught moral and philosophical principles. Here's a general example from a teacher named 'Egan':

Pugilists! [Boxers!] As your endeavours may stimulate you to improve in your science, be not unmindful to increase in character. Lift not your arm against the weak, intemperate, or the ignorant, who might provoke you to ridiculous combat...

The English martial-arts teachers seem to have emphasized prudence as a value for fighters, alongside courage and fighting skill. Prudence, as they described it, is the quality which enables the fighter to know how much force to use, when to use it, and when not to use it.

[Silver] There is no doubt but that the honourable exercise of the weapon is made right perfect by means of two things, to wit: Judgement and Force: Because by the one we know the manner and time to handle the weapon, and by the other we have the power to execute therewith, in due time with advantage.

[Lonnergan] Let courage and prudence be your insepa-rable guides in the execution of your attacks, defenses, and counter-attacks.

[Brown] Simplicity is efficiency's best friend.

English martial-arts teachers also discouraged bragging and boasting:

[Egan] Keep from boasting as it not only shows weakness of mind, but generally ends in disgrace.

[Lonnergan] Self-opinion is often hurtful, yet none at all is much more so... Be not over elated by the attacks you succeed with, nor despise those that succeed against you.

[Godfrey] True honour must be very intimate with honesty.

Finally, the Maisters observed that when a fighter kills someone, even in self-defense, the killing will affect his own mind.

[Godfrey] There is a Consciousness attends all actions, which is the strongest monitor; and that Consciousness will not leave a man undisturbed after his fellow-creature is laid bleeding at his feet, though from the highest provocation, and in his necessary self-defence.[159]

It appears safe to generalize that the 'warrior path' is concerned with courage, prudence and discipline, that is, with the knowledge and the talent to do no more and no less than what is necessary to protect oneself. Although there is perhaps not enough material with which to make a definitive summary statement, it seems that the preservation of these values is the root of one's honor. Indeed, these values appear more important than the capacity for deadly violence.

Modern Soldiers

I wanted to know if the soldiers in modern armies think similarly. I wanted to know what kind of people they are. So I interviewed a few soldiers myself. I asked a man who had done several tours of duty with the Canadian forces in Afghanistan why he joined the army. He answered:

I always had an interest in the military, ever since I was small. The idea of it fascinated me as I read through the stories and watched the movies. The British Empire especially grabbed me, the idea of exploring the world and the colonies and the battles and so forth. I remember reading a magazine about the Napoleonic Wars one summer over and over and over again. I loved it. Then when I was old enough, I joined the cadets and later the reserves. Soldiering stopped being fantasy and became reality, and it was an easy transition. It would be nice to say I had some altruistic reason to join up, but truth be told I wanted to soldier and be a soldier. That's about it really. (G. Barber, 2010)

A number of my informants also spoke of the sense of adventure, and of a desire to be part of "what's going on in the real world." Psychologist and philosopher William James, in *The Varieties of Religious Experience*, wrote of this feeling:

War and adventure assuredly keep all who engage in them from treating themselves too tenderly. They demand such incredible efforts, depth beyond depth of exertion, both in degree and in duration, that the whole scale of motivation alters. Discomfort and annoyance, hunger and wet, pain and cold, squalor and filth, cease to have any deterrent operation whatever. Death turns into a commonplace matter, and its usual power to check our action vanishes. With the annulling of these customary inhibitions, ranges of new energy are set free, and life seems cast upon a higher plane of power. (James, *The Varieties of Religious Experience*, p 283)

A sense of adventure, it would seem, and a sense of life 'on a higher plane', motivates some people to become soldiers. There are perhaps few other situations in which the highest immensities we know, life and death, are so constantly at stake. The desire to experience life at that higher plane can create in volunteer soldiers a strong desire to be on the front line of a battlefield: they actually *want* to fight the war. As a former American soldier told a journalist: "The root cause of the misunderstanding [between soldiers and civilians] is that the average person wouldn't actually want to volunteer for the military, so they don't understand that motivation to fight in a war zone in the first place."[160] But another soldier explained his motivations in these terms: "It's not like I was bloodthirsty and wanted to hurt people," he said. "It was more of a camaraderie feeling for me to fight alongside my brothers, travel to different countries and serve my duties as a Marine."(*Ibid*) Many soldiers who served in administrative or support positions, instead of in combat, returned to civilian life feeling disappointed, and sometimes even ashamed. It can be hard to explain this feeling to civilian friends.

Perhaps that sense of life 'on a higher plane' also explains why soldiers often speak of friendship and loyalty as the highest of their values. As another soldier told the BBC: "Everybody knows that at one point that your life could depend on the person next to you or vice versa. You don't feel that at a desk job." (*Ibid*) Every solder I spoke with described team unity and friendship as the highest of their values. When I asked why, they told me that fighting a war creates bonds of friendship and trust between people on the team which, my informants say, become stronger than any other kind of bond they know. The root of this bond appeared to be the knowledge that their buddies will die to protect them, and the knowledge that they themselves may have to die to protect their buddies. This theme recurred in just about everyone I spoke to. For instance, a woman who had been a signals officer in the Canadian navy told me what she thought was the most important relationship on a combat ship:

> I think it's the guys that you're with, in your unit or platoon, or on your ship. It all comes down to you and your mates. You can take away the kit and the vehicles and the arms, you can take everything else away, but if you take away your buddies, then you can't do anything. (K. Herlt, 10 Jan 2009)

Another informant told me a similar story. Combat solders tend to be proud of the fact that they have to do the hardest work, he said. They carry the heaviest gear, eat the worst food, sleep in the most uncomfortable conditions, go without showering or changing clothes for weeks, and get the most dangerous missions. These experiences, coupled with the aura of life-and-death that warfare imputes upon everything they do, makes life seem heightened, enlarged. The language of metaphysics finds a place here: this informant thought that civilian life, with its luxuries and comforts and distractions, was 'unreal'. He also thought regular civilian life effectively emasculates men, and makes them no longer real men. (I only paraphrase here: his actual words were not so polite.)

Some soldiers assert a curious relationship with their vehicles and equipment. As the soldier who had toured Afghanistan told me:

> The most important relationships I've found in soldiering are a split between the feeling of companionship with your comrades and your equipment. In my case as an armoured soldier and now an armoured reconnaissance soldier, I bond strongly with the crew I'm serving with and with the vehicle I'm crewing. My near obsession with vehicle and weapon maintenance reflects my thought that if I don't fail my weapons and equipment, they won't fail me. With the crew, it doesn't matter what your personal thoughts about each other

are in your off time. Once you're on the road you're one. Behind it all is my odd loyalty and love of the crown and the regiment, my pride as a soldier from British Columbia and my faith in the old gods. (G. Barber, 2010)

Thus, although a soldier has a personal and important relationship with his equipment, he has the strongest such relationship with his teammates. The values which he said sustain these relationships are: "Loyalty, bravery, courage, honour, honesty, fidelity. The usual culprits. These things mean different things to everybody, and everyone has a different extent to which they'll follow them. That said, these are the things I value as a soldier, and they're the standard that I try to uphold. These are the cornerstones of good morale, esprit de corps and unit cohesion." (*Ibid*)

Toughness and manliness were not mentioned very often by my informants, as values that inform their lives as soldiers, although I will relate one memorable comment I received. I asked a policeman why so many policemen wear moustaches. This wasn't intended as a serious question at first. The officer answered: "Because we like it." A nearby female officer overheard the question, and said: "They do it to intimidate people, show them who's boss. If you've got facial hair, you're definitely a man. So they wear moustaches to be men." Everyone laughed. But the laughter also seemed a little nervous. I decided to move to different questions.

By the way, warrior values like loyalty, bravery, honesty, and honor also appear in official military policy documents. One such document produced by the Canadian government described group unity and loyalty as an important component of honor, apparently equal to the humane treatment of prisoners and non-combatants:

Honour itself flows from practicing the military ethos. It

comes from being loyal to your unit and faithful to comrades in fulfilling your duties. It comes with adhering fully to the law of armed conflict, especially in the humane treatment of prisoners of war. Honour insists that all non-combatants be protected and accorded the dignity and other considerations their situation may entitle them to.[161]

This notion of loyalty also appears in the way the same document ranks the soldier's priorities: for one of the three core military values it describes is "service before self".[162] The other two, by the way, are "fighting spirit" (physical and psychological combat readiness) and "unlimited liability" (the acceptance of the fact that one might die in the line of duty), both of which, it seems to me, contribute strongly to the sense of heightened life which military adventuring can produce.

Do soldiers have any kind of relationship with, or at least an understanding of, their enemies? In fact some do. An outstanding example of this is an incident that occurred in the trenches of the First World War, around Christmas of 1914. Soldiers from both sides shouted Christmas greetings to each other from across the no-man's-land. A German soldier timidly climbed out of his trench, approached the British lines, and saluted. Soon many soldiers from both sides climbed out, traded cigarettes and chocolate with each other, and photos of each other's girlfriends back home. A British lieutenant reported that one of the Germans was heard to say, "We don't want to kill you, and you don't want to kill us, so why shoot?"[163] A Scottish soldier produced a ball and an impromptu soccer match started up, with German and Scottish hats for goalposts. The Germans won 3-2. In one case, German soldiers dragged their British counterparts by the legs to a Christmas dinner.[164]

In the Second World War, General Montgomery of England and General Rommel of Germany had portraits of each other on their office walls. When planning a battle, or a troop movement, or other operation, they would look at the portrait of their adversary to try and imagine what the other was thinking. In part this helped them to concentrate on the job, and it reminded them to not underestimate each other. Yet they were also the kind of soldiers who could recognize military excellence wherever they saw it, even in their enemies. Of course, not all soldiers think this way about their enemies. As one of them told me:

> I cannot speak for every soldier, only myself. I personally have no relationship (beyond the obvious one) with the enemy, nor do I sympathize with them or their ways or ideas… To me the insurgents who were trying their level best to kill us didn't rate a connection. In discussions with other soldiers, I have found that I am one of the few who harbour these sorts of thoughts. Others 'felt' for the opposition, or the plight of the locals. It just never got to me. (G. Barber, 2010)

Almost all of the current and former regular soldiers I spoke to expressed their choice to join their country's military in surprisingly spiritual terms. None mentioned God, nor did they mention some kind of visionary experience. But they did speak of a call to a kind of public service, and to participate in causes more important than themselves and their individual interests. Most also spoke of national pride. And all of them spoke of these commitments in very serious terms, since in pursuit of those commitments they were prepared to incur great personal risk, even to die.

The Cost of Honor

I'd like to affirm the goodness and the beauty of the relationships that combat soldiers develop with each other. I'd like to affirm the strong sense of honor which plays such an important role in the life of a warrior. But perhaps because I am a civilian, I find that affirmation difficult. War may be heroism and the immensification of life, but war is also destruction, oppression, and the killing of human beings and the ruining of landscapes on very large scales. Certainly, like his ancient and mediaeval counterparts, the modern soldier is still a man of violence. Canadian General Rick Hillier, while he was Chief of Defence Staff, observed this himself when he said: "We're not the public service of Canada. We're not just another department. We are the Canadian Forces, and our job is to be able to kill people."[165] It's also important to remember that the people who die in war are not always enemy soldiers, nor are they people who are 'guilty' of anything. On 12th July 2007, for instance, an American military helicopter opened fire on a group of unarmed people in a street in Baghdad, killing over a dozen people including two journalists, and wounding numerous others including two children. At first the incident was reported as "combat operations against a hostile force."[166] Video footage from the helicopter itself, released to the public in April of 2010 by the international whistleblowing organization WikiLeaks, clearly show that no one was armed, and no one was behaving in a hostile or aggressive manner. They also show that the pilots enjoyed the killing. One of the crew, observing aman wounded from the first round of shooting, is heard to say, "Come on buddy. All you gotta do is pick up a weapon."[167]

A short story by Mark Twain called *The War Prayer* reminds us that when we pray for victory and glory for our side of a battle, we also pray for the suffering and the humiliation of the other side:

O Lord our God, help us to tear their soldiers to bloody shreds with our shells; help us to cover their smiling fields with the pale forms of their patriot dead; help us to drown the thunder of their guns with the shrieks of their wounded, writhing in pain; help us to lay waste their humble homes with a hurricane of fire; help us to wring the hearts of their unoffending widows with unavailing grief; help us to turn them out roofless with little children to wander unfriended the wastes of their desolated land in rags and hunger and thirst...

(Mark Twain, *The War Prayer*, first published 1916 by *Harper's Monthly*)

War also inflicts misery and pain on the victorious fighters. 20% of American soldiers deployed in Iraq, for instance, now suffer from post-traumatic stress. Also, for the first time since the Vietnam war, the suicide rate among American soldiers grew higher than the civilian rate. In the 12 month period ending September 2009, 160 on-duty American soldiers took their own lives.[168]

I think there is an inescapable moral tragedy here, similar to the one we saw in the lives of hunters. Almost everyone recognizes the importance of the armed forces, for the protection of the nation, for disaster relief, for patrolling the territory, for peace-keeping, for the prevention of crimes against humanity, and so on. Yet so many of the things that an army must do, in pursuit of these noble purposes, are themselves terrible, as are so many of the consequences of what they do. We might comfort ourselves with the thought that the good consequences outweighed the bad, or that terrible things must be done to prevent even more terrible things from happening. But the person who outwardly accepts such a utilitarian view secretly knows that it is impossible to measure these things, and thus impossible to know whether he is right. In this paradox, heroic virtues like courage, valor, honor, and the like, serve also to reduce the force of the cognitive dissonance. We need such values in our warriors so that they can do the jobs we need them to do, without being transformed into monsters, nor cast into suicidal despair. Such virtues may also help the civilians understand fully what the warriors do, and not despise them for doing it. As one of my informants said to me: "A country that despises its army soon finds it has a despicable army."

We should also ask whether the heroic virtues must learned only through death. Is war the only field of human endeavor that teaches honor, courage, and the immensity of life? Are there no alternatives? Philosopher William James had the same worry:

Yet the fact remains that war is a school of strenuous life and heroism... [and] is the only school that as yet is universally available. But when we gravely ask ourselves whether this wholesale organization of irrationality and crime be our only bulwark against effeminacy, we stand aghast at the thought, and think more kindly of ascetic religion. One hears of the mechanical equivalent of heat. What we now need to discover in the social realm is *the moral equivalent of war*: something heroic that will speak to men as universally as war does, and yet will be as compatible with their spiritual selves as war has proved itself to be incompatible. (*Ibid*, p 284; emphasis added.)

The people of ancient Iron Age Heroic societies lived astonishingly violent lives compared to ours. Yet they created elaborate traditions, laws, honor codes and models of heroic virtue designed to *reduce* the violence. The custom of single combat, which was known to Celts, Anglo-Saxons, Norsemen and Germanic peoples, allowed battles to be decided on the outcome of only two fighters, one from each side, selected by the generals. In that way, battles could be decided with far less death. In some cases, religious figures such as Druids could declare that a battle was unjust and order the warriors to go home. They also invented *alternatives to killing* which provided the same, or similar, social rewards to victors like honor, glory, and the immensification of life.

We today need to find our own ways to check the killing

instinct, and prevent war. I have no doubt that war and killing has always been an ethical and social tragedy, for both winners and losers. But today, the armies of the world possess weapons far more dangerous than swords and spears. Chemical and biological weapons can spread disease and death to thousands of people and their surrounding natural ecosystems in days, or even mere hours. A nuclear weapon can destroy an entire city, flattening all its buildings to rubble, and killing tens of thousands of people, in as little as ten seconds. And a computer virus, attacking a banking network or a power grid, can cause as much if not more damage to an economy and to people's lives than any of the other weapons I've just mentioned. I simply cannot see how a modern soldier can earn his sense of personal and national honor with the use of such weapons.

It is time now to ask ourselves: What other relationships in public and private life could serve as the moral equivalent to war? Where can we experience life in a heightened state, and learn honor, without killing each other? These are some of the questions that will guide the next few studies.

14

Sports, Games and Athletics

We ended the last study with a difficult but serious question: what is the moral equivalent to war? Is there a way to experience honor, heroism, heightened life, and ecstasy, without killing? I asked various people what they thought could serve as the moral equivalent to warfare. The most consistent answer was sports and athletics. Let's give a quick look at four obvious ways that sports can be compared to war, to see if sports can substitute itself in the place of war.

Probably the first way that sports and warfare are alike is competition. Players compete against each other for victory and success. Second: both armies and sports teams wave flags, wear symbols and colors, sing anthems, and make other demonstrations of patriotism. Fans of the Montreal Canadiens hockey team, for instance, refer to the team's jersey as *La Sainte-Flanelle*, 'The Holy Cloth'. Being a supporter of a certain team, for some, is just as important as being a citizen of a certain nation, or a believer in a certain religion. Indeed the two may be blurred together. A nation's pride can be tied to its history of success and excellence in playing its 'national game', and the stories of outstanding athletes who came from that nation. Third: the camaraderie that exists between teammates also makes sports teams comparable to armies. Much like soldiers heading into battle, players in a team sport must strategize together, and rely on each other to do their part, in order to win. Shared sporting effort, and sporting victory, can create bonds of friendship between players much as other kinds of shared adventuring can do. This same bond can often be seen between fans and spectators, especially after a victory. When Canada's national hockey teams win at the

Olympics or at the World Juniors, all thirty-three million of us celebrate.

Some sports can be compared to warfare when they involve a risk of severe injury, or death. Rugby, boxing, martial arts, American football, downhill skiing, and so on, are interesting and beautiful precisely because they are also dangerous. On 12 February, 2010, Nodar Kumaritashvili, an Olympic luge sledder from Georgia, died while training for the Vancouver 2010 Olympic Winter Games. Near the end of the track, reputed to be the fastest luge track in the world, he lost control of his sled and was thrown off the track and into an unprotected concrete pillar. Depending on the nature of the sport, the prospect of death itself can hover over the sports field as over the battlefield, contributing to a similar sense of 'heightened life' that soldiers sometimes describe. But the main difference is that while an athlete might die on the field, no one took to the field intending to kill him. Victory is not contingent upon destroying the opponent: for one side to win, it isn't necessary for anyone on the other side to die. And athletes are not expected to die so that their teammates can continue to victory. We go to the sports field for different purposes. So let us turn to those different purposes now.

The Nature of Sport

Wars are usually fought to obtain material advantage: the victorious army gains land territory, oil fields, mines, control of trade routes, or other geo-political prizes. Athletes, by contrast from soldiers, compete for public honor and prestige. Professional athletes may be paid handsomely by their clubs, and some tournaments award cash prizes to winners. But the money is usually the second and not the first reason for pursuing a professional sports career. Observe the ecstasy on the faces of the players at the moment they win the most prestigious tournament in their profession: the FIFA World Cup (for soccer), the Stanley Cup Playoff (for hockey), the William Webb Ellis Cup (for union rugby), and the Olympic Gold Medal (for numerous other sports). The cash rewards that might be included here are not really comparable to the material gains of war-fighting, because the losing side does not foot the bill.

Athletic competition for honor and prestige alone may be as old as sport itself. Herodotus describes an occasion when Xerxes of Persia was investigating events in Greece, prior to an attempted invasion:

> A few Arcadian deserters came in – men who had nothing to live on and wanted employment; they were taken to Xerxes and questioned about what the Greeks were doing... he was told in reply that the Greeks were celebrating the Olympic festival, where they were watching athletic contests and chariot races. Xerxes asked what the prize was for which they contended, the Arcadians mentioned the wreath of olive leaves which it is our custom to give. This drew from Tritantaechmes, the son of Artabanus, a very sound remark... 'Good heavens, Mardonius, what kind of men are these that you have brought us to fight against – men who compete with one another for no material reward, but only for honor!' (Herodotus, *Histories*, p 533)

The implication we are to infer here is that the Greeks had a superior culture. (Herodotus was a Greek, after all.) But this is not the whole story: for Greek Olympic victors often did receive great material rewards once they returned home. It was believed that an Olympic success conferred honor not only on the athlete himself, but also on the city he came from as well. So the people of that city would reward the winner with lavish feasts at public expense for the rest of his life, and sometimes also a place in the civic government or the military. Furthermore the non-material reward of 'mere' honor and prestige may have included artworks, sculptures, and poems commissioned to commemorate his victory. Herodotus described how an Olympic victor was treated upon his return home from the ancient games:

> Phillipus was an Olympic victor and the best looking man of his day; and because of his good looks he received from the people of Egesta the unparalleled honor of a hero's shrine erected on his tomb, at which religious ceremonies are still held to win his favor. (Herodotus, *Histories*, p 357)

Thus an Olympic victor might win enough personal glory to carry his name into apotheosis – a form of immortality in which the story of a man's life continues to be told by others long after the man himself dies.

How do athletes earn this kind of honor? Obviously, one way to earn it is by winning games. As we saw in the quote from Herodotus, we sometimes praise them for non-athletic reasons too. But that is actually a clue to another understanding of sport. Some athletic performances attain degrees of excellence that are perhaps best described as *artistic*. Consider, as an example, "the goal that defied physics": Roberto Carlos' free kick goal during a pre-World Cup game in France, on 3rd June 1997. Carlos, playing for Brazil, curved the ball ten yards around the row of defenders and into the net. French goalkeeper Fabien Barthez was so astonished that he merely stood and watched it fly past him.[169] Similarly, we could look at Diego Maradona's two goals in the 1986 World Cup match against England: the "Hand of God" goal, and the "Goal of the Century". Both of them seemed very improbable, very unlikely goals, especially since they were scored within minutes of each other, by the same player. Yet both were enormously pleasurable and exciting to watch. Even the coach for the opposing team called the second one "a miracle, a fantastic goal."

We love performances like these even if the player or his team does not win the game. This suggests that sport has another purpose, another way for athletes to earn honor, separate from the scoring of points and the winning of games. That second purpose is *the demonstration of athletic excellence* such that the athlete's performance deserves to be judged *artistically*. We have seen something of this already, in the discussion of artists and craftspeople. This excellence can take the form of a performance beyond the expected, or even a performance beyond what was hitherto thought physically possible. But more generally, it consists in *the excellence of technique*. In this sense, athletes compete not so much against their opponents but against their own previous performances. The same ecstasy that one feels in winning the FIFA World Cup can also be found in scoring the perfect goal – regardless of whether it is the winning goal, and regardless of whether the game is lost or won at all. Here we are concerned with the perfect arc shot, the perfect free kick, the perfect long pass. Some sports, like kyudo (Japanese Zen archery), is concerned almost exclusively with the perfection of technique. Striking the target in the bull's eye is much less important than the *shin-zen-bi* (truth, beauty) and the *munen muso* (no-thought, or naturalness) of the shot.

The danger of the game need not be reduced or eliminated for the artistic element to appear. A good boxer's technique, for instance, can be elegant, artistic, even graceful. But the purpose of a boxing match is not to score more points than the opponent. It is to punch up that opponent so badly that he can no longer walk. Even so, the most memorable knockouts are not the ones that came easily and quickly to the victor. Rather, we remember the knockouts earned by strategy, technique, talent, endurance, and especially surprise. Think of Muhammad Ali knocking out George Foreman in The Rumble in the Jungle of 30th October 1974.

Sports can serve as a testing-field of human potential in this way in part because sports are always infused with chance, and so the results are always a surprise. Commentators and analysts might try to predict game results by mathematically extrapolating a given individual or team's past performance. But no one can know in advance how air turbulence might change the speed or direction of the ball, or how high the 'point man' will jump, or whether a butterfly will distract the goalkeeper. Thus one simply cannot know all the factors that may contribute to someone's scoring a winning goal at the last second. A sporting event is thus always characterized by irreducible dramatic tension. Since this is so, sporting excellence thus includes not only the athlete's own physical talent, but also his or her talent for capitalizing on his luck. The athlete has to be able to detect the 'tenor' of a match: the 'way' the match seems to be going, the 'sense' of who is likely to win, the 'feel' for the opponent's strategies, as well as the feel for his own. These feelings come about after a complex intellectual analysis of a very large amount of information, from the competitor's steps, movements, and facial expressions, to the sights and sounds of the audience. The tenor of a match can change unexpectedly: thus sports commentators often speak of turning points and moments of truth. The athlete must see what opportunities or risks these changes present, and he must make use of them. And she must be able to do all of this calculating and decision-making in a fraction of a second. This is not simply a matter of dexterity and stamina and strength: it is also a matter of athletic perceptual intelligence.

Similarly, sport tests not only the body: it also tests the will. Chrissie Wellington, the first woman to win the Ironman Competition, described how she was able to keep up her endurance. She said that she would recite inspirational poems or song lyrics in her head, such as Rudyard Kipling's *If*, a copy of which she carries with her at every race. "Because when you're 30k into the marathon it's not your body that's carrying you, it's your mind."[170]

Sport can serve as a circle of meaning not simply because it is a means of earning honor and experiencing ecstasy without killing. It also serves this way because its qualities resemble real human life. Like sports, ordinary human life, individually and socially, is infused with chance and luck. No one can accurately or reliably predict anything about the future. We can make extrapolations on the basis of previous events, of course, and these extrapolations may be reasonably reliable most of the time. But life always has occasional moments of absolute unpredictability. Talented people can rise to such occasions, or be consumed by them, just as often happens on soccer fields and boxing rings. Life also tests your will. You might lose your job, or learn that you have cancer, or watch your best friend die. But you have to go on living: you have to find or invent a reason and a will not to fall into malaise, nihilism, and suicidal despair. And finally, life also offers us moments of unexpected artistic excellence and delight. Tomorrow a stranger might be kind to you, and the sunrise might be more glorious than today. Sport is a circle of meaning when it replicates life in all of these ways.

15

Sailors, Ships and the Sea

In the year 2009, for the first time in my life, I went sailing. Not that it was the first time I had ever boarded a sailboat. But it was the first time I was invited to handle one. My brother-in-law controlled the main sail and the rudder of his 24-foot lake boat, and I controlled of the head sail. We practiced a few turns when the wind was not gusting too strongly. After about an hour I got used to the sound of the sail, and learned how strengthening or slackening my grip on its ropes affected our speed and direction, and the angle of our side-tipping. Of course, as it was only my first day sailing, I didn't get it right very often. The fact that I did not get thrown overboard was victory enough for me.

We were on a small reservoir lake in southern Ontario, Canada, on a sunny and warm day. If we got into trouble, we could swim to shore quite easily. We had nothing to fear. But those who sail on the open ocean face much bigger dangers. Ocean waves during storms can swell from seven to ten meters high. In the centuries before Europeans 'discovered' Turtle Island, people thought that Ireland was the western edge of the world, the physical frontier to the absolute unknown. No one knew of any lands beyond it: they knew only of its storms. Thus it was probably one of the most tangible source of fear in their lives. Furthermore they had Biblical stories of sea monsters, like the Leviathan, to make them even more afraid of venturing too far into the sea. As a frontier of the unknown, the ocean has historically represented a realm of fear. Thus it would have required great courage, will, and command of one's powers, to deliberately sail into the west, beyond the sight of land. Might *geographic exploration* be another alternative to war?

To answer this question, it may be helpful to look first at the relationships we have with water, with our ships, and with the sea.

Sacred Waters

Water is necessary and essential to human life survival. Without water for drinking and bathing, we die. It might be argued that air is more essential, since we can live without water for a few days, but we can live without air for only a few minutes. Yet I think that water is the more important element to human life because, at least until the last hundred years or so, air could not be packaged. Water, by contrast, can be packaged: it can be channeled in canals or aqueducts, stored for later in jars or pots, and sold as a commodity in a market. Thus water can play a larger role in human culture. For most of human history, water for drinking and cleaning was what economists call 'a free good': something that you can get without having to trade anything for it. In most parts of the world, people could collect as much as they needed for themselves by catching the rain in barrels or reservoirs, or by digging wells. There are exceptions, of course: the Kalahari Desert, for instance, where for ten months of the year there are no pools, lakes or streams. Water has to be obtained from fruit, plants like wild melons or tubers, or from animals. During the driest and hottest months, "the season of the brown hyena", people keep themselves hydrated by digging shallow holes, urinating in them, and lying down in them, remaining motionless for hours.[172] The Kalahari has a rainy season starting in January that lasts three months, which is full of celebration and thanksgiving. Yet in some years the rains are very light. And as pollutants and greenhouse gases warm our planet and change its climate, there are years in which the rains do not come at all. But even in climates where there is no dry season and where water is much more abundant, water still figures into our most important relationships in almost the same way as food and shelter. As we have seen, to share food with someone is to affirm that person's entitlement to life, and to shift the presumptions between strangers from fear to trust. Let us add here that water, whether it is scarce or abundant, and even when it is a free good, serves our relationships the same way. I can affirm someone's right to live by sharing water with her, in the same way that I do by offering food and shelter.

In the desert environment where the three Abrahamic religions began, water is also very scarce. It is perhaps natural, therefore, that hand-washing should take on such enormous religious significance for all of them. Clean hands are protected against disease and are therefore ready to handle food; this easily becomes a symbol for a soul, cleansed of sin, and ready to handle sacred things. For this reason Christians initiate new converts, and their infant children, into their community using water: the ritual is called baptism. St. Paul did not seem to think of baptism as a symbolic cleansing, however; it seems he thought of it more like a symbolic *drowning:*

> ... don't you know that all of us who were baptized into Christ Jesus were baptized into his death? We were therefore buried with him through baptism into death in order that, just as Christ was raised from the dead through the glory of the Father, we too may live a new life. For if we have been united with him in a death like his, we will certainly also be united with him in a resurrection like his. (Romans 6:3-5)

Non-religious rituals also use water to enact a similar transformation of someone's status. Sailors in modern navies who cross the Atlantic for the first time in their lives receive an initiation called the Line Crossing, or the Rites of Neptune. Similarly, a water ritual can affirm an entire community's relationship with the sea. The wealth of renaissance Venice, for instance, came from its fleet of ocean-going ships that traded precious commodities like spices and silks from Arabia, India, and Africa. Thus the Doge (the ruler of Venice) was ceremonially 'married' to the sea, once a year.

Finally, our use of water also demonstrates our values when we use it to hurt people. Drinking water can be poisoned, just as food can be. A dehydrated person can be thrown back into the desert. Enemies can be held with their heads or faces under-water, to be tortured, or killed. Religious fanatics in Europe, from the 1400s to the mid 1700s, used water to test whether someone was a witch. The suspect's hands and feet were tied together, and she was thrown into a lake. The idea was that if she was a witch, God's pure natural water would reject her, and she would therefore float. If, on the other hand, she sank (and drowned), she was innocent. The Catholic Counter-Reformation gave the world another form of water torture, which today we call water-boarding. A person is tied down to a plank, and a cloth is placed over his face. Water is then poured on the cloth from above. The experience for the victim is like drowning – and it is completely terrifying. When waterboarding was used by Catholics against various Protestants during Europe's Counter-Reformation, it took on a distinctly theological character. As observed by religious scholar William Schweiker:

Water as a form of torture is an inversion of the waters of baptism under the (grotesque) belief that it can deliver the heretic from his or her sins. It was believed – at least since St. Augustine – that punishment, even lethal in form, could be an act of mercy meant to keep a sinner from continuing in sin, either by repentance of heresy or by death. The background idea or purpose, then, was originally the claim that torture or punishment could save the sinner from further sin that would endanger his or her soul.[173]

Waterboarding torture is still used today. During the second Iraq

War, American military interrogators used waterboarding to gather information from prisoners. In October of 2010, A man from Nebraska was arrested for waterboarding his girlfriend.[174]

The religious significance of water is more than a symbol grounded in its practical usefulness. There is also a phenomenological dimension. A hint to this dimension appears in the way that ancient people used water to communicate with their gods. The heroic-age Celts, for instance, deposited swords and other valuable items into rivers, lakes, bogs, and wells, as sacrificial offerings. They built long causeways into the fenlands and bogs, and dropped their offerings just off to the sides of the causeways. Britons gave sword offerings into waters this way as late as the 14th century. They also built sanctuaries at the sources of important European rivers, such as the Seine, in France, where archaeologists found 190 woodcarvings, dating from the first century.[175] Here's the words of Strabo, describing a similar Celtic sanctuary near Toulouse:

> The country being rich in gold, with inhabitants both god-fearing and of frugal life, possessed treasures in many parts of Celtica; and the lakes in particular provided inviolability for their treasures, into which they let down heavy masses of silver and gold... in Toulouse, moreover, the temple was a revered one, greatly esteemed by the local inhabitants, and for this reason the treasures there were unusually large, since many made dedications and none would dare to profane them.[176]

It seems that water was used for sacrifices because water was the medium of passage to the Otherworld. Various stories in the Celtic corpus attest to this, such as the Voyage of Bran, and the Voyage of Máel Dúin, both of which involve teams of warriors visiting a series of magical islands. We also find this in the architecture of Newgrange, which features a great kerbstone at the entrance carved with spiral art that resembles the rushing water of a river. An ancient trackway from that entrance to the edge of the river Boyne suggests that the monument was intended to be approached from across the river.

The Celtic worldview also placed the lands of the dead on an island across the western sea. Plutarch noted that "the inhabitants of Britain located the lands of the dead in adjacent small islands," to the west, the direction of the setting sun.[177] Plutarch's account of how souls cross to these islands is as follows:

> On the ocean strand opposite Britain dwell certain fishermen; they hear a voice calling them and a knock at the door. Rising from their beds they find at the shore unfamiliar boats heavily laden. They grasp the oars, and in an hour are across, although their own boats would require one and a half days. When they arrive, although they see nobody, they hear a voice calling out the names of those who disembark.[178]

The island of Bull Rock, just off Dursey Island, county Cork, was once known as *Tech Duinn*, the House of Donn, a god of the dead whose name means roughly 'the dark one' or 'the black one'. Donn was a leader in one of the first mythological tribes to colonize Ireland. But as the story goes, he was drowned near that island before making landfall. Thus the original Celtic belief concerning death probably went something like this. Donn, the first man who died, became the god of the dead. He calls out to those who are on their deathbeds, and provides them with a rowboat for their journey his otherworldly island.

If sacrifices were offered to water because the way to the Otherworld is through water, then why was water imagined to be the way to the Otherworld? The answer, I think, is in the way water appears to come from the Otherworld, and back again. Psychologist Philip Carr-Gomm described magic as: "the experience we have when something emerges into light from the darkness, from the unknown." He mentioned as examples the sun rise in the morning, the birth of a child, the appearance of the stars at twilight. "And the earliest magical ceremonies were when people went down into the caves, and emerged with the sunrise, to be reborn."[179] The experience of magic, as a phenomenological event, is the experience of something emerging from hiddenness, and revealing itself to our senses. We can add many more examples here: flowers blooming in the morning, trees budding and producing leaves in the spring, and butterflies emerging from cocoons. Water in a natural setting seems to emerge from mystery in precisely this way. It emerged from springs and wells deep underground, flowed in rivers down from high hills and mountains, and fell from the sky. Then it flowed down to the sea, and presumably continued on beyond 'the ninth wave', the horizon, to another hidden world. A scientific understanding tells us that water does not emerge from the unknown. It moves through the environment in a defined and non-mysterious circuit of evaporation and precipitation, which we call the water cycle. But our Iron Age ancestors did not have this scientific information. What they *saw* was that water appeared to flow from an unseen source to an unseen destination. This makes it otherworldly, and magical. Water is thus not just a symbol for the values which are enacted when we use it for hygiene and survival. It is also a phenomenological encounter with the immensity of the unknown. This, I think, explains why the Celts gave offerings to their gods in pools and lakes and rivers, and why they located their Otherworld in islands across the sea.

Nor are the Celts the only people to treat water this way. The river Ganges, in India, is the embodiment of a Hindu goddess named Ganga who was created from the water of Brahmin's water-vessel, and sent to earth to help people pass on to their next lives. Many Hindus believe that bathing in the Ganges can release people from their sins and empower them for enlightenment, and that the soul of a deceased person will move on to heaven if their ashes are spread in the river. (There is a sharp irony in the fact that the Ganges is so saturated with industrial waste that it is one of the most polluted rivers in the world.) The Zamzam well, in Mecca, is revered by Muslims because, as the story goes, it was created by the angel Gabriel. Another version says it was created when Ishmael, while still an infant, scraped his foot on the ground and caused water to burst forth. Indeed the site of the Kaaba, which all Muslims face while praying, was chosen for its proximity to the well. Similarly, the magical presence of water is the reason why we use it in so many of our religious rituals. We drink it, share it, and wash ourselves with it, and do all the same things we normally do outside of ritual. But we do it religiously; that is, we do those things as part of a dramatized enacted affirmation of social, personal, and spiritual values, and as part of a relationship with the mysteries of the world.

Reading the Sea

As my brother-in-law and I sailed in circles around the lake, he explained how important it is to be aware of the shapes of the waves, the movement of birds and other animals, and the color of clouds. All those things are signs of how the winds will move next: whether it will change direction, whether it will gust strongly for a moment, whether it will suddenly calm. Similarly, he described the importance of listening to the flapping of the sail: the kind of sound it makes tells the sailor whether the boat is getting the most from the available wind, or whether the boat is about to flip upside-down. Sailing races, he said, are won or lost by the skipper's talent at reading the winds and waves, and manipulating the ropes and sails to make tight turns and to maximize speed. It quickly occurred to me that he was speaking of a kind of perceptual intelligence. The environmental signs that a sailor looks for, to know how to handle the sailboat, are similar to those which hunters use to follow animals at a distance. An experienced sailor must process in his mind hundreds of subtle environmental details, all in his head, in order to know what angle to hold the sail to, and how tight the tension on the ropes should be, and when to make turns, and so on. As I investigated this possibility further, I learned about the Polynesian Wayfinders, and about the *Hokule'a*.

In 1976, a group of Polynesians sailed from Hawaii to Tahiti, a distance of 4,400 kilometers, *without* modern navigational tools. The scientific paradigm of the day asserted that the trip must be impossible. The islands are too far apart, the prevailing winds and currents flow in the wrong direction, and the Polynesians are not smart enough to know how to do it. The islands must have been settled accidentally, by fishermen blown off course by storms. Furthermore, colonial governments from the middle of the 19th century had outlawed nearly everything about traditional Polynesian culture, and so the technique of wayfinding had almost disappeared. Thus when the *Hokule'a* arrived in Tahiti, successfully, 16,000 exuberant people came to the shore to cheer. The arrival of the *Hokule'a* restored in the people a sense of identity and pride.

Nainoa Thompson, one of the last living Polynesian wayfinders, and the navigator of the *Hokule'a*, explained how the voyage was possible. The navigator must study wind directions and speeds, and learn which way the winds go at different times of year. The prevailing winds on Polynesia blow from east to west, which is why early European explorers believe that Polynesia was colonized from South America. But there is a short period of time in which they change directions, making eastward travel easier; besides which, the Polynesian sailors knew how to tack into the wind. The navigator must also learn the character of clouds: different shapes and colors denote different weather fronts approaching, and the presence of islands. The wildlife, in the sea and in the sky, also point the way to nearby islands:

certain species of birds always travel back to their nests at night and so can be followed like guides. Distances to nearby islands can be gauged this way, as some birds venture further to sea than others. Navigators also memorize over 200 stars, and observe their rising and setting places on the horizon to know which direction the boat is facing. If any of these features are obscured by mist or stormy weather, the navigator also determines the ship's direction by feeling the rhythms of the waves striking the hull and rocking it up and down. Local disturbances produce one type of rhythm, distant storms produce another, and deep water currents produce a third. A Polynesian navigator, even when sitting inside the boat in the dark, can detect half a dozen wave rhythms affecting the boat at the same time. As described by anthropologist Wade Davis, following Thompson's description:

> The truly great navigators such as Mau [Thompson's teacher] can identify the presence of distant atolls of islands beyond the visible horizon simply by watching the reverberation of waves across the hull of the canoe, knowing full well that every island group in the Pacific has its own refractive pattern that can be read with the same ease with which a forensic scientist would read a fingerprint.[180]

Navigating at sea, using only one's bodily senses and one's mind to know distance and direction, requires profound perceptual intelligence. The navigator has to be able to internalize in his mind an enormous amount of information from wind, cloud, wildlife, stars, the sun and moon, and the waves, and even the quality of the light. Then he has to apply this information to the practical problem of traveling from one island to another in a territory of around 25 million square kilometers. Therefore Wade says, "The science and art of navigation is holistic."[181] This intense intellectual activity produces in the navigator the feeling of where the destination island is, and which direction to sail to get there. As the navigators themselves say, they "see the island in the mind", and they "pull the island out of the sea".

Reading the Ships

A sailor must know how to read his boat, as much as he must read the sea and sky. Certainly, maritime perceptual intelligence can produce in the sailor, if not a feeling of oneness, then a feeling of deep love, for his ship. Angus Walters, skipper of Canada's most famous racing schooner, the Bluenose, said he had only two loves in his life: his wife, and the ship. During night watch, he would walk from bow to stern and back, listening to the creaking sounds made by the boards and ropes, to learn whether anything was being unduly strained and whether anything needed repair. His sailors noted that he would talk quietly to the ship during these rounds. Walters said he knew how close to shore he was, even in foggy weather, by the sounds and the vibrations of the waves slapping against the sides. I think it likely this intimate knowledge, and this intimate love, is what made the Bluenose so successful. During its career as a working fishing vessel and as a racing boat, the Bluenose became world famous as the fastest sailing ship ever built. Except for its first race, it won every sailing competition it entered. When in 1946 the Bluenose sank in a sand shoal somewhere in the Caribbean, Walters cried without consolation for a month.

Another way that people build relationships with their boats appears in the way people 'humanize' them. We give sailboats personal names, for instance. We decorate them with carvings, ornaments, colorful paint, and we deck them out with colorful flags; these decorations are perhaps comparable to clothing and cosmetics. The sail, in particular, although an essential part of a sailing ship, is also a decoratable surface. The sail is where you put the patterns, designs, and symbols that identify the ship, the crew, and the home port. For centuries tall sailing ships had animal or human figures placed on the prow, to give the ship a sense of personhood and distinct identity. This practice long predates the galleons and triremes of the Renaissance. Consider the magnificent Oseberg Ship, a Viking dragon boat built around the year 800 and discovered by archaeologists near Oslo in 1904. It had a magnificent carving on its prow, starting with a coiled snake head, and flowing into an intricate series of animal designs. Consider, also, the practice of painting eyes on the prow of fishing boats. The ancient practice can be found in various parts of the world, including the Mediterranean, southeast Asia, the British Isles, and the First Nations of the Pacific coast of Canada. A fishing boat with eyes seems to have an intelligence of its own. Perhaps I have too much of an animist imagination, but when I look upon a fishing boat with painted eyes on its prow, I immediately imagine that the boat looks back at me. It seems to *know* who I am, and where it is going, and how to read the waves and the skies, and whether its crew is competent enough to handle it. Anthropomorphic art on ships suggests an animist relationship: sailors decorate and respect their ships *as if* the ship had a mind and spirit of its own. The art humanizes the ship, and in so doing, helps express the humanity of the sailors, and express the character of their relationship with their ship, and with the sea.

Do modern sailors still think about their boats in this personal way? I read an account of a team of modern adventurers who built a replica Viking knarr, the *Snorri*, and sailed it from Greenland to the Viking settlement on the northern peninsula of Newfoundland. Theirs was the first Viking ship to follow Leif Eriksson's route in over a thousand years. In the first few months of sea trials, however, their rudder never worked properly. In fact the designers of the replica ship never knew what shape of rudder to use: no Danish ships with their rudders had been discovered by archaeologists. Danish ship rudders were found elsewhere, but not attached to their ships! The designers eventually settled on a design based on a rudder found by archaeologists without its ship. But it was difficult to manage: it would whip around violently, sending the helmsman lurching forward and back, and it was easily damaged. One of the crewmembers gave himself the task of designing and making a new one. Bit by bit, he whittled small parts of it, a subtle fraction at a time. Then he observed its new behavior, noting whether the most recent subtle change made the ship easier or harder to manage. "We've been so careful to stick to the original rudders, but we have to remember that those rudders worked on the boats they were made for... Every boat probably has a different shaped rudder, depending on how it wants to go."[182] The attribution of *intentionality* to the ship is part of the process of humanizing technology. Perhaps it is not the ship that wants to go somewhere, but we perceive that it does because that is how our perceptual intelligence reports to us what needs to be done to make the ship work well.

Of course it's likely that no sailor in the world would admit to actually believing that his boat could think or reason, or that it had independent desires and feelings. Some latent animism may be involved in the way ships are decorated, but no one is really fooled by a pair of painted eyes into thinking that a ship is a person. Yet a ship can be loved and respected by its crew like a person. We hear the captain telling us to "treat her like a lady". It's not just a matter of calling a ship by a human name, and using human pronouns in reference to it, as sailors and boat owners often do. It also involves constant awareness of the boat's own needs. Respect for the ship involves awareness of the movements of the winds, the position of sails and ropes and rudders, and the loads they bear. It involves not straining the boat beyond its load-bearing capacity. Respect for the ship also involves surveying it for wear and tear, and making all necessary repairs. The ship thus depends on the people who use it, as much as the people depend on the ship. It *works* better when these interdependencies are undertaken with an attitude of respect. Boats and ships that are well-loved like that embody a way of being in the world.

The crew of the *Snorri* also gave sacrificial offerings to the ocean, in imitation of their Viking predecessors:

> Before we raised sail, a few of us made offerings to the waters to see us safely across. The idea was to give up something precious. Jan tossed in a hoarded Italian sausage; John Gardner, our bosun and assistant boat builder, sacrificed some rum; Homer and I dumped in loose tobacco. By nine o'clock that night we had erased 30 miles of the crossing. We could make it to Baffin in three days![183]

Similarly, when the crew had been rowing against the wind for weeks, the captain "became a little too superstitious. People get that way on boats, but on a Viking boat, stuck without wind, it can get a little out of hand." He had been reading about how the Norse god Frey had a boat that always got its following wind, and thought of how most people remember Odin and Thor but neglect the other Aesir. So he stripped himself naked, stood on a crossbeam and stretched out his arms to pray to Frey for a following wind. The following day, he got the wind.

Again, I don't want to suggest that any of the crew seriously believed in the existence of Odin or any of the Aesir gods, because I don't know that. Rather, I think it likely that they did those things partly out of frustration for the various setbacks they endured, partly for the sake of historical re-enactment, and partly for the fun of it. In a similar way, when they finally arrived at L'Anse Aux Meadows they swam the last 200 meters to the shore, just as their Viking predecessors would have done.

The Final Frontier

Geographic exploration puts the whole human organism to the test. Designing and building your ship, planning your journey, and navigating on the way tests your intelligence. Handling the ropes and rudders tests your physical strength, endurance, and dexterity. Setting out for unexplored areas and facing great storms tests your bravery. The prospect of death by drowning never goes away. On 24 October 2010, after two and a half years at sea, a replica Phoenician ship (the *Phoenecia*) arrived at its home port of Arwad Island, Syria, after circumnavigating Africa. From storms with seven meter swells, to the loss of the rudder, the captain said he and the crew had "an adventure every day."[184] In discovering new lands and new peoples, sailing and geographic exploration also opens up possibilities for wonder. In returning home again, it offers the prospect of glory and honor. Davis noted that the Aboriginal Polynesians who populated the entire Pacific did so because their society bestowed great prestige on those who discovered new islands.

> To sail off into the rising sun, quite possibly never to be seen again, was an act of considerable courage that brought enormous honour to a clan. Oral traditions suggest that as many as half of these expeditions may have ended in disaster. But as failure implied death, those left behind had a vested interest in imagining success, and in their dreams they envisioned new lands rising out of the sea to greet their departed relatives, men and women who acquired by their very acts the status of gods.[185]

Davis also noted that Polynesian society was strictly hierarchical, and the only way a second or third son could earn honor was by discovering new islands. Similar social pressures also existed in mediaeval and early modern Europe, when the first Europeans crossed the Atlantic to settle in North America. A young man not likely to inherit the farm (or the noble title) could make a name for himself by managing one of the colonies, and make money selling the new continent's wealth to European markets. In every important respect, exploration can produce the same benefits as warfare, but without the obligation to kill anyone. It can serve alongside athletics as a moral equivalent to war. Of course, the first Europeans to explore North America did kill thousands, perhaps millions, of Aboriginal people, either through the new diseases they carried, or through warfare. Examples of co-operation between Aboriginal communities and the visitors do exist, but examples of hostility and conflict are more like the norm. Thus the point must be taken with certain caveats. Exploration *could* serve as the moral equivalent to war that William James hoped for, although historically it has often accompanied and sometimes served the purposes of war. But in that respect, it is perhaps not much different from education, or health care, or leadership, or the market, or other models of human interaction which could either empower and enlighten people, or else oppress and destroy them, depending on the values and priorities of the participants.

I write these words in the early part of the twenty-first century. The whole surface of our Earth is now fully explored, and has been for more than a hundred years. Adventuring ships like the *Hokule'a*, the *Snorri*, and the *Phoenecia*, are wonderful examples of the rediscovery of human powers and potentials, but they do not discover new lands. Furthermore, human mechanical and industrial power is now capable of changing the planet on large scales. We can level an entire mountain with explosives and earth-moving machinery, to mine it for minerals. We can destroy forests many thousands of square kilometers in area with our lumber mills. We can alter the chemical balance of the atmosphere with aerosols, car exhausts, and industrial pollu-tants, thus accelerating a greenhouse effect and causing more storms. We can fly above the highest mountains in our aircraft, and touch the bottom of the sea with our submarines. Indeed we can even create earthquakes now. For example, the water in the reservoir behind the Zipingpu Dam in Sichuan Province, China, was 550 meters from a fault line. The weight of its water caused a 7.9 magnitude earthquake that killed an estimated 80,000 people and left 5 million more homeless.[186]

The Earth still stands as an immensity above the individual woman or man, and exploring it personally or in small teams can still be a spiritually uplifting experience. If someone climbs a great mountain and conquers its summit, there will always be more mountains, and never enough time in one life to climb them all. But the grandeur of the Earth is now eclipsed by the works of humankind. Thus for many people, the sea has lost its magic, and the Earth no longer holds us in awe and wonder. But there remains one more frontier of mystery where magic could still be found, and it stretches out above us, beyond the atmosphere of our planet. Space travel is already putting humanity's technological, intellectual and adventurous capacities to the test. Most planets in our solar system have been visited by our robotic probes, and a dozen people have walked on the moon. And space travel is just as dangerous as sea travel once was. Of the roughly 460 people who have left our atmosphere so far, 19 died during the trip. I venture to say that every element that makes warfare appealing to some people, such as the danger, the test of courage and power, the prospect of earning honor and glory, is present in space exploration. Alongside athletics then, the exploration of the stars may serve as a moral equivalent to war, of the sort William James was looking for. Space also presents us with a new frontier of the absolute unknown, and so a new face of the magical, just as water and the sea used to do. It also offers us a new realm of fear: we do not know very much about what is out there, and we tend to fear what we do not know. And we often imagine the worst. Consider how many 20th century horror films involve aliens, just as ancient sea-journey tales used to involve sea monsters, supernatural beings, and the dead. It is possible that if we encounter other civilizations out there, then space exploration will present us with new diseases, new modes of oppression, and new wars. But we may also find new realms of discovery too. We know that there are strange new worlds out there. Our telescopes and instruments have so far discovered more than 300 planets orbiting other stars. And there may be uncountable trillions more in each of the uncountable trillions of galaxies which our telescopes and instruments can detect. These facts are amazing! Thus outer space does not have to be approached with fear. It can also be approached with wonder.

16

Musicians

I was born into an Irish family, and traditional Celtic music was a big part of the 'soundtrack' of my childhood. In adulthood, after one of my sisters married a professional Celtic musician, my childhood home served as a performance venue for traveling Celtic musicians. My brother-in-law's musical ear is always close to the ground, alert to the work of other artists in the field, and to new innovations in the style. Thus a musician he respected who happened to be passing nearby would be invited to present a concert in our dining room. The audience is mostly made of neighbors, friends, and friends-of-friends. It was not exactly invitation-only, but you normally had to 'know someone' to find out about the show. And the musicians themselves are often delighted to perform in a comfortable and intimate place. We have fit as many as thirty people into the living and dining room, with a table on the side for snacks and drinks. The performer himself is given dinner and breakfast the next day, and invited to sell his CD's and to promote his next concert. He might also promote the concerts of friends of his. It's a marvelous kind of experience: informal yet organized, intimate and magical. And some of the performers may travel very far indeed. One performer who did a concert in my parent's dining room came all the way from Scotland, a continent and an ocean away.

It's the magic of the live performance that interests me here. Music, as just about everyone knows, can produce ecstasy. Part of this is biological. Our brains are biophysically structured in such a way that music induces the production of endorphins and other pleasure-stimulating neurotransmitters. Music performances also serve as the kind of shared experiences that can create friendship among people. The audience at the end of the concert can talk more freely with each other than they could do before. They now have an experience in common: the music itself, and the joy it can produce in the mind and body.

And since music can produce its magic and ecstasy without killing anyone, perhaps it can serve as a place where we can have the experience of 'heightened life' without war.

In the Heroic Hall

I suspect that the house concert is the modern-day equivalent of the experience people had with the mediaeval minstrel and troubadour, the Scandinavian and Germanic *scop*, and the traveling Celtic *fili* and the *bard*. Yet these figures had social and political functions in their respective societies which the contemporary independent musician performing at a house concert probably doesn't have. The traveling poet-musician in those ancient societies was a community's primary source of news and information about faraway people, places, and events.[187]

As explained by historian Stephen Pollington, the Germanic *scop* was also involved in promoting the power of his chieftain:

> The constant stream of praise for the lord from the warband's resident poet was a major part of the prestige underlying the leader's position. In a sense, the poet's position was not unlike that of the warrior: both freely offer service to their lord; both receive valuables and honour at the lord's discretion; both are bound into a reciprocal relationship with the leader in which support is offered in return for honour and public praise. (Stephen Pollington, *The Mead Hall*, (Frithgarth, Norfolk, UK: Anglo-Saxon Books, 2003) p 190)

The scop could also move more or less freely between social classes. At a *sumbel*, the scop "could be a unifying figure for both the lower and upper hall-ends. His performance would engage all who were present, allowing praise of the leader to be delivered in an engaging and entertaining manner to the delight of the whole assembly." (*Ibid*, p 190)

In Celtic countries, the *fili* (poet) and *bard* (musician) served a similar role. Unlike almost everyone else in Celtic society, the bard had legal rights outside of his own tribe. He was also the only non-religious professional person with independent legal standing: this meant that his legal standing was not tied to that of his chieftain or his lord. The poets were graded in a hierarchy of seven ranks: the highest, the *ollamh*, reserved for the very best and most respected poets, had the same honor-price as a king (Kelly, *A Guide to Early Irish Law*, p 48). It appears that Celtic society reserved special respect for performers of music and poetry. The *Instructions of Cormac*, for instance, affirms the value of "silence during a recital" in several places (*Teosca Cormac*, §4). In the same text, Cormac also advises his grandson to "be silent with the silent when a recital is being listened to." (*Ibid*, §30)

We also have some information about the level of technical excellence and the intensity of stage presence expected of the Celtic bard. Old Irish laws stipulate that a special kind of bard called a *cruit*, whose primary instrument was the harp, had to know how to perform three particular kinds of music, which the laws called the Three Noble Strains: *gentraige*, which induces laughter and happiness, *goltraige* which induces tears and sadness, and *fodána*, which induces the audience to sleep (Kelly, *A Guide to Early Irish Law*, p 64). The laws also state how much money a bard could demand as payment for his performances, and a successful bard could get very rich. But if his performance was excessively monotonous and boring, or if he overcharged his patrons, he could face various legal penalties. If his performances and his subject matter was consistently inadequate, he could lose his independent legal status and his honor-price.

A Celtic poet who specializes in satire was called a *rindile* or a *cáinte*, the latter name derived from a verb meaning 'to cut'.

However, the cáinte could not attack just anyone he wanted to at any time. In old Irish law, to satirize someone with verbal taunts, insults, mockery, or with a false accusation of moral wrongdoing, was a serious criminal offence. But satire was also one of the social pressures which induced people to get along with each other, to do their jobs and obey the laws. Thus the old laws distinguish between justified and unjustified satire. If the satire was legitimate, the satirized party might have to make 'a pledge to save his honor'. (A pledge, in old Irish law, is a bit like a 'peace bond' today. It was an object of special value, given to another person who holds it like a kind of hostage until the case is resolved.) To ignore legitimate satire was also treated as a criminal offence: even a king who ignored satire against himself could lose his kingly honor-price. If the satire was illegitimate, the satirist would have to pay the victim his honor-price, and in some cases also perform a poem or song in praise of the offended person, to put the offended party's reputation right again (cf Kelly, *A Guide to Early Irish Law*, pp 137-9). To some extent, the *cáinte* is comparable to the *thyle*, whom as we have seen is the person who challenges or criticizes people, especially when it would be unseemly or inappropriate for the chieftain to do so himself. We have already seen how Unferth, the *thyle* in the court of Hrothgar, treated Beowulf (and how Beowulf handled Unferth in return).

The Celtic bard's capacity for satire was also believed to be supernaturally powerful. Irish mythology contains numerous examples of poets and singers inflicting blemishes and physical disfigurements upon the bodies of those they satirize. Due to the Celtic legal requirement for kings to be without physical blemish, an attack by a bard that causes such a blemish could lead to a king's downfall. Indeed the story of the first satire ever recited in Ireland had just that effect: a bard named Corpre disfigured and thus deposed High King Bres, on account of the king's miserliness and refusal of hospitality. Nor are such stories limited to myths and legends: historical records also hold a few examples. The *Annals of Connacht* for the year 1414, for instance, record that Lord Lieutenant John Stanley was killed by "a poet's spell". Similarly, the *Annals of Ulster* for the year 1024 state that a murdered poet was able to live just long enough to recite a curse-poem against his attackers, which caused their bodies to rot within an hour (cf Kelly, *A Guide to Early Irish Law*, p 44). Leaving aside the supernatural element implied here, perhaps some part of the poet's power was invested in his capacity to induce shame upon his targets. Blushing after satire might have counted as a physical blemish under some circumstances (or, at least, in the eyes of a king's opportunistic political opponents). And perhaps a particularly true-shooting satirist could induce in his subjects a suicidal malaise.

The old Irish laws also state that a poet had to know three techniques of magical prophesy called the Three Illuminations. The first of them is called *imbas forosna*, ('encompassing knowledge which illuminates'). A 9th century description of this technique gives us the following. First the poet eats a small sample of the uncooked meat of a pig, dog, or cat, and he offers some of it to his gods. Next he goes to sleep while four other poets recite magical poems or chants or songs in a circle around him. The future is then revealed to the poet in his dream. The second of the Three Illuminations is called *teinm láeda* ('breaking the marrow'), about which little is known. The third is called *díchetal di chennaib* ('chanting from the head'). This one seemed to involve entering a mild trancelike state, and reciting spontaneous poetry which describes future events. As techniques for perceiving the future, it seems that the poets inherited these three magical techniques from the Druids. The Celts of continental Europe seem to have been educated as Bards first, then as Ovates (seers or prophets), before attaining the social rank of Druids.

Socrates, searching 5th century BCE Athens for people who actually did know what they claimed to know, also approached the musicians and poets. He described how they compose with the aid of some kind of mystical experience:

> I went to the poets, the writers of tragedies and dithyrambs and the others, intending in their case to catch myself being more ignorant than they. So I took up those poems with which they seemed to have taken the most trouble and asked them what they meant, in order that I might at the same time learn something from them... I soon realized that poets do not compose their poems with knowledge, but by some inborn talent and by inspiration, like seers and prophets who also say many fine things without any understanding of what they say. The poets seemed to me to have had a similar experience. (*Apology* 22b-c)

To Socrates, the similarity between religious inspiration and artistic composition was a reason to be suspicious, not admiring, of the artists. Being unable to explain the meaning nor the inspirational source of their work, Socrates concluded that the musicians and poets did not know what they professed to know. Socrates is at least partially correct. If a person cannot explain what he or she knows, nor explain how she knows it, then we have good cause to doubt that she knows what she says she knows. However, as most artists and creative people know, there is a definite psychological state in which artistic ideas flow freely, and much work can be accomplished in a short amount of time. Psychologists today sometimes call this condition 'flow' or 'fugue state'. An artist in this condition becomes enormously productive in a short burst of time, and may perceive the work as coming to him from a magical or divine source outside of himself.

In the Local Pub
Are any of these things still expected of contemporary musicians

and performing artists today? Or, are such talents expected of the best of them, if not them all? For the most part, modern people do not look to poets and storytellers and musicians for public news, as we once relied on the Germanic *scop* or the Celtic *fili*. Today we get our news now from journalists and the mass media, and we look to musicians and singers mostly for entertainment. But the Bardic prerogative to satirize people for shameful, dishonorable, or idiotic behavior is perhaps still alive and well. In the spring of 2008, for instance, a guitar belonging to Canadian musician Dave Carroll was severely damaged by United Airlines baggage handlers. After an entire year of being given excuses and dismissals by the company, he wrote a trilogy of songs to shame the company into taking responsibility for their negligence. The first of the songs, which was called *United Breaks Guitars*, was downloaded from the Internet by the eager public more than six million times, and the company was compelled to apologize.

Musicians, singers, live poets (beat poets, slam poets etc) and performing artists still need some of the same skills as their ancient Celtic counterparts. I spoke with about two dozen or so performers over a year, and all of them mentioned two or three of the following points:

- Obviously an artistic creative capacity is required here. A musician must use some of her free time to compose new songs, and to experiment with new possibilities for lyrics, melody, instrumentation, and the like. She must also practice regularly, preferably daily, because (as one informant put it) "the stage is not the place to learn new chords."
- He or she has to know how to project her voice, so that she can be heard by everyone, without straining herself and hurting her throat. She cannot always expect electric amplification, and has to be ready to perform without it. This is not as easy as it may seem to those who don't know how to do it (but I am informed that it is a *teachable* talent).

- Depending on the kind of artist that she is, she might be expected to perform at almost any time: parties hosted by friends or family, paying gigs that are booked at the last minute, and so on. She therefore must have a large part of her repertoire memorized, and always have her instrument in tune and close at hand.
- She must be able to assess the social situation in which she is asked to perform so that she can offer the right kind of performance.
- She may also be required to produce melodies or song lyrics on short order, for instance if a paying client wants original music for the occasion. I know musicians who were handed poems written by friends (or paying clients) and were then asked to set the poem to music, and given only twenty minutes to do so. A kind of constant artistic readiness, therefore, was required.
- Informants from the modern Druidic community stressed that the bard must be capable of magical or spiritual inspiration. Informants used the word *imbas* here, as well as the phrase-word 'Fire in the Head', the Welsh word *Awen*, and sometimes the Ojibway word *orenda*. These words were used by informants to mean knowledge transmitted to a person from the gods during a period of intense meditation and artistic productivity.
- Finally, musicians also need to listen to other musicians, and be 'up to date' with the styles, trends, and news in her community. Being a bard does not mean playing only one's own songs. And after all, musicians become better musicians by learning from and sharing with other performers.

Since professional musicians are often on the road for most of the year, they have to have a relationship with themselves too. Heather Dale, a well traveled independent musician and composer, felt that her most important relationship is with her own creative powers:

> It sounds a bit silly, but it's definitely with myself, my creative, private side. If I neglect myself, then I find my ability to create music and perform it effectively really suffers. It may simply be that my own songs are so personal; even if I'm telling quite an obscure story, I always try to find some element that touches me (and hopefully my listeners). I've gone through periods in the past where I've been so busy, so distracted by work or ill health or social stress, that I don't get inspired to write or sing at all, and it takes a solid amount of quiet time to regain that equilibrium, time when I'm putting my needs first and only entering the social whirl when *I* feel like I might need it. In those times I go for long walks, get back into nature, daydream, paint, play piano, whatever it takes to reconnect with that quiet soul inside me that can synthesize my experiences into a musical form. It's especially hard to keep that equilibrium when I'm out touring; the days really do fly by and so much personal energy is taken up by traveling and connecting with new people. I get lots of ideas on the road, but it's rare that I do much writing until I'm back home again. (H. Dale, 2009: www.heatherdale.com)

Another informant taught me that the bard's relation to herself must be strong enough to be able to hold back depression and loneliness. Bards are emotional people, and often have to go deep into their feelings in order to produce meaningful and memorable works of beauty. But this means going into all of her feelings, not just the happy ones. It also means examining sad times in one's life and experiencing the sadness of those times all over again.

> If we are honest artists, we can't be just singing about 'true love' all the time, the way pop stars do. Life is more complex

than that. And good art so frequently emerges from *problems*: broken hearts, big plans and dreams that suddenly disappear, and long lonely winter nights. A perfectly happy man is almost always a perfectly boring man. His story is too easy to tell. Nothing much really happens around him. But a troubled and tormented man is much more interesting: and we love to tell stories about people under pressure. (T. Foley, 2010)

This same informant also emphasized that artistic inspiration, *imbas*, emerges from turbulence and not from calm: "To be an artist is not to be at peace; and a true artist may not be a very happy man. That's why they make such lousy boyfriends!"

There is at least one further talent that a performer must learn which perhaps cannot be measured like the other practical skills, and indeed is comparable to magic: 'stage presence'. This is the ability to acquire and hold the attention of an audience, but it is also something more. It is only vaguely related to the performer's technical skill, or the artistic and cultural importance of the work of art he's presenting. Someone may be technically skilled and very well versed in 'the classics' and yet have no presence at all. Stage presence is more like the capacity to become 'larger', to fill a room with the here-ness and now-ness of her voice and image. It's not exactly something that one either naturally has or naturally lacks, because, like techniques for vocal projection, it can actually be taught. It is one of the things that actors learn at drama schools. Some bards have special warm-up habits which help put them in the right mood to project their stage presence effectively. One performer told me: "I always wear high heel boots when I perform: I feel tall, sexy, and powerful, and I need to feel that in order to make the magic." (T. Foley, 2010) But even with habits like these, there is still something about stage presence that resists definition. Stage presence transports the minds of both performer and audience to the site of the story. The intellectual activity involved is sometimes called 'visualization': people see the world of the story in their mind's eye, and emotionally respond to it as if they are actually there. An excellent performer with great stage presence can induce that effect in the audience. This was explained to me by a friend of mine who is a professional theatre actor: "Do you know what magic is? Magic is standing on a stage and convincing three hundred people that they are somewhere else." (C. Benson, 2009)

Performers with good stage presence are applauded and cheered, and the venue managers normally ask for them to return. Performers with poor presence are ignored by their audiences. If his stage presence is particularly bad, he may be heckled and booed off the stage. As the word spreads about his lack of talent, no one hires him for subsequent shows. No one likes a boring performer, even if what he is doing is artistically sound or culturally important. Those qualities alone are not enough to hold an audience's attention. Indeed, stage presence is distinct from a performer's technical talent and the artistic significance of his work because a particular performance might lack those two areas entirely, but the performer might captivate an audience's attention nonetheless. Furthermore, stage presence can work against the performer. The actor in playing a secondary character, who for some reason is on stage while the main characters have the majority of the dialogue, might nonetheless center the audience's attention on himself, by for instance engaging in curious or comical 'stage business' (rolling a cigarette, tying his shoe, etc). Stage presence thus has the effect of subjecting performers to an almost Darwinian selection process.

The songs we sing together reinforce the symbiotic identity, the profound togetherness, of a community, even while contributing new creative possibilities to that identity. All of the relationships and activities described in this book are ways that people present themselves to themselves and to each other, with the support of values that counteract fear and nurture meaning. But there is something special about live musical performance, because of the way live music concentrates into a single event so many things that support that purpose: literature, language and word play, bodily gesture and dance, music, performance talent, stage presence, perceptual intelligence of social environments, thought and emotion, history, artistic creativity, and magic.

The Bardic Circle

One of the highlight events of Kaleidoscope Gathering, an annual pagan culture festival which I regularly attend, is the Bardic Competition. Musicians, storytellers, and other performing artists sign up to sing a song, tell a story, demonstrate a dance, or even just rant and rave to entertain, for an audience of between two and three hundred people. A 'master of ceremonies' warms up the audience with a performance of his own, and helps keep the timing of the event flowing smoothly. At the Kaleidoscope Bardic, the Master of Ceremonies is a professional actor who plays the role of a Scottish highland chieftain. This character's antics have become so popular over the years that he is as much part of the festival as a whole, as he is part of the Bardic event.

Although the Bardic is a lot like an open stage at a pub, there are a few rules, such as:

- Time limits on competitor's performances, usually 5 minutes, including any introductory dialogue.
- A limit to the number of performers, in order to ensure the evening doesn't drag on forever.
- A requirement for performances to be 'family friendly' (i.e. no explicit adult sexual content, no racist language or hate speech, and the like).
- A prohibition on interrupting a performer in progress, although the MC may stop a performance that is offensive, or which goes beyond the time limit.

Festival staff judge the performances: these staffers may also have 'shenanigans' of their own, mostly to help keep the energy of the night lighthearted and fun. The winners receive various gifts, mostly donated by local artists and craftspeople, and the top winner receives free admission to the following year's festival. The winners are usually the performers who have the most original, attention-holding, artistically excellent, and professionally polished performance.

Some performers at the Bardic Competition also bribe the judges with ice cream, cookies, alcoholic drinks, decorative gifts, massages, and sometimes offers of unspecified 'other services' after the competition is over. But these bribes mean nothing when the judges come down to deliberating their final decision. The festival organizers assured me that there has never been a case in which a winner was chosen because of his bribe instead of his performance. On one occasion, a judged asked a performer, "What's your bribe?" The performer cheekily replied, "I don't have to give a bribe: my music is *that good*." And indeed he won the competition that year. The bribes all part of the theatre, although sometimes the judges' choice of best bribe receives an honorable mention.

The relationship between a performer and the audience can be especially visible in such environments. Since the audience sits in a circle around a fire (it's a theatre-in-the-round) a performer never stands more than ten feet away from the front row, and always has a few people behind her. But this also means that the performer can see almost all of the faces in the audience, and can know right away whether they are interested or bored. It's a tough challenge, even for those who have been doing it for many years. But it is enormously rewarding for everyone when it is successful. The fire in the center of the circle becomes the *axis mundi*, the center, radiating not just light and warmth, but also the ideas, feelings, and truths of the culture and its shared identity, which sustains the spirit as food and water sustain the body. The circular space around the fire, where the musician stands and performs, becomes sacred ground, august and hallowed, not to be entered by just anyone. Yet that ground is also enchanted and beautiful, a frontier of mystery from which only good things may come. A performer whose stage presence is similarly august and beautiful can make her song seem like a truth radiating from the very heart of the world. Then the audience itself forgets the differences that divide them, and they become one people, one community, one circle of meaning. There the immensities gather: the trees and the shadows and the stars become full of listening gods, the circle becomes our true and proper home.

We shall see more of the importance of artists and performers when we study storytellers. But let us turn next to another figure in the community whose work also dismantles our labyrinths of fear, and replaces them with circles of meaning.

17

Philosophers

This next proposition may seem a little ridiculous to some. I think that another alternative to war, where we may learn bravery and heightened life without killing anyone, is philosophy.

Twelve centuries ago, Europe's Atlantic coast was dominated by a people called 'Vikings': raiders and plunderers from Norway, Denmark, and other Scandinavian countries. They often targeted early Christian monasteries because that's where the gold was kept. Starting around the year 800, Vikings raided the monasteries on the coasts of Ireland at least once a year for forty consecutive years. In the year 837, sixty Viking dragon-ships were anchored at the mouth of the river Liffey, and sixty more sat by the mouth of the Boyne. More fleets of Viking ships were riding up the Shannon and other rivers into the very heart of the country. In the years 795, 802 and 806, Vikings sacked the monastery on the isle of Iona, killing most inhabitants each time. On the third occasion, the record says they killed "no less than sixty-eight monks." (Moody & Martin, *The Course of Irish History*, pp 92-94) Today, just about every historian understands that the Vikings were 'the victims of bad press'. After all, the accounts of their attacks were written by the very people they were attacking. But the palpable fear of the Norsemen should not be lightly dismissed. In this poetic fragment from the period, an Irish monk described the fear of the Viking in his gratitude for a winter storm that would keep them away:

The wind is rough tonight,
Tossing the white-combed ocean,
I need not dread fierce Vikings

Crossing the Irish sea.
(Marginalia in *Thesaurus Paleohibernicus*, ii, 290)

Refugees from the sacking of Iona came to the Abbey at Kells, in
the midlands of Ireland, bringing with them the last few
treasures that the Vikings either didn't find or didn't want.
Among them, they brought an unfinished illustrated folio of the
Gospels, known today as the Book of Kells. Welsh chronicler
Geraldus Cambrensis saw the Book of Kells (or another one like
it) in the abbey in Kildare, and described it as follows:

> Here you can look upon the face of the divine majesty drawn
> in a miraculous way; here too upon the mystical representa-
> tions of the Evangelists... And there are almost innumerable
> other drawings. If you look at them carelessly and casually
> and not too closely, you may judge them to be mere daubs
> rather than careful compositions. You will see nothing subtle
> where everything is subtle. But if you take the trouble to look
> very closely, and penetrate with your eyes to the secrets of the
> artistry, you will notice such intricacies, so delicate and
> subtle, so close together and so well knitted, so involved and
> bound together, and so fresh still in their colorings that you
> will not hesitate to declare that all these things must have
> been the result of the work, not of men, but of angels.
>
> (Geraldus Cambrensis, *Topographica Hibernia* (London:
> Penguin, 1982), p 84)

A treasure like the Book of Kells can be important, and worth
saving, even at a time when people's lives were in direct peril.
Books represent knowledge, and knowledge is the keel and the
rudder of civilization. As the Book of Kells was an illustrated
edition of the four Gospels of Christ, the refugees who brought it
to Kells probably thought of it as their light of religious hope in
a time of danger and fear. As it is also a complex and beautiful

treasure of art, perhaps it also represented a fragile sign of the goodness and the genius of humankind.

Over the next century, the Norsemen shifted their focus from plunder to colonization, and for various reasons lost interest in Ireland. In the year 1014 they were driven out of Ireland permanently by Brian Boru at the Battle of Clontarf. Later in the same century, Alfred 'the Great' of Wessex shut them out of Britain. But even while the Viking wars were in progress, Irish Celtic monks were traveling all over Europe. Their main purpose was not organized missionary evangelism. In fact they saw themselves as following in the footsteps of certain Old Testament patriarchs, such as Abraham, who sought isolated places to contemplate God without the distraction of worldly affairs. Therefore they sought remote and inaccessible places, such as hidden Alpine valleys, or small isolated islands. Yet they represented an alternative cultural force, an intellectual force, spreading not only the Christian religion, but also the whole preserved knowledge of civilization from before the fall of the Roman empire. From the 6th to the 8th centuries, Irish adventuring monks established nearly a hundred monasteries all over the continent of Europe (Moody & Martin, *The Course of Irish History*, p 75). Arabic scholars had also preserved the learning of the ancient world, and some of their books began to make their way back into Europe around the same time. With these books and the ideas contained within them, Europe began to rebuild its intellectual heritage.

Alfred the Great is remembered today as a warrior-king, but he was also a thinking man. After his victory over the Danes, he arranged for all the important books of the time to be translated from Latin into English, and he established a national campaign for literacy. In his orders he wrote:

It seems better to me... that we should translate certain books which are most necessary to know into the language that we can all understand, and also arrange it... so that the youth of free men now among the English people... are able to read English writing very well.[188]

Alfred hired scholars from all over Ireland and Britain to do most of the translating work, but he learned Latin himself and contributed personally to the project. He also ordered the creation of *The Anglo-Saxon Chronicle*, a year-by-year account of the history of Britain. It was the first document of its kind written in the English language. Similarly, Charlemagne, ruler of the Carolingian Empire and counted today as the first king of France, commissioned the construction of a library, to collect and copy as many books as possible. His scribes invented a practical yet beautiful form of lettering for the purpose, called Carolingian script, which is still used and little changed to this day. What little we know of the literature of the ancient Greek and Roman world is known to us largely because of the copies that Charlemagne commissioned. Like Alfred, Charlemagne also created a public education program: his decree, in part, said: "In every bishop's see [territory], instruction shall be given in the psalms, musical notation, chant, the computation of the years and seasons, and grammar."[189]

I think that Charlemagne and Alfred and all those traveling Irish monks created these centers of education because they understood something about the power of knowledge. "Civilised man," wrote historian Kenneth Clark, "must feel that he belongs somewhere in space and time; that he consciously looks forward and looks back. And for this purpose it is a great convenience to be able to read and write."[190] Clarke also observed that the ability to read and write separates the civilized person from the 'barbarian' (his term). It is not just that the person without civilization prefers to fight rather than to think. That would be a false dichotomy. But Clarke's point is that a civilized person has a different understanding of time, a different understanding of his relation to the past and the future, and a greater need to establish permanence in the world. Written words can survive time in a way that spoken words cannot. Spoken words belong only to the moment in which they are spoken. But written words – painted on paper, carved into stone, wrought in metal bars, and so forth – belong to all posterity. They can be remembered by the readers just the same as spoken words can, but they can be read and re-read as long as the surface they are written on survives. To write and publish a book, and indeed to build and maintain a library, one needs to have confidence in the future. Clarke used the culture of the Norse as a comparison:

> Civilisation means something more than energy and will and creative power: something the early Norsemen hadn't got, but which, even in their time, was beginning to reappear in Western Europe. How can I define it? Well, very shortly, a sense of permanence. The wanderers and the invaders were in a continual state of flux. They didn't feel the need to look forward beyond the next March or the next voyage or the next battle. And for that reason it didn't occur to them to build stone houses, or to write books.[191]

But Clarke is wrong here – the Norsemen *did* have their own books. They too were interested in sophisticated themes like history, justice, family life, romantic love, and scientific specu-lation, just like people in any other enquiring society. The impetus to write these books seems to have been the colonization of Iceland and Greenland, because those lands had no Viking ancestral burial mounds. Without those mounds, the stories in their oral history had no references in their landscape. This effec-tively left them without a history: and without a history, they were also without a home. So they decided to *create* history (and hence turn the new lands into homelands) by meticulously documenting all the major events of the colonial period. The books of the Norse colonists are called *sagas*. There are literally hundreds of them, and they reveal some of the same literary subtlety that one finds in the artwork of the Celts, and the literature of the Greeks and Romans. To this day modern Icelanders read them with national pride.

By the way, in studying the relations involved in scholars and books, we could also include maps, musical scores, mathematical computations, letters, star charts, paintings and drawings, photographs and films. We can include just about anything in which information and ideas can be set down for posterity. Many scholars use the word 'text' to mean any of these documents. A text can be just about anything on which knowledge can be recorded, and made accessible to anyone who knows how to read it, at any time. It is an account of someone's creation or discovery of knowledge, with which other people can make similar discoveries. A relationship with a book, in this sense, is a relationship with knowledge. It is also a relationship with the other people with whom we teach, learn, and share knowledge. And as some of the people who might read your book are people who will be born after you die, and as you can read a book written by someone who died long before you were born, it follows that a relationship with a book suggests a relationship with time. A large part of a scholar's work involves discovering, understanding, and sometimes criticizing the knowledge of the past, applying it to present-day problems, and preserving it and passing it on to the future. It also involved generating new knowledge to bequeath to the future. Obviously, the scholar's relation with his or her books is not the only relation in which knowledge and time are involved. Some relationships require specialized skills, such as a knowledge of obscure vocabulary, or of foreign languages. Some require deep familiarity with various materials, with natural processes, or with people. These are undoubtedly forms of knowledge. A scholar's relationship to knowledge requires these things too. But it also calls for confidence in the *worthiness of ideas* to be shared with others, and recorded for the future. The relationship with time, which is a great immensity, is a large part of what makes the scholar's relationship with books a spiritual one.

This may not seem very obvious to modern people. Probably the majority of written words that people produce and read today (in modern Western society anyway) are written not with ink and paper, but with electronic signals. We write blog posts, instant messaging notes, and social networking status updates on our computers. We write text messages on our phones. We don't expect anyone to save most of these messages for longer than the time it takes to read them and write a reply. We probably process more written words each day than anyone has ever had to process ever before in the history of the world. But we keep almost none of them: emails and text messages get archived away or deleted. Furthermore, with our free primary education, free public libraries, and relatively cheap adult literacy programs, we often take literacy for granted. There is also a certain popular prejudice which associates education with elitism and arrogant snobbery, and imagines that intellectual people have no emotions. So we have perhaps less appreciation of what a great achievement literacy really is. Clarke said, "For over five hundred years this achievement [literacy] was rare in Western Europe. It is a shock to realize that during all this time practically no lay person, from kings and emperors downwards, could read or write."[192] Even Alfred the Great, although he could read several languages, might not have been able to write any of them. It is likely that he dictated his books to a secretary.

But imagine what your life would be like if you couldn't read. All those posters, signs, billboards, shop fronts, emails, contracts, documents, restaurant menus, websites, sales receipts, magazines, newspapers, public monuments, and of course books, which are everywhere in our society, would be closed to you. You would know that they mean *something*, because you can watch

334

other people read them, and hear them talk about what they read. But you would not be able to share the experience which the literate person, standing next to you, is having. Illiterate adults in our society sometimes describe feelings of profound isolation from the world, and sometimes also shame and embarrassment. It is not only that they cannot read, but more generally that they feel that they live in a different world. I know that some people are illiterate for no fault of their own: they have a learning disability, for instance, or they come from poverty and therefore couldn't go to school. But I trust my point is clear. Literacy creates avenues for communication and self-expression that the illiterate person simply doesn't have. It is thus a remarkable accomplishment, and in my view literacy has great spiritual significance.

Incidentally, the word 'seeker', often used today to refer to a person who searches for knowledge in (non-intellectual) spiritual experiences, has a place in the history of literacy. It was first used in a spiritual context during the English Civil War, by soldiers in Oliver Cromwell's New Model Army. They used the word to refer to someone who read the Bible on his own and sought his own understanding of its meaning. Thus the notion of being a 'seeker' was tied to literacy right from the beginning.

The Spirit of Reason
The commitment to autonomous reason in the pursuit of knowledge is what makes the philosopher distinct from artists, poets, religious mystics, and just about every other kind of knowledge-seeker. Not that other kinds of seekers are necessarily less rational, or that their work has less philosophical value. But they do not place systematic reason at the center of their activity. The philosopher's commitment to reason would seem to pull her relationship with knowledge away from the sacred and closer to the secular. Indeed the usual definitions of reason and rationality tend to deliberately shy away from poetic

or mystical ornamentation. Let us define it here simply as a method for sound and clear thinking. To be rational simply means to have strong and valid *reasons* for believing whatever you believe. The comedians of Monty Python defined a rational argument as "a collected series of statements intended to establish a proposition." That's a perfectly good definition. But there is something else in the exercise of reason which I think makes it profoundly spiritual, and which that definition doesn't capture. Having given my adult life to philosophy, the spiritual dimension of reason is important to me. But I beg your patience, dear reader, as that significance is difficult to explain.

A relationship with knowledge requires *curiosity*, which after all is nothing less than *the desire for knowledge*. To be a scholar, and especially a philosopher, you have to be the sort of person for whom the simple explanations of things are not enough to satisfy you. A philosopher notices something new or interesting in her world: then she has to find out more about it. She asks what it is, where it came from, how it works, what its relations are, why it is here, and what else might be implied by its appearance. Curiosity is the philosopher's first virtue, and this curiosity has to run very deep. Indeed the desire for knowledge is built right into the very name for the activity itself: for as almost everyone knows, philosophy is *Philia Sophia*, the friendship with knowledge, the love of wisdom. He is not a philosopher if he does not care about knowledge, nor about his method for gathering knowledge.

A philosopher's curiosity is also *organized*. The lover of knowledge is not like a collector of antiquities who displays his treasures in a private museum. Nor does he jump from one shiny new intellectual trinket to another, like a kind of magpie. Rather, the lover of knowledge *has a plan*. He has a definite method of investigation, and that method matters to him as much as, if not more than, the discoveries which that method reveals to him. Systematic reason is that method; to care about that method is a mark of a good philosopher. Historian Mariateresa Brocchieri wrote of Abelard, one of the finest mediaeval intellectuals, that: "in all the areas he touched and at all the stages of his teaching career, he cared more for the method of investigation than its object; more for the theoretical process of analysis than for the topic itself." (Brocchieri, "The Intellectual", in Le Goff, *Mediaeval Callings*, pp 188-9) Thus I define reason as *organized curiosity*. But that does not tell us whether reason is *spiritual*. You see the difficulty of the task I have put before me!

I close my eyes. I think about what thinking is. I wonder about what I have been doing my whole life. I see my life and all my relations spread out before me, and I examine them. Who am I? Is the story of my life intelligible? Why am I here? Why is anyone here? Who is it that poses these questions? Has my life so far been worthwhile and meaningful? Reason and rationality, you see, is a process of *self-examination*: to examine oneself is *to take care of one's own soul*. This is an ancient and often repeated theme in the works of the great classical philosophers. We find it in the private meditations of Marcus Aurelius, who used to examine himself with questions like these:

> To what use, then, am I now putting my soul? Ask yourself this question on every occasion. Examine yourself. "What do I now have in this part of me called the directing mind? What sort of soul do I have after all? Is it that of a child? A boy? A woman? A despot? A beast of the field? A wild animal?"[193]

We find the spirit of self-examination in Epicurus' famous letter to his friend Menoeceus: "Let no young man delay the study of philosophy, and let no old man become weary of it, for it is never too early or too late to care for the well-being of the soul." We find it earliest of all in Socrates, who brazenly chastised the jurors at his trial, even while they had the power to sentence him to death.

Are you not ashamed of your eagerness to possess as much wealth, reputation and honors as possible, while you do not care for nor give thought to wisdom or truth, or the best possible state of your soul? (*Apology* 29e)

These writers held philosophical self-examination in such high esteem for two reasons. First, the rational person, they observed, is happier. We find this view in the dream of Boethius, who while wasting away in a prison, condemned for a crime he didn't commit, dreamed of the goddess Sophia telling him: "Why do you mortal men seek after happiness outside yourselves, when it lies within you"? (Boethius, *Consolation of Philosophy*, p 63) Cicero noted that neither pain nor pleasure, neither good fortune nor bad, can unseat the rational person's peace of mind: "Philosophy will ensure that the man who has obeyed its laws shall never fail to be armed against all the hazards of fortune: that he shall possess and control, within his own self, every possible guarantee for a satisfactory and happy life." (Cicero, *Discussions at Tusculum*, Ch V, p 63) Similarly, thousands of miles and many centuries away from Rome, the Chinese philosopher Mencius taught: "All things are already complete in oneself. There is no greater joy than to examine oneself and be sincere." (*Book of Mencius* 7A:4)

Secondly, reason gives you a chance to participate in the divine. "The philosopher," says Plato, "by consorting with what is ordered and divine and despite all the slanders around that say otherwise, himself becomes as divine and ordered as a human being can." (*Republic* 500d) And Marcus Aurelius says: "He lives with the gods who consistently shows them his soul, content with its lot, and performing the wishes of that divinity, that fragment of himself which Zeus has given each person to guard and guide him. In each of us this divinity is our mind and reason." (Marcus Aurelius, *Meditations*, 5.27, p 43) Reason and rationality thus has theological force because of the way it brings about a change within the mind and heart of the seeker, which harmonizes the seeker's life with the ways of the highest and deepest things.

Following all this self-examination, I open my eyes, and then open my door, step on to the footpath, and look upon the world. Here are gardens, forests, rivers, deserts, cities, towns, street lamps, sidewalks. Here are ships going out to sea and coming to port again. Here are airports full of people going this way and that way, from one side of the earth to the other. Here are stars, planets, and the sun and moon, making circles around the earth as if fixed to cosmic wheels. I walk about all these things, exploring them, feeling them, touching them, examining them. What is the world? Where did it come from? How did it come to be what it is? Why is it here? What things matter most? Is the world a totality of one thing, or an infinity of many things? Why is there *something* here, rather than nothing at all?

Questions like these are questions about the most ultimate problems in our lives. As I am a philosopher, I want to know about the totality and the infinity of things. I want to perceive the totality and the infinity directly with my own eyes and ears and body and mind. I'm curious and excited about these things – I want to *know* them! I find ignorance a deeply troubling state of being. I'm also full of amazement and wonder. I'm posing these questions, and as I investigate answers, I find myself discovering the universe, discovering myself, discovering dis-cover-y itself. Reason renders strange things intelligible, distant things graspable, mysterious things non-mysterious. I'm invigorated by excitement: philosophical questions are adventurous!

Knowledge must sometimes be struggled for. Philosophical questions are hard. I arrive at a seemingly cogent answer to a question but still find myself full of skepticism and doubt. I close my eyes again and summon my deepest beliefs to the eye of my mind. I consider whether they were deliberately chosen, or whether they were trained into me by habit, parental influence, culture, peer pressure, religion, the mass media, or some other form of unconscious education. I might find myself attached by nostalgia to a belief which, upon further examination, turns out to have the weakest logical integrity, and the flimsiest basis in the facts. If I find I have bad reasons for my beliefs, then I have to let them go. This can be very hard to do. My beliefs about the most ultimate questions are tightly tied into my worldview and my sense of identity. To reject one of them is to reject a piece of who I am, and also to change who I am.

I consider their alternatives, and find myself facing some very disturbing possibilities. Perhaps there are no gods. Perhaps life has no purpose or meaning. Perhaps there is no reason for me to do anything. Perhaps everything is permitted and nothing is true. To be a philosopher means that these prospects are not swept under the rug. They too are placed on the table, along with all their implications and consequences. I look at them and experience fear and trembling. I contemplate Being but also Nothingness. I feel the sickness unto death. I fully see how this is kind of doubt is at the start of a slippery slope that ends in misanthropy, nihilism, despair, and suicide. I gaze into the abyss anyway. The abyss also gazes into me. Philosophy requires curiosity, but also great *courage!*

Someone tells me, "The world is what it is because some god made it that way." A second person says, "It's completely impossible to know how everything began." A third, "You shouldn't trouble yourself with such matters, you should not disturb the mystery of things." A fourth, "Haven't you got better work to do? Isn't there an economy to rebuild, a GDP to maintain, a national budget to balance, a war to fight, a new car to drive, a child in a faraway famine-stricken country to feed, and a phone bill to pay!"

Most of these people have given up the philosopher's adventure far too soon. But a philosopher cannot be complacent. His mind must be active at all times: inquiring, puzzled, skeptical of that which is taken for granted. Reason will not let me sleep.

The simple and common-sense answers are not enough. We quickly find them to be uncommon; we often find them nonsensical. I won't simply repeat a clever quote from a television show or a pop song. I need to *know*, directly, clearly, honestly, and finally, the answers to my questions. I'm perfectly happy if my questions lead to more questions. This keeps me philosophizing! This makes the process of discovery ongoing and sustainable. I learn the world, and I learn myself: I also learn how much more there is to learn.

I'm doing all this in a distinctly relentless and uncompromising way, because I will not settle for the kind of answer that satisfies a simple mind. I won't stop until I have the very best possible answer. I go where the logic takes me. A well crafted proposition also offers directions to follow to a sound conclusion, if I know how to read it well. It's like I'm being led by Necessity or Destiny. To the list of a good philosopher's qualities, let us add systematic purposefulness, but let us call it by a more honest name: *stubbornness*.

Let us also add *skepticism*. For the philosopher who doesn't settle for the simple must be open to the prospect that things are not what they seem. There may be more to things than what meets the eye at first glance. And to skepticism, let us add *rebellion*. For I won't blindly accept what I am told by my parents, my friends, my church, my government, my newspaper columnist, my fashion consultant, my postman, or my marketing director. I have to be my own authority in these matters; I have to be *autonomous*, and do my own thinking. No one else can do my thinking for me. And I am under no obligation to follow anybody's party line. This autonomy can also be spiritual, for instance when God himself affirms it: "You shall not accept any information, unless you verify it for yourself. I have given you the hearing, the eyesight, and the brain, and you are responsible for using them." (*Koran* 17:36) Again, this requires courage!

A mediaeval person calling himself a philosopher would have

been regarded with a little bit of suspicion. Philosophers studied the books of the pre-Christian, pagan world, and might therefore study and teach dangerous, heretical ideas. Philosophers also seek knowledge primarily by means of human reason, and not primarily by mystical experiences, holy scripture, church authority, or divine faith. This kind of intellectual freedom opened the way to some very serious forms of non-conformity, especially including the most severe of all heresies: atheism. The emphasis on total intellectual freedom goes right back to one of the earliest philosophers, Socrates, who was accused by his opponents of being "a student of all things in the sky and below the earth." (*Apology* 18c) As if it was a criminal offence! But people tend to feel personally threatened by the systematic questioning of their own or their society's most unquestioned beliefs. Philosophers have often faced insults, ostracism, and loneliness for their work. And how many of them have found themselves run out of their homes when they spoke the truth for what it was, but what they said was contrary to the 'truth' being imposed on the country by some warlord! Philosophy can be dangerous not just personally, but also politically.

I'm doing all this in a distinctly *intellectual* way. I won't remain still with the answer that is easy, and emotionally gratifying, unless it is also true. Not that I am faced with a choice between being happy and being right. To me, that claim is clearly a false dichotomy. In fact the truth is probably that the non-intellectual is probably much *less* happy. One who lives entirely in terms of instinct is someone who is in an important sense not in control of his own life. He moves from one pleasure-stimulus to the next; he takes all criticisms of his choices and his ideas as personal affronts; and he only reacts to what he sees, having little or no capacity to anticipate them and plan for them. The person who lives entirely by the impulses of his instincts and passions soon becomes imprisoned by them, and imprisoned most of all by his instinct for fear. Second of all, so many people live in fantasy worlds, meticulously constructed by 'reality' television, market advertising, movies, shock-talk political commentary, and by popularity contests on social networking Internet pages. But no one who lives in a world of illusion, falsehood, fantasy, however temporarily pleasurable, is granted a sustainable and fully satisfying happiness. Reality eventually finds him, and if he is not prepared for it, then it will likely hurt him. The philosopher prefers to live in the real world. And to the philosopher, the real world is very large indeed. It spans 'all things in the sky and below the earth', from the microcosm of the atom beneath my visual reach, to the macrocosm of the furthest distant galaxies, also beyond my sight.

Realism, honesty, and *precision* are the next important qualities. The philosopher has to be able to see things and name things for what they really are. She says, "Stop, hey, what's that sound? Everybody look what's going down." (Incidentally, this is a quality which reason shares with education and the arts.) Confucius offered what I believe to be the very best argument for the importance of precision in our language: it appears in a teaching of his which today we call "The Rectification of Names":

> If names are not rectified, then language will not be in accord with truth. If language is not in accord with truth, then things cannot be accomplished. If things cannot be accomplished, then ceremonies and music will not flourish. If ceremonies and music will not flourish, then punishment will not be just. If punishments are not just, then the people will not know how to move hand or foot. (*Analects* 13:3)

The argument here is that words and language must be used properly in order to produce worthwhile lives for people. For if people do not say what they mean, nor mean what they say, then we will not be able to communicate properly. We will not know what ways of relating to each other are respectful or disrespectful, permitted or not permitted (this is part of the Confucian understanding of 'ceremonies and music'). Not knowing that, we will also not know whether or not something will cause harm, or result in punishment. We end up too afraid to do anything: too consumed by fear to move hand or foot.

I'd like to add here that when words and languages are rectified, it is harder for people in power to pull the wool over your eyes. Things have to be described for what they truly are, and not with clever euphemisms that distract and insulate people from reality. Think about the company that sells 'home-style' food, with 'real' and 'natural' ingredients, made on an assembly line using synthetic sugars and chemical preservatives and colors. Think of news editors who instruct journalists to report government budget cuts as 'savings', as happened at the BBC in early 2011.[194] Think of how public servants in Canada were instructed to describe the government of Canada as the "Harper Government", after the name of the Prime Minister, in all official communications.[195] Words are powerful things. They can heal and harm, they can configure reality, they can tune one's consciousness for a life of meaning, or a life of fear. It becomes vitally important, therefore, to use words correctly.

This does not mean that our language must become more mechanical, less living, more mathematical, less poetic. For another part of the spirit of reason has to do with *subtlety*. Subtlety is a small difference or a delicate detail which takes on greater importance the more it is contemplated. Subtlety has its role in perceptual intelligence: attention to subtleties in the environment helps the hunter know where the animals he is chasing are likely to be. In art or in literature or music or philosophy or any of the sciences, subtle shifts in the meaning of a single word or phrase or symbol can cast the whole work into a new significance. Subtlety is one of the marks of intellectual excellence. In a subtle text, some of the patterns and relations and

344

expressions of meaning are not obvious at first. They have to be discovered, 'unlocked' so to speak, by careful and dedicated observation and thinking. "Good thinking is subtle," my doctoral supervisor once taught me. "Good thinking takes time, and patience. If you think you understood a philosophical text on first reading, then you almost certainly have not!" Subtlety can appear in the arts too. The Book of Kells is an excellent example, since some of its designs are as dense as 100 lines per inch. Thus intellectual precision, in the mode of attending to the subtleties of things, actually opens up the magic and artistry of language. And by the way, the subtlety of the Book of Kells is the very polar opposite of the weapons of the invading Norsemen. After all, there's nothing subtle about a large, muscular, screaming man trying to kill you with an axe.

I open my eyes again. I examine the world; I examine myself. I draw conclusions from what I find. I then examine the conclusions, to see if they follow properly from their premises, or that they are supported by the evidence, or that they are consistent with other conclusions, or that there are no hidden unexamined presuppositions. I wonder about the implications of the conclusions I've reached, not only for the practical results in the world, but also for the person I would become, if I acted upon them. And I wonder what might be said of those conclusions by people I respect and admire. And overall, I'm using the power of my own thoughts to penetrate the mysteries of the universe.

Power and Enlightenment
Our stereotypes tell us that the rational man has no emotions. We imagine he never experiences love, nor enjoys the arts, nor feels indignation at some injustice, nor plays with his children. But I have never met such a man unless he was burdened by an electro-chemical dysfunction in his brain. When complete strangers tell me that I should balance my head with my heart, rationality with emotion, the intellect with intuition and instinct,

I cringe a little. For these statements presuppose so much! Most of all, it is presupposed that reason and inspiration are two different things. But there are not two things here: *there is one thing* – or perhaps I better say, there is one activity, and it is called the love of wisdom. Among all spiritual activities this love is the only one which addresses itself directly to the immensities. Reason is not just a method of critical thinking: it is a method of enlightenment.

Another stereotype tells us that ignorance is bliss. We should therefore ask, might an ignorant person nonetheless lead a happy life? Socrates told his accusers that "the unexamined life is not worth living." (*Apology* 38a) This motto has been interpreted up and down so often, it is almost completely worn out and wrung dry. But if nothing else, we can say that this proposition claims that the life of self-knowledge is *better* than the life of ignorance. Is that proposition true? Or, is ignorance actually bliss? One way to approach this question is to observe what knowledge can do for you. Although the historians I consulted didn't mention it, I suspect that both Alfred and Charlemagne established their literacy programs because they regarded knowledge as a form of *power*. In the history of ideas (in the English language anyway), the proposition that knowledge is power did not get an explicit treatment until five hundred years later, with the work of the Elizabethan scientist Francis Bacon. But the idea that knowledge is power is the kind of philosophical insight that anyone can discover. Knowledge is power for the simple reason that the more that you know, the more that you can *do*. You can travel farther, and faster, or build bigger buildings, or talk to people who live very far away. You can create an accounting ledger of the wealth of your kingdom, in order to tax it, or reallocate labor, or conscript people into the army. You can build bigger and more powerful machines, for whatever purpose you may wish. And if you can write down what you know, then you can share it with more people, and be more sure of it if your memory grows

346

fallible. Finally, with literacy as a source of knowledge (and hence power) you can pass your knowledge on to the future. Each generation can build upon the work of its predecessors, and no one needs to reinvent the wheel.

Yet Alfred and Charlemagne almost certainly knew of a second attitude towards knowledge, which they would have encountered in their study of classical Greek literature and philosophy. This attitude held that knowledge is *enlightenment*. It is an ancient wisdom, best articulated in classical Greek philosophy, that the ability to think and to reason is a spiritual thing. The classical tradition identifies the mind with the soul, 'the spark of the divine' within us: that phrase was first used by Aristotle, although it comes to us from other sources too. The idea that knowledge is enlightenment is the idea that knowledge is inherently valuable and edifying, and to be pursued for its own sake, whether or not it has any practical application. We who live in a utilitarian age should not be quick to dismiss this pursuit as something frivolous. Someone who meditates, for instance, or who studies the great works of philosophy and literature, or who researches history, or who does scientific work, or who discusses theology with his friends, contributes enormously to her own quality of life, and that of the people around her. But those contributions are often immaterial, and thus hard to quantify. Sometimes they are also hard to *see*. Yet they offer the kind of benefits which simply cannot be obtained any other way. Probably the first and most important benefit that knowledge confers is the release from fear. The more we understand the ways of the world, the less we will cower from it. Things might still be threatening and dangerous, and certain existential conditions like loneliness and death are not thus banished. But if we *understand* something, then we can face it courageously and confidently. We will have less need for fantasies and illusions to protect our minds from fear, especially the fear of the unknown. And we may be less vulnerable to the enervating despair that can strike when events unexpectedly turn toward the tragic. The pursuit of knowledge for the sake of enlightenment can bring you greater *self*-knowledge too, and with it greater conscious control of your own mind and thoughts. Advertising, political propaganda, peer pressure, or other forms of psychological manipulation will be less able to affect you. Finally, let me add that intellectual discovery can be very exciting and adventurous in its own right, and even wonderfully pleasurable. As Alfred himself wrote in his diaries: "The saddest thing about any man is that he be ignorant, and the most exciting thing is that he knows."[196]

Argumentation Without Conflict

If you study critical thinking at a college or university, you will probably be introduced to a catalogue of arguments: the categorical proposition, the syllogism, the enthymeme. You will be shown a long list of fallacies with unpronounceable Latin names. These things are useful to know. But they are only the tools of the philosopher's trade. Their purpose is to *serve* the philosopher's curiosity. An analogy may help explain. The carpenter must learn the types and cuts of wood that come from the trees and the lumber mills. He must learn the hammers, chisels, punches, files, and drills. These practical and technical matters serve him as he lovingly carves ornaments and delicate lines into his cabinets and tables and bookcases. Similarly, he who studies music must learn the major and minor chords, the time signatures, and so on. He must learn the structure of the sonata and the symphony, or the different rhythms of jazz or blues or rock or folk. These technical matters serve the musician as the raw materials of his art, just as the knowledge of the tools and the properties of different kinds of wood serve the carpenter. Nothing in the theory of music compels a composer to write a symphony for an orchestra, instead of a rock song for a garage band. And nothing in the mathematical description of a musical work tells you what it's like to *hear* the music. Reason serves the philosopher the same way. The principles of logic are his tools. For raw materials, he has the books written by his predecessors, the conversations he has with other rational people, the experiences of his own life, and all things below the earth and in the sky. Whatever your path in life, even if it is a religious path, the function of reason is to *clear the path*. It helps us identify everything that is irrelevant, and gently move it out of the way. It keeps us on track, avoiding all unnecessary digressions, side roads and dead ends. Reason helps keep wisdom from being interrupted. With all distractions set aside, the philosopher can devote himself to her proper calling, which is architecture and music.

In most cases, the principles of sound reasoning will be such that anyone anywhere can follow them, and easily share them with others. As an example, consider the words of Deganawidah, the mystic who founded the Great Peace of the Iroquois Confederacy. One of his followers asked him what the people who accept the great peace will be like. He answered:

> Reason brings Righteousness, and Reason is a power that works among all minds alike. When once Reason is established, all the minds of all mankind will be in a state of Health and Peace. It will be as if there were but a single person.[197]

This basic acknowledgement, that reason works the same way in the minds of all people, also appears in the works of Plutarch, and Confucius, and the unknown authors of the Vedas, and numerous writers in the Western tradition. It is a universal idea.

Consider as another example this passage from the *Instructions of Cormac*, written in Ireland some time in the 10th century. The text as a whole takes the form of a conversation between King Cormac Mac Airt, and his grandson Carbre, on various ethical questions. One of Carbre's questions concerns the proper way to debate ideas in a public assembly.

"O grandson of Conn, O Cormac," said Carbre. "What is the worst pleading and arguing?"

"Not hard to tell," said Cormac. "Seventeen signs of bad pleading, vis:

Contending against knowledge,

Taking refuge in bad language,

Much abuse,

Contending without proofs,

A stiff delivery,

A muttering speech,

Hair-splitting,

Uncertain proofs,

Despising books,

Turning against customs,

Talking in too loud a voice,

Shifting one's pleading,

Inciting the multitude,

Fighting everybody,

Blowing one's own trumpet,

Shouting at the top of one's voice,

Swearing after judgment."[198]

This short passage is a straightforward manual for sound logical reasoning. It identifies seventeen kinds of bad argument, from bullish tactics like insults, the threat of force, and playing the crowd, to more subtle things, like the absence of supporting evidence, or the absence of basic consistency. Remember, the author of this text lived in one of the cultures that those well-admired, highly civilized and efficiently organized Romans considered ignorant barbarians. Yet whoever he was, he knew that productive public debate requires standards of rationality, lest the debate descend into a popularity contest, or a brawl. Even a tribal society, like the Celts, knew and understood what reason and rationality is. Indeed each of these items could belong in a modern textbook on informal logic.

These principles could be favorably compared with contemporary moral theories, such as Jurgen Habermas' theory of discourse ethics. Habermas did not describe moral principles as such, but rather he described principles that have to be honored in order for people to discover their moral principles in a public discourse with each other. His only directly moral claim is that principles of philosophical importance should be subject to a free and fair debate in a public sphere. To ensure freedom and fairness, the speakers must follow a few basic rules of fair argumentation, such as:

- Anyone with the competence to speak and act is allowed to participate.
- No speaker may contradict himself.
- Different speakers may not use the same expression with different meanings.
- Someone wishing to debate a proposition not under discussion must provide a reason for wanting to do so.
- Every speaker may assert only what he or she really believes.
- Every speaker is allowed to question any assertion whatsoever.
- No one may be prevented by coercion from participating.[199]

To the list of the qualities of the spirit of reason, we must now add *communicative openness*. This is the quality which brings you into an intellectual relation with others. Communicative openness means listening to others, taking their views seriously, and treating their ideas with respect even while critically examining them. It means not resorting to fear and force when promoting one's own views, but rather presenting them in a way that leaves them open to the critical scrutiny of others. Communicative openness is a variation of what professional philosophers call 'the principle of charity'. This principle requires speakers to interpret and understand each other's ideas in the very best possible light. Listeners must assume that other speakers are rational, and that what they say is rational, even if that rationality is not immediately obvious. This is partly a professional courtesy that philosophers extend to one another. It also helps to ensure that, when one is critical of another's views, one has understood that person's views properly, and that one is critical for the right reasons. It also helps prevent intellectual or ideological differences from descending into personal grudges.

Enemies of Reason

Reason is fragile. This is not because the laws of logic are weak. Rather, reason is fragile because it is subtle. Reason asks for our time and our patience. Ignorance demands your attention with force. Reason tugs at your shirtsleeve with a gentle hand; ignorance bludgeons you in the face with a hammer. I'm almost sorry to admit it, but a crowd of intellectuals, no matter how deep their wisdom, can be shouted down by a single ignorant man.

As one who has given his whole adult life to the pursuit of reason, I find this very troubling. There are people who prefer ignorance, prejudice, and bellicosity, instead of knowledge. I have a hard time understanding why. To me, reason has always seemed so self-evidently beautiful that it hardly needs further explanation. But apparently it does: for the benefits it offers are simply not obvious to the ignorant man. As far as I can see, the explanation for why some people prefer ignorance and belligerence runs as follows. People's beliefs about the highest and deepest problems in life are tightly involved in their world-views and in their identities. Your beliefs concerning the *philosophical* questions of reality, truth, knowledge, good and evil, beauty, religion, and the like, shape who you believe yourself to be. They similarly shape how you interpret your place in the world, and what you think you should be doing with your life. Reason has the terribly annoying habit of occasionally placing those beliefs into question, pointing out problems, suggesting alternatives, calling for the rejection of unfounded or unsound ideas. The rational person thinks that by pointing out flaws in our thinking, she is doing others a service: she is helping us improve the quality of our thinking. But the ignorant person treats criticism of his deepest ideas as an offence on his very sense of self. When he hears criticisms of his beliefs, he thinks himself under personal attack, and he entrenches himself deeper in his (irrational) beliefs, and he attacks the person presenting the criticism.

Rational people tend to believe that if they present the facts of some case as clearly and precisely as possible, others will be convinced. But some psychological research is now showing that people do not actually make decisions that way. Most people's decision-making habits are designed to protect the sense of self and of identity, at almost any price. This includes protecting their place in the social world, protecting their status and reputation, their livelihood, and their way of being in the world. Clinical psychologist Drew Westen observed that people's emotional feelings tend to influence our judgments more than reasons do.[200] Similarly, cognitive scientist George Lackoff observed that if the facts of some case conflict with values that someone has already committed himself to, then the facts will not normally convince him to change his mind: "the facts bounce off."[201] A scientific study undertaken by psychologists at Duke University and Georgia State University found that people who have rigid, conservative, or fundamentalist beliefs tend to keep those beliefs even when presented with substantial evidence that their beliefs are false. Control groups of people, some identifying themselves as conservative and some as liberal, were shown items of political misinformation from the 2008 United States presidential campaign. A poll was then taken to see how many people believed what they were shown. Then, the participants were shown evidence refuting the misinformation. The evidence came from reliable sources, including former members of President Bush, Jr.'s cabinet. The poll was then conducted again. Those who were already predisposed to believe the misinformation tended to continue believing it, even after being shown evidence to the contrary. The experiment showed that a fundamentalist mind tends to automatically reject alternative points of view. The researchers theorized that "upon hearing a refutation [of misinformation], conservatives might 'argue back' against the refutation in their minds, thereby strengthening their belief in the misinformation."[202]

But the enemy of reason is not simply the person who doesn't want to hear different views than his own. He is, rather, the one who normally promotes his views with deception, rhetorical manipulation, slippery slopes, red herrings, straw men, or even with lies. Psychologists Barbara Forrest and Paul Gross studied the strategy employed by fundamentalist Christian groups to undermine scientific evidence for the theory of evolution. Here is how they summarized it:

… exploiting that modern, nearly universal, liberal suspicion of zealotry, you accuse the branch of legitimate inquiry whose results you hate, in this case evolutionary natural sciences, of – what else? – zealotry! Fanaticism! Crying "viewpoint discrimination" you loudly demand adherence to the principle of freedom of speech, especially in teaching, insist that your freedom is being denied your legitimate alternative view. You identify your (in this case, religious) view of the world as the victim of censorship by a conspiracy among most of the world's scientists, whom you label "dogmatic Darwinists" or the like.[203]

The enemy of reason also uses violence, the language of violence, and the threat of violence. Political assassinations are the most obvious examples. Just this morning as I write these words, a

Pakistani cabinet minister was shot dead by the Taliban because the minister opposed Pakistan's blasphemy laws.[204] But this can happen in any country, including those reputed to be very stable and secure. On 8th January 2011, someone opened fire on a peaceful political meeting in Tucson, Arizona, severely wounding a congresswoman, and killing half a dozen others, including a federal judge, and a nine-year-old girl. Clarence Dupnik, the county sheriff who investigated the crime, observed that the event was influenced by "the vitriolic rhetoric that we hear day in and day out from people in the radio business and some people in the TV business," and the effect of that rhetoric on "unbalanced people."[205]

The violence in the language of the enemy of reason isn't always obvious. Normally it is thinly concealed beneath weasel words, metaphors, hints, equivocations, and innuendo. For instance, when Greenpeace activists climbed on the roof of Britain's parliament building, Donal Blaney, leader of a group called the Young Britons Foundation, called upon police to "next time shoot them down... start with water cannon and if that doesn't work, maybe crank it up a level or two."[206] US congressional candidate Allan West urged his supporters to make his opponent "scared to come out of his house."[207] In 2006, a radical left-wing environmental activist told a scientist that "the rape of nature justified the rape of anyone who supported it."[208] Finally, the enemy of reason will claim 'censorship' or 'oppression', or claim the 'right to free speech', if they come under criticism. Just as Plato warned, over twenty-six centuries ago, a democratic society is "full of freedom and freedom of speech," but "its fiercest members do all the talking and acting." (*Republic* 557b, 564d/e)

The point of studying reason and logic is to show that *there is a better way for people to communicate with each other*. The belligerent and ignorant person can shout down a whole crowd of experienced and educated intellectuals. But that does not make him right, nor does it make his words true. The social function of a philosopher, or any intellectual, is to help prevent people from falling into hateful and destructive ways of communicating their ideas. Without her, the most bullish and violent of the fanatics in our midst will do all the talking, and we all descend into a world of fear.

The Wisdom Circle

The philosophers of ancient Greece and Rome who championed reason as a means of caring for the soul also emphasized that the work need not be done entirely alone. Socrates practiced philosophy by talking to people and asking them philosophical questions, whether in public places or in their own homes. His successors created schools for the purpose: Plato's Academy, Aristotle's Lyceum, for instance. The Stoics gathered in groups on the front porches (the *stoa* – hence the name) of public buildings to discuss philosophical matters together. Some aristocratic Roman families hired philosophers to serve in the household staff as teachers, advisors, and personal confidants. The Roman philosopher and medical doctor Galen of Pergamon recommended that those who wanted to take good care of themselves should seek good conversation with those reputed to be honest, outspoken, and wise. The Roman philosopher Seneca, in a letter to his friend Lucilius, described how philosophy can help deepen and strengthen pre-existing relationships:

> Skilled wrestlers are kept up to the mark by practice; a musician is stirred to action by one of equal proficiency. The wise man also needs to have his virtues kept in action; and as he prompts himself to do things, so he is prompted by another wise man.[209]

There are exceptions to this view. Cicero wrote that "a man who has the ability to commune with himself does not feel the slightest need for anyone else's conversation."[210] But these exceptions tend to be rare. For the most part the classical philosophers followed the Aristotelian teaching that "man is a social being" (*NE*, 1169b15), and that "it is by taking part in transactions with our fellow-men that some of us become just and others unjust." (*NE*, 1103b12)

A Wisdom Circle is a ritual gathering of people who talk of the things that matter most in life. It is called a wisdom circle, not because those who attend it are already wise, but because they are seeking wisdom together. It can happen just about any place where two or more people can have an uninterrupted conversation for as long as they wish. Thus it is not necessary to have access to a library, or for the members to be university educated. While I think that a society is greatly benefited by education, and that we cannot do without schools, libraries, and universities, still I find that philosophy belongs to everyone. A Wisdom Circle is a way to give philosophy back to the people.

A wisdom circle is a ritual, but not an especially formal one: it can coincide with a dinner party, a movie night, or a book club. The leader of the ritual is the host, who is usually the person at whose home the circle takes place. He or she has the privilege of the opening formalities, and the responsibility to ensure that the process is respected by everyone. It can be useful to have a short ritual formality at the beginning, to help everyone approach the occasion with seriousness and heart. The formality need not be elaborate. Mato-Kuwapi, an elder of the Santee-Yanktonai Sioux Nation, described how wisdom circles began among his own people:

> Before talking of holy things, we prepare ourselves by offerings... one will fill his pipe and hand it to the other who will light it and offer it to the sky and earth... they will smoke together... Then they will be ready to talk.[211]

In my tradition, the host initiates the event by lighting a flame in the center. It might be as small as a candle on a coffee table, or as large as a campfire in an outdoor clearing. My own preference is for three candles, which represent the 'fire in the head' and the candles which, in the ancient Irish triad, illuminate every darkness: truth, nature, and knowledge. Lighting the flame introduces the presence of the sacred into the circle. Then everyone is given a cup of tea, since sharing food is one of the activities that brings people together and helps people trust each other. These acts signify that the circle has begun. The host then poses the question which the members of the circle have come to explore together. Finally, he or she takes up the talking stick and offers it to the nearest person that he regards as an Elder, and invites that person to speak first. The wisdom circle can then continue as long as the participants wish it to continue. There is no minimum length of time: the only time requirement is that the circle may not end until everyone who wanted to speak was able to do so at least once. For this reason, it is often impractical to hold a wisdom circle with more than about thirty people at a time. But there is no minimum number of people. The most productive wisdom circles include about a dozen people, but some of the most memorable wisdom circles I attended had only three people, including myself.

Some people may want to use a talking stick in their wisdom circles, especially if the circle is very large (a dozen people or more). The talking stick is a custom for public discourse derived from certain Aboriginal cultures. It is a procedural principle, similar to 'having the floor' in a formal committee meeting or parliamentary debate, and is represented by a decorated staff which the host passes from one person to another. The idea is that the person holding the stick is the only person permitted to speak, and that no one may interrupt the person holding the stick. Indeed, in some Aboriginal traditions, participants pretend that they cannot hear anyone else. I've used a hockey stick, a painted rock, a pencil, and a conch shell (recalling the novel *The Lord of the Flies*). On one curious occasion in my experience, the talking stick was a stuffed animal representing a totem that was important to the host. In my experience, any group of people, even a group of friends, can degenerate into a cacophony of useless noise, unless there is a simple procedure like this one to keep things moving smoothly.

A wisdom circle can address just about any question which the people of the circle find important and interesting. At some circles the host chooses the question, but at others the members of the circle decide the question in advance. Here are a few examples from circles I have personally attended:

- Do the gods truly exist? Who (or what) are they?
- What is friendship?
- What is human nature?
- What is the best way to deal with 'burnout' among our leaders and Elders?
- Can genuine spiritual knowledge come with the use of drugs or alcohol?
- Should nationalism or national identity form part of one's spiritual path?
- What is the significance of our dreams?
- What happens to us when we die?

I have learned from experience that a wisdom circle should address only one question at a time. This helps keep the discussion focused and productive. Without that focus, philosophical knowledge is less likely to emerge. A discussion of randomly changing topics might be interesting, but tends not to delve very deeply into problems that deserve a deep exploration. If other interesting questions arise in the course of the discussion, they can be remembered for future circles. But I leave to each circle the matter of whether the circle should arrive at a single or final answer. Many philosophical questions are highly complicated, and admit of more than one possible good answer. Moreover, one evening of discussion may not be enough time to explore all of one question's possibilities.

A wisdom circle has a small number of rules, which serve to separate the wisdom circle from ordinary conversations, and help the circle run smoothly. Note that they are not *moral* rules: they do not define what topics may or may not be addressed, or what things may or may not be said. Rather, they are requirements of logic and of procedure. They enable everyone to discover philosophical knowledge without distractions or obstructions. (Some may say "There are no rules in our wisdom circle," and will say that this respects the right to freedom of speech. But in such circles covert or implicit or unspoken rules will govern the occasion nonetheless. The covert rules will normally involve a prohibition on criticizing or questioning the word of the most outspoken or aggressive personality. Thus the absence of explicit rules tends to actually stifle free speech, and does not enable it. But I digress.) Almost every wisdom circle I've ever attended had some variation of the following rules, and I think a true wisdom circle cannot do without them. They are:

- Everyone who comes to this circle may speak. The circle may not disband until everyone who wants to speak has had a chance to do so.
- Everyone who speaks must also listen.
- Everyone shall assume that all participants are rational, and shall interpret each other's words in the very best possible way.
- Speak clearly, consistently, and rationally.
- Speak only what you actually believe.
- Speak what understand to be true.
- Speak from the heart.

At some circles I've attended, rules like these were stated right at the beginning. This gave new members a better sense of what was going on, and reinforced for others the sacredness of the occasion. The rules I have presented here are derived partly from some of the principles of reasoning already mentioned, such as the Councils of Cormac. Other rules noted here are modeled after Jurgen Habermas' principles of discourse ethics. The first of his principles, for instance, reads: "Every subject with the competence to speak and act is allowed to take part in the discourse." (Habermas, *Ibid*, p 87) Habermas refers to these principles as "necessary for a search for truth organized in the form of a competition." Although I find much to admire in his explanation, I see no reason why a wisdom circle has to be a *competition*. A wisdom circle is not a college debating society. There are no points to be scored and no trophies to be won. Rather, there are questions to answer, and problems to solve. Some questions can admit of more than one excellent answer, so it is not always necessary for one answer to overcome the others. A wisdom circle is an organized collaborative effort to learn something about the most important, the highest, the deepest questions in our lives. To work properly, it has to be the kind of situation in which no one wins unless everyone wins. The quality of the knowledge that emerges from the circle should matter more than the short-lived prestige of being the person who thought up the big idea first.

The first two principles have priority because they affirm that everyone has a capacity for philosophical thinking, and that everyone can have something of worth and meaning to say. This is required here as a basic vote of confidence in humanity, and in every person's ability to speak with intelligence and heart. The requirement to listen is intended here in several ways. One is to assert that everyone's voice is equally important, and equally worth hearing. No one's voice is more worth hearing than anyone else's for reasons that are not relevant to her ability to think and to express herself. Thus no privilege is offered to the person who spent the most money on food and drink for the occasion, or who travelled the greatest distance to be there, or who has the most friends in the circle. If any privilege is granted to anyone, it is granted on the basis of that person's knowledge, eloquence, thoughtfulness, sincerity, and other *relevant* qualities of character. The last four guiding principles of the wisdom circle are intended to encourage those qualities. Some wisdom circles, for instance, invite experts in some particular subject to give a presentation as a special guest speaker. That special guest will be offered the talking stick first, and a little extra time at the beginning. Between 20 and 30 minutes is usually enough. But once the presentation is finished, she becomes but one speaker among many in the circle. Some privilege may also be granted to any Elders since, presumably, they became Elders precisely by possessing the knowledge, reason, and other relevant qualities. Otherwise, the circle is a meeting of equals. Even the host of the circle is no more important as a speaker than anyone else. His job as host is only to see that the rules of the circle are respected by all.

On a practical level, the requirement to listen also helps keep the circle moving. Everyone who speaks must get to the point quickly, say only as much as needs to be said to make the point, and then step down to allow the next speaker to step up. There should be no 'filibustering' here. Some groups I have known limit people to ten minutes; some limit them to five; some make no specific time stipulation but accord to the host the power to let a speaker know, with a signal, that he should finish. If a speaker feels he hasn't expressed himself fully, he can take another turn to speak later on. The requirement to listen also protects soft-spoken or timid individuals from being interrupted by more domineering personalities.

Equality of speaking and listening is also important because, ideally, all people in a wisdom circle are participants, and no one is a mere spectator. Wisdom is never achieved by passive reception: it requires involvement. The requirement to listen also implies certain rules of basic respect: for instance, no one may interrupt or interfere with another while she is speaking. Brief interjections to express agreement, or to ask for clarification, may be permitted (and the emphasis here is on 'brief'!). But no one may cut another off, or shout another down, or otherwise by violence or coercion silence someone's voice. Someone might object to what is said, but that is not a reason to prevent that person from speaking, unless the speaker is deliberately intending to insult or abuse someone. Anything said by anyone in the wisdom circle is open to criticism by anyone else, but the criticism must be rational and respectful. This is in part to avoid logical fallacies like *straw man* and *ad hominem*. But it also preserves the communicative openness in the circle. I think this principle is also important for the wisdom circle. The event will not work properly if participants fear receiving unfair or malicious criticism. If what someone says is clearly not rational, one must identify the irrationality with clarity and precision, and help correct it respectfully. If we cannot speak and listen to each other with this kind of respect, we're lost.

In a wisdom circle, no one may attempt to deceive another: hence the fifth and sixth rules. In an ordinary conversation, some people will habitually say what they calculate will influence and impress other people the most, without stopping to think first of whether they believe what they say, nor whether what they say is true. Some people automatically argue against whatever was said by a person they might dislike, regardless of what that person actually said, simply because they dislike that person. And some people get a perverse sense of fun from being contrary. But these strategies can often serve as obstacles to good critical thinking, and obstacles to the pursuit of wisdom, and so should be avoided. Some people enjoy taking on a 'devil's advocate' position, and argue against someone else's position, or even against his or her own beliefs, for the sake of a good debate. In a wisdom circle, one must be explicitly, absolutely, unambiguously clear about when one is playing devil's advocate, and when one is not. Even professional philosophers will occasionally entertain a hypothetical proposition, for instance by anticipating a criticism. But it is unhelpful here to misrepresent your actual views. The point is to remain honest and sincere, and to never deceive anyone, especially including yourself.

I have given the last, and perhaps most privileged, place on the list the requirement to speak from the heart. Yet it is hard to describe exactly what this means. It might be one of those things of which it is said, "You either already know what it is, or else you will never know." To speak from the heart can mean, very simply, to speak with as much clarity of reason and sincerity of emotion as you can, about the things that matter most. Of course, if that were all, then there would be nothing special about it. But I think 'speaking from the heart' also means speaking in a way that reveals to others something of who you are. It is to examine yourself at a very deep level, and to open yourself to examination by others. To speak from the heart is to lay yourself bare, make yourself vulnerable, make yourself fully open and fully revealed to others. Many people do not much like the thought of examining themselves under the gaze of others. Indeed some will prefer not to examine themselves at all. Yet I have included the notion of speaking from the heart as a requirement for a wisdom circle. The point is not to punish people for not speaking from the heart. It is, however, to create the social environment in which speaking from the heart is possible, and supported. Not all topics will require a comprehensive exposure of one's innermost thoughts and feelings. Individuals who don't feel ready to speak that way shouldn't feel pressured to do so (but should perhaps be warned in advance that other people will want to do so). But the wisdom circle should be able to address serious topics in a critical and heart-full way. To do so is to help counteract the frivolous banality of pop culture entertainment, the manipulative propaganda in the news media, and any other fantasies that keep people locked in their labyrinths of fear.

It may also strike some readers as puzzling that speaking from the heart needs to be established as a *rule*. Surely speaking from the heart should come naturally, and the need to do so should be obvious! Yet some people do not know what it means to speak from the heart. They've never seen it done before. They feel too afraid, or too proud, to show their hearts. Or, perhaps sadly, they simply do not know their own heart well enough to show it to others. If done well, a wisdom circle can help teach people something about themselves, and at the same time help people become more heart-full people. At the very least, it should serve as the kind of shared experience which creates and sustains meaningful friendships.

Finally, if anyone feels that the name 'wisdom circle' is too formal or pretentious, you can always call it a 'discussion night', rent a movie to talk about, and order pizza.

18

Teachers

After speaking of philosophers and books, it seems natural to discuss the relations between teachers and students. For your relationship with knowledge is also your relationship with the people with whom you share knowledge. And this relation, in a different way, underlies almost all of the other relations of the worthwhile life. If you wish to be a hunter, for instance, then you must learn how to handle your weapon, how to move quietly, and how to read the landscape where your quarry dwells. If you wish to become a scholar, you must read the classics in the field you wish to study, and learn how to interpret, analyze, and occasionally to criticize them. If you wish to be a sailor, you must learn how to handle the ropes and pulleys and other parts of your boat, and how to read the water. A person who wishes to do *anything* must first learn about it. She must learn its purposes, history, language, basic concepts, skills and talents, standards of excellence, and everything else that goes into its performance. She must also practice it, as long and as often as possible. Education underlies all human endeavor. Indeed, some of the relations already discussed have an educational dimension as part of its very meaning: parents, Elders, leaders, scholars, and storytellers all have a pedagogical role. Moreover, education can benefit you through the whole of your life. Scientists recently discovered that those who remained in education longer in their lives were better able to compensate for the degradation of their brains in old age, and thus better able to stave off conditions like dementia.[212]

Yet education is not just about acquiring information and developing skills. It may sound a little silly, but *being human on*

Earth is also a pedagogical process. Just as one must learn how to be a carpenter, a chemist, a musician, or whatever, one must also learn how to be a human being. Whatever it is you are learning, it's almost certain you are *also* learning about human relations and human realities. This understanding of education is often expressed in literature and art, for instance in the 1989 film *Dead Poets Society*, and in James Hilton's 1934 novel, *Goodbye, Mr. Chips*. Of all philosophers who discussed education, the one who asserted this point the strongest is probably Confucius. One of his analects runs as follows.

> One who loves humanity but not learning will be obscured by ignorance. One who loves wisdom but not learning will be obscured by lack of principle. One who loves faithfulness but not learning will be obscured by heartlessness. One who loves uprightness but not learning will be obscured by violence. One who loves strength of character but not learning will be obscured by recklessness." (*Analects* 17:8)

Confucius here asserts that moral virtues are themselves under-written by education. Someone could be courageous and strong-willed, but without education he could also be bigoted and cruel. And the ignorant man might imagine that racism or sexism is an important part of his integrity. Mencius, a philosopher of the Confucian tradition, may have had this thought in mind when he wrote:

> According to the way of man, if they are well fed, warmly clothed, and comfortably lodged but without education, they will become almost like animals.
> (*Book of Mencius*, 3A:4)

Quotations like these suggest that being human means being more than just a member of a species, or a possessor of a certain genetic code. It also means being something more. And whatever that may be, it is through education that we become so.

It's an appealing proposition. But is it true? There are, indeed, reasons to doubt it. Many people find, for instance, that education is a painful experience. And schools can be great crucibles of fear. Students fear failing their classes. Teachers often fear their students. Administrators fear budget cuts. It is likely that very few people in a formal school setting feel that they are learning much about being human. Does education enlighten and empower people, as Confucius believed, or does it demoralize and oppress people? Let us explore some arguments both for and against it, and see where they take us.

Dark Sarcasm in the Classroom

The uplifting and humanizing power of education just described may be very hard to see because of the prominence of a rival model of education. Following the education theorist Paulo Freire, let us call it the 'banking' model. Here is how he describes it:

> Narration (with the teacher as narrator) leads the students to memorize mechanically the narrated content. Worse yet, it turns them into 'containers', into 'receptacles' to be 'filled' by the teacher. The more completely she fills the receptacles, the better a teacher she is. The more meekly the receptacles permit themselves to be filled, the better students they are. Education thus becomes an act of depositing, in which the students are the depositories and the teacher is the depositor. Instead of communicating, the teacher issues communiqués and makes deposits which the students patiently receive, memorize, and repeat.[213]

In this model of education, students do not think. Indeed they may be positively discouraged from thinking. Freire wrote that teachers do all the thinking on the student's behalf, but I suspect that in this model the teachers don't do much thinking either. The curriculum and the textbook contain the only permissible thoughts, and the teachers act as mere messengers and interpreters of those thoughts. This model, because it discourages independent thinking, does not form the student into a human being. It forms her, instead, into a machine.

It's not difficult to see why the banking model became prominent. A human system of education for thousands or even millions of people would be a bureaucratic nightmare. It would need very small class sizes, almost unlimited access to resources like libraries and scientific equipment, and some kind of screening process to eliminate apathetic and uninspiring teachers. But the taxpayers who fund public education, and the politicians who manage it, often demand that the system produce the best results for the lowest possible cost. It's far more economically efficient to shove a hundred students into each hall, deposit in their minds a standard curriculum, and make them write standard tests. Aside from that, some teachers are perfectly happy to teach like bankers, because it's easy. They don't have to be encouraging, inspiring, or supportive: they just have to show up.

The banking model of education persists for another reason: it can be used as a tool of assimilation and oppression. Mary Wollstonecraft discussed this in her 1792 philosophical masterwork, *A Vindication of the Rights of Woman*. She observed that in her day, girls were educated to be docile, weak, and irrational. Thereafter, when they become adult women, they were told by their fathers and husbands that they were docile and weak and irrational by nature. But this is, as Wollstonecraft astutely observed, a ridiculous inversion of the reality. If women are not virtuous, she says, it is because "women are not allowed to have sufficient strength of mind to acquire what really deserves the name of virtue." (Wollstonecraft, *Vindication*, Ch II, p 21)

The government of my own country tried to do a similar thing to the Aboriginal people for over 150 years, using a system of residential schools. Starting in 1840, hundreds of residential schools were built in or near the reserves, funded by the federal government and operated by various Christian churches. Aboriginal children were brought there, often forcibly, to learn the white man's ways, and to be assimilated into the white man's culture. The justification for the assimilation was perhaps best articulated in 1888 by former Ontario premier Edward Blake, who said that Native people were "an inferior race, and in an inferior state of civilization."[214] Over 100,000 children passed through the system in the first half of the 20th century, and more than half of them died in it, mostly due to extremely poor sanitation.[215] I have personally met a number of residential school survivors, many of whom are Elders now. They described being verbally, physically, and sometimes sexually abused for speaking their own language or practicing their own religion. As one Elder told me, "If something happened, if we told the truth we were beaten, if we told a lie we were beaten worse." The result is they did not know what consequences their actions would create, and so did not know how to move or speak. Upon arrival on the first day, some had their hair forcibly shorn, and their clothing forcibly cut from their bodies and burned in front of them. The purpose of doing this is to attack the signs of Aboriginal identity, and replace it with a white identity. But the real result was that the victim becomes a nobody: having no dignity, no acknowledged worth, no meaningful reality. Many Elders I spoke with described how in their adult lives they grappled with these experiences by developing severe addictions to alcohol, to gambling, or to gasoline fumes. Some also described developing a disposition to commit acts of anger and violence. They effectively sought solace for their own pain by stepping into the role of the aggressor, to inflict upon others the same traumas once inflicted upon them. Since the closure of the last residential school in 1996, various reconciliation projects have been established, including a truth commission, and compensatory payments to victims. On 11th June 2008, Prime Minister Stephen Harper made a formal apology to all Aboriginal people on behalf of the government and the nation. Yet for many people, the wounds of the assimilation effort are still deep.

At the risk of losing my job, I'm sorry to say that another reason for the prominence of the banking model has to do with the students. The banking model seems to be the kind of education many contemporary students expect and demand. They think it will get them the highest grades, and therefore the best jobs. They also think that education is a kind of race in which higher grades matter more than knowledge gained or skills acquired. A teacher in an engineering program described to me how he once dealt with a student who had that attitude.

> In the university course, I gave a take-home midterm exam. They sound easy, but in engineering, they take about two days to complete properly. It was about designing a simple seawater supply system. Two young women students got it all wrong. I coached them and then allowed them to re-do the project with a suitable mark penalty (they did OK, second time). At the next lecture, another young woman, who is very competitive, asked me if I had allowed Ms X and Ms Y to redo the test. When I said yes, she came aboard me, stating it was unfair for me to do so. I explained that I was much more interested in students learning than her competitiveness, but if she did not like that the department head was right done the hall and he would be glad to see her. (R. Patterson, 2009)

Dr. Patterson had also been a career soldier, and he added that the competitive student's mistake was "trying to browbeat an old infantry officer." But other teachers might not be as willing or able to stand up to their students in the same way. A colleague of mine found the 'culture of entitlement' among his students so demoralizing that he eventually quit. Here are his words, describing his feelings on the matter.

> I wanted to be a friendly and approachable professor, but I also have high standards. I expect that students in the second year of university know how to compose a grammatically correct sentence, how to find a book they need in a library, and how to spell. It seems that instead of learning to do these things, some students would rather come to my office to demand explanations, appeal to my pity, bribe me, or threaten me, to get a better grade. If they scored poorly on a lab report, it was *my* fault for holding them down, never their fault for not doing the work. I do my best to show how biology can be inspiring, how it doesn't have to be just a collection of cold facts. But most of my students cared only about getting the highest possible grade and then getting out. I was becoming a jaded and uncaring teacher. But a jaded teacher has no business in the classroom. I felt it my responsibility, therefore, to quit the job, and when my contract expired six months later that's exactly what I did. (Name withheld by request, 2009)

Knowledge may be enlightenment and power, but it is clear that schools do not always enlighten and empower people. Let us now turn to an alternative model of education, to see whether it is possible to escape.

Teaching and Thinking

Let us say that a teacher is a person who has knowledge, experience, and talent in some field, and who passes them to others. Similarly, a student is the person to whom the teacher passes on what she knows. This may seem straightforward enough, and probably describes most of what happens in a formal classroom. But is this all that there is to education? When

372

I think of the teachers I admired and respected as a younger lad, I certainly knew them to be knowledgeable and talented people, and I looked up to them for it. But when I think of the things they did for me, the mere transmission of information does not loom large in my memory. I remember how they smiled when I said or did something that met their approval. I remember how my high school drama teacher drove me home one day, after a vandal slashed my bicycle tires. Now, in my career as a professor, I stand on the other side of the podium. Yet in that position I'm not sure that I pass anything on to anyone. It's not that my students don't 'pick up' the things that I am 'passing on': most of them certainly do. But the students of mine who merely reproduce my lectures in their tests and essays eventually prove that they haven't learned much, even while their grades are high. They may be able to repeat Aristotle's Doctrine of the Mean word-for-word, but they cannot explain what it means, nor how their lives might be different if they lived by its logic. One could say that they have no understanding, but that doesn't seem right to me. These people are not idiots. But the students who do 'get it' the most are almost always *not* those who do nothing more than memorize and repeat. What do those students do differently?

It seems to me that the students who do actually learn something in my courses are those who ask questions, suggest counter-arguments, and imagine variations. They are also the ones who complain when something they are being taught about the world does not fit their actual experiences. In short, *they do their own thinking*. Further, they do their thinking in accord with some, if not all, of the principles I described earlier as the qualities of the spirit of reason: organized curiosity, struggle and courage, skepticism, autonomy, rebellion, intellectual precision, subtlety, and communicative openness. Without thinking, education becomes more like psychological programming, and what could become a mature and intelligent adult becomes instead a child in a grown man's body.

As noted in the previous study, knowledge is both enlightenment and also power. Yet knowledge cannot empower nor enlighten unless students are allowed to think for themselves. Teachers cannot do their thinking for them. But this prompts the question: if students are doing their own thinking, what do teachers do? Are teachers not to do any thinking of their own?

To help answer this question, allow me to relate some of my own experiences as a teacher. When I taught at a major university in southern Ontario, Canada, I often had between 50 and 150 students in each lecture. The last course I taught there had 175 students. My relationship with my students was almost non-existent. By the end of the term, the only students I knew by name were a few who sat in the front row. My colleagues recommended that I maintain a friendly, approachable demeanor, and a respectful attitude, but also a certain professional distance. All I had to do was stand at the podium, lecture, answer questions, grade papers, and go home. But when I was hired by a regional college in western Quebec, I had to change almost everything I did in my classroom. I still prepared lectures and graded essays and the like. But I also had to learn about my students' lives, and allow them to learn a few things about my life. Students felt offended if I didn't know everyone's name by the end of the sixth week. A very different standard of 'professional distance' prevailed. They would ask about other jobs I've had besides teaching, and what my life was like when I was their age. They asked about my dog, and my girlfriend, and about funny things that happened when I lived in Europe. And students were often surprisingly open about their lives. I've a young man right now who is starting a garage band with a few of his friends, and he seemed eager to know that I liked their music. A young woman wants a career as a model and fashion designer and she occasionally asks my opinion of her outfits. Not all the things students tell me of their lives are fun, however. Some come from families that are falling apart. Some were in school only because they felt pressured by parents to be there. Some were in trouble with the law. Usually, students came forward with information like this because they wanted to explain why they missed a class, or needed an extension on an assignment. But they also needed to know that I cared about them *personally*, and not just as a group. They needed to be recognized as human beings and as people, and not as numbers. Perhaps they expressed these needs more than my university students did because the college was smaller, and had more students from working class families. But it soon became clear to me that if I gave them that kind of personal respect, as much as I was able, then the right kind of environment for critical thinking emerged. I still have around 100 students each term, although they are now spread over four or five classes, instead of concentrated into one. But I also have a much more satisfying experience as a professor.

The personal rapport with the student helps to create a social and interpersonal environment for that student in which he or she can think. For when we think, we do not think in pure disembodied abstraction. When we think, even about the most theoretical topics, we do not suddenly forget who we are. We do our thinking in a certain time, in a certain place, surrounded by certain people. That environment is either helpful and supportive for thinking, to some degree, or it is not. And in that, I think, is the answer to the question about what teachers should do: they have to create that environment in which students can freely, intelligently, and productively do their own thinking. Teachers can offer ideas, resources, and possibilities which students have perhaps never seen or considered before. They can also try to set a personal example, by which students can see they care about what they are teaching. When stonemason Bobby Watt, for instance, teaches at the school for stonemasons that he established in Whitby, Ontario, he tries to instill "the real pride of who you are and what you're doing for a living and why what you're doing is so important. If you've got an apprentice whose head is in it and whose heart is in it, you'll pretty sure be able to make sure his hands go along."[216] But above all else, teachers create the environment for thinking by *posing problems* and *asking questions* which students and teachers, together, can investigate. Good thinking begins with good questions, and clear perceptions. The teacher who wants her students to do their own thinking must pose the very best questions, and then assist students in their own process of investigating the best answers. It is perhaps only through good questions that we are able to see the world for what it truly is. Even in the presentation of factual information, questions can still be posed, such as how one may find out what the facts are, and what those facts might mean in our lives. The relation of teacher to student, then, is more like a collaborative partnership.

Much therefore depends on the talent and the character of the teacher. We've all had a few deadbeat teachers in our lives. Yet much also depends on certain dispositions in the student. Curiosity, as in the spirit of the scholar, of course, will be one of them. The teacher must trust the student's intelligence, and the student must have some confidence in herself. There may still be exams to write, and standards of excellence to measure progress, and goals to reach. There may still be a possibility for failure. But even the standards of excellence are themselves among the problems which education investigates. Overall, in this model of education, students do most of the work of educating themselves, and teachers simply present themselves as one of the resources that students can use in that effort. Teachers may end up learning as much from the students as the students learn from teachers.

Incidentally, the proposition that a human being is a thinking being can be subject to the same process of pedagogical questioning as any other proposition. Teachers and students are free to ask what thinking is, and what it means to be a thinking being. But in order to doubt or deny the importance of thinking, *one must be thinking*. The importance of thinking is thus self-evident.

It is this act of autonomous and original thinking which, so it seems to me, makes the process of growing up not just biological but also pedagogical. Without this kind of education, we are more susceptible to propaganda, more likely to commit crimes, more likely to develop a substance addiction, less innovative in the sciences and arts, and less happy. Without this kind of thinking, we may as well be machines. For this reason, I would like to call this model of education the human model. In a human education, students learn to be cooks, carpenters, musicians, and managers, just as they do in any other model of education. But along the way, they *think*, and in thinking, they become human beings.

Ideology and Indoctrination

In his discussion of the education of the guardians, Plato wrote: "You know, don't you, that the beginning of any process is the most important, especially for the young and tender? It's at that time that it is most malleable and takes on any pattern one wishes to impress on it." (*Republic* 377b) He then claimed that educators must control the curriculum very carefully, censor the poems and stories that children may hear, and even tell them lies. It's probably undeniable that the kind of education we receive while young profoundly influences the kind of adult we become. For that reason, parents, community leaders, governments, militaries, religious groups, and corporations worry about what the students are learning. Many fear that the students will grow up to think and live differently than the way they want them to think. Schools, school boards, and universities thus become fields of conflict where various ideological and religious factions compete to shape the minds of future generations. So we should pose a critical objection: could the human model of education described here be used to *indoctrinate* people rather than humanize them? And by doing so, could it teach people to believe in falsehoods, or to count evil deeds as justifiable and right?

We've already seen an example from history. The very point of the Indian Residential School system was precisely "to kill the Indian in the child" and transform the child into a white-assimilated subject of the British empire. Today, the vanguards of ideology influence school curricula and policy using PTA organizations, elected school boards, and school trustees. It is often in the name of 'letting students decide', 'teaching the controversy', or 'teaching both sides' that ideologically rigid political or religious doctrines, with little or no basis in reality, are wedged into school curricula alongside well-substantiated historical narratives and sound scientific theories. In 2005, for instance, the Kansas State Board of Education voted to insert Intelligent Design, a religious ideology, into the high school science curricula.[217] Similarly, in 2010 the Texas Board of Education voted to change the social studies and history curriculum to emphasize conservative political and social values. These changes included removing references to the contributions of Latino and black people in American society and culture. A dissenting member of the board, Mary Helen Berlanga, said: "They can just pretend this is a white America and Hispanics don't exist... They are rewriting history, not only of Texas but of the United States and the world."[218]

Cash-strapped schools sometimes accept donations of money and supplies from private corporations. In return these companies sponsor school activities and market their products directly to the children, right inside the classroom. Corporations like Modern Talking Pictures Systems and Lifetime Learning Systems create educational videos for big corporations like Dow Chemical, Proctor & Gamble, and Exxon. These materials present the company's perspectives on issues such as public health, energy security, global warming, and so on, as if those perspectives were facts. Whittle Communications, an advertising agency, produces educational videos in its *Channel One* program, with thirty-second advertising spots, just like regular television. Companies are willing to pay almost $200,000 for these spots, since the students are effectively a captive audience. The contracts between Whittle and the school which uses their materials stipulate that 90% of the children in the school must watch the programs, and teachers may not interrupt or stop the programs. Whittle also specifically targets schools in low-income areas with a disproportionate number of black students.[219] Teachers and curriculum writers, unwilling to 'bite the had that feeds', may be much less prepared to create educational materials which question the corporate perspective. This undermines the school's ability to help students think critically and independently about important social problems. Non-profit groups which represent other perspectives, such as charities or environmental activist groups, simply do not have the funds to compete with big businesses, and so their perspectives are pushed out.[220]

The objection that a human education can too easily become indoctrination is a serious one. In the human model of education, the aim is to open and not to close avenues for critical intellectual discovery. An ideology and its propaganda normally presupposes only one idea of what it is to be human, and with it only one ideal mode of politics, religion, culture, and social value. But in a human education, there can be many such modes. Indeed, if human education allowed only one understanding of what it is to be human, whether conservative or liberal or religious or whatever, then a major avenue of critical and free thinking would be closed, and it would no longer be fully human education. This may make education appear vulnerable to hijacking by an anti-life or anti-rational ideology. But there is at least one proposition to remember: it is the claim that to be human is to be a thinking being, animated by the spirit of reason, and all its special qualities. While communicative openness is certainly one of those qualities, it does not follow that one must be 'open' to ideas which are scientifically unsound, historically false, morally corrupt, or ideologically closed. Such ideas eventually demand the suspension of reason, the distortion or suppression of evidence, or the hardening or narrowing of compassion. Because propaganda and ideology must circumvent reason to succeed, the manner of teaching it always eventually reverts back to the banking model. Indoctrination is not education: for indoctrination merely deposits truth-claims in the student's mind without a chance for the student to do her own thinking.

A human education could still be a conservative one. It is neither left wing nor right wing in its own leaning, nor does it favor one religion over another. It favors only reason and reality. So long as one's educational enquiries are rational, then there is no limit to what one may think, and no limit to what more and what else it may mean to be human. The question should thus be, what kind of people do we want to be? And what kind of education should we pursue in order to become the kind of people we want to be?

19

Storytellers

While considering ways in which knowledge is transmitted from one person to another, and from one generation to the next, we should also consider storytelling. For classrooms are obviously not the only places where people learn from each other.

Once each month, in a certain Irish pub in Montreal, there is a storyteller's night. On each occasion people gather, order food and beer, and make small talk, much as one would do at any other night. I was invited by a friend who was learning to be a traditional storyteller himself, and who considered one of the tellers presenting that night to be his mentor. I noted a certain camaraderie between him and his mentor, like old friends, yet also a certain deference too: for instance, my friend made sure that the seat the older teller wanted was kept free. A second older man arrived a short while later, and he took himself to the storyteller's chair, and made casual conversation with the people around him. Most everyone continued on with their conversations with each other, but they kept one eye on the man in the storyteller's chair, to be sure not to miss any signal he might give indicating that he was ready to begin. When he began to confer with the other teller about which stories to tell that night, and enquired about whether the music from the other side of the bar could be turned down, people gathered around. Some sat on the floor to be near enough to hear everything.

Most people in the audience were of college and university student age. This is the very generation that many journalists, sociologists, and pundits describe as apathetic, disinterested, entitlement-minded, and self-absorbed. One would not expect such people to want to hear an old man do nothing but talk for two and a half hours. But the storytelling night in the pub had no such fancy flashy accoutrements. It was simply an elderly gentleman from county Kerry telling old stories to whoever wanted to come and listen. Yet he held his audience completely rapt. No one rustled in their seats, no one checked their watches or cell phones; no one coughed or sneezed; no one gave up waiting for the end and left early. As other patrons of the pub walked by, they would slow their pace, watch and listen, and smile before continuing. Thus even those who did not wish to participate seemed to know what was going on, and seemed to sense the aura of history and of knowledge that surrounded us.

The most significant signal of the storyteller's readiness to begin, it seemed to me, was his *silence*. When he finished conferring with his colleague he closed his eyes and crossed his elbows on his lap, and seemed to be thinking very carefully about the right words to begin. This silence interested me: the dignity of the man was such that there was no need for someone to hush the crowd, or for the barman to ring a bell and call for quiet, or for anyone to explicitly demand anyone's attention. The sight of the seannachie silently thinking through his story to himself was the only necessary sign. For this kind of a signal to work, everyone involved has to be paying attention to the wider picture of their social world. Their minds, while they may be doing other tasks requiring conscious attention, such as eating, or settling the bill with the barman, or carrying on a conversation, nonetheless must at the same time be vigilant to the subtleties happening around them. When others turn their heads in the direction of the storyteller's chair; when others cease their conversations; when the seannachie himself sets his pint down in a certain definitive way which suggests he will be leaving it there for a while, then one may draw the conclusion that the time has come to listen. The more of these signals one sees, even if one sees them only unconsciously, the stronger the conclusion will be. Yet the silence that followed the acknowledgement of all these signals, the silence in which the seannachie took us to another time without a word nor a gesture, was the most powerful signal of all.

The seannachie I heard that evening in Montreal broke the silence with a formulaic opening expression. Most of us know the one that was made famous by the Brothers Grimm: "Once upon a time... " The teller in the Montreal pub began with what I later learned was his own signature opening, which out of respect for him I will not reproduce here. The expression was a lot like the opening gesture of a ritual: it created a frame in time around the story, with an established beginning, and anticipation of a completion to come. With his opening signature, and each descriptive word that followed, we listeners slipped further into his world. Upon hearing the invocation of time, I felt I knew where I was: I felt invited to enter the world the storyteller was about to describe.

A storytelling session cannot have that effect unless everyone involved has learned the etiquette. Yet I think the etiquette here is not a matter of following the rules or the laws, as a computer might follow its program. No one is issuing commands that must be obeyed. Nonetheless there is an ethical understanding in play. This understanding is rational and intellectual, since it must be learned. There must be a talent for observation involved, and a talent for drawing conclusions based on those observations. Some part of the understanding here is also involved in one's perceptual intelligence, since it depends on an ability to detect subtle social signals which may pass beneath the conscious notice of most people while they are doing something else. The eyes and ears receive these signals, and the mind processes them in a complicated analysis, which in each moment considers the likely explanation for what is observed, compares the experience with similar experiences in the past, remembers what happened in the past in similar situations, looks and listens for further information to confirm or disconfirm the explanation, and then decides what to do. The process of perceptual intelligence is always hard at work.

Further, one has to be aware of the *value* of the storytelling session, the value of the knowledge that such a session imparts. That knowledge is at the same time the knowledge of how to behave during such an occasion, and how to tell the difference between a right way and a wrong way to do things. One must know how much respect and deference to the storyteller is too little, and how much is too much. One must also know what would constitute a slight, an insult, or an offence. The latter can also be subtle, as in the case of someone who insults another by declining to shake that person's hand. There must also be an understanding of what to do about disruptive or disrespectful people. Overall, together with the perceptual intelligence that discerns 'the tenor of the now', there must also be an understanding of the ethical significance of all the elements of the event. That understanding includes the knowledge of how to be a good teller, how to be a good listener, what a good story is, and what it is to be involved in a storytelling session.

Storytelling events, like the one I attended that night in Montreal, certainly have been part of my own life for a very long time. My father was born, bred, and buttered in Ireland and, through him, some of the Irish storytelling culture was part of my childhood. When I went to live in Ireland, I went to a few storytelling nights in local pubs. This was not always as simple as going to hear a local band. Many of these events were not advertised nor publicized. To attend one, you had to know someone who knows someone who knows someone. I was invited to one only after I had lived there for a few years, long enough for a few local people to decide that I could be trusted. I suspect that the reason for making the event semi-private was to prevent interruptions, and to ensure everyone in the audience knew the etiquette and the values involved.

Tellers and Audiences

I asked a few local storytellers about how they understood their relationship to their audiences. One friend told me: "The Bardic path is the only path where you are allowed to break down someone else's emotional and psychic barriers, to make them experience something." (D. Thew, 2010) In reply, another associate of mine offered the following:

> While it is true that a Bard's magic can reach deeply into a person and move them like no other art form, the Bard still needs to earn that power from the audience every time he performs. The audience members always retain the power to cut the Bard out of their space if he is unprepared, uninspiring, or disrespectful of their attention. Audiences can turn on a Bard in a heartbeat; it's an ugly thing to watch, and it's even worse to experience. The Bard and the listener both enter into a pact where the listener pledges to open themselves to the bard, and the bard pledges to share something inspiring. The chances of the Bard failing in this pact are as epic as the legends of old, and if the Bard is not ready to move his listeners, his listeners will move away, leaving the Bard powerless.
>
> (J.D. "Hobbes" Hickey, 2010)

The relation between teller and audience can also appear in the way that a teller may ask for a critique of his performance from select members of the audience. Thus, after one of his stories, the seannachie in Montreal asked the audience for their honest opinion about the quality of the performance. It seems that an audio recording for a local tourist promotion agency was planned, and the teller wanted to refine his performance for the sake of that recording. After hearing the audience's comments, he began a semi-private conversation with another senior teller. I later learned that the teller was asking someone he regarded as a peer for more detailed and more critical opinions about the night's performance, again for the sake of the recording. He had been planning his performance in advance, not just for the few minutes before the beginning, but actually for several days. Every word, every gesture, every change of tempo, and every pause was carefully visualized in advance. For each sentence, he had to decide which word would receive his vocative emphasis. For each event in the story, he had to decide how much time to give it, and how much detail to describe. For every part of the world of the story, he had to decide how much to show to the listeners, and how much they would have to fill in for themselves. Thus although the performance gave the listeners the impression that the story came from deep within the storytellers mind, heart and soul, nonetheless what we saw and heard was exactly what he wanted us to see and hear. No part of the performance was 'off the cuff'. A good teller probably *does* feel as if the performance wells up from a source within him or beyond him. That is part of the magic of *imbas*. Musicians, actors, teachers, and even stand-up comedians often describe the same feeling. But it is still the case that excellence requires special skill, talent, discipline, and meticulous rehearsal. Anyone can tell a story, but perhaps only a few of us are called to be storytellers. (I hesitate to say that some are born to be good at some craft, while others are not. Yet it does seem to be the case that some people lack the disposition to learn and excel at certain crafts, and others who possess the disposition do not develop it to its full potential. But I shall leave that point aside for now.) The conversation I observed between the teller and his peer concerned those very points of performance planning, and how well he deployed the skills of his craft that evening. For although the storytelling night took place in a pub instead of a purpose-built theatre, nonetheless we were an audience for a professionally rehearsed and produced theatrical event. I am sure that storytelling is a true craft, on a level rank with stage acting, dance and choreography, musicianship, and other performing arts. I am also sure that the bards, poets, scops and storytellers of ancient cultures also held an informal post-performance conference with their peers and their apprentices. Such dialogues were probably one of the ways that standards of excellence were decided upon, and used to evaluate each performance.

What Stories Can Do

At one of the storytelling nights in Galway, Ireland, that I attended in the early 2000s, I had a brief chance to ask the seannachie whether he thought storytelling could do things which radio, television, and cinema could not. At first he gave me a look which suggested he thought my question a little annoying. To him, the power and importance of storytelling was so obviously greater than that of the modern mass media that the question didn't need to be asked. But after a beat, he smiled and said that he had been warned by others that I might ask a philosophical question. And for his answer, he leaned forward and said, "You know, storytelling can raise the dead, so it can."

The seannachie didn't explain his meaning to me. I suppose he wanted me to think about it for myself. "Put that in your academic pipe and smoke it," he said next, as it was late at night and he wanted to go home. Over the years, I have indeed been thinking about it. I suspect his meaning has to with the way that storytelling can create in the mind of both teller and listener the presence of the story's characters. A good storyteller can make those characters appear just as real as the other people in one's life: the person is *here*, present before the mind's eye, because someone is telling her story. There need not be anything supernatural about this process. It can be explained sufficiently with reference to the power of language and of words and gestures. Such things are the elemental units in the 'technology' of storytelling. They represent the interior world of the speaker: in the sense of *re-presenting*, or making something present again, after it has first been made present in the speaker's mind. An excellent performance can represent the speaker's interior world so well that audiences reproduce that world in their own minds. Well-chosen words and phrases and gestures can thus act as forces in the world, changing the way people think and act and relate to each other. In so doing, they bestow presence upon the characters and events that the story speaks of.

The seannachie I spoke with that night may also have been thinking of an important concept in the life of his heroic-age predecessors: *apotheosis*. This is the process by which a person achieves a kind of vicarious immortality through the story of his life, as others continue to tell it long after he dies. So important was this idea in Europe's early Iron Age that many of its mytho-logical heroes swear oaths to achieve it. The Irish hero Cú Chulainn, for instance, while still a seven year old child, declared: "It is little I would care... if my life were to last one day and one night only, so long as my name and the story of what I had done would live after me."[221] We find the desire for apoth-eosis in the words of other characters from other countries in Europe's Heroic Age. In the *Iliad*, for instance, Hector of Troy says: "Let me not then die ingloriously and without a struggle, but let me first do some great thing that shall be told among men hereafter." (*Iliad* 22:304-5) Perhaps apotheosis is possible because, as described in the chapter on friendship, human life and human relations are naturally structured in the form of a narrative. When a living person is before us, we recognize who she is by the way her words, choices, and movements enact a coherent story. When the living person is absent, or dead, but her story is told, some part of her presence is revived.

What else can storytelling do? It seems that storytelling can also have a kind of tempering, or 'curative' influence on our minds. This effect was described by Aristotle in a text called *The Poetics*. As a first premise, he says that during the course of living one can accumulate various emotional and experiential burdens, such as stress, anxiety, inhibition, frustration, obsession and, most of all, fear. When we attend a theatrical performance of a tragic story, we experience these unpleasant emotions again, because we emotionally respond to and identify with what we see on the stage. But in the course of the performance, the energy and the work that is required to feel these emotions is spent away. We can thus look upon the world and our lives afresh again. Aristotle called this process *catharsis*, a word which means cleansing or purging.

I asked the friend who brought me to the storytelling night in Montreal what he thought storytelling could do. His answer had to do with the way that storytelling can transmit knowledge to people. Here is part of what he said:

> Myth allows us to understand concepts that cannot be fully grasped by logical definition. Let's say that you have never heard the word 'courage' and are completely in the dark with the concept of it. From a logical standpoint, I could read you the dictionary definition of Courage and you could still not truly understand its meaning. Instead, I would tell you a story about a boy who sets his fear aside to battle a dragon that is determined to destroy his village. In the moment when the boy lifts his trembling arms to point the sword at the dragon's heart, you would have the opportunity to understand the true meaning of Courage without even using the word. This is the heart of mythic knowledge.
>
> (J.D. "Hobbes" Hickey, 2009)

If I understand his argument correctly, he is saying that story-telling can serve a pedagogical function. It allows people to have 'vicarious' experiences of life and of the world. It also allows people to learn things that perhaps cannot be learned so easily by analytic discourse. Certainly, people tend to respond favorably to ideas presented in the form of narrative discourse.

Analytic discourse does not normally appear so dramatic and exciting. Stories that explore mythic knowledge may be amusing and entertaining. They may even explore important ideas using the devices of fantasy: trees that can walk and talk like human beings, or spacecraft that can travel to faraway stars. Nor must the story embody those truths in the manner of a 'moral tale', with an obvious (perhaps highly pretentious) 'lesson' to be learned. Some stories do not wear their meanings on their sleeves. But a story may be 'true' in the sense that it teaches, explores, examines, experiments with, and expounds upon what it is to be human. It examines our values, problems, possibilities, and limitations. It speculates about what our place in the world is, or could be, or can not be.

But storytelling is fiction, some critic might say, even if it is the story of a real person's life. The story is only a later account of an event, which may be full of the teller's own embellishments and alterations. The 'biopic' film, for instance, never depicts events as they actually were: they depict events as the filmmaker is best able to reproduce them on screen. This objection was addressed by Ricoeur, who said: "this would be to misunderstand aesthetics itself." In his words:

> In the unreal sphere of fiction we never tire of exploring new ways of evaluating actions and characters. The thought experiments we conduct in the great laboratory of the imaginary are also explorations in the realm of good and evil. Transvaluing, even devaluing, is still evaluating. Moral judgment has not been abolished; it is rather itself subjected to the imaginative variations proper to fiction.[222]

Perhaps this observation, that narrative fiction is 'the laboratory of ethics', can help us understand why some stories are told and re-told and others are not, why some people's lives achieve apotheosis and others do not. A story which embodies a mythic truth about human life (to use my informant's term) is a story that people will want to hear, again and again. This can be the case even if the story is about other people, long since gone. We regularly recognize ourselves (our values, our problems, our possibilities, our limitations, etc) in the stories of other people. This is, for instance, the meaning of the hero tale. As Ricoeur says:

> To a large extent, in fact, the identity of a person or a community is made up of these identifications with values, norms, ideals, models, or heroes, *in* which the person or the community recognizes itself. Recognizing oneself *in* contributes to recognizing oneself *by*. The identification with heroic figures clearly displays this otherness assumed as one's own, but this is already latent in the identification with values which make us place a 'cause' above our own survival. An element of loyalty is thus incorporated into character and makes it turn towards fidelity, hence toward maintaining the self.[223]

As I read this passage from Ricoeur, I got the impression that he was aching to use the word 'Messiah' instead of 'hero' (Ricoeur is a Huguenot Protestant Christian). Jesus, obviously, is a figure whose story embodies the values of millions of people around the world. But this can be true of any hero: we need not be limited to one religion. Millions of people recognize themselves in the stories of Mohammed, or Krishna, or Buddha, or Kwan Yin, or Mithras, and so on. Nor must we be limited to religious stories in general. We recognize ourselves and our lives in the stories of mythological figures from thousands of cultural pantheons. Nor must we be limited to mythological tales. We also recognize ourselves in the stories of historical people, and fictitious characters. The longest of the stories presented at the storytelling night in Montreal was the tale of four whiskey bootleggers in the Eastern Townships of Quebec during the "Dirty Thirties". In the telling of that story, I think I observed this relation directly. The Frenchman, the Abenaki Native, the Scotsman, and the Irishman each had a story of how their family came to settle the area, and what life had been like for their ancestors. This was by no means a happy story. Winter storms, racial discrimination, diseases, injustices, famines, mass evictions, and untimely deaths, wrought each character's life in sadness. Yet the young audience followed the old seannachie's every word and gesture very attentively. The seannachie was telling us not only an account of our history as a people and a nation. He was also telling us who we are.

Similarly, this notion of mythic truth may tell us why some stories have a cathartic effect and others do not. Much depends, of course, on the skill and talent of the teller as a performing artist. But much also depends on the extent to which a story brings us back to a clear proposition about who we are. I think this is the case because I cannot see how catharsis could be achieved by escapism, or illusion. A fantasy story may be amusing and entertaining, and have some value in that. But if it aims to distract us from the truth of things, and to instill in us a complacent lethargy, or even encourage us to believe a glamorous lie, then it is only a straw man. Such stories may do this by substituting a cheap and superficial adage in the place of an exploration of real problems. They may do this by allowing us to pretend that our real problems are not so bad. They may make us worry about something that in fact is not especially important. They may even tell us that we don't have any real problems at all. But in no case does the straw-man story prepare anyone for life in the real world, where real problems are faced by real people who, afterwards, often need real healing. Without that grasp of reality, catharsis cannot happen. I think that I observed something like this process of catharsis happening in the audience after the seannachie finished telling the story of the whiskey bootleggers. Everyone appeared calm, introspective, peaceful. They asked questions about the real historical events mentioned in the story, and where he heard the story from, and what his influences might have been. Some felt an urge to tell a short anecdote about their own ancestors and predecessors, in similar situations. They thanked him too, and some offered to buy his next pint.

The Tellers of Our Time

Most people, when they want to hear a good story, do not seek out their local seannachie. Instead, they turn on the television, go to the movies, open a pulp fiction novel, log on to a computer-delivered social network, or play a video game. Traditionally storytellers are still among us, but now we also have filmmakers, novelists, poets, actors, playwrights, stand-up comedians, and journalists. The nature of mass media technology need not make the stories themselves much different, except insofar as technology opens or closes various possibilities for how stories are told. (I tip my hat to Marshall McLuhan here.) However, the vast majority of the stories we find in the mass media are straw men. They do not seek the curative effect of catharsis, even if they promise us catharsis. They are not much interested in describing, criticizing, exploring, or teaching any truths of human life. Mass media entertainment is funded by advertisers, and directed by network executives concerned primarily with maximizing viewer ratings and shareholder value. These people prefer the stories that appeal to the simplest and lowest parts of our nature, because those stories tend to sell best of all. Indeed the stories themselves are manufactured, advertised, packaged, and delivered just like any other consumer product in the market economy. As such they are judged primarily by their popularity and profitability, and not primarily by their aesthetic qualities, or the cultural importance of their topics. Indeed we regularly judge the excellence of a new movie by the money brought in from ticket sales in the first seven days. Some stories in the news media serve to actually distract us from the realities of the world, or manipulate our perception of them. For example: internal memos written by Bill Sammon, managing editor of the Washington office of Fox TV News, required on-air journalists to "refrain from asserting that the planet has warmed (or cooled) in any given period without IMMEDIATELY pointing out that such theories are based upon data that critics have called into question."[224] The same manager also required Fox News staff to deliberately bias its description of President Barak Obama's proposed 'public option' health insurance plan. Instead, he wanted it referred to as the (more fearful) 'government option'.[225]

The observation that television serves to distract us from reality is not new. Perhaps the first person to identify this problem was the American journalist Edward Murrow. In a speech at a meeting of the Radio and Television News Directors Association, delivered more than fifty years ago, Murrow said:

We have currently a built-in allergy to unpleasant or disturbing information. Our mass media reflect this. But unless we get up off our fat surpluses and recognize that television in the main is being used to distract, delude, amuse and insulate us, then television and those who finance it, those who look at it and those who work at it, may see a totally different picture too late.

(Edward R. Murrow, "Wires and Lights", 15th October 1958)

Murrow was worried here about how quiz shows, game shows, and comedy programs were displacing investigative news reporting on most television and radio networks. He didn't ask for a complete reversal of this trend. Rather, he called upon his distinguished audience to give a small fraction of their broadcast time each week to serious public affairs investigation and analysis, advertising-free. It didn't happen. Similarly, I am not saying we should throw out our televisions and cancel our Internet services. Rather, I think we should make more time in our lives for better stories. I'm saying we should rebuild and cherish the social environment in which better stories can be told, and enjoyed, by everyone. And we should support, encourage, and show respect to the talented storytellers among us, no matter who they are.

20

Leaders

Many centuries ago, Aristotle famously wrote that "man is by nature a social being." He might have added that every social group, whether large or small, has leaders. The hockey team has a coach, the neighborhood volunteer group has its head, a church has its priest or minister, a school has its principal, a business has its manager, a corporation has its CEO, a nation has its governor. A simple definition of a leader is a person whom others follow. And a simple definition of leadership is the talent or the skill in leading one's followers. The leader might be someone who holds an institutional position and who issues orders. But she might just be someone who is more loved, envied, knowledgeable, wealthy, feared, or in some way more *influential* than others. The members of a counterculture farming commune might claim to be a collective, and they might make their decisions by democratic consensus. But there will still be some few who are more respected than others, and whose voice carries more weight than others. Even the very smallest and the least technologically advanced of human communities, an Aboriginal band of only 30 people, has a 'big man'.

Whatever one's model of leadership, it will necessarily involve some relation between the leader herself and her supporters and followers. The Roman philosopher Cicero described the importance of supporters as follows:

No leader, either in war or in peace, could ever have performed important or beneficial actions unless he had gained the co-operation of his fellow men. Panaetius cited Themistocles, Pericles, Cyrus, Agesilaus, and Alexander, none of whom, he pointed out, could have achieved their great successes if they had failed to enlist supporters.[226]

This is obviously true of those twentieth century leaders who brought profound changes to human life 'single handedly', as is often said of them. Mohandas Gandhi, Martin Luther King, Jr., etc, could not have done anything if they did not have the help of others. In a similar way, Confucius wrote that leadership depends on supporters and followers. One of his analects runs as follows:

Tzu-kung asked about government. Confucius said, "Sufficient food, sufficient armament, and sufficient confidence of the people." Tzu-kung asked, "Forced to give up one of these, which would you abandon first?" Confucius said, "I would abandon the armament." Tzu-kung said, "Forced to give up one of the remaining two, which would you abandon first?" Confucius said, "I would abandon food. There have been deaths from time immemorial, but no state can exist without the confidence of the people." (*Analects* 12:7)

In the place of a 'state', here, one can insert just about any group of people assembled for some purpose, from hockey teams to multinational corporations.

The old Irish laws are fairly clear about who is and who is not the leader of a tribe: "He is not a king who does not have hostages in fetters, and to whom no royal tribute is rendered, and to whom no fines for breach of promulgated law are paid" (cited in Kelly, *A Guide to Early Irish Law*, p 19). A sense of *realpolitik* is evident here: the king has to be able to actually enforce his laws if he wants to remain king. With these comments in mind, let us add to our definition that leaders must procure more than just other people's non-interference. It must enlist people's respect and help. I might decide not to get in the way, and to that extent I may be helping. But I am certainly not being led by her, because I am not proactively doing anything in accord with her purposes or her instruction. A leader must be able to motivate others to positively do things, whether with her or for her. But this, obviously, says nothing about the many ways that a leader could obtain the support of her people. Another old Irish text fills in a few more details:

> ... there are only four rulers: the true ruler and the wily ruler, the ruler of occupation with hosts, and the bull ruler.
>
> The true ruler, in the first place, is moved towards every good thing, he smiles on the truth when he hears it, he exalts it when he sees it. For he whom the living do not glorify with blessings is not a true ruler.
>
> The wily ruler defends borders and tribes, they yield their valuables and dues to him.
>
> The ruler of occupation with hosts from outside; his forces turn away, they put off his needs, for a prosperous man does not turn outside.
>
> The bull ruler strikes [and] is struck, wards off [and] is warded off, roots out [and] is rooted out, pursues [and] is pursued. Against him there is always bellowing with horns.
> (*Testament of Morann*, § 58-62)

The true ruler, according to the author of this text, is loved by his supporters: they 'glorify him with blessings'. The wily ruler is one who maintains his leadership through some kind of trickery or deceit. The ruler of occupation is one who has lost the trust and respect of his own people, and so he has to pay foreign mercenaries (outside contractors?) to enforce his laws. Finally, the bull ruler is constantly harried by opponents and attackers: the horns bellowing against him are the battle-cries of his enemies. Eventually, the bull ruler is overthrown.

It isn't explicitly stated, but it may be that the 'ruler of occupation' uses his mercenaries to impose fear on his people. Let us look at what happens when a leader tries to do that.

Breaking the Fear Barrier

The relation of leader to follower is perhaps more subject to fear than any other. For one thing: no one likes to think of herself as a follower, nor often willingly admits to following another. Images of dictators like Idi Amin, Pol Pot, Benito Mussolini, and Adolf Hitler, are among the most powerful symbols of evil in Western culture today. Indeed images of depraved Roman emperors like Caligula and Nero are still potent symbols of evil, even after many centuries. We use the word 'draconian' to refer to laws or policies that seem excessively harsh. This word refers back to a 7th century BCE Athenian lawmaker, Draco, for whom the punishment for breaking any law, no matter how trivial, was death. And as Plato wrote, people in a democratic society are always fearful of threats to their freedom, and quick to accuse their leaders of being oligarchs and tyrants (*Republic* 562d).

We associate leadership with fear in this way because, as noted already, one of the most effective ways for a leader to gain and keep power is by using fear. Political scientists such as Machiavelli wrote that a leader should use fear to maintain his rule. "For love is secured by a bond of gratitude which men, wretched creatures that they are, break when it is to their advantage to do so; but fear is strengthened by a dread of punishment which is always effective."[227] Around a century or so afterwards, Thomas Hobbes wrote that the sovereign has to be powerful and fearful, in order to prevent war and ensure social stability. "For by this authority, given him by every particular man in the commonwealth, he hath the use of so much power and strength conferred on him, that by terror thereof, he is enabled to conform the wills of them all, to peace at home, and mutual aid against their enemies abroad."[228]

But what becomes of the person who uses fear this way? It

almost always happens that he ends up trapping himself in a labyrinth. People close to Joseph Stalin, for instance, observed that he was often very lonely. But no one wanted to accept his occasional overtures of friendship, because they worried that he would accuse them of disloyalty and order their deaths. Nikita Khrushchev wrote of him that: "When he woke up in the morning, he would immediately summon us, either inviting us to the movies or starting some conversation which could have been finished in two minutes but was stretched out so that we could stay with him longer."[229] Milovan Djilas, another of Stalin's immediate circle, said: "He became himself the slave of the despotism, the bureaucracy, the narrowness, and the servility he imposed on his country. It is indeed true that no one can destroy another's freedom without losing his own."[230] As Plato wrote, many centuries ago, "Someone with a tyrannical nature lives his whole life without being friends with anyone, always a master to one man or a slave to another, and never getting a taste of either freedom or true friendship." (*Republic* 576a) In that way, leadership through fear becomes a labyrinth that traps the leader himself, as surely as it traps his followers.

We might also look at the kind of society that leadership through fear creates. Muammar Gaddafi, within a few years of assuming power in Libya, created what he called a Jamahiriya, or government by the people. The idea was that power would be exercised primarily through local committees. But in practical terms, his government was a paranoid and murderous police state. As much as 20% of the population was involved in spying on other Libyans.[231] Ordinary people would refuse to talk to journalists about their lives, because government 'minders' would watch from nearby, and take notes. Political dissidents were 'disappeared', held without charge, beaten and tortured, and sometimes executed in public, and on live national television. Gaddafi banned the teaching of foreign languages in schools, and made it an offence to talk to foreigners about politics, punishable by three years in prison. He placed propaganda posters, statues, and images of himself everywhere. A schoolteacher told a journalist: "There were so many billboards of Qaddafi, he used to appear in our dreams."[232] A journalist who spoke with one of Gaddafi's 'inner circle' wrote of how fear dominated the minds of his closest supporters:

> To tremble with fear is a cliché. However, on two occasions I noticed officials in his [Gaddafi's] presence start to shake. I wondered if they were ill, then realised that they were unable to control their fear, sweating and twitching and trying to edge out of his direct gaze. I once asked one of his inner circle – we were not in Libya – why his close colleagues behaved that way. He thought and then said that the Colonel's rages were occasionally so terrible that many thought he might kill. "It's terrible," he said. "But what can we do? He has the power. There are no alternatives in this kind of world. I'd rather not talk about it."[233]

But as is well-known, leadership through fear is ultimately unsustainable: a leader who becomes a "bull ruler" is eventually overthrown. Gaddafi should have been reading his Machiavelli more closely, especially this part: "The prince must none the less make himself feared in such a way that, if he is not loved, at least he escapes being hated."[234] The people of Libya eventually had enough of living in fear, and in February 2011 they started a rebellion against him.

The uprising in Libya followed other uprisings in other north African countries, notably Tunisia and Egypt. On 18ᵗʰ January 2011, Asmaa Mahfouz, 26 years old, decided that she had enough of the corruption in her country's government and the brutality of the police. Therefore she posted to the Internet a video in which she described her intention to go to Tahrir Square, in downtown Cairo, and start protesting, and she invited others to do the same. A certain amount of fear attended her decision. Later on she told a journalist: "I felt that doing this video may be too big a step for me, but then I thought: For how much longer will I continue to be afraid and hesitant? I had to do something." Ms. Mahfouz is a very visible example of leadership by action. A single person's initiative and bravery became the most important link in a long chain of cause-and-effect which resulted in removal of Egyptian President Hosni Mubarak from power, only twenty-four days later. It is important to note that in all the democratic uprisings in north Africa in the first two months of 2011, the Islamic fundamentalist terror group Al Qaeda played absolutely no role whatsoever. Nor did the protesters in those countries use violence to achieve their goals. They simply occupied major public squares in their cities and refused to leave until their demands were met. Mariam Soliman, another Egyptian activist, described herself as follows: "I am not socialist, I am not a liberal, I am not an Islamist. I am an Egyptian woman, a regular woman rejecting injustice and corruption in my country."[235] Indeed it must be observed that most of the protest leadership were women, and that the protests were generally peaceful because it was led mainly by women.[236]

There was violence at these protests. But the overwhelming majority of it was instigated by the corrupt politicians attempting to cling to power. Mubarak of Egypt, for instance, hired poor people from rural parts of Egypt to come to Cairo and beat up the protesters.[237] In the first few days of protesting in Libya, Muammar Gaddafi claimed that the protests were caused by Al-Qaida, and by drugs in young people's coffee. In the first few days of the protest he deployed snipers on the rooftops of buildings, killing at least 15 people. He also destroyed the minaret of a mosque full of protesters using anti-aircraft missiles.[238] Thus the governments of these countries used fear to maintain their rule: fear of Islamic terrorists, and as well as fear of their own police and military. But this kind of fear cannot be effective forever. As Mahfouz said, "Everyone used to say there is no hope, that no one will turn up on the street, that the people are passive. But the barrier of fear was broken."[239]

Setting the Example

What would leadership be like if the leaders did not need to use fear to keep their followers? As I investigated this question, I found myself impressed most of all by the way Aboriginal people understand leadership. There are hundreds of Aboriginal languages and cultures on Turtle Island, all of them in various ways different and distinct from each other. But one of the fairly consistent cultural themes is the way that leadership depends on the personal qualities of the leader. Basil Johnston wrote that even though leaders in Ojibway society had to be admirable people, no one felt under any strong obligation to obey them. "Even when circumstance demands leadership," he wrote, "the act of leading is without compulsion. The followers follow freely and are at liberty to withdraw."[240] He also said the following about leadership among the Ojibway:

> As the crane calls infrequently and commands attention, so ought a leader exercise his prerogative rarely and bear the same attention in the discharge of his duties. He speaks infrequently lest he be considered shallow. A leader having no other source of authority except for his force of character and persuasion did not jeopardize his tenuous ability. Moreover a leader was first in action, not merely a commander; as a speaker he did not utter his own sentiments, but those of his people... He was as leader by example and the first of speakers only.

Crowshoe & Manneschmidt wrote the following about leadership in the Peigan Nation:

The civil chief controlled the destiny of his people only so long as the strength of his personality and the obvious correctness of his judgement seemed to indicate his authority.[241]

Daniel Paul, of the Mi'kmaq Nation, wrote:

In contrast to most of the cultures of Europe, where the divine right to rule was the province of the aristocrat, the Mi'kmaq people held that a leader had to earn the right to lead. The standards were rigid for men who aspired to leadership. Aspirants had to be compassionate, honourable, intelligent, brave, and wise. The term of office was indeterminate, and if a leader conducted himself well, his leadership could continue until death. Grand Chief Membertou, the greatest Mi'kmaq chief in living memory, remained a leader until his death at an age said to be well over one hundred.[242]

In all three of these cases, from Aboriginal societies far distant from each other in space and in language, the authority of the leader stems primarily from his personal qualities. What qualities, then, should a leader have? Much of the time, something like 'eloquence', or the ability to speak persuasively, will be among them. As Johnston wrote, "leadership was predicated upon persuasion."[243] Paul listed compassion, honor, intelligence, bravery and wisdom as additional necessary qualities for a Mi'kmaq leader. Johnston wrote that among the Ojibway, people born under a leadership totem would be trained for leadership from childhood. "… they studied history, tradition, grammar, and speaking. Part of the training fostered eloquence, wisdom, and generosity." Similarly, McMillan wrote that among the Interior Salish some chiefs were hereditary, but even so a prestigious family lineage was still not enough to secure a chief's authority:

A chief could lead only by persuasion and example, not by coercion… chiefly positions tended to be hereditary, as the son of a wealthy and influential chief had a great advantage over other possible candidates. However, he still had to prove worthy of the position or his leadership would not be recognised.[244]

Note that although there were leadership castes and hereditary chieftains in some Aboriginal societies, it was nothing like a hereditary aristocracy. Johnston asserts that: "Merit was the criteria for assessing the quality of a candidate. Thus, if a person, born of another totemic group, were deemed to possess a greater capacity for leadership than one so prepared, he would be preferred."[245]

I asked a few friends of mine who were in leadership positions themselves about what they thought leadership required. P. Fletcher, who for twenty years organized Kaleidoscope Gathering, Canada's largest pagan cultural festival, taught me what she thought the values of a good leader should be.

- Act in a way that sets an example. Do not ask someone to do something that you would not do yourself.
- Try to keep ego out of it as mush as possible. Reflect on your thoughts and actions to understand your own motives. It hurts when you fall from a pedestal especially one you have placed yourself on.
- Be thoughtful in your actions and decisions, to benefit the greater good with honesty and integrity. Sometimes, this does not make you popular.
- Really listen to those you serve and those you trust; you can not know everything and you will better understand the needs of your community.
- Delegate to those you trust to do the best job they can, it empowers those you work with. They will often do better than yourself and you can learn from them.

- Be kind in your words, even if you are not feeling positive inside; you may have to eat them later. I always to try to say "Please" and "Thank you." People really enjoy being appreciated.

   (P. Fletcher, 2010)

Fletcher stepped down in 2009, and passed the torch to others. Although the festival community was very confident in the new leadership, they were also sad to see her go. The bards composed songs in her honor. (*Sweet Pamela*, sung to the tune of Neil Diamond's *Sweet Caroline*, is still a Bardic favorite after three years.) Spontaneous acts of gratitude and thanks flowed freely, such as this one, which occurred at the festival's closing ceremony:

> A woman came into the middle of the circle with me to say her thank you to me. This was very touching for me, but she felt the need to kneel at my feet. I could not accept this behaviour and despite my pleas for her to please get up, that no one should ever kneel before me, she would not. So, the only thing I could think to do was to lie at feet to let her know how much I truly appreciated everything the community had actually given me and taught me. (P. Fletcher, 2010)

And at the end of the closing ceremony, over a hundred people from the community Fletcher served for twenty years came forward in a giant 'group hug'.

Outpourings of love like these are simply not given to leaders who rely upon fear. They are the reward for those who lead by good personal example.

21

Healers

No relationship is immune from problems. Even the most harmonious, happiest, and most fruitful relationships are stressed and fractured from time to time. Even the relation which seems healthy enough to last forever may some day break down. For this reason we need healers: these are people involved in repairing and restoring broken or damaged relationships.

The Hippocratic Oath

Medical doctors, when they finish their training, must swear a special ceremonial promise, called the Hippocratic Oath, in which they promise to 'do no harm'. The original oath appears in an ancient Greek manuscript called *The Hippocratic Writings*, so named for its author, Hippocrates, the 'Father of Western medicine'. Here is a translation of the original Oath in its entirety.

> I swear by Apollo the healer, by Aesculapius, by Health and by all the powers of healing, and call to witness all the gods and goddesses that I may keep this Oath and Promise to the best of my ability and judgment.
>
> I will pay the same respect to my master in the Science as to my parents and share my life with him and pay all my debts to him. I shall regard his sons as my brothers and teach them the Science, if they desire to learn it, without fee or contract. I will hand on precepts, lectures and all other learning to my sons, to those of my master and to those pupils duly apprenticed and sworn, and to no other.
>
> I will use my power to help the sick to the best of my ability and judgment; I will abstain from harming or

wronging any man by it.

I will not give a fatal draught to anyone if I am asked, nor will I suggest any such thing. Neither will I give a woman means to procure an abortion.

I will be chaste and religious in my life and in my practice.

I will not cut, even for the stone, but I will leave such procedures to the practitioners of that craft.

Whenever I go into a house, I will go to help the sick and never with the intention of doing harm or injury. I will not abuse my position to indulge in sexual contacts with the bodies of women or men, whether they be freemen or slaves.

Whatever I see or hear, professionally or privately, which ought not to be divulged, I will keep secret and tell no one.

If, therefore, I observe this Oath and do not violate it, may I prosper both in my life and in my profession, earning good repute among all men for all time. If I transgress and forswear this Oath, may my lot be otherwise.[246]

No modern medical doctor swears exactly this Oath anymore: most medical schools have their own (although they still call it The Hippocratic Oath). But the oaths of most schools have a few elements in common with the original Oath, for instance the requirement 'to help the sick', and to 'do no harm or injustice'.

It may be worthwhile to examine the original oath more closely. The first and last parts in this Oath are like the frame of a picture. The oath-taker starts by invoking various deities, perhaps to assert the seriousness and importance of the deeds which the oath-taker is about to promise to do. The second through to the seventh parts constitute the promises which the oath-taker makes. The first of them (paragraph 2) establishes the doctor's relationship with other doctors, and especially his teacher. A doctor should treat other doctors like family, and the sons of his teacher like his own brothers. This effectively asserts that the relationship of a teacher to a student is as strong and as significant as the relationship between a father and son. I think it is significant that the original Hippocratic Oath mentions a doctor's relationship to other doctors before mentioning his relationship to his patients. I see it as a kind of guild-solidarity clause. This is perhaps intended to preserve the integrity of the profession, and of the knowledge that is passed on during a doctor's apprenticeship. The third paragraph is where the doctor's relationship with his patients appears: it takes the form of the famous requirement 'do no harm'. The next parts forbid the doctor from performing abortions and from euthanizing their patients, and from performing surgery, presumably even if the patient asks for those procedures. This may in part be because the requirement to 'do no harm' demands it. But there is some ambiguity here. That part of the oath also includes a kind of guild-protectionist clause: the reason a doctor is not allowed to surgically remove ulcers is because there are other practitioners who specialize in surgery, and the doctor should stand back and let them do their job. Similarly, the reason that a doctor is forbidden to procure abortions or to euthanize a patient might be because those jobs belong to other specialists: midwives and apothecaries, perhaps. But it is clear that this oath requires doctors to make the patient's good health his highest priority. This is further clarified in the last parts, where the oath requires doctors to behave 'professionally', and also affirms doctor-patient confidentiality. One can infer a lot, with these statements, about what doctors were like in Hippocrates' time. It seems plausible that in Greek society around the time of Hippocrates, the profession of medicine had fallen into disrepute, as people claiming to be doctors were taking advantage of their patients. Hippocrates says as much elsewhere in his writings: "Although the art of healing is the most noble of all the arts, yet, because of the ignorance both of its professors and of their rash critics, it has at this time fallen into the least repute of them all."[247] He also gripes about the absence of legal penalties for malpractice. The requirement to abstain from sex with patients might be a sign that many medical doctors at the time were doing exactly that. After all, no one makes a law to stop people from doing things that they are not already doing. (Imagine a sign on a beach that says, "Please, do not eat the sand.") Including this requirement might have been an attempt to improve the trust between doctor and patient. A patient has to trust that his doctor is thinking about the patient's health, and nothing else. He shouldn't expect to be harmed or taken advantage of. Also, when a condition is potentially fatal, or is socially stigmatized (the patient has AIDS, to use a modern example), then he might not want the world to know about it. So he has to trust that the doctor will keep things confidential.

Trust, it seems to me, is an essential part of the relationship between a healer and a patient. Someone who has taken an oath like this one at the beginning of his medical career offers to his potential patients, and to society as a whole, greater reason to trust him. A doctor needs to have that trust: he might not be able to do his job properly without it. Moreover, patients who don't trust their doctors might lie about their symptoms, or they might not allow the doctor to do a proper examination. A professional oath, like this one, affirms social values in a practical and public way: it is the oath-taker's public statement of commitment to those values. It therefore has the social effect of entitling the oath-taker to certain benefits if he embodies those values well (benefits such as public trust), and also extra punishments if he embodies those values poorly. That, I think, is the function of the final paragraph of the oath.

Healing the Body

Obviously, the public good that doctors and others in the healing professions pledge to uphold is the good of health. But it may not be so obvious what health really is. In my own studies of the philosophical literature of the subject, it seems to me that there are three outstanding (and sometimes competing) definitions of health. Any definition of health that you may find, no matter where you find it, is likely to be a variation of one of these four.

The first of my definitions of health is scientific in nature. Health is *homeostasis*, which is the condition of a living body that can function on its own, without the need for outside mechanical assistance like respirators or dialysis machines. This definition has the advantage of being objective: it establishes precise criteria for a doctor to work to achieve. And most of the time, it will be highly useful. A broken arm, for instance, is a broken arm, and obviously in need of outside support in the form of a splint or a cast. But sometimes things are not so obvious. Consider someone like Stephen Hawking, the world's foremost astrophysicist, whose body is possessed by cerebral palsy. Yet his condition has not impaired his ability to do advanced scientific work.

To resolve a case like this, we might turn to a Utilitarian definition: health is the condition of a body in which the pleasurable and useful experiences of the working of one's own body outweigh the troublesome and painful experiences. This has the benefit of being similarly objective, yet a little more flexible. But it too can have exceptions. Someone in a persistent vegetative state is probably feeling no pain, but we should be reluctant to call that person healthy.

The third definition of health I shall call Aristotelian, since it is loosely based on his Doctrine of the Mean. It states that a person is healthy when there is a balance between what a person aims to do (with the use of her body), and what her bodily condition enables her to do. Dr. Edmund Pellegrino, author of an influential paper on the subject, reached a similar definition: he wrote that health is "an equilibrium established between inborn or acquired diseases or limitations and the use of our bodies for trans-bodily purposes – to advance a person's interests, plans, or aspirations."[248] Thus, someone is healthy when he or she is able to do (with her body) whatever she may wish to do. We could call a disabled person healthy this way, if her disability does not impede her pursuit of her plans and aspirations. Of course, this definition might designate someone as 'unhealthy' if her goals are well beyond her body's abilities. Imagine someone who wants to be an Olympic track runner, and who is obviously not in good enough shape to finish, let alone win, a race, but is otherwise healthy. She could train herself so that a year or so in the future, she could compete. But if the aspiration is entirely unrealistic, it may be a form of *mental* ill health. It might fall to psychologists, councilors, and mental health support workers to help people set more rational goals for themselves.

My own preference is for this third definition. Even with its problems it still opens the possibility for a dialogue between healers and patients, in a way the other three cannot do. It allows for the goal of medical treatment to be decided collaboratively. Each person, with the help of her doctors and other health professionals, can decide for herself what she wants, and what is best for her, and what kind of health-related goals she can work to achieve. It might involve alleviating pain from some disease, or repairing an injury, or undertaking various preventative measures, or even empowering the body so that it can go 'faster, higher, stronger', as the Olympic motto says. Then the doctor can evaluate the likelihood of success in that aim, and develop a treatment plan to achieve it. Although I prefer this definition, it may not be strictly necessary to eliminate the other three. When a healer pledges to uphold health as a public value, she could have in mind any one of them, or even all three of them.

I have suggested that a public oath to uphold a public good entitles a doctor to her patient's trust, and to the public's trust. How does the relationship of trust break down? Why is it that so many people still distrust doctors, despite the oath, despite heavy government regulation of the health care industry, and despite the intimate nature of health issues which would seem to require doctor and patient to trust each other? In America, the breakdown of trust may, in part, be a product of the privatized and profit-seeking health care system, in which a trip to a doctor is expensive. Prospective patients therefore convince themselves that the doctors will do them no good anyway, and thus they save their money. New Age healers often promote the idea that pharmacological solutions are unnatural, or that the medical establishment is corrupt. This also contributes to a general distrust of doctors in mainstream society. But I think the distrust of doctors is based mainly in the impression that doctors treat their patients as the site of a biomechanical breakdown, instead of as a person. The scientific approach to medicine seems to encourage this point of view. A central question in medicine thus becomes: does a doctor primarily treat the person, or does she primarily treat the disease? And which one *should* the doctor treat first?

My view, as you might guess, is that a doctor should consider her patients as people first. Sometimes, social and economic forces get in the way of this. When the medical profession is organized as a for-profit industry, as it is in America, doctors and hospitals have a monetary incentive to treat patients as cash cows instead of as people. Economic indicators will measure success in terms of its profitability, and its contribution to gross domestic product, instead of in terms of lives saved. Yet patients deserve to be treated as human beings, and not as factors of an economic calculus. Countries where health care services are mostly public are not without their own problems, and sometimes also measure success using economic indicators. But the care is generally more compassionate and humane. Patients have less anxiety since they know that their injury or illness will not bankrupt and impoverish them. Public health care is also more economically efficient. In 1996 researchers found that the privatized American system cost $1,000 per capita more than the Canadian public system.[249] In 2009, more than 50 million

Americans had no health insurance coverage at all. Almost 60% of those who had no insurance were part-time workers or the unemployed.[250]

Some of the distrust in doctors might be generated in the frustrations that can take hold of a doctor's mind when her patients are uncooperative or demanding. Dr. Joseph Collins, writing in Harper's Magazine in 1927, made the most eloquent expression of professional jadedness that I have ever read. "The longer I practice medicine the more I am convinced that every physician should cultivate lying as a fine art," he said.[251] This is because "to tell the whole truth [to a patient about his condition] is often to perpetrate a cruelty of which many are incapable." He also wrote that "many experiences show that patients do not want the truth about their maladies, and that it is prejudicial to their well-being to know it."[252] He cited numerous examples, mostly from his own experience, of how patients given the whole truth about their condition refused to believe it, and thus didn't follow his instructions, and died. He also described cases when he told his patients a white lie, and so spared the patient much anxiety and worry. These patients lived better and longer than they might otherwise have lived. Part of Collins' argument has to do with professionalism: he asserted that a doctor shouldn't pronounce a diagnosis before she is absolutely sure about it. But he also asserts a rather misanthropic claim about people: "No one can stand the whole truth about himself." I appreciate that Dr. Collins wants to spare his patients from fear, which he says is "the medium in which disease waxes strong." Yet there is something of the taste of sour grapes here: a doctor who assumes from the outset that patients can't handle the truth about their own health probably can't be completely trusted. Certainly a major part of a doctor's trustworthiness stems from her honesty. Without that honesty, a productive dialogue between doctor and patient about health goals and treatment plans cannot occur. There are compassionate and sensitive ways for a doctor to convey unpleasant truths about a patient's condition. It may be incumbent upon doctors to find those ways, so that patients and doctors can make informed decisions about treatment plans, and be spared the fear that concerned Dr. Collins so much.

Another way that trustworthiness might break down has to do with the attitudes of patients themselves. Several of the doctors and nurses who I spoke with taught me that the majority of their patients visit them only to demand prescriptions for drugs, and for no other reason. This kind of patient does not wish to give the doctor the time and freedom to investigate the condition properly. Nor does this kind of patient want to take much of a role in the maintenance of his own health. All the rhetoric of 'team building' between doctor and patient and other medical professionals is entirely lost on such people. In that situation, a doctor must ask herself which aim must take priority: healing the patient to the best of her ability, or simply doing whatever the patient demands of her. One doctor said to me: "The simplest, easiest, and most effective way to get an uncooperative patient out of my office is to write him a prescription. They don't really want to know what the problem is. They just want me to give them a pill to get rid of it." (Name withheld by request, 2009) This informant described how, on one occasion, when he "tried to act like a doctor" and investigate a patient's condition both scientifically and humanely, the patient threatened to sue him for malpractice. He wrote a prescription for a strong painkiller and a referral to a specialist, and never saw that patient again. I was given the impression that the more demanding and selfish the patients are, the more emotionally distant a doctor is likely to become. Yet I do not wish to say that only the patients are entirely to blame. In fact I think the situation is a product of a vicious circle. Selfish patients cause their doctors to become disinterested in other patients, and disinterested doctors cause patients to become cynical and distrusting of the whole medical profession.

A sound and flourishing relationship between a healer and a patient is one in which both partners respect and trust each other. Patients accord to doctors the autonomy to do their jobs, and doctors approach the patients as people, with lives to live and stories to tell.

Healing the Community

Relationships between people also break down, just as relations between the body do. Some Aboriginal nations in Canada have created procedures and techniques for restoring peace between people which are worth investigating here. These techniques have been used, experimented with, altered where necessary, and refined over 50,000 years, and it is not difficult to imagine why. In a small community of hunter-gatherers, where everyone relies on everyone else for survival, ill will between two or more members of the group can threaten the survival of the entire group. Offending individuals might not go hunting and gathering, or in their anger they might decide not to share their meat. Thus moral values had to emerge which would help reduce or calm tensions before they got out of hand. Personal virtues such as constant agreeableness, and temperance – in this context, the virtue of never ever losing one's temper – are two of them. The healing circle, which is more like a technique of ethics than a value, is another, and here I shall attempt to describe it.

A healing circle may be defined as "a First Nations way of repairing harm to people and communities through dialogue among all the affected parties in a carefully controlled and private setting under the leadership of Elders."[253] In Canada, if an Aboriginal person charged with a crime pleads guilty, he or she can be diverted from the courts to a healing circle. When the process has been followed properly the decision of a healing circle has the same force as a judicial sentencing.

One of the Elders I consulted taught me that in the traditions of his people:

... the last stage involves a community meeting which is presided over by a male and a female Elder, and with the offender and his family on one side, and the victim and his family on the other. Also attending the meeting are the Chief, his assistant, and the council. There must also be a fire in the centre of the meeting place. At that meeting it would be decided whether the offender had properly done the things asked of him, and whether the matter was finally settled.

In other Aboriginal traditions, the community meeting may or may not be the last stage. But it is always the most important stage. Indeed the community meeting, in the circle, is where the most important healing work is done.

Elder H.C. of the Peigan nation described to me what a healing circle in the tradition of his people looks like. First of all, a Sacred Bundle is placed on an altar on the west side of the circle, across from the entrance in the east. The bundle's caretakers sit on either side of it: the woman on the left or south side and the man on the right or north side. On the right side of the bundle and its keeper sits the offender. Next to him are his family and supporters. He emphasized that the offender's supporters are not like 'defence attorneys'. Their job is not to make the offender look good. Rather:

... their job is to support the offender, help him to understand what he did, and what problems or consequences were created by his actions. They might help explain why the offender did what he did, for instance if the offender's parents died recently. Yet they will also describe what they are willing to do to help the offender acknowledge what he did and learn to do better in the future.

On the left side of the bundle sits the victim, and next to him are his family and supporters. Their purpose is to help explain the victim's point of view, but not necessarily to elicit sympathy for him. The healing circle is not an arena where two parties with opposed interests compete with each other. Therefore the victim's supporters are not like prosecuting attorneys. But the victim's supporters do have the job of helping the offender fully understand the true consequences of his actions, and to take responsibility for them.

There are a few other functionary positions in the healing circle. Two Elders stand on either side of the door, one male and one female. Their job is to see that the process of the circle is done properly. There are also four positions traditionally referred to as 'drummers' who sit in a row on the left (south) side, next to the fire. Their job is to make sure that the decisions of the circle are enforced. The drummers could be anyone with a relevant professional expertise or knowledge that can be brought to the situation to help. Elder H.C. referred to these people as "technical support workers." Thus if an offender is on probation, for example, one of them could be his probation officer. If there are children involved in the incident, one of them could be a child welfare officer and another a social worker. Once the opening prayers and purifications (i.e. smudging with sweetgrass or sage) are done, then:

> The victim speaks first, then the victim's supporters, one at a time. Then the offender speaks, and then the offender's supporters. It goes around the circle. Everything has to happen by consensus. Once all the explanations and descriptions and so on are done, everyone, starting with the offender, gets a chance to suggest a course of action or a decision, what the offender should do to make amends with the victim and the whole community.

Thereafter, the process continues in accord with a few simple ground rules. Each of these rules, in various ways, represent distinct values. Here I shall describe what appears to be the six most important ones.

1. The first 'rule' is really the purpose of a healing circle, which is to restore the relationships which the incident disrupted. Offender and victim are forced to confront one another. This is what several Elders told me they like about the circle the most. The victim shows who he is and the full extent of the incident's consequences. The offender may present his own case for why he did what he did, and this may go a certain length toward enabling the victim to forgive. But the offender must *earn* that forgiveness primarily by making an honest effort to understand the consequences of his actions, understand the victim's point of view, and change his own point of view. This is not an easy task. Yvonne Boyer wrote, "The impact of a youth looking a victim in the eye and saying 'I am sorry' is very powerful experience."[254]

2. Ethical teachings such as the Seven Grandfathers must be observed at all times. Again, respect is among the most important of these. As a sign of respect, and in order to allow each person to fully express their thoughts and feelings, no one is permitted to interrupt anyone who is speaking. Honesty and trust and truthfulness are also very important. There is no question, in the healing circle, of a victim exaggerating his situation in order to improve his position and get a 'better deal'. Similarly, an offender must take responsibility for his action. The offender who assents to a healing process effectively pleads guilty to the offence automatically. This is in part because the Criminal Code of Canada requires offenders to accept responsibility for their actions before they can consent to an alternative form of justice.[255] But the larger reason is because the very purpose and point of a healing circle is to *compel* the offender to take responsibility for his actions. This would not happen if the offender insists upon his innocence or denies his guilt. In the healing circle, there is opportunity for the offender to explain himself, but no option for an offender to simply plead innocent.

Similarly, the offender cannot attempt to improve his position by, for instance, casting doubt on the facts of the case, or attacking the credibility of witnesses or victims. This makes the healing process very difficult for offenders. One of the workers in the Biidaaban program (the traditional justice program used by the Mnjikaning First Nation, Ontario) said:

> We, by no shape or form, ever want to be seen as giving a 'get out of jail free card'. Our program is not free. It's tough. It's easier to go to jail than it is to have a look at yourself and be in front of your peers and be accountable for the wrongs you've done to whoever it is and how that has affected the community. They [the offenders] have to plead guilty and take responsibility for their actions, number one. They need to say they're sorry and they need to right the wrongs. Restitution. To ensure the community that it will never happen again.[256]

For these reasons, among others, the perception that offenders 'get off easy' in the healing circle is simply false. Acknowledging responsibility for having harmed someone, and facing the victim of one's actions and the victim's family in order to make that acknowledgement, is very hard for many people to do.

3. A healing process involves many people, not just the offender and victim and a judge. It involves as many people in the community as are affected, or who have an ability to help. Most of all, it involves the victim's and offender's families. An Elder taught me that the reason for this is:

> The healing work must also be done with the offender's family. For instance, if a young person is required to perform a certain number of hours of community service, and yet his parents are both alcoholics, then the community service may not benefit the offender, and may not go very far to heal him. The root problem has not been attacked: and so the conditions

which created the disposition to offend still exist.

Part of the reason why families must be involved is exactly as Elder Louttit stated it here. If the offender is going to return to an environment of broken relationships, then the healing work is likely to be undone. Officer Louise Logue affirmed this as well when she said the family outreach is one of the most important stages in the process that diverts Aboriginal offenders from the courts to the circle. In her words, "The diversion process is less likely to be successful if the child is only going to return to a damaged or broken home." But another part of the reason may have to do with the attribution of responsibility not only to the offender himself, but also to the people around him. Each person involved in the offender's life, especially the members of his family, has to take his or her share of the responsibility (I do not say 'blame'). As Elder Joseph Lacroix taught, "Everyone who commits a crime, it's that person's choice. Society is never to blame. But society can be responsible for producing the want to do it." Similarly, Yvonne Boyer, former Director of Justice for the Saskatoon Tribal Council, wrote that in the circle, the offender must confront everyone who may care about him, and explain himself to them, and that this can be extraordinarily difficult to do: "It is far more difficult for a youth to explain to his or her grandmother why they committed the offence than it is to a judge in a robe on a bench."[257]

The reason for involving the family and community may also be stated as follows. In the Aboriginal worldview, there is an expanding circle of responsibility which starts from the self and extends out to include all one's relations in ever-increasing circles of comprehensiveness. All these broken or disturbed relationships will need to be healed, therefore the offender has to explain himself and apologize to everyone involved. Similarly, everyone involved must accept their share of the responsibility for the incident, and for the healing. As one participant in the

Biidaaban healing program put it, "To set people free is a wonderful thing and it takes a whole team of people to do that."[258]

4. A healing process takes a long time to complete. Elder T.L. taught me: "A healing process might take many years. People say, 'the days of the 60s Scoops are over, why not just get over it?' Because healing doesn't happen in just one day. It can take many years." Since that is so, one of the police officers I spoke with was therefore very critical of the way some police services attempt to 'short cut' the healing process in the interest of getting fast results. She said:

> There is a process that the government has been encouraging police forces to use, called 'reintegrative shaming'. It is the use of shunning and humiliation in a controlled manner, followed by a formal reacceptance, all in the same event, taking about three hours or so. But it is just a cheap way for the government to contribute to Native culture. And not altogether helpful because it doesn't go to the source of the problem.

It seems clear, on the basis of these remarks, that there is no such thing as a quick-fix for a damaged or disrupted relationship. Each incident, and each person involved, must be given all of the time that is necessary to complete the process.

5. A healing process must involve sincere and intense expressions of thought and feeling. An Elder who worked with court diversions to healing circles taught me that: "Tears are part of the healing. At many sessions tears flow freely." Workers in the Biidaaban program say similar things about the emotional force of the circle, and the healing power of the free expression of emotions. For instance, one worker told the following story about a probation officer who attended a healing circle which was dealing with a sex offender. The occasion moved her to reveal her own pain after having been abused many years previously.

...the police officer was in tears as she described how his [the offender's] statement had affected her. She had worked in our community from the far North for a number of years and she had been raised in one of our communities in the North and she was actually disclosing publicly for the first time how she had been abused and was saying how overwhelming it was to her being moved into tears. She couldn't believe what she was hearing because she never before heard an offender take responsibility for the wrongs that he had done and apologize for it.[259]

Another Elder I consulted taught me that, "Healing has to involve humour." He observed that in his own experience in the formal court system, "everyone is terribly serious all the time. The element of humor, which to my people is essential to the healing process, was completely missing." At a court hearing, he was asked by a judge why he was always looking away, turning his ear to the judge instead of looking at him directly. He answered, "My one ear has a hearing aid, and I turn that one to you, so I can hear you. The other is full of potatoes. It's no good at all." The judge smiled. The sincerity of the emotional expressions, in both laughter and sadness, are often taken as signs that the people involved are facing their situation and their responsibilities directly and honestly. As one Biidaaban program participant described the circle:

I wish you could see the faces on the people after the Gathering. The relief. They feel good about themselves and they don't have to hide the stuff anymore. No more hiding and lying. All the weight comes off their shoulders. You can see their eyes smiling. It's hard work. It's gut-wrenching work. Sometimes we have horrible circles to get through and we'll start at 9:00 in the morning and go to after 11:00 at night but it's worth every second.[260]

It may be inferred, therefore, that sincere and heartfelt expressions of emotion are part of the very meaning of healing, in the Aboriginal justice tradition. Again, for this reason among others, offenders who go through an Aboriginal healing circle are not 'getting off easy'. They are forced to face difficult realities, both within themselves and in the lives of others, and they are forced to make difficult choices.

6. Finally, the healing is offered to everyone, including the offender: indeed the circle must help the offender to see the good in himself. The aforementioned police officer taught me that: "The offender himself may not know what he brings, and what he has to contribute. If no one ever tells you that you are worth something, then you might not know it." An offender who had been through the Biidaaban program described the effect this had on him: "I didn't know people cared about me or that they saw the good things in me too. I thought they'd all be against me. It [the circle] stopped the gossip. Now they knew the truth and I can live with that."[261] This point has deep roots in Aboriginal culture. It appears, for instance, in the story of Hiawatha. His propensity for cannibalism was healed after he saw the good in himself, through the reflection of the Peacemaker's face in the water of his kettle. An offender who is shown the good in himself by his supporters, family, and community is better able to deal with his problems (and of course, much less likely to reoffend).

It may strike some readers of this study as unusual or puzzling that the *offender* must be healed, as well as the victim. This is in part for reasons given earlier, in the discussion of self-awareness. Many offenders were themselves victims of abuse or trauma. When they offend, they replay the same story again in their later lives, only having reversed the roles. Offenders need to have their own wounds healed so that they will no longer be disposed to harm others. This attitude is embodied in an Aboriginal Legal Services of Toronto document from 1991 which states:

424

> At the heart of the Community Council must be a real, conscious feeling of kindness and respect for both the offender and the victim. When the offender and victim realize that the Council members actually care about them and respect them, then the message of the Council has a better chance of getting through.[262]

If the offender is treated with respect, then the healing process which traditional Aboriginal justice aims for is more likely to succeed. But deeper than this practical reason is the ethical reason: everyone, even the offender, possesses a spirit, and therefore deserves respect.

I asked several of my informants, What does success look like? One of the Elders answered, "Part of it is learning to forgive again." A policewoman said: "Success is when the offender does not re-victimize others again. Success is when the kids are able to handle their realities again. They can cope with stressors, and engage with bettering themselves, for instance through education, the arts, a skilled trade." She also said that success is the permanent inculcation of a certain group of virtues into the offender's character. In particular, she mentioned "courage, honor, humility, respect, and integrity." Note the emphasis on what Canadians might understand as 'rehabilitation'. The offender does not 'pay a debt to society'. The vocabulary of economics, implied by words like 'payment' and 'debt', does not fit the case. Rather, the healing process, if it is successful, involves *a transformation of the offender's character*. The purpose of this transformation is not only to prevent the person from committing offences again. Rather, it is to transform the offender into a better person.

A critic might ask, What if there is no obvious relationship between offender and victim to disturb in the first place? What is the point of characterizing justice as the healing of damaged relationships, when an offender can victimize a stranger? I think the answer that an Aboriginal Elder would give to this question might go like this. It is an important part of the Aboriginal worldview to affirm that just as everyone has within him or her a spirit, likewise the world has within itself a Great Spirit. In that way, everyone already has a spiritual relationship with everyone and everything else. This is true whether or not the parties also have other relationships such as being a neighbor, a family member, a work associate, a friend, and so on. If, therefore, an offender harms a stranger, he damages the spiritual relationship that obtains between him and his victim, and, correspondingly, he damages himself and his relationship to the Great Spirit. The harm to the spiritual relationship and to his own integrity will require healing. And it is often precisely through the meeting with the victim, in which he gets to know him and his life story, and hears him describe the impact of the offence, which heals these wounds to his spirit.

22

The Gods

We have come a long way together, you and I, through twenty-one different ways of relating to the sacred. We explored a few natural relations, such as those which arise with our animals, with landscapes, with our families, and within our own bodies. We explored a few personal relations, such as with our friends and lovers, those with whom we share food and drink, and those who we invite into our homes as guests. With these relations as our materials we built a community, and learned what it is to have a home. Then we enriched our community with the work of craftspeople and artists, and built markets to trade the things they make. We protected our community with courageous and honorable warriors. We invigorated it with athletes, explorers, musicians, and leaders. We struggled to empower and enlighten ourselves with our philosophers, teachers, Elders, and story-tellers. And when we had problems, we turned to our healers to restore us to peace.

In the opening pages of this book, I defined the sacred as that which serves as a partner in the search for the highest and deepest things. I had hoped to show that we find these things in our relationships. I also hoped to show that by treating our relationships as circles of meaning, we can avoid the labyrinth of fear, and create worthwhile and fulfilling lives. Although these ideas were explored only anecdotally, we may well ask, here in the last few pages of our time together, was the search successful? And what, at the end of the day, finally *are* the highest and deepest things?

A Pseudo-History of The Gods

In the summer of 2004 I stood across the road from the Elisabethkirche, the mediaeval Gothic cathedral in Marburg, Germany, and I set up my camera for the picture. It is a truly marvelous building: with its tall narrow stained glass windows, its lovingly carved foliate arch over the front door, its magnificent tall towers. Once I had my shot I crossed the road and stepped inside, into a space equally as awe-inspiring. The pillars supporting the ceiling were like the trunks of ancient trees, to my mind resembling the trees of the mighty Germanic forests not far from the city. Family crests, statues of saints, and side altars attest to the presence of the many people over the centuries who have used and loved this public space for centuries. When the battery on my camera died, my companion said it was just as well, since I was seeing most of the cathedral through its lens instead of through my own good eyes. So I put the camera down and looked around properly. Light from through the windows is constantly in motion, as clouds pass before the sun, and as the sun passes from east to south to west. At the end of the apse is a kind of screen which conceals the view of the high altar in the nave. I let my imagination slip momentarily into the mode of a pilgrim, arriving here after weeks of walking. With that image in my mind, I found myself standing only a few strides from a gateway to the throne room of God, in a building deliberately designed to give its visitor a momentary glimpse of the kingdom yet to come. How wonderful, how utterly entrancing, to stand within a building perfectly designed to make the visitor feel that he has left the Earth, and entered a better place! And how sad and empty must be the culture of my own time, the twenty-first century, when our grandest monuments are office towers, dedicated to commerce, open only to those with official business. But despite this aesthetically powerful image, this scale model of the royal court of Heaven, I could not drive from my mind the thought that *this building was not made to glorify God. It was made to edify Man.*

Why is that? One reason is because cathedral building in the mediaeval world was big business. The cathedral served first of all as a demonstration of the technological power, political consensus, artistic talent, and engineering skill of the people that built them. They also demonstrate the wealth of those who paid for them. Mediaeval nobility and royalty were involved in a kind of 'arts race' with each other, using their cathedrals. Whoever could build the tallest, largest, most impressive cathedral, would win the greatest prestige. And for the financiers, building a cathedral was often a very high-performing investment. For if your cathedral housed some truly fabulous art and architecture, and perhaps also the relics of a famous saint or two, then you could attract pilgrims from all over Europe. Before and after they kneel to pray before the toenails of their favorite saint, they leave a little offering in the jar. If the pilgrims are rich then they leave big offerings in your jar: enough perhaps to fund a monastery or a college nearby. They also spend their money in your town's hostels, bars, theatres, and restaurants (and maybe the brothels too). In this political and economic sense, it's plainly obvious that a cathedral glorifies human beings rather than God. But there is another, more serious reason why cathedrals have more to do with man than with God, and to explain it I must go through some intellectual history.

The very first religious idea ever to occur to human beings is *animism*. This is the idea that just about everything in the world has an invisible, immaterial spirit dwelling within it. But animism is more comprehensive still. Every knoll in the woods and every tree that grows there, every cloud that bursts with thunder and rain, every animal from the tiniest fish to the highest-flying eagle, possesses a spirit. Even the bright bodies of the cosmos, the sun, moon, and stars, have spirits. And some of these spirits are entirely disembodied, such as ghosts, angels, totemic animals, djinnis, and ancestors. We meet them in our dreams, or in mirages, or in shadows that move in the corner of the eye. Some may be purely conceptual, as when we speak of the 'spirit of friendship', or the 'spirit of freedom'. And some may be very sophisticated indeed, such as the Atman, or the Buddha Nature. Every religion in the world is but an elaboration or a variation of animism. Where differences exist, they tend not to question the plain existence of spiritual beings. Instead the differences between religions concern the nature, number, and interests, of such spirits, as well as the means of communicating with them, and their role in human affairs. As explained by the anthropologist Marvin Harris:

> ... the basis of all that is distinctly religious in human thought is animism, the belief that humans share the world with a population of extraordinary, extracorporeal, and mostly invisible beings, ranging from souls and ghosts to saints and faeries, angels, and cherubim, demons, jinni, devils, and gods. Wherever people believe in the existence of one or more of these beings, that is where religion exists... animistic beliefs [are] to be found in every society, and a century of ethnological research has yet to turn up a single exception.
> (Harris, *Our Kind*, p 399)

Animism presents us with a first, very preliminary understanding of the sacred. The highest and deepest things are the spirits themselves, and the objects, events, and places in which they dwell, whatever those may be.

Some of the those spirits seem to be 'greater' than others. Perhaps their sphere of influence is wider and more encompassing, or their relation to human beings more intimate. They have names, and stories, and ritualistic practices associated with them. We've seen examples already, with animal totems, and with a family's distant ancestors. One or more special spirits, the stories might say, were present at the beginning of the world, or even involved in the world's creation. The root of religion is animism, yet the root of *organized* religion is *theism*. This is the idea that the spirit world is arranged in a hierarchical order with a pantheon of high-ranking spirits on the top, who are called gods, and various ranks of lesser spirits below. There might be just one god at the top: that is the opinion of monotheism. There might be two gods at the highest rank, one of whom is male and the other female, who relate to each other as lovers, and to humanity as parents. There may be a canonical pantheon of a fixed number of gods, each with a specific area of concern. There may be hundreds, millions, or some giganormously huge number of gods, impossible to count. By being uncountable they achieve the same conception of infinity as monotheism does. Whatever the number of gods, there will certainly be an established body of literature about them. Whether that literature is purely oral, or whether it is written down, the stories of the gods take on as much significance as the experience of their presence in dreams, visions, trances, and environmental perceptions. Theism thus offers us another possible understanding of the sacred. The highest and deepest things are the things which belong to the Gods, or which are reserved for the gods. The stories will become as important a way of knowing the god as a trance-induced personal visionary experience. This probably explains the sacredness of things that are obviously associated with religion, like temples, relics, books, taboos, rituals, and holidays.

Theism is consistent with the origin of the word 'religion' itself, which is the Latin word *religio*, meaning 'to reconnect' or 'to rejoin'. When Latin-speaking people in ancient Europe used the word, they were very specific about what they were reconnecting to. We call something sacred if it allows us to rejoin with the primordial forces and events of the beginning of time. Thus Romans used the word religion as a question: where we today might ask, "Are you religious?", a Roman would have asked,

"What do you connect back to?". Contemporary pagans mean something similar when they ask, "What is your path?" Another translation of the word 'religion' is "an obligation with respect to the divine", with the implication that the obligation normally took the form of a prohibition or a taboo.[263] Thus the question "Are you religious?" could also mean "what are your obligations with respect to the divine?" And this, in turn, is a complicated way of saying, "What is your path?"

Theism, the basis of organized religion, can become more intensely organized still. Somewhere along the way, the prophets and priests will claim that the gods do not just preside over various environmental phenomena, or various social interests. They also make certain demands from us in relation to their spheres of concern. At first the demands may be relatively simple, and may indeed be nothing but elaborations or standard-izations of rituals and taboos that people had been living with all along. But somewhere along the way the demands get a little more, well, demanding. Now the gods want more than just a certain kind of offering, in return for a certain kind of boon. Now they also want us to act, to behave, to organize our societies, and perhaps also to think, in a certain kind of way. They give us rules to follow. They may assign rewards for those who follow the rules, and punishments for those who break them. At some point in the life of a religious tradition, the gods become lawmakers, and organized religion becomes *legalist* religion. The laws, issued by the gods in some kind of assembly among themselves (in a polytheist legalism) or else issued by the One God (in a monotheist legalism), become just as important as the simple presence of the god, and the god's actions in the mythologies. Consider, for instance, the preamble to Hammurabi's Code, first promulgated around 1700 BCE:

When Anu the Sublime, King of the Anunaki, and Bel, the lord of heaven and earth, who decreed the fate of the land,

432

assigned to Marduk, the overruling son of Ea, God of right-eousness, dominion over earthly man, and made him great among the Igigi, they called Babylon by his illustrious name, made it great on earth, and founded an everlasting kingdom in it, whose foundations are laid so solidly as those of heaven and earth; then Anu and Bel called by name me, Hammurabi, the exalted prince, who feared God, to bring about the rule of righteousness in the land, to destroy the wicked and the evil-doers; so that the strong should not harm the weak; so that I should rule over the black-headed people like Shamash, and enlighten the land, to further the well-being of mankind.[264]

Most of the rest of the preamble is a long-winded speech in praise of Hammurabi himself. Then it finishes off with a further affirmation of how the god Marduk sent Hammurabi "to rule over men, to give the protection of right to the land," and to bring about "the well-being of the oppressed." (*Ibid*, p 2) Notice how Hammurabi proclaims that his right to create laws was given to him by the gods. The law thus has supernatural power, aligned with the immutable and eternal elements of reality itself, such that the kingdom is "everlasting" and has foundations as solid "as those of heaven and earth."

Consider as another example, from a very different time and place, the preamble to the Lombard Laws. The Lombards were a Germanic tribe who seem to have originated in the area around the mouth of the river Elbe, and who migrated into a region of northern Italy which still bears their name (Lombardy). One of their kings, Rothair, composed and distributed a standardized law-code, and its preamble runs as follows:

In the name of the Lord, I, the most noble Rothair, seven-teenth king of the Lombards, [issue this lawbook] with the aid of God in the eighth year of my reign and the thirty-eighth year of my life... The collection which follows makes evident how great was and is our care and solicitude for the welfare of our subjects; for we recognize that it is not only the numerous demands of the wealthy which should carry weight, but also the burdensome trials of the poor are important. Therefore, trusting in the mercy of Almighty God, we have perceived it necessary to improve and to reaffirm the present law...

(K.F. Drew, trans, *The Lombard Laws*, (U of Pennsylvania Press, 1973) p 39)

Several things are interesting here. One is that the law is said to flow from the ruler's "care and solicitude for the welfare of our subjects," not only the rich, but also the poor. This may be compared to Hammurabi's statement that the laws are enacted in order to protect the weak and the oppressed. But most important for our present purposes, Rothair says that the law is issued 'with the aid of God'. As with the Code of Hammurabi, supernatural powers are invoked to lend legitimacy and force to the laws.

If these examples seem remote, one could also appeal (with some irony) to God himself. The first of the Ten Commandments reads: "I am the Lord thy God, which brought thee out of the land of Egypt, from the house of bondage. You shall have none other gods before me." (Deuteronomy 5:6-7) This law is really an enabling or annunciating clause, which lends divine force to the laws which follow, much like the preambles to the law codes already mentioned. Aside from outstanding miraculous events like the creation of the world, God's most important acts in the Old Testament are the proclamation of laws. For instance, God also told Moses that "If you will diligently hearken to the voice of the Lord your God, and will do that which is right in his sight, and will give ear to his commandments, and keep all his statutes, I will put none of these diseases upon thee, which I have brought upon the Egyptians: for I am the Lord that heals you." (Exodus 15:26) Similarly, the prophet Ezekiel, whose text is otherwise full of bizarre psychedelic visions, affirmed that the rule of law is

God's highest concern: "I [God] gave them my statutes, and showed them my judgments, which if a man do, he shall even live in them. Moreover also I gave them my Sabbaths, to be a sign between me and them, that they might know that I am the Lord that sanctify them." (Ezekiel 20:10-12) Again, a few lines later: "As I live, says the Lord God, surely with a mighty hand, and with a stretched out arm, and with fury poured out, will I rule over you." (Ezekiel 20:33) The prophet Sirach said, "Moreover he [God] gave them instructions, and the law of life for an inheritance. He made an everlasting covenant with them, and he showed them his justice and judgments." (Sirach 17:9-10) The author of the Psalms veritably petitions God to teach him the law: "Teach me, O Lord, the way of thy statutes; and I shall keep it unto the end. Give me understanding, and I shall keep thy law." (Psalms 119: 33-4) The same psalm also establishes that the speaker's relation to God is that of a servant to his master (cf Psalms 119:38). It is clear, I think, that in the Old Testament, God's primary concern is the law.

The Old Testament's law is a covenant between God and an entire community. With Christianity the relationship is more individualist. But God's preoccupation with law does not change. Jesus Christ's most important teachings are not metaphysical, but moral. The Beatitudes ('blessed are the poor...'), the Golden Rule ('do unto others...'), the Great Commandment (love your neighbor...') the various instructions he leaves for his apostles at the Last Supper, and finally the Great Commission (to spread the gospel, make converts, etc) are all principles of a primarily social, moral, and also political nature. They are spiritual only because they happen to have been promulgated by Jesus. Saint Paul reaffirms the divine lawmaker role this when he says, "Let every soul be subject unto the higher powers. For there is no power but of God: the powers that be are ordained of God. Whosoever therefore resists the power, resists the ordinance of God." (Romans 13:1-2) Later in the Christian tradition, a theologian like Thomas Aquinas can claim that "the end [the purpose] of God's governance is God himself, and his law is indistinguishable from himself." (*Summa Theologica*, Q 90)

The legalist understanding of God also appears in the work of the 20th century theologian Rudolph Otto, who defined the sacred as follows:

> In every highly-developed religion the appreciation of moral obligation and duty, ranking as a claim of the deity upon man, has been developed side by side with the religious feeling itself. None the less a profoundly humble and heartfelt recognition of 'the holy' may occur in particular experiences without being always or definitely charged or infused with the sense of moral demands. The 'holy' will then be recognized as that which commands our respect, as that whose real value is to be acknowledged inwardly. It is not that the awe of holiness is itself simply 'fear' in the face of what is absolutely overpowering, before which there is no alternative to blind, awestruck obedience. '*Tu solus sanctus*' is rather a paean of *praise*, which, so far from being merely a faltering confession of the divine supremacy, recognizes and extols a value, precious beyond all conceiving. The object of such praise is not simply absolute might, making its claims and compelling their fulfillment, but a might that has at the same time the supreme *right* to make the highest claim to service, and receives praise because it is in an absolute sense worthy to be praised.[265]

I very much appreciate Otto's understanding of 'the holy' as that which absolutely commands respect. Yet the important lines here are the first and the last ones, where it is implied that God's commandments have that aura of holiness, and that moral obligations and duties always accompany religious feelings.

We can now make a clear statement of how a legalist religion understands the sacred. The highest and deepest thing that a legalist religion recognizes is the law. Indeed in such a worldview, God *is* the law, and the law *is* God, and when one worships God, one worships the law. To be more precise, God is the personification of a particular model of political, economic, and social order. Like a kind of divine Big Brother, the idea of God is an elevation of the idea of law, transforming the law from a straightforward social and cultural phenomena into a supernatural personification. By corresponding the laws in this way to the most awesome force in the world, namely the creator of the world, the law can take on the properties of that creator: omnipotence, authority, majesty, and glory. Moreover, this elevation of the law also elevates those who wield the political authority to make and to enforce the laws. The state, its sovereign, and its ministers, can present themselves as agents and as spokespersons for the unquestionable, ultimate power of the universe itself. With God as one's ally, one cannot be defeated. In any legalist tradition, that is all that God is. That is why cathedrals edify Man rather than glorify God. When God and the law become one and the same, we are only worshipping our own social and political order.

Fear of the Lord

From the simplest forms of animism to the most sophisticated theologies of legalist traditions, religion can generate fear in the minds of the faithful. Aboriginal people are perfectly capable of imagining a world full of monsters: think of the Wendigo, or the Bunyip, for instance. The local shaman may also use this fear to enforce conformity to certain social norms. As Harris observed, in times of drought, famine, or disease, the shaman will accuse a freeloader of being a witch, and will have him driven out of the settlement. In a more organized religion, one might believe that the gods will punish a community for failing to perform a required ritual. Queen Djehami, a practitioner of Voudon and a queen in one of the traditional kingdoms of Benin, stated that Haiti was struck by the earthquake of January 2010 because the people did not give the traditional sacrifices to their ancestors.[266]

Here's a story about the original Olympic games of ancient Greece, which reminds us that religion and spirituality need not always be connected to morality. It concerns not a winner but a 'loser' who perhaps should have been a winner. An athlete named Cleomedes, from the island of Astypalaea, won an Olympic wrestling match against Iccus of Epidaurus: in fact Cleomedes was such a powerful wrestler that he actually killed his opponent. The judges ruled against his victory, not because of the killing blow, but because of a breach of the rules concerning allowable techniques. Cleomedes was so furious that he ran home, and uprooted the foundation of a school, killing all the children inside. Witnesses to his crime pelted him with rocks, so he ran into a nearby temple and hid in a chest. When his pursuers found the chest, they smashed it open, only to find it empty: Cleomedes had vanished. Messengers were sent to the Oracle at Delphi to find out what became of him, and the Oracle said:

Last of the heroes is Cleomedes of Astypalaea.
Honor him with sacrifice; he is no longer mortal.[171]

Why did the Oracle say this? Perhaps because Cleomedes' rage was pure, and therefore inhuman, and therefore divine. Greek religious thought could turn everything into a deity. It mattered not whether it was good or evil, it mattered only that it was living and that it *immensified* what it is to be alive. We might not like this way of thinking today: we want to impute an ethically good constitution upon our divinities. But I suspect that this may misunderstand what religion truly is. I risk of stirring controversy with this statement: but it seems obvious that gods can be dangerous. For there is nothing in religion, or in the idea of the holy, which *necessarily* makes the gods good, nor makes religious people good people. Their committed followers can be killers, and their holy places can be full of thorns or poisonous snakes. But they are no less gods for that.

But a legalist tradition is where fear can be concentrated into a full-grown labyrinth that traps its practitioners into dogmatism, hate, and terror, preventing the very liberation which the religion promises. By itself, the legalistic conception of God is not objectionable. The laws ordained by the god may well be very good laws. They might forbid obviously unjust behavior such as murder, thievery, and lies. They might call upon the believer to shelter the homeless, feed the hungry, clothe the naked, heal the sick, and empower the powerless (cf Isaiah 58:6-8, Matt 25:34-40). Following such principles as a spiritual path can surely bring out the best in us. But since the foundation of a legalist tradition's moral authority is the dictate of God, then a legalist tradition may well produce very bad laws, and people will still feel compelled to follow them. Consider, for instance, the fact that there is not one single word anywhere in the Bible which categorically condemns slavery. Actually we find numerous places where God endorses slavery, and orders slaves to be obedient to their masters. Such passages appear in both the Old and New Testaments (Ephesians 6:5-8, 1 Timothy 6:1, and Titus 2:9-10 as examples). There are a few statements about the wrongness of mistreating slaves. The book of Deuteronomy says that if you have a fellow Hebrew as your slave for six years, you must set him free on the seventh. But this is not the same as a categorical prohibition on slavery. Indeed the same chapter says that if after seven years your slave wants to stay, then you can nail his ear to the doorpost and thereby make him yours for life (cf. Deuteronomy 15:12-17). Perhaps the idea was to give the slave an incentive to leave. Yet we should expect a prohibition on slavery from a God who says he loves us all and who created all of us, even the slaves, in his own image. It's true that the campaign to eradicate slavery in the British Empire was begun by an English protestant, William Wilberforce, around the year 1790. But it was the humanist philosophers of the age, such as Adam Smith and Thomas Paine, who did the most to argue for the end of the slave trade.

Similarly, someone might believe his religion requires him to kill. The Laws of the Talmud, for instance, state that if a member of your own family invites you to the worship of a different god, you must kill him. If an entire city turns to the worship of a different god, you must kill everyone in it, and burn it to the ground (cf Deuteronomy 13:6-16). A notorious line from the Koran called "the Sword Verse", frequently quoted by terrorists, requires the believers to "slay the idolaters wherever you find them. Arrest them, besiege them, and lie in ambush everywhere for them." (*Koran* 9:5) This law comes with certain caveats, for instance one is not to fight non-believers who honor their treaties with Muslims, or who seek asylum, or who are generally peaceful and good-willed (cf *Koran* 60:8). But a fanatic might not care about such caveats; he may even argue that since the law is God's law, it takes precedence over human laws. For instance on 4th January 2011, Salman Taseer, the governor of Punjab province in Pakistan, was murdered by his own bodyguard. The killer, Mumtaz Qadri, was following a radical fundamentalist Muslim cleric who issued a death fatwa against Taseer, who opposed a strict blasphemy law. The following day, when asked how one could justify the killing of a democratically elected leader, Qadri's defense lawyer said: "The law that says that Mr Qadri is a murderer was not drawn in accordance with Islam."[267] A legalist tradition builds a fear labyrinth around itself when it believers claims that its laws, because they come from God, are perfect, untouchable, immutable, and unquestionable, even as they require people to do barbaric and terrible things.

A legalist tradition can create a second kind of labyrinth of fear if it assigns terrible punishments upon those who disregard, disagree with, or break the laws. In several places in the Gospels,

Jesus threatened disbelievers and sinners with fire and brimstone. In one memorable scene, Jesus shouts at a group of Pharisees: "You snakes! You brood of vipers! How will you escape being condemned to hell?" (Matt 23:33) Elsewhere in the same Gospel, Jesus teaches his followers to fear God's punishment: "Do not be afraid of those who kill the body but cannot kill the soul. Rather, be afraid of the One who can destroy both soul and body in hell." (Matt 10:28) Contemporary religious leaders still use supernatural terrors to gain the loyalty and the obedience of followers. For example, in 2007 Pope Benedict XVI included the following remark in one of his sermons: "Hell exists and there is eternal punishment for those who sin and do not repent... those who close their hearts to Him will be condemned to eternal damnation. Only God's love can change from within the existence of the person and, consequently, the existence of every society, because only His infinite love liberates from sin the root of every evil."[268] One cannot expect the leader of a major Christian church to say that salvation could be gained without God. Nonetheless the Pope's words here are an extortion threat: 'believe in God, or else suffer forever in Hell'.

Yet the punishment for disobedience need not be postponed until the afterlife. It could be imposed on people during their lifetimes. In the Old Testament, for instance, God inflicts natural disasters, military defeats, and foreign oppression upon entire cities and whole nations for the few sinners and nonconformists among them. Contemporary believers, drawing upon such stories, sometimes interpret contemporary events in the same way. Shortly after the destruction of New York's World Trade Center, and the damage to the Pentagon on the same day, the American fundamentalist preacher Jerry Falwell told a television audience, "I really believe that the Pagans, and the abortionists, and the feminists, and the gays and the lesbians who are actively trying to make that an alternative lifestyle, the ACLU, People For the American Way – all of them who have tried to secularize

America – I point the finger in their face and say 'you helped this happen'." Pat Robertson, sitting beside him, said "I totally concur."[269] A Catholic parish priest in Austria, Gerhard Wagner, told his followers that Hurricane Katrina was sent by God to destroy the city of New Orleans, because of that city's permissive attitude towards sexuality, and especially homosexuality. A short time later, in a move widely seen as an endorsement of Wagner's views, Pope Benedict XVI promoted him to auxiliary bishop.[270] On 15th March 2011, a Christian evangelical organization called Generals International claimed that the earthquake and tsunami which struck near Japan four days earlier, damaging one of its nuclear power facilities, was sent by God as punishment for the practice of Shinto and other non-Christian religions.[271] I am reminded of the words of the philosopher Blaise Pascal: "Men never do evil so completely and cheerfully as when they do it from religious conviction."[272]

The rigorist commitment to bad laws can turn around and harm the believers themselves. For example, the members of the Westboro Baptist Church, based in Kansas, believe that they are the only true Christians in the entire world. They believe, among other things, that God's laws require them to picket the funerals of soldiers and of gay people, with colorful fear-mongering signs that declare: "God hates fags", "Obey or perish", and "You're going to Hell". Yet these antics earned for them enormous public outrage. A family whose funeral they picketed is suing them for millions. And some of their members, including the daughter of one of the church's highest-ranking members, are leaving the church, and refusing to have anything to do with it or any of its members, including their families. As observed by a BBC filmmaker who made two documentaries about them:

> I was seeing a family that through its own tortured logic was involved in a long process of tearing itself apart, while denying at every stage what it was plainly doing. Many of

their activities are deeply repellent and yet it is also possible to see the Westboro Baptist Church as human beings who, in a weird way, are victimizing themselves along with all those they picket.[273]

The legalist tradition may also entertain a darker, more insidious fear. In its logic of identifying God with the law, it may claim that people cannot be moral without God, and that they cannot know the difference between right and wrong without God. Thus without God, people would produce an unjust, corrupt, and chaotic society: violent, unstable, inhumane, and depraved. This idea originates with the philosopher Immanuel Kant, over 200 years ago, and was popularized in Dostoyevsky's famous warning: "If God does not exist, then everything is possible." This is not the fear of being punished by God. This is the fear of what may follow from the *absence* of God. The weight of this possibility was eloquently expressed by the philosopher Freidrich Jacobi:

...the human being has such a choice, this single one: Nothingness or a God. Choosing Nothingness, he makes himself into a God; that is, he makes an apparition into God because if there is no God, it is impossible that man and everything which surrounds him is not merely an apparition. I repeat: God is, and is outside of me, a living being, existing in itself, or I am God. There is no third. (Jacobi, *Letter to Fichte*, 1799)

Without God, Jacobi is saying, each person becomes a lawmaker-god to himself, but in a world where nothing truly matters. Even one's own existence would have no higher or deeper meaning. And in such a situation *everything*, even the very worst of evils, is possible. Instead of threatening people with punishment in the afterlife, this fear threatens people with punishment in *this* life.

And instead of claiming that punishments would be handed down by God, in the form of natural disasters and military conquest, disbelievers would punish themselves and each other.

Yet this belief, can be tested by statistical research. Psychologists David and Susan Larson found that religious people have lower rates of alcoholism and suicide,[274] which certainly leans in favor of the benefits of being religious. But on a wider scale, sociologist Gregory Paul found that:

> ... in general, higher rates of belief in and worship of a creator correlate with higher rates of homicide, juvenile and early adult mortality, STD infection rates, teen pregnancy, and abortion in the prosperous democracies... The data examined in this study demonstrates that only the more secular, pro-evolution democracies have, for the first time in history, come closest to achieving practical 'cultures of life' that feature low rates of lethal crime, juvenile-adult mortality, sex-related dysfunction, and even abortion. The least theistic secular developed democracies such as Japan, France, and Scandinavia have been most successful in these regards.[275]

Thus the claim that people cannot know morality without God is false. Indeed the evidence points in the opposite direction: religiosity correlates to violence and social dysfunction. In this we see another example of the labyrinth. By following the divine law we're doing something that we think is in our interest, but we produce instead a situation that no one wants.

But let us clarify something. The problem here is not that a religion is legalist in nature. Nor is the problem religion as such. The problem, let us remember, is fear. Legalist religion tends to be more susceptible to fear than other kinds of religion. But whether a given religion is legalist or not, we should reject any part of it that would rather frighten people into submission than reason with them or inspire them. We should declare, as the Sufi mystic Rabi'a al-Adawiya declared:

> I want to pour water into hell and set fire to paradise so that these two veils disappear and no one worships God out of fear of hell or in hope of paradise but just for the sake of his own eternal beauty.[276]

Legalist religion tends to be more subject to fear than animism, or theism, or other –ism's. But we are not necessarily looking to dispense with legalist religion, nor for that matter with religion as such. We are looking for ways to dispel fear, with all of its attendant suffering, and we are looking for ways to create meaningful and worthwhile lives. Is there a way to relate to the gods that does not require fear?

The Highest and Deepest Things

When most religious people think about God, they think about something else besides laws and moral principles. They also think of their God as a *person*, whose presence informs the world. And when they think about religion and spirituality, they think about the *experience* of that person's presence. This can be true whether one is monotheist or polytheist, whether one is an animist or a legalist, whether one is Christian, Pagan, Muslim, Hindu, or Jew. The religious devotee imagines her God as a *being*, one who thinks and feels, who speaks and can be spoken to, who hears us and can be heard by us. Most everyone, even those who are not religious, have an idea what the word God normally means: a being infinite, perfect, eternal and immortal, who created the world and continues to inform the world with power and presence. But imagine what that means in terms of a personal experience. A God is someone utterly and completely *awesome*, a being of *overwhelming presence* that occupies all the senses, and pervades the highest and deepest places in the sky and below the earth. And that person also cares about you, even with all your flaws, mistakes, and shortcomings: *isn't that just the most exciting and amazing news that you have heard all day?*

So where do we find this person? Most religious people would like to say, "Everywhere." For everything belongs to the gods, everything links back (*religio*) to the gods, and therefore everything is sacred. This statement surely delivers the force, the weight, the seriousness of being religious. But most of the time, we don't look for the gods just anywhere. We look for them in places that are special, places that stand out, places that seem unusual.

The notion that the sacred is something that stands out appears in the very origin of the word 'temple'. The Greek word for that kind of place is *temenos*, which derives from the verb *temno*, meaning 'to cut off'. Similarly the related Latin word *templum*, means 'a space cut off or marked out'. The English word 'temple' comes from these ancient sources. Today it means a building, but originally it would have implied an entire landscape. The only building permitted within it was a shelter to house a statue of a god. Therefore, by the term 'sacred place' Europeans understood a sanctuary or a precinct which was deliberately marked off from the landscape surrounding it. The area was set aside for the god: no trees could be felled for lumber or fuel, and no animals hunted, and no crops sown or harvested. The word 'temple' has come to be associated with just the building with the statue of the god, but it once referred to the whole of the sacred landscape. To emphasize the sacredness of the place, there would normally be a physical boundary between it and the non-sacred space surrounding it, such as a wall.[277]

Yet the sacred stands out from the world in a very particular way, and not just because someone built a wall around it. The sacred does not appear in the manner of something in which you happen to have fixed your attention. It is not like the way that the sounds of numerous voices in a room fade into the background when you are listening for the voice of just one person. Rather, it is something which seems to grip *you* in its presence, and call forth your attention, in the manner of what Otto calls "mysterium tremendum":

> The feeling of it may at times come sweeping like a gentle tide, pervading the mind with a tranquil mood of deepest worship. It may pass over into a more set and lasting attitude of the soul, continuing, as it were, thrillingly vibrant and resonant, until at last it dies away and the soul resumes its 'profane', non-religious mood of everyday experience. It may burst in sudden eruption up from the depths of the soul with spasms and convulsions, or lead to the strangest excitements, to intoxicated frenzy, to transport, and to ecstasy.[279]

This feeling, as Otto describes it, tends to be prompted by that which is unknown, mysterious, and somehow beyond knowledge: the experience "may become the hushed, trembling, and speechless humility of the creature in the presence of – whom or what? In the presence of that which is a *mystery* inexpressible and above all creatures." (*Ibid*, p 14). This tells us a third feature of the sacred. Along with being something that stands out from the world, and something which grips one with the force of something tremendous, it is also the presence of something unknown, unseen, mysterious.

What things tend to produce this experience? Well, one might say God does. But this, too, is an evasion of the question: God only appears to us in, or through, or with, something, even if that something is a dream. We could rephrase the question: what things tend to produce the experience of God? Or, what things tend to produce the experience of *mysterium tremendum* which is so often declared to be the presence of God? Now that is a question that we can study, and try to answer.

It seems obvious to me that the first object in the life of humanity to prompt such powerful feelings is the earth. For the

earth is obviously 'great' in the sense that it is our home, the stage
for all the plays of our lives, the realm from which we emerge as
animals, and return to when we die. As noted in the discussion of
the sea, the earth has places and phenomena that apparently
represent frontiers of the unknown. Water wells and springs were
mentioned: we might here add mountain spires, deep forests,
caves, and the horizon itself. The earth always has such frontiers,
for the earth is always greater than any one person's ability to
grasp and understand, in a single lifetime. And as noted in the
discussion of landscapes and the circle of life, human beings are
entirely dependent upon the earth and its products for continued
existence. This perhaps explains why, in most of the world's
sacred stories, the earth is the first of the gods to emerge into
being from the primordial nothingness, or else the first object
created by the transcendental creator-God. In the biblical book of
Genesis, God first "created the heavens and the earth", although
at first the earth is "formless and empty". In the first two days he
differentiates the features of the world, separating day from
night, and water from sky. In the *Theogony* of Hesiod, the mythological account of the origins of the Greek gods, the earth is the
first god to emerge into being, where before there was non-being:
"First came the Chasm, and then broad-breasted Earth, secure
seat for ever of all the immortals who occupy the peak of snowy
Olympus..."[280] And the Buddha, although his spiritual victory
was accomplished by his own effort, called upon the earth to
witness it. Moreover, aside from its features as a whole, the Earth
also has places of outstanding aesthetic character, where we feel
ourselves in the presence of something powerful and mysterious.
The Roman philosopher Seneca described this feeling as follows:

If ever you have come upon a dense grove of ancient trees
rising to an unusual height and blocking the sight of the sky
with the shade of branch upon branch, the loftiness of the
forest, the solitude of the place, and the marvel of such thick

and unbroken shadow out in the open generate belief in a divine presence. And any cave where the rocks have been eaten away deep into the mountain it supports, not made by human hands but hollowed out into a vast expanse by natural forces, will suggest to your spirit some need for religious observance. We venerate the sources of great rivers: the sudden eruption of a tremendous stream from its concealment causes altars to be built. Hot springs are worshipped, and the darkness and immeasurable depth renders certain pools sacred.[281]

And finally, in our relations with animals, landscapes, and with our own bodies, we discovered spiritual significance in corporeal embodiment itself. Yet at first that significance appeared mainly in the 'negative': that is, in the wrongness of denying or under-valuing embodiment. We named that denial *misercorpism*. But we moved on from there, in search of something more positive: we studied landscapes, seascapes, animals, and our homes. There we found a way of knowing the earth which draws us into a visceral and intimate relation with our surroundings. We named it *perceptual intelligence*. With this wonderful form of knowledge, the earth opened itself to us in all of its complexity and beauty, and we learned what it was to belong somewhere, and be at home. As the theologian-philosopher Paul Ricoeur says, "The Earth here is something different, and something more, than a planet: it is the mythical name of our corporeal anchoring in the world."[282]

We also have experience of *mysterium tremendum* in the presence *other people*. Here we may restore the glory and majesty of cathedrals, temples, and sacred places, which I may seem to have 'written off'. Such structures are designed not just to represent but to positively *embody* the things we associate with the divine. For one of the ways to seek the experience of the divine is to deliberately create the conditions for the experiences using works of art, music, and architecture. Cathedrals embody the stories and mythologies of the gods and heroes, the laws that the gods supposedly gave us, and the very experience of *mysterium tremendum* itself. If it has been designed well, temples and cathedrals spare such things from the world of work, and allow them to unfold in their own way. (One of my life's ambitions is to some day design and build a great temple.) Paul Ricoeur described how temples both presuppose the way the sacred stands out from the ordinary, but also embodies and even provokes that very stand-out experience itself:

> What is most remarkable about the phenomenology of the sacred is that it can be described as a manner of inhabiting space and time. Thus we speak of sacred space to indicate the fact that space is not homogeneous but delimited — *templum* — and oriented around the "midpoint" of the sacred space. Innumerable figures, such as the circle, the square, the cross, the labyrinth, and the mandala, have the same spatialising power with respect to the sacred, thanks to the relations these figures establish between the center and its dimensions, horizons, intersections, and so on. All these phenomena and the related phenomena by which the passage from profane to sacred space is signified — thresholds, gates, bridges, pathways, ladders, ropes, and so on — attest to an inscription of the sacred on a level of experience beneath that of language.[3]

Here in the temple, we can also find the various ways we represent theological principles and divine experiences in human form. The work of philosopher Friedrich Nietzsche is informative here. Imagine a monk or a nun kneeling in prayer before the statue of a saint. Nietzsche asks, to whom is he praying? Surely not to the saint — for Nietzsche believed that God is dead and so there is no question of the supernatural being of a saint making his presence known in the statue. So the believer at prayer is caught up in a massive case of self-delusion (which, in other writings, Nietzsche claims is the case). Or, he is doing something a little more subtle, perhaps so subtle it is hidden even from himself: he is giving honor to a representation of human power and greatness.

> So far the most powerful human beings have still bowed worshipfully before the saint as the riddle of self-conquest and deliberate final renunciation. Why did they bow? In him – and as it were behind the question mark of his fragile and miserable appearance – they sensed the superior force that sought to test itself in such a conquest, the strength of the will in which they recognized and honored their own strength and delight in dominion: they honored something in themselves when they honored the saint.[283]

Nietzsche is saying that when we kneel down before the image of the saint, we are actually kneeling down before an image of ourselves. Humanity is not made in God's image: rather, Nietzsche argues, the truth is that God is made in humanity's image. But where Nietzsche saw this as a reason why all religion is an empty sham, I see in this a reason why *being human, here on earth, is spiritual*. The uplifting and the elevating of what it is to be human is a perfectly legitimate spiritual activity. For as the poet William Blake observed:

For Mercy, Pity, Peace, and Love
Is God, our father dear,
And Mercy, Pity, Peace, and Love
Is Man, his child and care.
For Mercy has a human heart
Pity a human face,
And Love, the human form divine,

And Peace, the human dress.[284]

Surely we have seen the evidence of this proposition all along! When we studied how we share food and drink, and share the shelter of our homes, we learned how the things we do enact moral principles: generosity, and hospitality, in particular. We also found that perceptual intelligence can have a purpose beyond itself to strive for: the creation of a good and worthwhile life. In our families we found that blood and history can produce strong feelings of solidarity and loyalty. Our friends and lovers taught us that shared life experiences and shared adventures produce shared stories. Then the relations previously based on social rituals can instead be based on *symbiotic identity*, which is the knowledge of how our stories overlap each other, and make our very identities intertwine with each other. We learned about *courage and honor* from our warriors, even while we also learned that courage and honor sometimes come with a heavy cost in human lives. From athletes and from artists and craftspeople we learned about *excellence*. In music, on the sports field, and in sexual lovemaking, we discovered sources of ecstasy which could act alternatives and as rivals to doctrinarian forms of spiritual knowledge such as theology and scriptures. And in the philosopher's library and in our school classrooms we learned that reason and rationality is deeply spiritual. It attends to the immensities directly, and does so with curiosity, courage, subtlety, openness, and a host of other ennobling qualities. When these values appear in our lives, the very experience of *mysterium tremendum* has a chance to appear in and through our relations with others. For surely we may find the experience of wonder, of power, of eternity, and of absolute and unconditional love, in the arms of our parents, children, lovers, and friends.

With this in mind, we can look afresh at the laws, which earlier I argued were the part of spiritual thought most at risk of being trapped in fear. With other people, and our relations with them, at the center of our attention, we can define a law as a representation of a relationship. If we followed the law just because it is the law, we are much more at risk of oppressing each other and harming ourselves. But if we follow the law for the sake of the relationship, then the law becomes secondary to the relationship, and the health of the relationship becomes paramount. We can thus follow the laws which work, modify them or reject them as they fail, adopt new ones as our needs require, and in every case preserve the health and the flourishing of the relationship, which is what truly matters anyway. Here we can also add ritual procedures, traditional customs and norms, and other 'laws' which might not explicitly moral in nature. They, too, have moral and spiritual force because of the relations with other people that they represent or involve. For instance, I have a friend who described his relationship with a Celtic goddess, as follows:

I had a problem with my girlfriend, and I petitioned *Herself* for guidance. I went down to the river with three apples and a bottle of whiskey. I sent the apples into the river, took a swig of the whiskey and poured the rest on to a nearby stone, and just sat down and started talking. Within a few days, I started to get a kind of weird feeling every time I noticed the footprint of a woman's shoe in the snow in front of me. This feeling started slowly, but grew over a fortnight, and I noticed it particularly if I happened to step in one. So I went down to the river again, with my apples and my whiskey, and had another chat about it, as well as how things were going with my original problem. After about six weeks I realised that Herself had given me another *geis* [a Celtic taboo]. It seems She agreed to help me with my relationship problems, but in return I am not allowed to erase a woman's footprint. At first this was impossible: it was the middle of winter, and women's footprints are everywhere. But then I experimented a little, and spoke about it with a trusted friend, and found that the new *geis* applies to stepping in a woman's footprint when I enter or leave my home or my place of work. But the interesting thing is, this *geis* isn't really a silly taboo. What it really does is force me to remember the women in my life, and the things they do for me.

(Name withheld, 2011)

There remains a third and last source of the sacred. When we studied water and the sea, we learned that magic has something to do with the way things emerge from the darkness into the light. We learned that human beings arrange themselves in relation to the divine by addressing themselves to the frontiers of the unknown. For when we relate to the gods, we do more than just follow their laws. We also pray, meditate, make offerings, write praise poems, sing songs, tell stories, create artworks, and (although I may seem to have dismissed it earlier) build temples and monuments. All of these things serve in their own way to initiate a kind of dialogue with the gods. And to send our messages to the gods, we set our offerings in places where they may pass from the light into the darkness. We drop them in deep waters, set them adrift on rafts on the sea, burn them in sacrificial fires, or bury them under the earth. I wrote earlier that the final frontier is interstellar space. Already people are addressing themselves to the mystery by launching the ashes of their deceased loved ones into space, in suborbital rockets. But there is another final frontier, which stands before us not in space but in time: that frontier is *death*, the most ineffable and inescapable of immensities. Here the highest and deepest things take on a most august and dreadful disguise: for here we address ourselves to the one final fear which almost everyone possesses and almost no one acknowledges.

Violence and murder has a curious place in religious culture. Consider the abundant evidence that Bronze Age and Iron Age

European societies enacted rituals which climaxed in the killing of a human being. Sometimes the victims were condemned criminals, sometimes captured prisoners of war, sometimes the society's own king, and sometimes another member of the tribe who temporarily took the place of a king. The bodies of around one hundred ritually killed human beings have been discovered in bogs and marshes across western Europe. This suggests that the practice was widespread, frequent, and (in some sense of the word) 'normal'. Lindow Man is perhaps the best known example: his body was discovered in a peat bog on the 1st August 1984, where it had been preserved for two thousand years. He was simultaneously stabbed in the side, garroted, and clubbed in the back of the head, before being drowned in the bog. The three methods of death suggest that his life was given to three different gods simultaneously. Furthermore, the angle of the blow on the back of the head suggests that he was kneeling at the time, and so that he took the blow willingly, or at least that he did not struggle. Why would someone consent to be killed in such a vicious way? To raise a question like this is to place the question of the meaning of life in its sharpest form, bringing the deepest problems and the highest stakes into play. For we don't really want to know whether the gods will send us famines if we don't kill some of our people in their names. What we really want to know is *whether life is for any reason valuable*; whether life is worth having and keeping, and at what cost, if any. We can ask whether death is necessary for the preservation of the circle of life. But what we really want to know is *whether the circle of life should go on*. We want to know whether life is worth preserving, caring for, and respecting; whether being alive is a blessing or a curse; whether the problems and miseries and injustices of life outweigh the pleasures and benefits; and whether, if we find that the miseries do outweigh the pleasures, it might be noble to carry on living anyway. Finally, knowing that death is a destiny for us all, we want to know whether there is such a thing as a noble death, and even whether there are reasons to seek out death for its own sake. Death forces such questions: death compels us to seek answers to them.

It may be useful here to consider the Irish mythological heroine Deirdre of the Sorrows. She was the most beautiful woman who ever lived in Ireland, and perhaps she was one of the greatest beauties of the whole world. Cathbad the Druid foretold before she was born that she would be beautiful, and that on account of her beauty, wars would be fought and many men would die. Determined to live her life her own way, she chose exile and poverty in Scotland with her lover Naoise, and his two brothers Ardan and Aillen, instead of a life of wealth and comfort with a man she hated, King Conchobor mac Nessa. The king sent her and her men away because she rejected his love. But some years later, he softened his heart, changed his mind, and no longer wished to oppress them. So he sent his champion, Fergus McRoy, as an emissary, to invite them back home. Yet Conchobor was crafty, and when he learned that her beauty was as wild and perfect as ever, he lusted for her again. He tricked Fergus into abandoning the small group of returning exiles, leaving them unprotected. He then ordered his Red Branch guards to set upon them, disarm them, kill Naoise and his brothers, and make Deirdre a prisoner. Perhaps today we would say that trickery, deceit, and murder are not fine ways to win the heart of a woman. But such is the logic of obsessed kings.

Deirdre's prison was an Iron Age palace, supplied with the sweetest foods and drinks, and furnished with the most precious things of beauty. But Deirdre enjoyed none of it: a prison full of luxuries is still a prison. So she rejected every gift, and never once smiled for her jailer, as her way of fighting him. In a last act of desperation, Conchobor sent her into the custody of the worst man anyone knew, so that she might appreciate the king's 'kindness'. But on the way, Deirdre threw herself from the chariot, deliberately cracked her head on a passing stone, and ended her own life.

Suicide is the darkest of all dark thoughts. I apologize to you, dear reader, if someone you know has recently taken his or her own life, and so this theme troubles you. (I have known such people too.) Yet suicide serves as an excellent (if morbid) way to explore the questions of life and death. It may indeed be the clearest way to discern whether life is truly meaningful. For the question of suicide is the very question of whether one's life is worth *continuing*. It also approaches the question of whether anything in the world, least of all your own self, deserves your care and respect. The person who finds life worthless, empty, more full of misery and suffering than of worth and meaning, *and yet does not take her own life*, enacts the proposition that *something* about her life is meaningful and worthwhile.

Between these three special presences in the world we have three great immensities: the earth, other people, and death. A fourth hangs over them: the solitude of the individual seeker, who faces the other three. Between them we have gathered our own 'fourfold', spared them from work and freed them in peace, to unfold and reveal themselves in their own way. These immensities constitute the highest and deepest things. For they are unavoidable and inevitable: every person must meet them, at some time in his or her life. They stand beneath everyone, supporting her existence; they also stand above everyone, beyond any one single person's ability to fully understand and control. Having such qualities, they call one's life into question. But they do not tell you what to do. For the sacred is not a commandment to be obeyed. It is a presence to be experienced. Thus if we see meet these immensities, face them, speak to them, and relate to them with humanity, integrity, and wonder, then we may achieve *eudaimonia*, the good and beautiful destiny.

Annotated References

1. Martin, *Philosopher's Dictionary*, p 187
2. MacDonald, *1914-1918: Voices and Images of the Great War* (Penguin, 1991), p 42
3. Roger Sauvé: *The Current State of Canadian Family Finances 2010 Report* by the Vanier Institute of the Family, 17 February 2011
4. T. McAllister, "US Military warns oil output may dip causing massive shortages by 2015" The Guardian, 11 April 2010
5. Allan Maki, "Waterloo football player makes doping history" The Globe and Mail (online edition) 8th September 2010.
6. Lou Dobbs, "Buffet: 'There are lots of loose nukes around the world'" Cable News Network, online edition, 19 June 2005
7. Grenier, "Calculating risk: terror warnings" Al Jazeera (online English edition) 8 October 2010
8. Malidoma Somé, "Ritual: Power, Healing and Community" (Penguin, 1997) pp 62-3
9. The Doctrine of the Mean § 20, as cited in Wing-Tsit Chan, *Chinese Philosophy*, p 105
10. The Book of Mencius, 3A:4, as cited in Wing-Tsit Chan, *Chinese Philosophy*, pp 69-70
11. Taittiriya Upanishad, I.xi.2, as cited in Radhakrishnan & Moore, eds, *A Sourcebook in Indian Philosophy*, p 58
12. "The Words of the High One", in Paul Taylor & W.H. Auden, trans, *The Elder Edda* (New York: Vintage / Random House, 1970) p 37
13. The Rubáiyát of Omar Khayyám, verse XI
14. di Pellegrino, L., Fadiga, L., Fogassi, L., Gallese, V. & Rizzolatti, G. (1992) "Understanding Motor Events: A

Neurophysiological Study". *Experimental Brain Research* 91:176-180

15. Preston, S. & de Waal, F., (2002) "Empathy: Its ultimate and proximate bases." *Behavioral and Brain Sciences*, 25, 1-72

16. Clark, *Civilisation*, p 85

17. *Ibid*, p 87

18. Cicero, "The Dream of Scipio", cited in *On The Good Life*, p 353

19. *Samyutta Nikaya*, III.66, cited in *Ibid*, pp 280-1

20. *Maitri Upanishad*, I.3, cited in *Ibid*, p 93

21. "God and the Brain: How We're Wired for Spirituality" *Newsweek*, 5 July 2001; "Meditation associated with structural changes in brain" Press release from Massachusetts General Hospital, 11 November 2005.

22. The attraction to the idea of losing a limb; the desire to become an amputee.

23. The inability to identify with the gender of one's own body; the desire to become the opposite sex.

24. Casey, *Pagan Virtue*, pp 39-40

25. *Katha Upanishad* III.3-4, as cited in Radhakrishnan & Moore, eds, *Indian Philosophy*, p 46

26. Umberto Eco, *Foucault's Pendulum*, p 362

27. Bartky, "Foucault, Femininity, and the Modernization of Patriarchal Power" in Diamond & Quimby, eds, *Feminism and Foucault: Reflections on Resistance* (Boston: Northeastern University Press, 1988)

28. Public court proceedings: *In re A.C.*, 533 A.2nd 611 (District of Columbia, 1987)

29. Harasty, J.; Double, K.L., et al. "Language-associated cortical regions are proportionally larger in the female brain." *Archives of Neurology*, February 1997, 54(2), pp 171-6

30. Lise Eliot, "Out with pink and blue: Don't foster the gender divide" *New Scientist*, Iss 2769, 19 July 2010

31. Cordelia Fine, Ph.D., cited in Robin McKie, "Male and

female ability differences down to socialisation, not genetics" *The Observer*, 15 August 2010

32.   Michael Babyak, et al. "Exercise Treatment for Major Depression: Maintenance of Therapeutic Benefit at 10 Months" *Psychosomatic Medicine* 62:633-638 (September/ October 2000)

33.   "Effect of Exercise on Reducing Major Depression Appears to be Long-Lasting", Press release, *Duke Medicine News and Communications*, first published 21 September 2000, updated 29 September 2005

34.   *Inanna*, pp 57

35.   Julius Caesar, *The Conquest of Gaul*, VI.21, p 143

36.   Dame Fiona Reynolds, quoted in Stephen Morris, "Britons 'terrified' of the countryside, National Trust warns" *The Guardian* (online edition) 30 October 2010

37.   Margulis, *The Symbiotic Planet*, p 15

38.   Quoted in Rogers, *Cities for a Small Planet*, p vi

39.   M. Wackernagel and W. Rees, *Our Ecological Footprint: Reducing Human Impact on the Earth*, p 3

40.   Stuart Bond, *Ecological Footprints*, p 7

41.   Quoted in Richard Rogers, *Cities for a Small Planet*, pp 111-2

42.   R. Ross, *Dancing with a Ghost: Exploring Indian Reality* (Markham, Ontario, Canada: Octopus Publishing Group, 1992) p 70

43.   Z. Bharucha & J. Pretty, "The roles and values of wild foods in agricultural systems" *Philosophical Transactions of the Royal Society*, B.2010, 365, pp 2913-2926

44.   Ross, *Ibid*, p 72

45.   Ross, *Ibid*, p 73

46.   Ross, *Ibid*, p 74

47.   Ross, *Ibid*, p 74

48.   Gick & Derrick, "Aero-tactile integration in speech perception" *Nature*, #462, pp 502-504, 26 November 2009

49.   McLuhan, Touch the Earth, p 22

50. McLuhan, Touch the Earth, p 90

51. *The Collected Poems of W.B. Yeats*, (New York: McMillan, 1956) p 469

52. Mark Colvin / Paula Kruger, "Change of heart from climate skeptics" *ABC News* (online edition) 31 August 2010

53. Cordula Meyer, 'Science as the enemy': The traveling salesman of climate skepticism" *Der Spiegel* (online English edition) 8 October 2010

54. "Harper's letter dismisses Kyoto as 'socialist scheme'" *CBC News* (online edition) 30 January 2007

55. John Collins Rudolph, "An Evangelical Backlash against Environmentalism" *The New York Times*, 4 January 2011

56. The full text of the declaration is available at the Cornwall Alliance website: www.cornwallalliance.org

57. Patrick Symmes, "History in the Remaking" *Newsweek*, 19 February 2010; Sandra Scham, "The World's First Temple" *Archaeology*, Vol 61 No. 6, Nov/Dec 2008

58. Frazer, *The Golden Bough*, p 548

59. Rotherham, *Ibid*, pp 172-3

60. Frazer, *The Golden Bough*, p 803

61. Rotherham, *Ibid*, pp 172-3

62. "Behavioral responses, he reasoned, are regulated by a fine balance between neurotransmitters and hormones at the level of the whole organism. The genes that control that balance occupy a high level in the hierarchical system of the genome. Even slight alterations in those regulatory genes can give rise to a wide network of changes in the developmental processes they govern. Thus, selecting animals for behavior may lead to other, far-reaching changes in the animals' development." Lyudmila N. Trut, "Early Canid Domestication: The Farm Fox Experiment" cited in *American Scientist*, Vol 87, March-April 1999, p 162

63. Bill Marsh, "A Hen's Space to Roost", *The New York Times*, 14 August 2010

64. Catherine Friend. *The Compassionate Carnivore* (Da Capo Lifelong, 2008)

65. Hagen, Ann. *A Second Handbook of Anglo-Saxon Food and Drink* (Hockwold cum Wilton, UK: Anglo-Saxon Books, 1995) p 43

66. Visser, Margaret. *The Rituals of Dinner: The Origins, Evolution, Eccentricities and Meaning of Table Manners* (Toronto: Harper Collins, 1991) p 3

67. Cited in Nevin Halici, *Sufi Cuisine* (London: SAQI, 2005) p 31

68. Taittiriya Upanishad II.2, as cited in Radhakrishnan and Moore, *Indian Philosophy*, p 59. The word here translated as 'panacea' is *sarvausadham*, which according to the translator can also mean 'consisting of all sorts of herbs'.

69. Régis Marcon, *Marvelous Recipes from the French Heartland* (English edition: Ici La Press, Woodbury, CT USA, 2002) p 12

70. Marcon, *Ibid*, p 13

71. Marcon, *Ibid*, p 12

72. Tacitus, *Germania*, § 22, p 120

73. E. Fitzgerald, trans, *The Rubáiyát of Omar Khayyám* (Avenel Books) verse XLII

74. "The Many Wines" in C. Barks, trans, *The Essential Rumi* pp 6-7

75. Veldhuizen, Urbanoski, and Cairney, "Geographic Variation in the Prevalence of Problematic Substance Abuse in Canada" *Canadian Journal of Psychiatry*, Vol 52, No. 7, July 2007

76. Tacitus, *Germania*, §23, p 121

77. Barry Estabrook, "Politics of the Plate: The Price of Tomatoes", *Gourmet Magazine*, March 2009; Fred Grimm, "How about a side order of human rights?" *The Miami Herald*, 16 December 2007

78. Jane Black, "A Squeeze for Tomato Growers" *The Washington*

Post, 29 April 2009

79. "More than 1 billion don't have enough to eat: UN agency" *CBC News / The Canadian Press* (Toronto, Canada) 19 June 2009; "World hunger 'hits 1 billion'" *BBC News* (London, UK) 19 June 2009

80. Alex Renton, "Is this the end of cheap food?" *The Observer / The Guardian* (Manchester UK), 20 January 2008; David Loyn, "World hunger 'near breaking point'" *BBC News* (London UK), 26 January 2009

81. "Price Increases are Costing Millions of People Their Health" *Spiegel International*, 25 August 2010

82. Robin McKie and Heather Stewart, "Hunger. Strikes. Riots. The food crisis bites" *The Observer / The Guardian* (Manchester, UK) 13th April 2008; "The cost of food: facts and figures" *BBC News* (London UK) 16 October 2008

83. Thomas Walkom, "Mutant Food Products Hard to Swallow", *The Toronto Star*, 2 June 1998, p A2

84. Andrew Malone, "The GM Genocide: Thousands of Indian farmers are committing suicide after using genetically modified crops" *The Daily Mail*, 3 November 2008

85. Gonzalo Oviedo, "Unnatural Roots of the Food Crisis" *BBC News* (London UK) 2 June 2008

86. Gonzalo Oviedo, *Ibid*

87. George & Hirnschall, *The Best of Chief Dan George*, p 43

88. The Book of Mencius, 4B:30, as cited in Wing-Tsit Chan, *A Sourcebook in Chinese Philosophy*, p 77

89. Macalister, trans, *Lebor Gabála Érenn*, Book V, 1956, p 27. Nuadu Airgetlám is one of the chief gods of the Irish pantheon, and the first of their kings.

90. Julius Caesar, *The Conquest of Gaul*, VI.18, p 142

91. Sturlson, *The Prose Edda*, (Penguin 2005) pp 6, 8

92. Chief Dan George and Helmut Hirnschall, *The Best of Chief Dan George*, (Surrey, BC, Canada: Hancock House, 2004) p 52

93. Study by Karen Fingerman; cited in Zosia Bielski, "The grown-up kid's secret weapon: mom and dad" *The Globe and Mail*, 17 January 2010

94. The Centers for Disease Control and Prevention and the National Institute of Justice, Extent, Nature, and Consequences of Intimate Partner Violence, July 2000. The Commonwealth Fund, *Health Concerns Across a Woman's Lifespan: 1998 Survey of Women's Health*, 1999

95. Allstate Foundation National Poll on Domestic Violence, 2006. Lieberman Research Inc., Tracking Survey conducted for The Advertising Council and the Family Violence Prevention Fund, July – October 1996)

96. Colleen Ross, "A better way to say hello" *CBC News* (Online edition) 9 November 2010

97. Kinsella, trans, *The Táin*, p 30

98. Stephen Pollington, *The Mead Hall*, (Frithgarth, Norfolk, UK: Anglo-Saxon Books, 2003) p 99

99. Visser, Margaret. *The Rituals of Dinner: The Origins, Evolution, Eccentricities and Meaning of Table Manners* (Toronto: Harper Collins, 1991) p 121

100. Posidonius was quoted in Athenaeus, *Deipnosophistae* 4.151-152

101. A particularly prestigious demand for a musical performance since the person called upon could not refuse to perform without incurring enormous dishonor.

102. Stephen Pollington, *The English Warrior: From Earliest Times till 1066*, Expanded edition (Frithgard, Norfolk, UK: Anglo-Saxon Books, 2006) pp 39-40

103. George & Hirnschall, *The Best of Chief Dan George*, p 67

104. G. Nakhnikian, "Love in Human Reason", *Midwest Studies in Philosophy*, Vol 3 (1980) p 294

105. "History as Narrative and Practice," *Philosophy Today* 29 (1979) p 214

106. MacIntyre, *After Virtue*, p 213

107. Wolkstein & Kramer, *Inanna: Queen of Heaven and Earth*, p 34

108. Ed Pilkington, "$1bn 'don't have sex' campaign a flop" *The Guardian*, 16 April 2007

109. M. Regnerus, *Forbidden Fruit: Sex & Religion in the Lives of American Teenagers*, pp 127, 137

110. L. Finer, "Trends in Premarital Sex in the United States", *Public Health Reports*, Vol 122 Iss 1, Jan/Feb 2007, p 73

111. "Neanderthal 'make up' containers discovered" *BBC News* (online edition) 9 January 2010

112. *The Autobiography of St. Teresa of Avila*, (Rockford, Illinois, USA: TAN Books, 1997) XXIX:17-18, pp 266-7

113. Adams, Wright, Lohr, "Is Homophobia Associated with Homosexual Arousal?" *Journal of Abnormal Psychology*, August 1996, 105(3), pp 440-5

114. Noon, *Law and Government of the Grand River Iroquois*, (New York USA: Viking Fund Publications in Anthropology, 1949) p 38

115. Borrows, *Indigenous Legal Traditions in Canada*, p 9

116. Johnston, *Ojibway Heritage*, p 63

117. George & Hirnschall, *The Best of Chief Dan George*, p 35

118. *Ibid*, p 85

119. Noon, *Law and Government of the Grand River Iroquois*, p 25

120. cf "Transfer Rites" in Crowshoe & Manneschmidt, *Akak'stiman*, pp 29-35

121. "Old traditions, crumbling with time" *The Irish Times*, online edition, 4 January 2011

122. Heidegger, "Building Dwelling Thinking" in *Basic Writings*, pp 347-8

123. *Ibid*, p 351

124. *Ibid*, p 352

125. *Ibid*, pp 351-2

126. *Ibid*, p 352

127. "Homelessness 'chronic' in Canada: study" *CBC News*, 26 June 2007

128. Judith Maxwell, "Bad policy creates the poverty trap" *The Globe and Mail*, 22 March 2011

129. Kim Covert, "Housing crisis 'inevitable' if prices outpace income', *Financial Post*, 3 March 2011

130. T.C. McLuhan, *Touch the Earth*, p 121

131. *Ibid*, p 74

132. "Parks help narrow health gap between rich, poor: study" *CBC News* (online edition) 7 November 2008

133. Susan Semenak, "Guerrilla Gardeners", *Canwest News Service / The Montreal Gazette*, 26 May 2008

134. "The Cultural Space of Djamaa el-Fna Square, Morocco" *United Nations Educational, Scientific, and Cultural Organization*, press kit published on 18 May 2001

135. Richard Rogers, *Cities for a Small Planet*, pp 152-3

136. Maria Cook, "Bobby the Brave" the *Ottawa Citizen*, 30 November 2009, p B1

137. Ruskin, *The Seven Lamps of Architecture* (New York: Wiley, 1854) p 154

138. Adrian Tierney-Jones: "Coopering: roll out the barrel" *The Telegraph*, 27 February 2011

139. Nancy Durham, "Roll out the barrel for the last cooper" *CBC News*, 23 January 2009

140. Nancy Durham, "Roll out the barrel for the last cooper" *CBC News*, 23 January 2009

141. Karl Marx, "Estranged Labor", as cited in Robert Tucker, ed, *The Marx-Engels Reader* (New York: Norton, 1972) p 60. Emphasis his.

142. Harris, *Our Kind* (HarperPerennial, 1989), p 190

143. Harris, *Our Kind*, p 191

144. Sinclair Stewart and Paul Waldie, "How it all began" *The Globe and Mail* (Toronto) 19 December 2008

145. Marcus Gee, "Global Trade Slump Raises Talk of 'Deglobalization'" *The Globe and Mail* (Toronto) 13 March 2009

146. Chris Palmeri, "Over One Million People Lost Their Home in 2008" *Business Week*, 14 January 2009

147. Edmund Andrews, "Economy shed 598,000 jobs in January" *The New York Times* (New York, USA) 6 February 2009

148. Jeannine Aversa, "US sheds 467,000 jobs, rate rises" *The Globe and Mail / The Associated Press*, 2 July 2009

149. "Income, Poverty, and Health Insurance in the United States", report by the US Census Bureau, September 2010, p 14

150. Nouriel Roubini, "We will have Even More Crises In The Future", *Der Spiegel* (online edition) 10 May 2010

151. "The Global Economy 'Still Has Deep-Seated Structural Problems'" *Der Spiegel* (online edition) 14 September 2010

152. Edmund Andrews, "Greenspan Concedes Error on Regulation" *The New York Times*, 23 October 2008

153. Andrew Clark, "Mervyn King: Bankers exploit gullible borrowers to pay for their bonuses" *The Guardian*, 5 March 2011

154. C.S. Lewis, The Screwtape Letters (New York USA: McMillan, 1971), p 128

155. "Analects of Confucius", 4:16, as cited in Wing-Tsit Chan, *Chinese Philosophy*, p 28

156. "Senior Freddie Mac executive found dead in Virginia home" *CBC News / The Associated Press*, 22 April 2009

157. Posidonius' words are quoted by Athenaeus, *Deipnosophistae* 4.151-152

158. Gregory, *Gods and Fighting Men*, pp 156-7

159. These last four quotes: Terry Brown, *English Martial Arts*, (Anglo Saxon Books, 1997) pp 221-3

160. "Frustration for the US soldiers who never went to war" *BBC News* (online edition) 20 July 2010

161. *Duty with Honour: The Profession of Arms in Canada* (Ottawa: Department of National Defence, 2003) p 32

162. *Duty with Honour*, p 26

163. McDonald, *1914-1918: Voices and Images of the Great War* (London, 1988) pp 46-8

164. Denis Winter, *Death's Men: Soldiers of the Great War* (London 1978) pp 220-1

165. Bruce Campion Smith and Les Whittington, "Hillier: Mission accomplished" *The Toronto Star* (Toronto Canada) 15 April 2008

166. Rubin, Alissa, "2 Iraqi Journalists Killed as US Forces Clash with Militias" *The New York Times* (online edition) 13 July 2007

167. Video footage, transcripts, and other information found at www.collateralmurder.com, a website maintained by the Wikileaks organization. Accessed 12 December 2010

168. Perrine Mouterde, "Soldiers confront the psychological cost of war" *France 24 News* (online edition) 26 November 2010

169. A team of scientists studied the goal, and found that it had not defied physics at all. They discovered that a spinning sphere moving in a fluid (like air) and unaffected by other factors (like wind turbulence or gravity) naturally moves in a spiral shape. cf Victoria Gill, "Roberto Carlos wonder 'no fluke' say physicists" *BBC News* (online edition) 1 September 2010

170. Lena Corner, "Chrissie Wellington Interview: The Iron Lady" *The Guardian* (online) 2 January 2011

171. Pausanias, *Description of Greece*, 6.9.8

172. Davis, *The Wayfinders*, p 21

173. W. Schweiker, "Torture and Religious Practice" *Dialog: A Journal of Theology*, vol 47 No 3, Fall 2008

174. "Man accused of waterboarding girlfriend he thought was unfaithful" *USA Today*, 29 October 2010

175. Chadwick, *The Celts*, p 140

176. Strabo, cited in Ó h-Ógáin, *The Sacred Isle*, pp 42-3

177. Cited in Ó h-Ógáin, *The Sacred Isle*, p 57

178. Cited in Ó h-Ógáin, *The Sacred Isle*, p 57

179. Philip Carr-Gomm, *Beyond Belief*, presentation delivered at the Glastonbury Symposium, July 2009

180. Davis, *The Wayfinders*, p 59

181. Davis, *The Wayfinders*, p 60

182. Rob Stevens, crewmember of the Snorri, as quoted in W. Hodding Carter, "Discovering Vinland: the voyage of Snorri", *Wooden Boat: the magazine for wooden boat owners, builders, and designers*, iss 148 (June 1999) p 67

183. W. Hodding Carter, "Discovering Vinland: the voyage of Snorri", *Wooden Boat: the magazine for wooden boat owners, builders, and designers*, iss 148 (June 1999) p 66

184. Lina Sinjab, "Replica Phoenician Ship ends round-Africa journey" *BBC News* (online edition) 24 October 2010

185. Davis, *The Wayfinders*, pp 49-51

186. Malcolm Moore, "Chinese earthquake may have been man-made, say scientists" *The Telegraph*, 2 February 2009

187. I suspect that the collapse of the commercial music industry, predicted by so many pundits and explained as a consequence of pirated music available on the Internet, will not equate to the demise of *music* as such. There are more independent musicians than ever before, and more of them deliberately choosing not to sign contracts with big music distributors. I suspect that a resurgence in regional musical folklore and tradition may ensue.

188. R. Lacey & D. Danziger, *The Year 1000: What Life was Like at the Turn of the First Millennium* (London UK: Little, Brown & Co, 1999) p 32

189. Part of Charlemagne's actual decree concerning public literacy, as cited in Clark, *Civilisation*, (Harper & Row, 1969) p 19

190. Clark, *Civilisation*, p 17

191. Clark, *Civilisation*, p 15

192. Clark, *Civilisation*, p 17

193. Marcus Aurelius, *Meditations*, 5.11, p 39

194. "BBC faces political pressure allegations" *Morning Star Online*, 4 March 2011; Sunny Hundal, "EXCL: BBC journalists told to use 'savings' instead of 'cuts' in news" *Liberal Conspiracy*, 3 March 2011

195. "A rebranding of the 'Harper Government'" *CBC News*, 4 March 2011

196. Lacey & Danziger, *The Year 1000*, p 32

197. *Ibid*, p 41

198. Kuno Meyer, trans, *The Instructions of King Cormac Mac Airt* §22:1-20 (Dublin: Royal Irish Academy, Todd Lecture Series vol XV, 1909) p 41

199. cf Habermas, *Moral Consciousness and Communicative Action* (MIT Press, 1992) pp 87-9

200. Westen, et al, "Motivation, Decision Making, and Consciousness: From Psychodynamics to Subliminal Priming and Emotional Constraint Satisfaction", in Moscovitch, and Zelazo, eds, *Cambridge Handbook of Consciousness* (Cambridge: Cambridge University Press, 2007) p 690

201. Lackoff, G. *Don't Think of an Elephant! Know your Values and Frame the Debate* (White River Junction, VT: Chelsea Green Publishing, 2004) p 17

202. S. Vedantam, "The Power of Political Misinformation" *The Washington Post*, 15 September 2008

203. Forrest and Gross, *Creationism's Trojan Horse: The Wedge of Intelligent Design* (OUP 2004) p 16

204. Declan Walsh, "Pakistani minister Shabhaz Bhatti shot dead in Islamabad" *The Guardian*, 2 March 2011

205. "Political rhetoric draws online fire" *The Seattle Times* (online edition) 8 January 2011

206. Robert Booth, "'Tory madrasa' preaches radical message to would-be MPs" *The Guardian*, 6 March 2010

207. David Weigel, "You've got to make the fellow scared to

come out of his house" *The Washington Post* (online edition), 6 April 2010

208. Emma Marris, "In the Name of Nature", *Nature*, vol 443, No 5, October 2006, p 501

209. Seneca, *Letters to Lucilius*, 109, 2; trans R.M. Gummere: Loeb Classical Library

210. Cicero, "Discussions at Tusculum" Ch V, in *On the Good Life*, p 114

211. McLuhan, *Touch the Earth*, p 35

212. Caroline Parkinson, "Education helps brain compensate for dementia changes" *BBC News* (online edition(26 July 2010

213. Freire, P. *Pedagogy of the Oppressed*, pp 52-3

214. Francis, Jones & Smith, *Destinies*, p 198

215. Curry & Howlett, "Natives died in droves as Ottawa ignored warnings" *The Globe and Mail*, 24 April 2007

216. Maria Cook, "Bobby the Brave" *The Ottawa Citizen*, 30 November 2009, p B1

217. Peter Slevin, "Kansas Education Board First To Back 'Intelligent Design'" *The Washington Post*, 9 November 2005

218. James McKinley Jr., "Texas Conservatives Win Curriculum Change" *The New York Times*, 12 March 2010

219. Michael Morgan, "Channel One in the Public Schools, Widening the Gap" Report published by the Dept of Communications, University of Massachusetts, Amherst MA, October 1993

220. For more discussion of corporate influence over education, see Barlow & Robertson, *Class Warfare*, (Key Porter Books, 1994), pp 77-111

221. Gregory, "Cuchullain of Muirthemney", in Clare Booss, ed, *A Treasury of Irish Myth* p 356

222. Ricoeur, *Oneself as Another*, p 164

223. Ricoeur, *Oneself as Another*, p 121

224. Kat Stoeffel, "Leaked Fox News Memo: Keep Global Warming a 'Debate'" the *New York Observer*, 15 December

2010; "FOXLEAKS: Fox Boss ordered staff to cast doubt on climate science" *Media Matters For America*, 15 December 2010

225. Kat Stoeffel, "Leaked Fox News Memo: Don't Call It the 'Public Option'" the *New York Observer*, 9 December 2010; "Leaked Email: Fox boss caught slanting news reporting" *Media Matters For America*, 9 December 2010

226. Cicero, "On Duties", cited in *On the Good Life*, p 127

227. Machiavelli, *The Prince*, (Penguin, 2003) Ch XVII, p 54

228. Hobbes, *Leviathan*, Ch 17, p 114

229. Khrushchev, *Khrushchev Remembers*, p 299

230. Djilas, *Conversations with Stalin*, (Harmondsworth, 1963) p 103

231. Mohammed Eljahmi, "Libya and the U.S.: Qadhafi Unrepentant" *The Middle East Quarterly*, vol 13, No. 1 (Winter 2006)

232. "A New Flag Flies in the East" *The Economist*, 24 February 2011

233. Katie Adie, "The Gaddafi I knew", *The Guardian*, 2 March 2011

234. Machiavelli, *The Prince*, Ch 17, p 54

235. Scott Shane, "As Regimes Fall in Arab World, Al Qaeda Sees History Fly By" *The New York Times*, 27 February 2011; Mona El-Naggar, "Equal Rights Takes to the Barricades" *The New York Times*, 1 February 2011

236. Naomi Wolf, "The Middle East feminist revolution" *Al Jazeera* (English edition) 4 March 2011

237. Volkhard Windfuhr, "Rural poor paid to attack opposition supporters" *Der Spiegel*, 4 February 2011

238. "Libyan snipers fire on mourners" *CBC News*, 19 February 2011; "Gadhafi blames al-Qaeda for Libyan riots" *CBC News*, 24 February 2011

239. El-Nagger, *Ibid*

240. Johnston, *Ojibway Heritage*, p 61

241. Crowshoe & Manneschmidt, *Akak'stiman*, p 17
242. Paul, *We Were Not the Savages*, p 18
243. Johnston, *Ojibway Heritage*, p 61
244. McMillan, *Native Peoples and Cultures in Canada*, p 158
245. Johnston, *Ojibway Heritage*, p 63
246. J. Chadwick & W.N. Mann, trans. *Hippocratic Writings*, (London: Penguin, 1983) p 67
247. *Ibid*, p 68
248. Edmund Pellegrino, MD., "Health Care: A Vocation to Justice and Love" cited in Francis Eigo, ed, *The Professions in Ethical Context: Vocations to Justice and Love* (Villanova, PA, USA: Villanova University Press, 1986) p 101
249. Ralph Nader, "Stop Americanizing Medicare" *CCPA Monitor* (Ottawa, Canada) February 1996, p 17
250. US Census Bureau, "Income, Poverty, and Health Insurance Coverage in 2009" (doc. P60-230), pp 22, 26.
251. Joseph Collins, "Should Doctors Tell the Truth?" in *Harper's Monthly Magazine*, # 155 (August 1927), pp 320-26
252. Collins, *Ibid*
253. B. Thommpson, "Removing the Cloak of Shame: A Report on a Healing Circle in Alkali Lake" p 5, cited in *Esketemc First Nation Traditional Justice Proposal*
254. Boyer, *Community Based Justice Initiatives*, p 4
255. Section 717(1) of the Criminal Code of Canada reads:
"Alternative measures may be used to deal with a person alleged to have committed an offence only if it is not inconsistent with the protection of society and the following conditions are met:
e) the person accepts responsibility for the act or omission that forms the basis of the offence that the person is alleged to have committed."
256. Couture & Couture, *Biidaaban*, p 35
257. Boyer, *Community Based Justice Initiatives*, pp 3-4
258. Couture & Couture, *Biidaaban*, p 45

259. Couture & Couture, *Biidaaban*, p 44

260. Couture & Couture, *Biidaaban*, p 45

261. Couture & Couture, *Biidaaban*, p 45

262. "Elders and Traditional Teachers Gathering, Birch Island", August 27-30, 1991. Cited in C. Proulx, *Reclaiming Aboriginal Justice, Identity, and Community*, p 47

263. cf Rives, *Religion in the Roman Empire*, (Blackwell 2007) pp 13-4

264. *The Code of Hammurabi*, trans L.W. King, (Kessinger Publishing, 2004) p 1

265. Otto, *The Idea of the Holy*, p 52

266. "Benin: Voodoo rituals to calm the spirits in Haiti" *Radio Netherlands Worldwide* (online edition) 14 January 2010

267. M. Ilyas Khan, "Salman Taseer murder: Is Pakistan past tipping point?" *BBC News* (online edition) 7 January 2011

268. Nick Pisa, "Hell Exists – deny it and you'll end up there" *The Scotsman*, 27 March 2007

269. cf *The 700 Club* television broadcast of 13 September 2001

270. Mark Tran, "Pope promotes pastor who said hurricane was God's punishment" *The Guardian*, 1 February 2009

272. Pascal, *Thoughts*, § 894

273. Louis Theroux: "Westboro Baptist Church Revisited" *BBC News*, 31 March 2011

274. Larson & Larson, "The Forgotten Factor in Physical and Mental Health: What Does the Research Show?" (National Institute for Healthcare, 1994)

275. Paul, Gregory S. "Cross-National Correlations of Quantifiable Societal Health with Popular Religiosity and Secularism in the Prosperous Democracies: A First Look". Journal of Religion and Society 7 (2005)

276. Annamarie Schimmel, *Islam: An Introduction* (SUNY Press 1992) p 105

277. Hughes & Swan, "How much of the Earth is Sacred Space?" in Pierce & VanDeVeer, eds, *People, Penguins, and Plastic*

Trees p 351

278. Ricoeur, *Figuring the Sacred*, p 50
279. Otto, *The Idea of the Holy*, pp 13-4
280. Hesiod, *Theogony*, p 6
281. Seneca, "Epistles" 41.3, cited in Rives, *Religion in the Roman Empire*, p 90
282. Ricoeur, *Oneself as Another*, p 150
283. Nietzsche, *Beyond Good and Evil* § 51, p 65
284. "The Divine Image", cited in William Blake, *Poems and Prose* (Fount Classics, 1997) p 16, 5 March 2011.

About the Author

Brendan Cathbad Myers's interest in mythology and ethics was inspired by Celtic storytelling and culture, taught to him by his Irish parents as a child. His Ph.D. doctorate is in ethics and philosophy. He has appeared on many US radio stations and podcasts, and writes a regular column in several Pagan magazines. He lives in Canada.

Moon Books invites you to begin or deepen your encounter with Paganism, in all its rich, creative, flourishing forms.